Journal of the Early Book Society
for the Study of Manuscripts and Printing History

Edited by Martha W. Driver
Volume 19, 2016

Copyright © 2016
Pace University Press
41 Park Row
New York, NY 10038

All rights reserved
Printed in the United States of America

ISBN: 978-0-9619518-8-7
ISSN: 1525-6790

Member

Council of Editors of Learned Journals

♾ ™ The paper used in this publication meets the minimum requirements of American National Standard for information Sciences—Permanence of Paper for printed Library Materials,
ANSI Z39.48—1984.

The *Journal of the Early Book Society* is published annually. *JEBS* invites longer articles on manuscripts and/or printed books produced between 1350 and 1550. Special consideration will be given to essays exploring the period of transition from manuscript to print. Authors are asked to follow *The Chicago Manual of Style*. A Works Cited list at the end of the text should include city, publisher, and date. Manuscripts are to be sent, in triplicate, along with an abstract of up to 150 words, to Martha Driver, Early Book Society, Department of English, Pace University, 41 Park Row, New York, New York 10038. Only materials accompanied by a self-addressed, stamped envelope (or international reply coupon) will be returned. Members of the Early Book Society who are recent authors may send review books for consideration to Susan Powell, Reviews Editor, 7 Woodbine Terrace, Headingley, Leeds LS6 4AF, England. Brief notes on recent discoveries, highlighting little-known or recently uncovered texts and/or images, may be sent to Alexandra Gillespie, Centre for Medieval Studies, 125 Queen's Park, 3rd Floor, Toronto, ON M5S 2C7, Canada. Subscription information may be obtained from Martha Driver or from Pace University Press.

Those interested in joining the Early Book Society or with editorial inquiries may contact Martha Driver by post or e-mail (MDriver@Pace.edu). Information may also be found at <www.nyu.edu/projects/EBS>. For ordering information, call Pace University Press at 212-346-1405 or visit http://www.pace.edu/press. Institutions and libraries may purchase copies directly from Ingram Library Services (1-800-937-5300).

The editor wishes to thank Gill Kent, the Pace University Press Graduate Assistants Taylor Lear and Rachel Diebel, and Manuela Soares, Associate Director, Pace University Press, for their help and advice on this issue.

Journal of the Early Book Society
for the Study of Manuscripts and Printing History

Editor:
Martha W. Driver, *Pace University*

Associate Editors:
Susan Powell, *University of Salford*
Daniel Wakelin, *University of Oxford*

Editorial Board:

Matthew Balensuela, *DePauw University*
Julia Boffey, *Queen Mary, University of London*
Cynthia J. Brown, *University of California, Santa Barbara*
Richard F. M. Byrn, *University of Leeds*
James Carley, *York University*
Joyce Coleman, *University of Oklahoma*
Margaret Connolly, *University of St Andrews*
Susanna Fein, *Kent State University*
Alexandra Gillespie, *University of Toronto*
Vincent Gillespie, *Lady Margaret Hall, Oxford University*
Stanley S. Hussey, *Lancaster University*
Ann M. Hutchison, *Pontifical Institute of Mediaeval Studies and York University*
Michael Kuczynski, *Tulane University*
William Marx, *University of Wales, Lampeter*
Carol M. Meale, *Bristol University*
Charlotte C. Morse, *Virginia Commonwealth University*
Daniel W. Mosser, *Virginia Polytechnic Institute and State University*
Ann Eljenholm Nichols, *Winona State University*
Judy Oliver, *Colgate University*
Michael Orr, *Lawrence University*
Steven Partridge, *University of British Columbia*
Derek Pearsall, *Harvard University*
Pamela Sheingorn, *Baruch College and The City University of New York Graduate School and University Center*
Alison Smith, *Wagner College*
Toshiyuki Takamiya, *Keio University*
Andrew Taylor, *University of Ottawa*
John Thompson, *Queen's University, Belfast*
Ronald Waldron, *King's College, University of London*
Edward Wheatley, *Loyola University*
Mary Beth Winn, *SUNY Albany*

Contents

Articles

The Harley Scribe's Early Career: 1
New Evidence of a Scribal Partnership in MS Harley 273
    SUSANNA FEIN

The Secrees of Old Philisoffres and John Lydgate's Posthumous   31
Reputation
    RORY G. CRITTEN

Dating William Forrest's *The Seconde Grisilde*   65
    OLIVER WORT

"Classicising Friars," Miscellaneous Transmission, and MS Royal   97
7 C.i
    RALPH HANNA

Selling Forbidden Books: Profit and Ideology in Thomas Godfray's   125
Printing
    ALEX DA COSTA

The Politics of Dedicating Printed Books and Manuscripts to King   149
Henry VII
    VALERIE SCHUTTE

Nota Bene: Brief Notes on Manuscripts and Early Printed Books Highlighting Little-Known or Recently Uncovered Items or Related Issues

"ȝet þer is a streinant witȝ two longe tailes":   175
English Musical Terminology in the "Chorister's Lament"
    REBECCA WEST

Loose Leaves, Lost Leaves, and the Text of *Piers Plowman*   187
    RALPH HANNA

A Trilingual Version of "Erthe upon Erthe" in The National   197
Archives of the United Kingdom, E 175/11/16
    MARJORIE HARRINGTON

An Unnoticed Fragment of the Anglo-Norman *Miroir* by Robert Gretham in Marsh's Library, Dublin NIAMH PATTWELL	217
A New Text of the *Marvels of Merlin* ERIC WEISKOTT	227
A Brief Note on Geoffrey Spirleng, Co-Scribe of MS Hunter 197 (U.1.1.), and His Compilation of the Old Free Book of Norwich, NRO, NCR Case 17c RUTH FROST	241
Prenes en gre All Over Again KATHLEEN L. SCOTT	249

Descriptive Reviews

Virginia Blanton, Veronica O'Mara, and Patricia Stoop, eds. *Nuns' Literacies in Medieval Europe: The Kansas City Dialogue* LAURA SAETVEIT MILES	267
Margaret Connolly and Raluca Radulescu, eds. *Insular Books: Vernacular Manuscript Miscellanies in Late Medieval Britain* MICHAEL JOHNSTON	271
Aidan Conti, Orietta Da Rold, and Philip Shaw, eds. *Writing Europe, 500-1450: Texts and Contexts* PAMELA ROBINSON	277
Janet Cowen, ed. *On Famous Women: The Middle English Translation of Boccaccio's 'De Mulieribus Claris'* VERONICA O'MARA	281
Susanna Fein, ed. *The Auchinleck Manuscript: New Perspectives* MARGARET CONNOLLY	285

SCALA Arts and Heritage Publishers
Julie Gardham   289
*Ingenious Impressions: Fifteenth-century printed books from the
University of Glasgow Library*

M. E. J. Hughes   290
*The Pepys Library and the Historic Collections of Magdalene College
Cambridge*

James Kelly, ed.   291
Treasures of Ushaw College: Durham's Hidden Gem
    SUSAN POWELL

David Greer   293
Manuscript Inscriptions in Early England Printed Music
    MAGNUS WILLIAMSON

Patrick J. Horner   297
*The Index of Middle English Prose: Handlist XXI: Manuscripts in the
Hatton and e Musaeo Collections, Bodleian Library, Oxford*
    SUSAN POWELL

Michael Johnston and Michael Van Dussen, eds.   301
The Medieval Manuscript Book: Cultural Approaches
    DANIEL HOBBINS

Carolyne Larrington and Diane Purkiss, eds.   305
Magical Tales: Myth, Legend and Enchantment in Children's Books
    SHAUN TYAS

Angela M. Lucas
The Index of Middle English Prose: Handlist XXII: Manuscripts   311
*in Christ's, Emmanuel, Jesus, Selwyn and Sidney Sussex Colleges,
Peterhouse and Trinity Hall, Cambridge*
    SUSAN POWELL

Peter E. Pormann, ed., with Jane Eagen.
A Descriptive Catalogue of the Hebrew Manuscripts of Corpus Christi 315
College, Oxford
    RALPH HANNA

Jaclyn Rajsic, Erik Kooper and Dominique Hoche, eds. 319
The Prose Brut and Other Late Medieval Chronicles. Books Have Their Histories: Essays in Honour of Lister M. Matheson
    JOHN THOMPSON

Kari Anne Rand 323
The Index of Middle English Prose: Index to Volumes I to XX
    VERONICA O'MARA

Jonathan Wilcox, ed. 327
Scraped, Stroked, and Bound: Materially Engaged Readings of Medieval Manuscripts
    PAMELA ROBINSON

About the Authors 331

The Harley Scribe's Early Career: New Evidence of a Scribal Partnership in MS Harley 273

SUSANNA FEIN

The life and labor of the Harley scribe have long attracted interest because of the important collection of lyrics and fabliaux found on folios 49 to 140 of London, British Library MS Harley 2253, which were copied by him from around 1340 to 1349.[1] Filling out the scribe's known corpus are holographs of forty-one extant legal writs and miscellaneous instances of his hand in British Library MSS Harley 273 and Royal 12.C.xii. These surviving documents offer tantalizing clues by which to observe the professional practices, reading habits, and intellectual environment of a man who acquired and reproduced an eclectic array of texts, doing so in a manner that exhibits compilatory flair and literary wit.

The regional provenance of the Harley scribe, the idiosyncratic nature of the book's mixed contents, and the presence of his hand alone on the remarkable folios 49 to 140 have led to a general opinion that he operated independently, apart from any organized scriptorium. Comparing him to the scribe of Oxford, Bodleian Library MS Digby 86, a similarly eclectic miscellany made in the vicinity of Worcester around 1272 to 1282, Keith Busby notes the scribes' most telling difference and similarity:

Whereas Digby 86 may have been copied by an amateur, Harley 2253 seems to have been written by a professional scribe who produced both court documents and literary texts in different localities in the Ludlow area at the request of paying customers; in neither case are we dealing with a *scriptorium,* monastic or secular.[2]

While the Harley scribe clearly sometimes worked as a scrivener for hire, he was, we tend to think, similar in his purpose to what is observed of other makers of household miscellanies; that is, he created Harley 2253 privately to suit his personal tastes, holding in mind the needs of the household in which (or for which) he produced it. We tend to imagine him as an avid reader and collector, a man of diverse skills, training, and interests—and also (the crux of my intervention here) as someone who often worked apart from communities of other scriveners. A typical and entirely plausible view is that he was "a tutor in a baronial household whilst waiting for ecclesiastical appointment."[3]

Because the Harley scribe owned two more manuscripts, we have a precious opportunity to enlarge knowledge of him by examining work done during his early training and scrivening career. We can refine our understanding by taking into account numerous indicators that he worked alongside and in collaboration with other copyists, seemingly, indeed, in a scriptorium. Even late in his career, during the making of Harley 2253, he must have associated with others having scrivening skills, for the first perceptible user of that book adds recipes for the preparation of manuscript colors on folio 52v—that is, this early user was also a scrivener. He picked up Harley 2253, found one and a half columns of blank space, and filled them with tricks of the trade.[4]

In this article I report several empirical observations—and their logical implications—regarding the early career of the Harley scribe. Paleographical and codicological evidence in Harley 273 reveals that he enjoyed a period of extremely close collaboration with a prolific scribe from Ludlow whose work is known solely from that manuscript. The affiliation took place when the Harley scribe was a young man, around 1314 to 1315, decades before the making of Harley 2253. The other scribe, given his polished formal script and lead role, was likely the older of the pair and may well have acted as the young man's mentor in both clerical training and scrivening, for in all their joint work the Harley scribe assumes secondary place: rubricator, glossator, user.

The data in full suggest that items being jointly produced for what is now Harley 273 were created for the Harley scribe's personal benefit—or, at least, they wound up being in his personal library, presumably alongside

Royal 12.C.xii and Harley 2253. To judge by the collaborative relationship between the two hands, Harley 273 is a book of instructive texts formed by a master teacher-scribe for the purpose of passing them to a student-scribe assistant, that is, a young novice-clerk in training. Ronald N. Walpole notes, "The book seems indeed to have been written and compiled by clerics for clerical readers."[5] Seeing it as "made for devotional and instructional purposes," Carter Revard observes how Harley 273 holds "matter that a young priest or chaplain would need," and how the scribe's traces indicate that it was "his own book or easily accessible in a way suggesting familial ownership if not personal possession."[6] The products made by the two copyists fill five discrete booklets, which someone (most likely the Harley scribe) bound together with two other booklets to create Harley 273.[7]

Among the various anonymous hands found in the Harley scribe's books, the scribe who worked extensively with him in Harley 273 emerges as the most dominant scrivening presence after the Harley scribe himself. He writes a textura formata script to produce works of doctrine, devotion, and liturgical practice, primarily in French but with frequent Latin headings or other Latin as needed. Indeed, this hand constitutes Harley 273's *main* hand, occupying more than four-fifths of its 218 folios. The hand is responsible for the contents of folios 1r to 181r, a long stint that opens with a calendar of feast days and stops during the *Manuel des pechés*. And, significantly, at the end of the scribe's long run there intrudes, in an obvious way, an indicator of the collaboration: the main hand copies most of the *Manuel*, beginning on folio 113ra but stopping at the base of folio 181rb. There, mid-text, after more than 360 pages of continuous copying, the main hand of Harley 273 ceases, and at this unlikely point the ever-present secondary scribe—the Harley scribe—completes the text alone. He copies the remainder of *Manuel* (beginning on fol. 181va), concludes it (fol. 191vb), and fills the remainder of the booklet with new material (fols. 192ra–198vb).[8]

Does this cessation of the main scribe's hand indicate a real-life hiatus: that he had died or become incapacitated, thus leaving the remainder of the task to his apprentice? Or might he have simply delegated the end to the young man? Given the abrupt visual change from a formal textura script to the Harley scribe's anglicana, the decision to conclude the text with a radically new hand must have had an unavoidable cause behind it.

Because paleographical study of the Harley scribe has generally been limited to isolating his oeuvre and dating his hand, no one has thus far subjected Harley 273 to a complex, multi-scribe analysis.[9] I propose to bring to light here the nature of the main scribe's oeuvre—its range, date, provenance—and to characterize what can be factually detected and reasonably hypothesized about his working relationship with the Harley scribe.

The Harley Scribe's Paleographical Presence in Harley 273

The Harley scribe's proprietary presence in Harley 273 is now well known, although it had not yet been discovered when the EETS facsimile of Harley 2253 was published in 1964.[10] The scribe's familiar anglicana script in Harley 273 is most fully characterized by Revard and its presence is reported succinctly in the *British Library's Digitised Manuscripts (BLDM)* description, where it is taken for granted that the Harley scribe is the book's "compiler." The BLDM offers this account:

> Origin: England. Assembled by a cleric or scribe from Ludlow, southern Shropshire: the dedication date of the parish Church of St. Laurence at Ludlow written in red ink at 13 February, 'Dedicacion de la eglise seint Laurence de Lodelawe' ('lodelowe') (f. 1v).... The same scribe is also responsible for the copy of large portions of Harley MS 2253 (ff. 49r–141v) and Royal MS 12 C. xii (see Revard 2000).[11]

This description implies that it was the "cleric or scribe from Ludlow"—that is, the Harley scribe—who inserted the dedication date of the Ludlow Church of St. Laurence. But, as Revard suggests but does not elucidate, the line of dedication belongs to the corpus of the *main* scribe, a man who would also seem to have been from Ludlow.[12] Next, adhering to Revard's appraisal, the *BLDM* description itemizes several instances of the Harley scribe's hand that, looked at in total, occupy relatively little space in the manuscript (fewer than ten folios).

The following is a record of the scribe's anglicana script in brown ink in Harley 273:[13]

- Folio 7r. Two indulgences and two drawings added after the Calendar in booklet 1 (hand dated 1318–1321).[14]
- Folio 82ra. Two corrections to Robert Grosseteste's *Rules* in booklet 3.[15]
- Folio 85vb. A charm for staunching blood, added at end of booklet 3 (hand dated 1318–1322).
- Folio 112va-b. Three charms—against bleeding, wounds, and fever—added at end of booklet 4 (hand dated ca. 1317–1321).[16]
- Folio 114v, lower margin. Latin verses on the length of Adam's stay in hell, added below the *Manuel des pechés*, in booklet 5 (hand dated 1314–1315).[17]
- Folio 116v, lower margin. A Credo in Latin verse, added below the *Manuel* (hand dated 1314–1315).
- Folios 123va–162rb. Marginal notations of exempla, marked *.ex.*^{m} (i.e., *exemplum*), added to the *Manuel*.
- Folio 131va, margin. One correction (*cote*, replacing *chose*) to *Manuel*.

- Folios 181va–190vb. Completion of the *Manuel*, with exempla still marked *.ex.*ᵐ (hand dated 1314–1315).
- Folios 190vb–191r. A table of venial and mortal sins involving swearing, appended to the *Manuel* (hand dated 1314–1315).
- Folios 191va–194ra, 195va–197vb. Most of *Purgatoire de s. Patrice* (hand dated 1314–1315), completing booklet 5.[18]
- Folio 214r–v. Corrections in brown in booklet 7.[19]

Taken together, these instances of the scribe's anglicana in Harley 273 provide the basis for scholars' confident attribution of the role of "compiler" to the Harley scribe. They show him adding brief material to blank space at the ends of booklets 1, 3, and 4, reading and correcting Grosseteste's *Rules* on husbandry and the *Manuel des pechés*, completing the work of the main scribe by finishing the *Manuel*, adding new material in order to see booklet 5's last quire filled and finished, and studying material in booklet 7.

In addition to these verifiable instances of his presence, one can readily discern his hovering shadow by delving into the paleographical clues more globally. The Harley scribe's hand occurs in two red explicits in booklet 3, where he applies his uneven textura—a script seen more frequently in Harley 2253 and Royal 12.C.xii than in Harley 273.[20] These specimens conclude two items in booklet 3:

- Folio 81ra. Explicit to Richard de Fournival's *Bestiaire d'amours*: "Issint fine Bestiaire damours."
- Folio 85va. Explicit to *Rules of Friendship*: "Explicit."

And, moving beyond text-script to look at more applications of color ink, one finds the Harley scribe's handiwork in red or alternating red/blue: large capitals added methodically and ubiquitously to the main scribe's five booklets.

Proof of this presence is shown in the ink used for the *Rules of Friendship* explicit on folio 85va. As can be seen in the *BLDM* color facsimile, this ink matches the rest of the red ink on the page: the capitals *C, J,* and *P;* the paraphs; and the compartmented square that illustrates a charm against wounds. Thus the Harley scribe's hand is present on this page not just in the brown anglicana charm for blood-staunching but also in the red textura explicit and the additional uses of red ink that embrace many functions: large capitals, punctuating paraphs, a small drawing. Here he rubricates his own charm and, significantly, he rubricates text written by the main scribe. Extrapolating this finding backward and forward into the rest of booklet 3 and potentially into booklets 1–2 and 4–5, one may reasonably wonder whether the young Harley scribe had been assigned the task of finishing the main scribe's products—a responsibility that could well be detectable by paleographical methods. Indeed, it can be shown that he did. But before addressing my broad finding that the Harley scribe operated regularly as an initialer in colored ink, it is necessary that we survey the newly identified corpus and paleographical features of Harley 273's main scribe.

The Corpus of the Main Scribe of Harley 273

In five booklets (the second lacking its end), the main scribe of Harley 273 copied the following major texts:

- Liturgical Calendar (booklet 1);
- Anglo-Norman Psalter and Book of Hours (booklet 2, ends imperfectly);[21]
- Richard de Fournival's *Bestiaire d'amours* and Robert Grosseteste's *Rules* (booklet 3);
- *Pseudo-Turpin Chronicle*, with a sermon on penance (booklet 4); and
- The major share of the *Manuel des pechés* (most of booklet 5).

As noted above, the maker of the liturgical Calendar is the volume's main scribe—a fact that affects how we read the provenance of the manuscript and its two primary scribes. The notation for February 13 commemorating the dedication of the Ludlow church is in the main scribe's hand, even though it is often implied to be a location marker for the Harley scribe, corroborating the localization of his legal holographs in the environs of Ludlow. Thus the inference about the Harley scribe's connection to the Calendar notation should be qualified: the dedication of the Ludlow church primarily indicates the interests of the actual copyist, the main scribe of Harley 273, and *both* scribes were deeply familiar with Ludlow. As Revard reminds us, the writs combined with Royal 12.C.xii's *Fouke fitz Waryn* demonstrate how the Harley scribe "knew Ludlow Castle and its chapels and the environs of Ludlow intimately."[22] The Calendar in Harley 273 leads to this conclusion, too, but in a secondary way for the Harley scribe, who acquires the Calendar from another Ludlow scribe and then gives it its finishing details.

Beyond the main scribe's listing of the Ludlow church, there are other indications of regional loyalties—undoubtedly shared by the scribes. The Calendar lists feasts of saints who are celebrated in Harley 2253, as well as some others from localities that stretch from Ludlow to Leominster and Hereford:

- Folio 1v. In March, Saint Milberga ("Mileburge virgine"), daughter of Mercian King Merewald, patron of Saint Etfrid (Harley 2253, art. 98).[23]
- Folio 3r. In June, Saint Ethelbert, patron saint of Hereford Cathedral (Harley 2253, art. 18).[24]

- Folio 4v. In September, Saint Laurence, patron saint of the Ludlow church.[25]
- Folio 5v. In October, Saint Thomas Cantilupe of Hereford (inserted by a later hand, perhaps the Harley scribe),[26] thirteenth-century chancellor of England and bishop of Hereford, canonized in 1307.
- Folio 5v. In November, Saint Etfrid ("adfrid prestre"), patron saint of Leominster Abbey (Harley 2253, art. 98).[27]

The main scribe's hand is a formal gothic book script, officially called *littera textualis semiquadrata formata* in a former online British Library catalogue description that has been supplanted by the new *BLDM* and *British Library Catalogue of Illuminated Manuscripts (BLCIM)* descriptions.[28] In this and other descriptions of Harley 273, no one has tried to compare hands and delineate individual scribal oeuvres. The fullest attempt is by Walpole, editor of the *Pseudo-Turpin Chronicle*, but he commits errors, saying, for example, that the hand of the Calendar and *Bestiaire* differs from that of the Psalter, then contradicting himself by saying that the Calendar hand is the same as that of the Psalter, then wrongly suggesting that the text of Nicholas Bozon's *Pleynte d'amour* in booklet 6 is also by that hand.[29]

The hand of the main scribe is quite consistent, and although it fluctuates from text to text in size and/or shade of ink, it is always readily distinguishable from other scripts appearing in the Harley scribe's manuscripts. It never appears in Royal 12.C.xii, Harley 2253, or booklets 6–7 of Harley 273. It is, however, the dominant presence in Harley 273's booklets 1–5, where (except for the Calendar) the main scribe adopts a two-column format distinctive among the Harley scribe's booklets.[30] The fullest description of the script to date is provided by Walpole:

> The writing is a rather formal book-hand with few cursive features. I note the following details: *a* is still open at the top. Round *s* is common at the end of a word, occasionally at the beginning, but long *s* is used there too and is general within the word. *r* takes the round form after *o, p, d* and sometimes after *a*, but it is upright elsewhere. *i* is often but not regularly marked with a hairline curving to the right. *y* often replaces *i*. . . . The *y* is marked with a dot. For the most part *t* does not show above the bar, but there are a few cases where there is just a suggestion of such protrusion. The ligature between *s* and *t* and the merging of rounds in *de, be, pe, ce, bo, co, po, pa* are typical. . . . At the top of the shaft of *l* the scribe adds a short diagonal stroke forming a crotch with the shaft.[31]

The biting ligature between letter-pairs described by Walpole is one marker by which to identify the hand, but there are many other distinctive features: the long *s* with a slight medial notch to the left, the abbreviation for *vus* (the arms of the *v* curved to the left), the unchanging forms of *a, e, d, q*, and *g*. But even more corroborative are the distinctive capital letters. The scribe has a frilly style of initial that can be seen in the fourth column of the Calendar (especially *D, K, N*), where he may add multiple right-hand notches. This penchant for ornate, overdesigned initials appears often in lines that head columns in the *Manuel des pechés*, where he even adds comic dogheads to the style. His more routine textura capitals are also distinctive, especially the *C* with an inner hook, the *E* with a sharp left-side point, and the *Q* drawn like a spiral with a tail. In fact, it is the main scribe's alphabet of capitals—a very attractive earmark style—that best serves to confirm the identification when other signs are present.[32]

The following list isolates the sizeable corpus of Harley 273's main scribe, most of which remains inedited.[33]

Booklet 1
    1. Latin/French Liturgical Calendar, fols. 1r–6v (inedited).[34]

Booklet 2 (ends imperfectly; double columns, 36 lines/column)
    2. Anglo-Norman (AN) prose. Oxford Psalter, with Latin headings, fols. 8ra–53rb (*ANL* 445).[35]
    3. AN prose and verse. Canticles and other liturgical pieces (*ANL* 457; inedited).
        a. Seven Canticles from the Old Testament, fols. 53rb–55vb.
        b. *Te Deum*, fols. 55vb–56rb (for verse version, see 4.a.iii).
        c. Three Canticles from the New Testament, fols. 56rb–57ra.
        d. Athanasian Creed, fol. 57ra–vb.
        e. Litany, fols. 57vb–58vb.
        f. *Pater Noster* in verse, fols. 58vb–59ra (*ANL* 840; unique).
        g. *Ave Maria* in verse, fol. 59ra (*ANL* 821, printing the text; see also 4.a.xvii).
        h. Six short prayers, fol. 59ra–b (*ANL* 860).
    4. Book of Hours (inedited).
        a. AN verse. Hours of the Virgin (*ANL* 828).[36]
            i. *Venite*, fol. 59va–b (*ANL* 868; translation of Psalm 94).
            ii. *Quem terra pontus ethera*, fol. 59vb.
            iii. *Te Deum*, fols. 60vb–61rb (for prose version, see 3.b).
            iv. *Benedicite omnia opera*, fol. 61va–b.
            v. *O admirabile*, fol. 62rb (repeated at 4.a.x).
            vi. *O gloriosa domina*, fol. 62rb (*ANL* 814).

vii. *Benedictus,* fol. 62va (for prose version, see 3.c).
viii. Prayer to Saint Thomas, fol. 62vb (*ANL* 939, printing the text).
ix. *Veni creator,* fol. 63ra (*ANL* 838).
x. *O admirabile,* fol. 63vb (see 4.a.v).
xi. *Ave maris stella,* fol. 65va–b (*ANL* 811).
xii. *Magnificat,* fols. 65vb–66ra (*ANL* 823; for prose version, see 3.c).
xiii. *Cum jocunditate,* fol. 66va.
xiv. *Virgo singularis,* fol. 66va–b (*ANL* 815).
xv. *Nunc dimittis,* fol. 66vb (*ANL* 835).
xvi. *Salve regina,* fols. 66vb–67ra (*ANL* 827).
xvii. *Ave Maria,* fol. 67ra (*ANL* 821, printing the text; see also 3.g).
xviii. *Omnipotens sempiterne,* fol. 67ra (*ANL* 834).
xix. *Credo in Deum patrem,* fol. 67ra–b (*ANL* 680).
xx. *Miserere mei Deus,* fol. 67rb–va.
  b. AN prose. Office of the Dead, fols. 68ra–69vb (*ANL* 829; unique; ends imperfectly, breaking off at the beginning of the sixth lesson).[37]

Booklet 3 (double columns, 37 lines/column)
  5. French (or AN?) prose. Richard de Fournival, *Bestiaire d'amours,* with line drawings, fols. 71ra–81ra (not in *ANL*).[38]
  6. AN prose. Robert Grosseteste, *Rules,* fols. 81rb–85ra (not in *ANL*).[39]
  7. AN prose. *Rules of Friendship,* fol. 85ra–va (*ANL* 246).[40]
  8. AN prose. Charm against wounds, with diagram, fol. 85va–b (not in *ANL*).[41]

Booklet 4 (except for item 14, double columns, 36 lines/column)
  9. French prose. *Pseudo-Turpin Chronicle,* fols. 86rb–102v (not in *ANL*).[42]
  10. AN prose. *On Penance,* fols. 103ra–110ra (*ANL* 672).[43]
  11. AN verse. *Prayer on the Five Joys of Our Lady,* fol. 110ra–b (*ANL* 772; inedited).[44]
  12. AN verse. A short prayer on the efficacy for absolution, fol. 110rb (*ANL* 891; inedited).
  13. AN verse. Instruction for saying the preceding prayer (or the following prayer) thrice daily, promising absolution, fol. 110rb (*ANL* 951; inedited).[45]
  14. AN prose. *Guide to Nightly and Daily Meditation,* with diagrams— left hand (fol. 111r), right hand (fol. 112r)—and Latin mnemonics, fols. 110va–112rb (*ANL* 861; inedited).
  15. AN verse. The Seven Gifts of the Holy Spirit, fol. 112va (*ANL* 615; inedited).

Booklet 5 (double columns, 38 lines/column)
   16. AN prose. William of Waddington, *Manuel des pechés*, fols. 113ra–190vb (*ANL* 635).[46]

The Harley Scribe as Rubricator

As mentioned above, the evidence in red ink on folio 85va, where one finds the Harley scribe's explicit to *Rules of Friendship*, reveals that he applied decorative elements and a few instances of *ordinatio* in colored ink—explicits, diagrams, large initials, paraphs—not only in finalizing his own short charms but also in finalizing items copied by the main scribe of Harley 273. This finding ought not to be surprising, for the Harley scribe applies red ink to finish his own products as a normal practice in Harley 2253.[47] As I show elsewhere, such decorative rubrication is a constant feature there in texts of his own making (fols. 49–140), and he also adds red ink to texts inherited from another scribe (fols. 1–48).[48]

A cursory glance through the long series of folios filled by the main copyist (fols. 1r–181r) reveals a notable uniformity in style for the hand that adds large initials in red or blue (following the main scribe's guide letters). Thus, here, in this feature of Harley 273, rests more strong evidence of an established, long-term, collaborative relationship: the main scribe copying vast amounts of text, the young Harley scribe adding finishing touches of color. The main scribe also applies some instances of colored inks, when he inserts, for example, red Latin headings throughout the Psalter and red or blue notched display letters in the Calendar. But in the main, throughout the corpus one may observe a continuous division of labor and a clear system of collaboration. In appearance, the most anomalous of the texts is the *Bestiaire d'amours*, produced in brown ink in a taut version of the main scribe's textura and accompanied by a set of fine drawings. The initials here also seem a bit different because they too are taut and brown in color. However, these mannered differences fall well within the range of usage seen elsewhere, and the script and initials match those of the main scribe and the Harley scribe. What this copy of the *Bestiaire* seems to indicate is a disciplined joint effort to produce a deluxe specimen of this challenging item, accompanied by miniature illustrations, intelligently planned and carefully executed. The explicit added by the young clerk on folio 81ra, "Issint fine Bestiaire damours," may convey, in part, a sense of joint accomplishment.

According to my paleographical assessment of the Harley scribe's three manuscripts, his rubricating hand appears in twenty-one of twenty-two booklets. The only one that lacks his hand is booklet 6 of Harley 273, which contains Bozon's *Pleynte d'amour*.[49] The analysis begins with evidence found in Harley 2253, where the Harley scribe initials and paraphs his own texts on folios 49 to 140. He conveniently presents a full alphabet of his large colored initials in *ABC of Women* (fols. 49r–50v).[50] Here is a display script that is entirely different from the scribe's anglicana and textura scripts. In general, the rubricator follows miniature guide letters inserted faintly by whoever is the main scribe.[51] This procedure reliably occurs in texts that the Harley scribe copied himself and in texts copied by other scribes. And it is the standard operating method for the scrivening partnership that existed between the main scribe of Harley 273 and the Harley scribe.

The following list summarizes the Harley scribe's letter-forms for large colored capitals, using the *ABC of Women* alphabet as a reference-point:

- Letters consistent in form (matching the *ABC*): B, C, D, E, F,[52] G, H, I/J,[53] K,[54] L, M, N, O,[55] P, Q, R, S,[56] U, X,[57] Y, Z.[58]
- Letters with two verifiable forms (one matching the *ABC*; the other found elsewhere in Harley 2253): A,[59] T.[60]
- Letters not appearing in the *ABC*: Þ, V, W.[61]

The Pattern of Collaboration

What remains to be shown is how the collaboration worked, booklet to booklet and text to text, between two scribes from Ludlow, the seasoned one leading an aspirant young clerk through material essential for his devotions and desirable for a future career as priest or chaplain in a parish or a secular household. Table 1 presents a collation of Harley 273 by quire, booklet, and contents, showing how all parts copied by the main scribe were finished by the Harley scribe, who later on added charms or indulgences at booklet ends, indicating his ongoing possession of the final products. It also presents the makeup of booklets 6 and 7, which were not part of the two-way collaboration but were clearly part of the Harley scribe's collection of instructive clerical lore. In booklet 7, his hand appears as a corrector (thus reader) and also as initialer. But nothing in it points firmly to a personal interaction between the booklet 7 scribe and the Harley scribe; I suspect that here he simply finished a technical clerical text that fell into his hands for study and reference.

Booklets 1 to 5 appear to be in sequence—chronological and pedagogical—because they begin with devotional matter (Calendar, Psalter, Book of Hours) and progress through instructional matter, with the main scribe disappearing from booklet 5 before it concludes. If this inference is right, then the whole collaboration in booklets 1 to 5 represents the earliest known period in the Harley scribe's corpus, around 1314 to 1315 (the date Revard gives to the Harley scribe's anglicana hand in booklet 5). The Harley scribe's five earliest known legal writs, dated December 18, 1314, to October 10, 1316, are all located narrowly in Ludlow, mainly along Corve and Old Streets. The first two deeds of transfer involve an Old Street property next to "the tenement of *Austin Friars*."⁶² Might this fraternal house be where mentor and assistant made booklets 1 to 5 of Harley 273?

One may observe, moreover, that shortly after the joint activity evident in booklets 1 to 5, the Harley scribe created the *Short English Metrical Chronicle* (ca. 1316–1317), his original redaction based on the *Brut*,⁶³ which survives in Royal 12.C.xii, folios 62r to 68v. And very shortly thereafter he annotated and inserted initials and paraphs in the prose *Mirour de Seinte Eglise* (Royal 12.C.xii, fols. 17r–32v; ca. 1317–1318).⁶⁴ His charms and indulgences in Harley 273 show him to be using the manuscript from around 1316 to 1329. So in these paleographically dated works one can trace the young Harley scribe's progress in schooled reading, mainly in French, sometimes in English—all of it overlying a bedrock of scriptural, liturgical, and scientific Latin—alongside years of applied scrivening that reinforced his studies. Recognizing the full extent of the collaboration with the main scribe of Harley 273, and collating it with Revard's precise dating of the Harley scribe's output, one can thus trace the sequential lineaments of the Harley scribe's clerical training when he was likely just a teenager.

Besides showing in the table how the two Ludlow scribes partnered in producing texts, I also note special instances of illustrative material appearing in booklets 2 to 5 (the only booklets where they exist). Some instances are planned—for example, the puzzle initials, the illustrations in the *Bestiaire*—but others—the marginal drolleries, the dogheaded capitals—are pure whimsy. Evidently humming with convivial camaraderie, the scriptorium was a place where clerks could express "their lighter moments."⁶⁵

Table 1. Booklets, Scribal Collaborations, and Contents of MS Harley 273

booklet 1, fols. 1*, 1–7
(1 leaf + 1 quire: a⁶ + 1 leaf)

Collaboration: Calendar
Harley scribe only: Two indulgences at end, added later

Main scribe: The master's formal hand inscribes most of the Calendar, orchestrating the controlled aesthetic. The red and blue patterning alternates from page to page, so that a page headed with a blue initial always follows a page headed with a red initial. The ornate, notched capitals in column 4 (1–2 lines high) are all his, as are the entries of saints and almost all of columns 1–3. He leaves guide letters for the Harley scribe's initials.
Harley scribe: In column 2, the Harley scribe inserts the flat-top *A*s. He makes the large *KL* (*Kalendar*) at the top of each page and he also inserts over guide letters the red or blue initials that open each saint's day.

booklet 2, fols. 8–69
(5 quires: b¹² c¹² d¹² e¹⁴ f¹²;
ends imperfectly)

Collaboration: AN Psalter, AN Canticles, AN Book of Hours

Main scribe: Texts in brown; Latin headings in red. Three initials with zoomorphic heads: dogs facing right on *D*s (fols. 18va, 51ra); camel facing left on *N* (fol. 48va).
Harley scribe: Enlarged initials at the beginning of each Psalm verse (1–2 lines high), with occasional paraphs in alternating red and blue ink following the main scribe's guide letters. Similar application of colored initials and occasional paraphs throughout the Canticles and the Book of Hours.
Harley scribe?: Nine puzzle initials (5–6 lines high), typically created by two applications of ink: (1) red and blue bodies, (2) fine-line flourishes and fills in slightly darker red and blue inks. Eight initials mark Psalms 1, 26, 38, 52, 68, 80, 97, and 109 (fols. 8ra, 15rb, 19vb, 23vb, 28ra, 33ra, 37vb, 42vb), following the monastic division of Psalms into eight groups of nocturnes. The ninth puzzle initial appears on folio 23va, marking Psalm 51.⁶⁶ Simpler dual-color initials appear on folios 47va and 59va. It is probable that the initialer (i.e., the Harley scribe) made these display initials because the body inks appear to match the regular enlarged initials.⁶⁷
Either scribe: Drolleries drawn in the margins: leaping rabbit in brown (fol. 23rb); hand in brown, pointing to gap for a red Latin heading (fol. 38va); clover in red (fol. 44rb); two-legged hybrid with cowled head, goat beard, rabbit ears, and camel hump in red (fol. 58rb);⁶⁸ hybrid with cowled head in red (fol. 59rb). The red drolleries are drawn with the fine-pen darker ink that flourishes and fills puzzle initials.

booklet 3, fols. 70–85
(2 quires: g⁸ h⁸)

Collaboration: Fournival's *Bestiaire*, Grosseteste's *Rules*, *Rules of Friendship*, Charm against wounds
Harley scribe only: Charm at end, added later

Main scribe: Texts in ink varying from light to dark brown.
Harley scribe: *Bestiaire* initials (generally 1–2 lines high) added after the drawings, mostly dark brown, but two at the opening are blue (fol. 70ra, 70rb) and some others are red (fols. 72rb, 72vb, 76ra, 78vb, 80va), with one red paraph (fol. 72ra). Four red initials and many red paraphs (with upper line extended to the right) in Grosseteste's *Rules*, *Rules for Friendship*, and charm. Two red explicits.
Harley scribe?: Fine-line red flourishes on three initials (fols. 70ra, 70rb, 85ra) in the manner of the puzzle initials in booklet 2.

Either scribe: *Bestiaire* miniatures in light brown fitted into rectangular spaces, not inserted last but instead copied in alternation with text.

    booklet 4, fols. 86–112   **Collaboration:** *Pseudo-Turpin*
    (3 quires: i¹⁰ j¹⁰ k⁶)   *Chronicle*, *On Penance*, prayers,
                                     meditative guide, *Seven Gifts*
                                     Harley scribe only: Three charms
                                     at end, added later

Main scribe: Texts in brown, including Latin mnemonics inserted in the hand diagrams of the meditative guide.
Harley scribe: Enlarged initials (2 lines high) in alternating red and blue in *Pseudo-Turpin Chronicle* and *On Penance*. Red initials (1–2 lines high) in French instructions of the meditative guide. All of these initials follow guide letters.
Harley scribe?: Fine-line red fill of a blue initial *P* (fol. 99rb) in the manner of the puzzle initials in booklet 2.
Either scribe: Hand diagrams in red (fols. 111r, 112r). Drolleries drawn in the margins: claw-footed hybrid with cowled head in brown (fol. 95va); woman's head with hairnet in brown (fol. 102vb).⁶⁹

    booklet 5, fols. 113–198   **Collaboration:** major portion of
    (8 quires: l¹² m¹² n¹² o¹² p¹²   *Manuel des pechés*
    q¹² r⁸ s⁶)   **Harley scribe only:** rest of
                                     Manuel, tables of sins
                                     Harley scribe & Scribe D: *Purgatoire de s. Patrice*

Main scribe: *Manuel* text in brown with French section headings in red (to fol. 181rb). Many top-of-column initials with zoomorphic heads and stacked or notched flourishes: dogs facing right on *Ds* (fols. 137rb, 155va); man facing right on *D* (fol. 138vb); man facing left on *U* (fols. 142vb), or *A* (fol. 155vb), or *L* (fol. 156rb); odd shape on *L* (fol. 145ra); snake facing right on *L* (fol. 158ra); snake tail on *D* (fol. 165va); stacked *Ds* (fols. 137va, 144vb, passim), *Ps* (fols. 138rb, 139vb, passim), and *Ss* (fols. 143ra, 163rb); notched *K* (fol. 157ra), *M* (fol. 157rb), and *Ns* (fols. 164ra, 170va).
Harley scribe: Colored initials (1–7 lines high) and numerous paraphs, mostly in red, with some in blue (as on opening page), continuing to fol. 184v, where all of the colored additions end. Exempla marked .*ex.*ᵐ in *Manuel* margins in light brown, with other marginal additions present (fols. 114v, 116v, 131va). *Purgatoire* is completed in brown by a secondary collaboration with Scribe D.

THE HARLEY SCRIBE'S EARLY CAREER 15

booklet 6, fols. 199–203　　　　***Pleynte* scribe only**: Bozon's
(1 quire: t$^{6-1}$)　　　　　　　　　　*Pleynte d'amour*[71]

booklet 7, fols. 204–217　　　　***Colors* scribe**: Miscellany of
(1 quire: u^{12})　　　　　　　　　　prayers (fols. 204r–209r), color
　　　　　　　　　　　　　　　　　　recipes (fols. 209r–212r), and
　　　　　　　　　　　　　　　　　　med ical recipes and charms
　　　　　　　　　　　　　　　　　　(fols. 212r-215v), chiefly in Latin

***Colors* scribe:** Texts inscribed in black with red headings.
Harley scribe: Initials in red in Harley scribe's style appear throughout booklet (written over guide letters). Two corrections in brown (fol. 214r–v). Direct collaboration unlikely.

Conclusions: The Harley Scribe in the Scriptorium

It is generally accepted that the Harley scribe operated alone in the making of Harley 2253, folios 49 to 140 (booklets 3–7). The determination of a single scribe derives not just from his consistent dark-brown anglicana used for texts but also from all instances of red ink, which are demonstrably added by the same copyist. Rubrication evidence in Harley 2253 is important because it shows the scribe doing his own finishing and it sets a paleographic standard for comparison with the other manuscripts. In Harley 273 and Royal 12.C.xii, too, the Harley scribe rubricated texts that he himself copied. It is now apparent that he also rubricated almost every additional item in his library of booklets as we know it. The evidence drawn from all three manuscripts indicates that early in his scrivening career, the Harley scribe performed colored initialing for other scribes. He clearly had means by which to acquire texts when they still lacked the finish of red ink, and he may have routinely performed this finishing work without knowing the copyists personally.

Among scribal hands in the Harley scribe's manuscripts, only two bear undeniable indicators that the scribes worked in immediate collaboration with him. Both are in Harley 273. Detecting their presence in this chronologically earliest portion of his holdings allows a picture of the scribe as a young man to emerge. In this period he *did* operate among colleagues—that is, in a formal scriptorium or school or site of clerkly service. Envisioning the scribe in a collaborative setting among scribes modifies the view we have had of his later solitary activity. While it does not necessarily alter the standard inference that the last manuscript, Harley 2253, was created as a private endeavor, perhaps for a household, it does amplify the Harley scribe's biography by revealing a social setting during his formative schooling.

In Harley 273 and Royal 12.C.xii, one finds the hands of twelve scribes operating beside that of the Harley scribe. Four make only random insertions, usually late, and because they are detectible nowhere else, they are of peripheral importance to this study. Six others copy single texts or booklets owned by the scribe: in Harley 273, Bozon's *Pleynte d'amour* and the Latin miscellany of prayers and charms; in Royal 12.C.xii, the AN *Mirour de Seinte Eglise, Ami et Amiloun*, the Latin *Liber experimentarius*, and the AN *Treatise on the Mass*. Their hands appear nowhere else in the Harley scribe's library, and they therefore exhibit no discernible relationship to him. Eliminating them leaves only the two scribes whom I note as being of particular interest: the main scribe of Harley 273, booklets 1 to 5; and Scribe D, the joint copyist of *Purgatoire de s. Patrice* and accounts keeper for a Mortimer household in Ireland (whose accounts are found on the flyleaves of Harley 2253).[72] Because Scribe D probably also inserted two corrections to the main scribe's copy of the *Pseudo-Turpin Chronicle*, he would seem to have been present in the same Ludlow milieu. These clues strongly suggest a textual community of scribes and readers that influenced the young Harley scribe.

By and large, the paleographical evidence in Harley 273 suggests that booklets 1 to 5 were crafted by a master scribe directly for the Harley scribe. They were designed to be finished by the young man, whose main function was not copyist but instead initialer in colored ink. They were to become his own copies as an aspirant professional cleric. His possession of them was part of an educative collaboration with a senior cleric in Ludlow who used pen-and-inksmanship as part of the lesson. The collaboration must have lasted over a significant time (months or years), perhaps beginning prior to 1314. The Harley scribe was presumably expected to *know* texts that he was given to finish off with red and blue, and he would have thereby absorbed a good deal of his clerical training. At the same time, a level of playfulness between mentor and student surfaces in the cartoonish drolleries inserted here and there in the Psalter and the *Manuel des pechés*.

Further research is needed on the fascinating insertion of artistic, sometimes humorous elements in Harley 273 in order to determine which types, if any, belong to the corpus of the Harley scribe. The eye-catching, fancifully overstacked, notched, or zoomorph-headed initials at the tops of columns in the Psalter and the *Manuel* are amusements that can convincingly be attributed to the main scribe, but authorship of others—the fantastical hybrids, the delightful *Bestiaire* miniatures—requires future careful study of inks, pen styles, and sequences of copying to confirm their attribution to one scribe or the other. The puzzle initials, too, require more forensic study before they can be confirmed as products by our scribe.

The scrivening presence of the Harley scribe is a common denominator across three manuscripts. The evidence points overwhelmingly to him as owner, user, and binder of twenty-two booklets dating from early to late in his life. The seven-booklet Harley 273 represents a collection he acquired early on, inscribed mostly by others. The eight-booklet Royal 12.C.xii preserves, in contrast, many lengthy items he redacted himself, notably, the *Short English Metrical Chronicle* and *Fouke fitz Waryn*.[73] In around 1340, in possession of these fifteen booklets plus two more of a larger format, the scribe began the significant project that became Harley 2253.[74] How the Harley scribe's youthful period of clerical study combined with scrivening eventually blossomed into the making of five booklets during his mature period—booklets that record extremely rare traces of a once-vital literary culture—remains a mystery wherein circumstances luckily met with a man's wont to collect and inscribe. Without knowing how that happened, we may now, at least, see with greater precision the mentor, the scriptorium, and the steady manner of training that helped form the literary consciousness and desires of the Harley scribe.

Kent State University

NOTES

1. The Harley scribe has also been called the "Ludlow scribe," an appellation that avoids confusion with scribes of other major Harleian manuscripts. By current consensus, however, he is now the "Harley scribe." See, e.g., Matthew Fisher, *Scribal Authorship and the Writing of History in Medieval England* (Columbus: Ohio State University Press, 2012); Keith Busby, "Multilingualism, the Harley Scribe, and Johannes Jacobi," in *Insular Books: Vernacular Manuscript Miscellanies in Late Medieval Britain*, ed. Margaret Connolly and Raluca Radulescu, Proceedings of the British Academy 201 (Oxford: Oxford University Press, 2015), 49–60; and Susanna Fein, "Literary Scribes: The Harley Scribe and Robert Thornton," in *Insular Books: Vernacular Manuscript Miscellanies in Late Medieval Britain*, ed. Margaret Connolly and Raluca Radulescu, Proceedings of the British Academy 201 (Oxford: Oxford University Press, 2015), 61–79. See, too, the landmark study, Carter Revard, "Scribe and Provenance," in *Studies in the Harley Manuscript: The Scribes, Contents, and Social Contexts of British Library MS Harley 2253*, ed. Susanna Fein (Kalamazoo, MI: Medieval Institute, 2000), 21–110. For the dates assigned in this article to the Harley scribe's corpus, I am indebted to Revard's study.
2. Keith Busby, *Codex and Context: Reading Old French Verse Narrative in Manuscript*, 2 vols. (Amsterdam: Rodopi, 2002), 2:512. On likenesses between these two manuscripts, see also Marilyn Corrie, "Harley 2253, Digby 86, and the Circulation of Literature in Pre-Chaucerian England," in *Studies in the Harley Manuscript: The Scribes, Contents, and Social*

Contexts of British Library MS Harley 2253, ed. Susanna Fein (Kalamazoo, MI: Medieval Institute, 2000), 427–443; John Scahill, "Trilingualism in Early Middle English Miscellanies: Languages and Literature," *Yearbook of English Studies* 33 (2003): 18–32, esp. 26–28; John Hines, *Voices in the Past: English Literature and Archaeology* (Cambridge, UK: D. S. Brewer, 2004), 71–104; and Susanna Fein, "The Fillers of the Auchinleck Manuscript and the Literary Culture of the West Midlands," in *Makers and Users of Medieval Books: Essays in Honour of A. S. G. Edwards*, ed. Carol M. Meale and Derek Pearsall (Cambridge, UK: D. S. Brewer, 2014), 60–77.

3. Tony Hunt, Julia Boffey, A. S. G. Edwards, and Daniel Huws, "Vernacular Literature and Its Readership," in *The Cambridge History of the Book in Britain: Volume II 1100–1400*, ed. Nigel Morgan and Rodney M. Thomson (Cambridge, UK: Cambridge University Press, 2008), 367–396, at 375. Both the Harley and Digby scribes seem to have been, according to Scahill, "Trilingualism," 28, "clerics in partly secular environments." See also Revard, "Scribe and Provenance," esp. 29–30; and Jason O'Rourke, "Imagining Book Production in Fourteenth-Century Herefordshire: The Scribe of British Library, MS Harley 2253 and His 'Organizing Principles,'" in *Imagining the Book*, ed. Stephen Kelly and John J. Thompson (Turnhout, Belgium: Brepols, 2005), 45–60.

4. See my discussion of Scribe C in Susanna Fein, "The Four Scribes of MS Harley 2253," *Journal of the Early Book Society* 16 (2013): 1–23, at 6–8.

5. Ronald N. Walpole, *The Old French Johannes Translation of the Pseudo-Turpin Chronicle: Supplement* (Berkeley: University of California Press, 1976), 36.

6. Revard, "Scribe and Provenance," 65, 67, 58, observes that the Harley scribe had detectible access to Harley 273 for at least fifteen years, ca. 1314–1329.

7. A table of contents written ca. 1400 at the back of the manuscript indicates that the booklets were bound early; Walpole, *Old French Johannes*, 33.

8. The Harley scribe leads this process but is aided by Scribe D, the only other scribe who demonstrates an acquaintance with him; Fein, "Four Scribes," 9–11. D's hand appears both on the flyleaves of Harley 2253 and in Harley 273, booklet 5's *Purgatoire de s. Patrice*, jointly copied with the Harley scribe, where D copies five medial columns (fols. 194rb–195rb). I wish to newly report that D appears, too, to be the correcting hand in the *Pseudo-Turpin Chronicle* (Harley 273, booklet 4): *Agolant* (fol. 90ra), *Dauid* (fol. 99va), *mavez* (*m* interlined above main scribe's *avez*; fol. 99va). On these corrections, see Walpole, *Old French Johannes*, 36–37.

9. In discussing the main scribe's work, Walpole was not aware of the Harley scribe's joint presence; *Old French Johannes*, 29–40. The British Library

Digitised Manuscripts (BLDM) description (s.v. "Harley MS 273") mentions the presence of two scribes but details only the Harley scribe's activity (http://www.bl.uk/manuscripts/FullDisplay.aspx?ref=Harley_MS_273.). I reference the main hand in Fein, "Four Scribes," 14 n. 15.
10. N. R. Ker, intro., *Facsimile of British Museum MS. Harley 2253*, EETS o.s. 255 (London: Oxford University Press, 1965). The discovery, made by Christopher Hohler, was reported in E. J. Hathaway, P. T. Ricketts, C. A. Robson, and A. D. Wilshere, eds., *Fouke le Fitz Waryn*, ANTS 26–28 (Oxford: Basil Blackwell, 1975), xxxviii; see Revard, "Scribe and Provenance," 26.
11. "Harley MS 273," *BLDM* description and color facsimile (see note 9).
12. According to Revard, the notation means that "the manuscript's owner used it in that church" and that the Harley scribe's "early studies were done either in Ludlow or by a man closely connected with Ludlow"; Revard, "Scribe and Provenance," 26, 69. Aside from the initial letter D, which the Harley scribe inserted (following a guide letter), the dedication is wholly the main scribe's product.
13. This list is indebted to the *BLDM* description and Revard, "Scribe and Provenance," 57, 67–68; I have added my own observations and precise indicators of location.
14. The indulgences were granted by Pope Innocent Urbanus IV (1261–1264) and Pope John XXII (1316–1334), respectively. Two drawings follow the indulgences, apparently in the same ink: an outline of "ihs" in large gothic letters and a floral design. Two late entries in the Calendar, written in a loose, hasty anglicana, might be by the Harley scribe; see note 26.
15. Revard, "Scribe and Provenance," 68; see also Elizabeth Lamond, ed. and trans., *Walter of Henley's Husbandry together with an Anonymous Husbandry, Seneschaucie, and Robert Grosseteste's Rules* (London: Longmans, Green, 1890), xliv.
16. For these charms, see Tony Hunt, ed., *Popular Medicine in Thirteenth-Century England: Introduction and Texts* (Cambridge, UK: D. S. Brewer, 1990), 88–89. In booklet 7, the Harley scribe's hand appears only on fol. 214r–v and in the rubricated initials, which consistently match his style. The *BLDM* description erroneously names charms on fol. 213r–v as being his; his script does not appear here. If he is the initialer, however, matching ink suggests that he underlined charms on fol. 213r–v.
17. Another version appears in Royal 12.C.xii, fol. 6v; Revard, "Scribe and Provenance," 68.
18. Johan Vising, ed., "*Le Purgatoire de Saint Patrice* des manuscrits Harléien 273 et fonds français 2198," *Götesborgs Högskolas Årsskrift* 22 (1916): 1–87. On the collaborating hand of Scribe D, see note 8 above.

19. Revard does not date these corrections, but they have the scribe's early form of *i* (pre-1331); Revard's latest date for Harley 273 is 1329. Revard also notes that the correction on dismal days (fol. 214v) was used later by the Harley scribe for a French prose text in Royal 12.C.xii, fol. 90v; Revard, "Scribe and Provenance," 68.
20. Fein, "Four Scribes," 14 n. 18.
21. A vernacular Psalter designed "for a secular rather than a regular cleric"; Revard, "Scribe and Provenance," 69.
22. Revard, "Scribe and Provenance," 29.
23. Susanna Fein, ed. and trans., with David Raybin and Jan Ziolkowski, *The Legend of Saint Etfrid, Priest of Leominster*, in *The Complete Harley 2253 Manuscript*, ed. and trans. Susanna Fein, with David Raybin and Jan Ziolkowski, vol. 3 (Kalamazoo, MI: Medieval Institute, 2015), 260–267. On Milberga's local reputation, see William Smith, *The Use of Hereford: The Sources of a Medieval English Diocesan Rite* (Burlington, VT: Ashgate, 2015), 54.
24. Susanna Fein, ed. and trans., with David Raybin and Jan Ziolkowski, *The Life of Saint Ethelbert*, in *The Complete Harley 2253 Manuscript*, ed. and trans. Susanna Fein, with David Raybin and Jan Ziolkowski, vol. 2 (Kalamazoo, MI: Medieval Institute, 2014), 50–59.
25. On the Calendar and the suggestions for the Harley scribe's identity, see David Lloyd, Margaret Clark, and Chris Potter, *St. Laurence's Church, Ludlow: The Parish Church and People, 1199–2009* (Wooten Almeley, UK: Logaston Press, 2010), 17.
26. On fol. 5v, an informal anglicana adds two saints to the Calendar: "*thome herford*" (Saint Thomas Cantilupe, feast day October 2) and "*sancte ffydes*" (Saint Foy, feast day October 6). This hand could be the Harley scribe's. The other late additions are not in his hand.
27. Fein, *Legend of Saint Etfrid*, 260–267
28. That description (removed and replaced in 2012, now irretrievable) characterized the hand by that name in several consecutive texts but did not specify that the hand is the same. For other descriptions of Harley 273 (besides the current one at *BLDM*), see "Harley MS 273" in the *British Library Catalogue of Illuminated Manuscripts (BLCIM)*, which names the hand "gothic"; Humfrey Wanley, D. Casley, et al., *A Catalogue of the Harleian Manuscripts in the British Museum* (1759; rev'd and repr. in 4 vols. London: British Museum, 1808–1812), 1:102; and H. L. D. Ward and J. A. Herbert, *Catalogue of Romances in the Department of Manuscripts in the British Museum*, 3 vols. (London: British Museum, 1883–1910), 1:587–589, 2:471–474, 3:272–284.
29. Walpole, *Old French Johannes*, 30–31. The first and third of his observations are false.

30. This two-column layout governs the look of each page. See the detailed description in ibid., 30.
31. Ibid., 35–36.
32. They are rare in the Psalter because each verse begins with the rubricator's initial in red or blue. The rubricator is a different scribe—I argue here that he is the Harley scribe. The main scribe's capitals are therefore chiefly evident in Latin headings appearing in red throughout the Psalter.
33. Omitted from the list are texts written by other hands (all brief later insertions). The digitized facsimile provides direct access to this corpus. *ANL* refers to Ruth Dean, with Maureen B. M. Boulton, *Anglo-Norman Literature: A Guide to Texts and Manuscripts*, ANTS o.p.s. 3 (London: Anglo-Norman Text Society, 1999).
34. The *BLDM* description of Harley 273 incorrectly joins booklets 1 and 2. They were probably used as a unit, but codicologically the Calendar is a separate gathering (with a cover) and ruled differently. A later medieval hand (one not found elsewhere in the Harley scribe's books) wrote four lines of Latin verse on its back cover (fol. 7v).
35. This item has been edited twice from its earliest witness, Oxford, Bodleian Library MS Douce 320. See Ian Short, ed., *The Oxford Psalter (Bodleian MS Douce 320)*, ANTS 72 (Oxford: Anglo-Norman Text Society from St Peter's College, Oxford, 2015); and Francisque Michel, ed., *Libri Psalmorum versio antique gallica* (Oxford: e typographeo academico, 1860). On its importance, see Geoff Rector, "The *Romanz* Psalter in England and Northern France in the Twelfth Century: Production, Mise-en-page, and Circulation," *Journal of the Early Book Society* 13 (2010): 1–38.
36. Because the AN Hours of the Virgin is inedited, my list of its internal items is representative, not exhaustive. In compiling this profile, I am indebted to Dean and Boulton's work in *ANL*, supplemented by access to the manuscript and the *BLDM* facsimile of "Harley MS 273."
37. *ANL* 829 reports that 4.a is in a different hand from 4.b. It is the same hand, only larger.
38. French text critically edited in Cesare Segre, ed., *Li Bestiaires d'amours di maistre Richart de Fornival e li response du Bestiaire* (Milan: Riccardo Ricciardi, 1957). Translation: Jeanette Beer, trans., *Master Richard's Bestiary of Love and Response* (Berkeley: University of California Press, 1986). See also Jeanette Beer, *Beasts of Love: Richard de Fournival's Bestiaire d'amour and a Woman's Response* (Toronto: University of Toronto Press, 2003). The presence of this text in Harley 273, nicely illustrated with line drawings, accounts for the manuscript's 2012 selection by the British Library for a digitized facsimile.

39. Lamond, *Walter of Henley's Husbandry*, 122–145, printing the text from Oxford, Bodleian Library MS Douce 98 with corrections from Harley 273 (xliii–xliv); and Dorothea Oschinsky, ed. and trans., *Walter of Henley and Other Treatises on Estate Management and Accounting* (Oxford: Clarendon, 1971), 11, 191–99, 487–415, printing the text from London, British Library MS Harley 1005. See also S. Harrison Thomson, *The Writings of Robert Grosseteste, Bishop of Lincoln 1235–1253* (Cambridge, UK: Cambridge University Press, 1940), 158–159; and James McEvoy, Robert Grosseteste (Oxford: Oxford University Press, 2000), 147.
40. The second and third parts of a three-part treatise. For an edition, see Tony Hunt, "Anglo-Norman Rules of Friendship," *French Studies Bulletin* 30 (1989): 9–11. This work also appears in Oxford, Bodleian Library MS Digby 86, fol. 207va–b.
41. For an edition, see Hunt, ed., *Popular Medicine*, 88. Ibid., 89–90, also edits a set of medical charms in a mixture of French and Latin from booklet 7 of Harley 273 (fol. 213r–v).
42. For an edition from a French manuscript, see Ronald N. Walpole, ed., *Le Turpin français, dit le Turpin I* (Toronto: University of Toronto Press, 1985). For a translation of a Latin redaction, see Kevin R. Poole, ed. and trans., *Chronicle of Pseudo-Turpin: Edition and Translation* (New York: Italica, 2014). For the AN version, see Ian Short, ed., *The Anglo-Norman Pseudo-Turpin Chronicle of William de Briane*, ANTS 25 (Oxford: Basil Blackwell, 1973). For the ME translation, see Stephen H. A. Shepherd, ed., *Turpines Story: A Middle English Translation of the Pseudo-Turpin Chronicle*, EETS o.s. 322 (Oxford: Oxford University Press, 2004).
43. This text has been edited and translated; see Tony Hunt, ed., and Jane Bliss, trans., *"Cher alme": Texts of Anglo-Norman Piety*, French of England Translation Series (FRETS) o.p.s. 1 (Tempe: Arizona Center for Medieval and Renaissance Studies, 2010), 294–319.
44. This item is also found in Harley 2253, fol. 134v; see Susanna Fein, ed. and trans., with David Raybin and Jan Ziolkowski, *Prayer on the Five Joys of Our Lady*, in *The Complete Harley 2253 Manuscript*, ed. and trans. Susanna Fein, with David Raybin and Jan Ziolkowski, vol. 3 (Kalamazoo, MI: Medieval Institute, 2015), 274–275 (art. 104).
45. This item of guidance is followed by a short prayer to Mary in AN verse (fol. 110rb; *ANL* 781; inedited), inserted by a later hand (one not found elsewhere in the Harley scribe's books). According to *ANL* 951, it typically accompanies either this prayer or the one preceding it in Harley 273.
46. Begun by the main scribe, who continues to fol. 181r, the text thereafter is copied by the Harley scribe. For an edition based on MSS Harley 273

and Harley 4657, see F. J. Furnivall, ed., *Robert of Brunne's "Handlyng Synne," A.D. 1303, with Those Parts of the Anglo-French Treatise on Which It Was Founded, William of Waddington's "Manuel des pechiez,"* Part I, EETS o.s. 119, 123 (London: Kegan, Paul, Trench, Trübner, 1901). On the challenge of identifying William of Waddington, "an English priest, who probably flourished towards the end of the 13th cent.," see Ward and Herbert, *Catalogue of Romances,* 3:272–284, at 272–273 (written by Herbert). As Herbert shows (ibid., 280–283), its exempla sometimes bear a derivative relationship with some in *Vitas patrum*—an AN work found in Harley 2253, fols. 1ra–21vb; Fein, *Complete Harley 2253 Manuscript,* 1:18–201 (art. 1). See also E. J. Arnould, *Le Manuel des pechés: Étude de littérature religieuse anglo-normande* (Paris: Droz, 1940), 361–367; and Klaus Bitterling, ed., *Of Shrifte and Penance: The ME Prose Translation of "Le Manuel des péchés,"* Middle English Texts 29 (Heidelberg, Germany: C. Winter, 1997).
47. Harley 2253 may now be viewed in color facsimile at the *BLDM* website: "Harley MS 2253," *British Library Digitised Manuscripts,* http://www.bl.uk/manuscripts/FullDisplay.aspx?ref=Harley_MS_2253.
48. Fein, "Four Scribes," 5–6.
49. Bozon was a Franciscan friar and prolific Anglo-Norman author (fl. ca. 1330s) who was apparently from the East Midlands or East Anglia. His writings circulated actively in the West Midlands, however, as is evident in the book of William Herebert, a friar of the Franciscan community of Hereford (London, British Library MS Additional 46919). Both had ties to the University of Oxford.
50. Fein, *Complete Harley 2253 Manuscript,* 2:18–33 (art. 8).
51. Because my focus here is on the Harley scribe's early collaboration with Harley 273's main scribe, I include data from Royal 12.C.xii only where it supplies necessary corroborating evidence.
52. In Royal 12.C.xii's *Fouke fitz Waryn,* where *F* is a prominent letter, the Harley scribe sometimes adds a descender to the first stroke or extends the top and lower horizontal bars. The basic form, however, agrees strongly with that found in the *ABC*. In Harley 273, the scribe's *F* appears in the Calendar (fol. 1r–v), frequently in the Psalter, and in booklet 7 (fol. 211v).
53. A playful "broken" *J*, designed to fit at the base of a column, is seen only in Harley 273, occurring in the Psalter and the *Pseudo-Turpin Chronicle* (fols. 64vb, 108rb). A capital *J* on fol. 207r (booklet 7) is made by the copyist, not the Harley scribe.
54. *K* always matches the *ABC* letter-form except when the Harley scribe uses it in a liturgical context: *KL* repeated at the top of each Calendar page (fols. 1r–6v), and *K* in *Kyriel* in the *Manuel* (fol. 68rb, two times).

The liturgical form is angular and lacks the right-side curviness of the normal form.

55. *O* is a consistent letter-form except for two instances in Harley 273 that have a tail on top (fols. 73r, 205v), like an upside-down *Q*, appearing beside many instances of the usual form. This rare variation helps to confirm that the same rubricator finished the *Bestiaire* in booklet 3 and the *Colors* text in booklet 7.
56. *S* is always a swirl with a right-hooked top, generally with closed (or near-closed) loops, resembling an 8. The main variation involves the left-side tail length. Forms with short, medium, or long tails appear randomly in both Harley 273 and Royal 12.C.xii. The letter appears only twice in Harley 2253, with short and medium tails (fols. 50r, 53v).
57. The two rare instances of *X* found in Harley 273 (fols. 68r, 106v) match the *ABC* letter-form.
58. *Y* and *Z* appear only in the *ABC* and one time each in Royal 12.C.xii (fols. 40r, 86v).
59. In Harley 273, he uses only the flat-top *A* found in *ABC*; the letter-form is frequent, particularly in the Calendar, Psalter, and *Bestiaire*. An odd habit of omitting the crossbar occurs in Royal 12.C.xii (fol. 32r) and nine times in Harley 273. A peaked variant (often with a long left descender) occurs frequently in Royal 12.C.xii and twice in Harley 2253 (fols. 54v, 55v). A long left descender also occurs frequently in Harley 273's flat-top *A*.
60. Two forms of *T* can be confirmed as belonging to the Harley scribe's repertoire by their appearance in Harley 2253: the squared-off *T* in the *ABC* (fol. 50r) and a curly-footed *T* in *The Life of Saint Ethelbert* (fol. 54v). *T* is a ubiquitous capital, very common in Harley 273. Both types occur in the Psalter, *Bestiaire*, and the *Pseudo-Turpin Chronicle*. The variants can be observed twice on a single folio (fols. 59r, 61r).
61. Þ appears only in Royal 12.C.xii (fols. 62v, 67v, 68r). *V* is frequently found in Harley 273, especially in the Psalter, matching the letter-form found once in Royal 12.C.xii (fol. 25r). The Harley scribe never uses *W* as a colored initial.
62. Revard, "Scribe and Provenance," 91. The fifth deed pertains to property in the Dinham/Christcroft district of Ludlow, where the Austins' first house was established in 1254. On the Austin friars of Ludlow, see Michael Faraday, *Ludlow 1085–1660: A Social, Economic and Political History* (Chichester, UK: Phillimore, 1991), 52 (map), 60–61; David Lloyd, *The Concise History of Ludlow* (Ludlow, UK: Merlin Unwin, 1999), 49–50 (drawn reconstruction of the friary—"one of the order's leading houses in England"—based on excavations); and Hines, *Voices in the Past*, 84 (map), 88. Faraday identifies many persons (bailiffs,

attorneys, etc.) who are named in these early writs; see, e.g., Faraday, *Ludlow*, 8, 25–26, 52, 80, 183–184.
63. See Fisher, *Scribal Authorship*, 100–145; and Una O'Farrell-Tate, ed., *The Abridged English Metrical Brut Edited from London, British Library MS Royal 12.C.XII*, Middle English Texts 32 (Heidelberg, Germany: C. Winter, 2002).
64. The A and B versions are edited in A. D. Wilshere, ed., *Mirour de Seinte Eglise (St. Edmund of Abingdon's Speculum Ecclesiae)*, ANTS 40 (London: Anglo-Norman Text Society, 1982). The Royal 12.C.xii text is from the A family.
65. Walpole, *Old French Johannes*, 36.
66. Psalm 51 receives a puzzle initial perhaps by accident (anticipating Psalm 52), and it is the wrong letter (*P* not *Q* for *Quid*). On the monastic division, see Rector, "The *Romanz* Psalter," 8.
67. Compare the puzzle initial that opens Harley 2253, fol. 1r, likely made by the Harley scribe (Fein, "Four Scribes," 5). There are subtle differences between the filler/flourish style of the Harley 273 puzzle initials and that of the opening *E* in Harley 2253, though they bear a general similarity. If the Harley scribe made them all, the chronological distance of two or three decades may explain the divergent style in Harley 2253.
68. In *Fouke fitz Waryn*, redacted by the Harley scribe, the hero Fouke encounters fantastical monsters, including a "venomous beast that had the head of a dog, a thick beard like a goat, and ears like a hare," said to be one of the creatures "St. Patrick had driven from Ireland." See Thomas E. Kelly, trans., *Fouke fitz Waryn*, in *Medieval Outlaws: Twelve Tales in Modern English Translation*, ed. Thomas H. Ohlgren, 2nd ed. (West Lafayette, IN: Parlor Press, 2005), 165–247, at 223.
69. This drollery sports a distinctive head fashion of the early fourteenth century, which Luttrell Psalter artists likewise display on woman-headed hybrids (fols. 60v, 274r). See the *BLDM* color facsimile: "Add. MS 42130," *British Library Digitised Manuscripts*, http://www.bl.uk/manuscripts/Viewer.aspx?ref=add_ms_42130_fs001ar. Compare, too, the mockery of this same fashion—a bun over each ear, secured with hairnets and bands—in a Harley lyric; see Susanna Fein, ed. and trans., with David Raybin and Jan Ziolkowski, *On the Follies of Fashion*, in *The Complete Harley 2253 Manuscript*, ed. and trans. Susanna Fein, with David Raybin and Jan Ziolkowski, vol. 2 (Kalamazoo, MI: Medieval Institute, 2015), 108–111 (art. 25a).
70. On Scribe D, see note 8 above.
71. The Harley scribe's hand does not appear in this booklet.
72. See note 8 above; Revard, "Scribe and Provenance," 23–25; and C. M. Woolgar, ed., *Household Accounts from Medieval England, Part I*:

Introduction, Glossary, Diet Accounts (I), Records for Social and Economic History n.s. 17 (Oxford: Oxford University Press, 1992), 174–177.
73. For both these items, the Harley scribe is, in the broad sense, an *author*. Each one has been individually altered from its exemplar. The changes made to *Fouke* transform the scribe's verse exemplar to prose. Those made to the *Short English Chronicle* add comments on history and specific places.
74. The Harley scribe's five booklets were appended to two booklets of Anglo-Norman religious narratives copied by an earlier scribe (Harley 2253, booklets 1–2), which the scribe had also acquired and partly rubricated at some point. These booklets had a larger format than those of Harley 273 and Royal 12.C.xii, and the scribe followed the grander scale in making the booklets designed for Harley 2253. See Fein, "Four Scribes," 39.

WORKS CITED

Primary Sources

British Library MS Additional 42130 (Luttrell Psalter).
British Library MS Harley 273.
British Library MS Harley 2253.
British Library MS Royal 12.C.xii.

Secondary Sources

"Add. MS 42130." *British Library Digitised Manuscripts (BLDM)*. http://www.bl.uk/manuscripts/Viewer.aspx?ref=add_ms_42130_fs001ar.
Arnould, E. J. *Le Manuel des pechés: Étude de littérature religieuse anglo-normande*. Paris: Droz, 1940.
Beer, Jeanette, trans. *Master Richard's Bestiary of Love and Response*. Berkeley: University of California Press, 1986.
———. *Beasts of Love: Richard de Fournival's Bestiaire d'amour and a Woman's Response*. Toronto: University of Toronto Press, 2003.
Bitterling, Klaus, ed. *Of Shrifte and Penance: The ME Prose Translation of "Le Manuel des péchés."* Middle English Texts 29. Heidelberg, Germany: C. Winter, 1997.
Busby, Keith. *Codex and Context: Reading Old French Verse Narrative in Manuscript*. 2 vols. Amsterdam: Rodopi, 2002.
———. "Multilingualism, the Harley Scribe, and Johannes Jacobi." In *Insular Books: Vernacular Manuscript Miscellanies in Late Medieval Britain*, ed. Margaret Connolly and Raluca Radulescu, 49–60. Proceedings of the British Academy 201. Oxford: Oxford University Press, 2015.
Corrie, Marilyn. "Harley 2253, Digby 86, and the Circulation of Literature

in Pre-Chaucerian England." In *Studies in the Harley Manuscript: The Scribes, Contents, and Social Contexts of British Library MS Harley 2253*, ed. Susanna Fein, 427–443. Kalamazoo, MI: Medieval Institute, 2000.

Dean, Ruth, with Maureen B. M. Boulton. *Anglo-Norman Literature: A Guide to Texts and Manuscripts (ANL)*. ANTS o.p.s. 3. London: Anglo-Norman Text Society, 1999.

Faraday, Michael. *Ludlow 1085–1660: A Social, Economic and Political History*. Chichester, UK: Phillimore, 1991.

Fein, Susanna, "The Four Scribes of MS Harley 2253." *Journal of the Early Book Society* 16 (2013): 27–49.

———. "The Fillers of the Auchinleck Manuscript and the Literary Culture of the West Midlands." In *Makers and Users of Medieval Books: Essays in Honour of A. S. G. Edwards*, ed. Carol M. Meale and Derek Pearsall, 60–77. Cambridge, UK: D. S. Brewer, 2014.

———. "Literary Scribes: The Harley Scribe and Robert Thornton." In *Insular Books: Vernacular Manuscript Miscellanies in Late Medieval Britain*, ed. Margaret Connolly and Raluca Radulescu, 61–79. Proceedings of the British Academy 201. Oxford: Oxford University Press, 2015.

———, ed. and trans., with David Raybin and Jan Ziolkowski. *The Complete Harley 2253 Manuscript*. Vols. 1–3. Kalamazoo, MI: Medieval Institute, 2014–2015.

———, ed. and trans., with David Raybin and Jan Ziolkowski. *The Legend of Saint Etfrid, Priest of Leominster*. In *The Complete Harley 2253 Manuscript*, ed. and trans. Susanna Fein, with David Raybin and Jan Ziolkowski, 260–267. Vol. 3. Kalamazoo, MI: Medieval Institute, 2015.

———, ed. and trans., with David Raybin and Jan Ziolkowski. *The Life of Saint Ethelbert*. In *The Complete Harley 2253 Manuscript*, ed. and trans. Susanna Fein, with David Raybin and Jan Ziolkowski, 50–59. Vol. 2. Kalamazoo, MI: Medieval Institute, 2014.

———, ed. and trans., with David Raybin and Jan Ziolkowski. *On the Follies of Fashion*. In *The Complete Harley 2253 Manuscript*, ed. and trans. Susanna Fein, with David Raybin and Jan Ziolkowski, 108–111. Vol. 2. Kalamazoo, MI: Medieval Institute, 2015.

———, ed. and trans., with David Raybin and Jan Ziolkowski. *Prayer on the Five Joys of Our Lady*. In *The Complete Harley 2253 Manuscript*, ed. and trans. Susanna Fein, with David Raybin and Jan Ziolkowski, 274–275. Vol. 3. Kalamazoo, MI: Medieval Institute, 2015.

———, ed. and trans., with David Raybin and Jan Ziolkowski. *Vitas patrum*. In *The Complete Harley 2253 Manuscript*, ed. and trans. Susanna Fein, with David Raybin and Jan Ziolkowski, 18–201. Vol. 1. Kalamazoo, MI: Medieval Institute, 2015.

Fisher, Matthew. *Scribal Authorship and the Writing of History in Medieval England.* Columbus: Ohio State University Press, 2012.

Furnivall, F. J., ed., *Robert of Brunne's "Handlyng Synne," A.D. 1303, with Those Parts of the Anglo-French Treatise on Which It Was Founded, William of Waddington's "Manuel des pechiez."* Part I. EETS o.s. 119, 123. London: Kegan, Paul, Trench, Trübner, 1901.

"Harley MS 2253." *British Library Digitised Manuscripts (BLDM).* http://www.bl.uk/manuscripts/FullDisplay.aspx?ref=Harley_MS_2253.

"Harley MS 273." *British Library Catalogue of Illuminated Manuscripts (BLCIM).* http://www.bl.uk/catalogues/illuminatedmanuscripts/searchMSNo.asp.

———. *British Library Digitised Manuscripts (BLDM).* http://www.bl.uk/manuscripts/FullDisplay.aspx?ref=Harley_MS_273.

Hathaway, E. J., P. T. Ricketts, C. A. Robson, and A. D. Wilshere, eds. *Fouke le Fitz Waryn.* ANTS 26–28. Oxford: Basil Blackwell, 1975.

Hines, John. *Voices in the Past: English Literature and Archaeology.* Cambridge, UK: D. S. Brewer, 2004.

Hunt, Tony, ed. *Popular Medicine in Thirteenth-Century England: Introduction and Texts.* Cambridge, UK: D. S. Brewer, 1990.

———. "Anglo-Norman Rules of Friendship," *French Studies Bulletin* 30 (1989): 9–11.

———, ed., and Jane Bliss, trans., *"Cher alme": Texts of Anglo-Norman Piety,* 294–319. French of England Translation Series (FRETS) o.p.s. 1. Tempe: Arizona Center for Medieval and Renaissance Studies, 2010.

———, Julia Boffey, A. S. G. Edwards, and Daniel Huws. "Vernacular Literature and Its Readership." In *The Cambridge History of the Book in Britain: Volume II 1100–1400,* ed. Nigel Morgan and Rodney M. Thomson, 367–396. Cambridge, UK: Cambridge University Press, 2008.

Kelly, Thomas E., trans. *Fouke fitz Waryn.* In *Medieval Outlaws: Twelve Tales in Modern English Translation,* ed. Thomas H. Ohlgren, 165–247. 2nd ed. West Lafayette, IN: Parlor Press, 2005.

Ker, N. R., intro. *Facsimile of British Museum MS. Harley 2253.* EETS o.s. 255. London: Oxford University Press, 1965.

Lamond, Elizabeth, ed. and trans. *Walter of Henley's Husbandry, Together with an Anonymous Husbandry, Seneschaucie, and Robert Grosseteste's Rules.* London: Longmans, Green, 1890.

Lloyd, David. *The Concise History of Ludlow.* Ludlow, UK: Merlin Unwin, 1999.

———, Margaret Clark, and Chris Potter. *St. Laurence's Church, Ludlow: The Parish Church and People, 1199–2009.* Wooten Almeley, UK: Logaston Press, 2010.

McEvoy, James. *Robert Grosseteste*. Oxford: Oxford University Press, 2000.
Michel, Francisque, ed., *Libri Psalmorum versio antique gallica*. Oxford: e typographeo academico, 1860.
Oschinsky, Dorothea, ed. and trans. *Walter of Henley and Other Treatises on Estate Management and Accounting*. Oxford: Clarendon, 1971.
O'Farrell-Tate, Una, ed. *The Abridged English Metrical Brut Edited from London, British Library MS Royal* 12.C.XII. Middle English Texts 32. Heidelberg, Germany: C. Winter, 2002.
O'Rourke, Jason. "Imagining Book Production in Fourteenth-Century Herefordshire: The Scribe of British Library, MS Harley 2253 and His 'Organizing Principles.'" In *Imagining the Book*, ed. Stephen Kelly and John J. Thompson, 45–60. Turnhout, Belgium: Brepols, 2005.
Poole, Kevin R., ed. *Chronicle of Pseudo-Turpin: Edition and Translation*. New York: Italica, 2014.
Rector, Geoff. "The *Romanz* Psalter in England and Northern France in the Twelfth Century: Production, Mise-en-page, and Circulation," *Journal of the Early Book Society* 13 (2010): 1–38.
Revard, Carter. "Scribe and Provenance." In *Studies in the Harley Manuscript: The Scribes, Contents, and Social Contexts of British Library MS Harley 2253*, ed. Susanna Fein, 21–110. Kalamazoo, MI: Medieval Institute, 2000.
Scahill, John. "Trilingualism in Early Middle English Miscellanies: Languages and Literature." *Yearbook of English Studies* 33 (2003): 18–32.
Schmitt, Rudolf, ed. *Der Pseudoturpin Harley 273: Der Text mit einer Untersuchung der Sprache*. Würzburg, Germany: Druck von Richard Mayr, 1933.
Segre, Cesare, ed. *Li Bestiaires d'amours di maistre Richart de Fornival e li response du Bestiaire*. Milan: Riccardo Ricciardi, 1957.
Shepherd, Stephen H. A., ed. *Turpines Story: A Middle English Translation of the Pseudo-Turpin Chronicle*. EETS 322. Oxford: Oxford University Press, 2004.
Short, Ian, ed. *The Anglo-Norman Pseudo-Turpin Chronicle of William de Briane*. ANTS 25. Oxford: Basil Blackwell, 1973.
———, ed. *The Oxford Psalter (Bodleian MS Douce 320)*. ANTS 72. Oxford: Anglo-Norman Text Society from St Peter's College, Oxford, 2015.
Smith, William. *The Use of Hereford: The Sources of a Medieval English Diocesan Rite*. Burlington, VT: Ashgate, 2015.
Thomson, S. Harrison. *The Writings of Robert Grosseteste, Bishop of Lincoln 1235–1253*. Cambridge, UK: Cambridge University Press, 1940.
Vising, Johan, ed. "Le Purgatoire de Saint Patrice des manuscrits Harléien 273 et fonds français 2198." *Götesborgs Högskolas Årsskrift* 22 (1916): 1–87.
Walpole, Ronald N., ed. *The Old French Johannes Translation of the*

Pseudo-Turpin Chronicle: A Critical Edition. Berkeley: University of California Press, 1976.

———. *The Old French Johannes Translation of the Pseudo-Turpin Chronicle: Supplement.* Berkeley: University of California Press, 1976.

———, ed. *Le Turpine français, dit le Turpin I.* Toronto: University of Toronto Press, 1985.

Wanley, Humfrey, D. Casley, et al. *A Catalogue of the Harleian Manuscripts in the British Museum.* 1759; rev'd and repr. in 4 vols. London: British Museum, 1808–1812.

Ward, H. L. D., and J. A. Herbert. *Catalogue of Romances in the Department of Manuscripts in the British Museum.* 3 vols. London: British Museum, 1883–1910.

Wilshere, A. D., ed. *Mirour de Seinte Eglise (St. Edmund of Abingdon's Speculum Ecclesiae).* ANTS 40. London: Anglo-Norman Text Society, 1982.

Woolgar, C. M., ed. *Household Accounts from Medieval England, Part I: Introduction, Glossary, Diet Accounts (I).* Records for Social and Economic History n.s. 17. Oxford: Oxford University Press, 1992.

The Secrees of Old Philisoffres and John Lydgate's Posthumous Reputation

RORY G. CRITTEN

The Secrees of Old Philisoffres is a Middle English verse translation of the pseudo-Aristotelian *Secretum Secretorum*, a mirror for princes that imagines the aged philosopher sending letters of advice to Alexander the Great on topics ranging from the arts of kingship to alchemy, physiognomy, and diet. Traditionally dated to the year of the author's death in 1449, it is normally presented as the last work written by the Benedictine monk and highly prolific poet, John Lydgate.[1] This is a distinction that the *Secrees* cannot be said to deserve in any unambiguous way, however, for its identity as a posthumously published, dual-authored production is routinely advertised in paratextual material surviving in the extant medieval witnesses and within the text of the poem itself. Thus after line 1491 of the copy of the work in London, British Library MS Sloane 2464, there comes a rubric announcing a change in authorship: "here deyed this translator and nobil poete and the yonge folowere gan his prologe on this wyse" (fol. 36r). There then follows a corresponding change of voice as, in a prologue introducing his work, the young follower laments his inexperience. He contrasts this with the expertise of the author of the first part of the poem, whom he is quick to identify as John Lydgate:

> Off Iohn lydgate / how shulde I the sotyl trace
> Folwe in secrees / celestial and dyvyne,
> Sith I am nat aqueynted / with the musys nyne?
> (1503–1505)[2]

This article elaborates upon two observations pertaining to the transferal of the authorial function in the *Secrees*. First, while Lydgate was clearly not shy when it came to asserting his authorship—indeed, he names himself in more texts than any other Middle English writer[3]—I am keen to register that it is the continuator of the *Secrees*, not Lydgate himself, who identifies Lydgate as the author of the text's opening section. To begin, I look at the agency of the continuator in the production of the *Secrees* and at the extent to which his attribution of the first portion of the poem to Lydgate can be understood as a self-interested bid for respect and, perhaps, reward. Then I go on to consider the significance of the author's death rubric, which is written not in the voice of the continuator but in that of an unidentified third person. I want to think about who speaks these lines and about how they structure our understanding of the relationship between the continuator and the author of the first part of the poem; within the context of a survey of the extant manuscript and early print situations in which the *Secrees* survives, I pay particular attention to the ways in which the author's death rubric implicates the poem's medieval reproducers in the process of developing Lydgate's posthumous reputation.

The success of the *Secrees* was considerable. According to the *Digital Index of Middle English Verse*, where it is listed as item 1544, the poem is extant in twenty-four medieval copies; an annotated list of these witnesses is appended to this article for convenience.[4] While the appeal of the work must have derived in part from the popularity of its source and from its handling of such current themes as good governance and medicine, I argue that a significant portion of the extant medieval witnesses to the text demonstrate an interest among both bookmakers and readers in developing and promoting Lydgate's authorial profile. Like the continuator of the *Secrees*, I suggest, the medieval reproducers of the poem could manipulate the idea of Lydgate's posthumous reputation with a view to exciting the curiosity of their audiences and accruing benefit to themselves. This approach to the *Secrees of Old Philisoffres* and its earliest witnesses thus offers a fresh opportunity to review a range of topics that are crucial to any understanding of English literature in the second half of the fifteenth century: the promotion of Chaucer and his first disciples by their followers; the currency of Middle English authorship as an idea that might give structure to a text or a book; and the motivations, commercial and otherwise, that could drive Middle English book production in the decades immediately before and after the advent of print in England.

The Authors and Their Poem

First, then, the question of attribution: Who wrote the *Secrees*? Where the continuator assigns the first portion of the poem to Lydgate, he also clarifies his position vis-à-vis his work. Lydgate's death provides the rationale for the continuator's composition, which the reader is invited to view both as a careful tribute to the memory of the dead poet and as a response to the command of an unnamed but impatient patron. In the opening lines of the text of the prologue preserved in Sloane 2464, the continuator mentions that he is late finishing his text:

> Tendirnesse of age / and lak of Elloquence,
> this feerful matere / savyng supportacioun,
> me hath constreyned / to put in suspence
> From yow, my lord / to whoom Recommendacioun
> I mekly do sende / with al Subieccioun
> The dulnesse of my penne. (1492–1497)

The abject pose in which the continuator depicts himself both here, before the commissioner of the work, and throughout his prologue will be familiar to readers of fifteenth-century poetry. Most often it is before Chaucer that the later Middle English poets prostrate themselves. In his retelling of the story of Troy, for example, Lydgate repeatedly looks back to the example set by his predecessor in *Troilus and Criseyde*. Indeed, we would do well to read the *Troilus*, Lydgate asserts, since it was Chaucer who first gilded "owre englishe" through his poetry and who first began to magnify our tongue and to adorn it with his eloquence:

> Þe hoole story Chaucer kan ȝow telle
> Ȝif þat ȝe liste—no man bet alyue—
> Nor þe processe halfe so wel discryue:
> For he owre englishe gilte with his sawes,
> Rude and boistous firste be olde dawes,
> Þat was ful fer from al perfeccioun,
> And but of litel reputacioun,
> Til þat he cam, &, þoruȝ his poetrie,
> Gan oure tonge firste to magnifie,
> And adourne it with his elloquence. (III. 4234–4243)[5]

Once viewed straightforwardly as evidence of Lydgate's awareness of his supposed inferiority to Chaucer, readers from Seth Lerer onward have reinterpreted such gestures towards the pre-eminence of the earlier poet as aspects of a strategy designed by Lydgate and his peers to justify their own literary projects in a climate that had only recently seen English-language poetry return to cultural prominence.[6] Thus in his reading of the continuation of this passage, Robert J. Meyer-Lee highlights Lydgate's retrospective construction of Chaucer as England's first poet laureate.⁷ Chaucer should be praised, Lydgate declares,

> So þat þe laurer of oure englishe tonge
> Be to hym ʒoue for his excellence,
> Riʒt as whilom by ful hiʒe sentence,
> Perpetuelly for a memorial,
> Of Columpna by þe cardynal
> To Petrak Fraunceis was ʒouen in Ytaille (III. 4246–4251)

While Lydgate confines his own ambitions to an attempt "So as I can, hym to magnifie / In my writynge, pleinly, til I dye" (III. 4261–4262), where he announces his intention to "magnifie" Chaucer just as Chaucer magnified English, Lydgate pictures himself in a role that is comparable to that performed by his predecessor, and he implicitly identifies himself as the earlier poet's heir. If he could establish Chaucer as a viable literary model, an early fifteenth-century poet like Lydgate would have a tradition of Middle English writing into which he might insert himself; by presenting himself as Chaucer's follower he might also hope to bask in the reflection of the glory with which he invested the departed poet and thus to increase his chances of attracting patronage and other forms of support, for himself and for his order. It is a testimony to Lydgate's success in establishing the currency of this authorial strategy that at least one of Lydgate's successors installed Lydgate in the position that Lydgate had reserved for Chaucer. The opportunistic mourning of Chaucer by the poets of Lydgate's generation had provided the foundations on which they could build their own poetic monuments. By the same logic, Lydgate's own death might be manipulated by a mid-fifteenth-century writer engaged in constructing his own literary reputation. I think that this is what is going on in the *Secrees of Old Philisoffres*.

The approach that I am advocating invites readers to view precisely those aspects of the *Secrees* that have rendered it unpopular in modern criticism as part of a deliberate attempt by the text's continuator to present an emotive portrait of Lydgate's demise. The brief critical history of the *Secrees* is not flattering. Walter F. Schirmer comments upon the negative impression left by the work of a "jumble," both in terms of its content and its formal disposition,⁸ and Derek Pearsall amplifies this criticism, pronouncing the poem to be "as nearly worthless as any that Lydgate penned."⁹ These assessments respond first and foremost to the complex opening section of the *Secrees* (ll. 1–637), which compiles a series of formal prologues taken over from the most likely multiple Latin and/or French versions of the *Secretum Secretorum* from which it was translated.¹⁰ These prologues contain much duplicated material. The process whereby the *Secretum* was translated into Latin is narrated twice and attributed to two different men without further elaboration, for instance (ll. 211–301; 603–637). In a uniquely sensitive reading of the *Secrees*, Margaret Bridges notes the likelihood that the author of the first section of the poem inherited a part of this confusion from his sources, a common feature among parallel French and English versions of the *Secretum* being the misattribution of the initial work of translating the text into Latin to Philip of Paris rather than to John of Spain, the writer now credited with producing the earliest Latin version of the *Secretum*; Bridges also points out that duplication of the kind met in the poem's opening lines is "consonant with [Lydgate's] penchant observable elsewhere for multiplying textual genealogies."[11]

Hospitable readings such as that pursued by Bridges are to be welcomed. It is difficult to imagine that Pearsall's and Schirmer's low estimation of the *Secrees* can have been current in the Middle Ages, given the frequency with which it was reproduced. At the same time, it is difficult to deny the justice of Pearsall's and Schirmer's objections outright. As well as containing several instances of repetition akin to that already described,[12] the portion of the text attributed to Lydgate seems unusually disconnected. There are unexplained shifts between third- and first-person narration, for instance, which frustrate the reading process considerably (ll. 225–231; 617–623).[13] While criticism has evolved beyond the need to make value judgments of the kind that characterize Schirmer's and Pearsall's mid-twentieth-century studies, it thus makes sense to try to work with as well as against their responses to the poem. Indeed, if I am right about the *Secrees*, their reactions might ultimately be imputed not to any deficiency in the work but to its potential cleverness.

The moment at which the death of Lydgate is announced in the *Secrees* appears to have been chosen for maximum impact. The stanzas leading up to this point contain a moralized reflection on the four seasons (ll. 1296–1491); according to the fiction developed in the *Secretum* tradition, this was one of the forms in which Aristotle delivered his advice to King Alexander. Thus we read that remembrance of spring should alert Alexander to the choice that he had to act either wisely or foolishly in his youth; summer should evoke for him the necessary relationship between desert and divine reward; autumn should be interpreted as a sign of the coming of old age; and winter should prompt recollection of the inevitability of death. This point is reinforced in the section's last stanza:

> Off this forseyd / take the morallite,
> Settith a syde / alle materys spooke in veyn:
> The foure sesouns / shewe in ther degre,
> First veer and Estas / next Autumpne with his greyn,
> Constreynt of wyntir / with frostys ovir leyn,

> To our foure Ages / the sesouns wel applyed;
> deth al consumyth / which may nat be denyed
> (1485–1491)

With this, the portion of the poem attributed to Lydgate ends, and the poet dies, as it were, before our eyes. Where the extant manuscripts have not suffered damage and do not present an extracted text, the next thing we read is the previously mentioned death rubric.[14] Thus we are led to believe, in Pearsall's words, that "the pen slipped limply from [Lydgate's] fingers, and the aged monk slumped to the floor."[15] In such a reading context, the previously mentioned infelicities in the poem's structure might be reprocessed as evidence of the author's senility and the ebbing of his literary powers. Indeed, the poem contains multiple allusions to the great age of Aristotle, the putative original author of the *Secretum Secretorum* that might also be thought to refer to Lydgate. According to the logic established by the posthumous attribution of the first portion of the *Secrees* to the English writer, the translating labors of the old poet can be read in parallel to the work of the old philosopher, who in the text's opening prologues is repeatedly said to have sent Alexander the letters compiled in the *Secretum* when he had fallen into great age (ll. 50–56; 477–483; 596–602; 645–651). Thus at the same time as the *Secrees* confirms Lydgate's fame, it renders him obsolete, clearing the ground for new writing.

As the text's nineteenth-century editor, Robert Steele, wryly noted, the apparent conjunction of literature and life, whereby Lydgate is said to have died having just penned his reflections on the inevitability of death, is "one of those coincidences which look like design."[16] Pearsall concurs, suggesting that before the continuator of the *Secrees* began the portion of the poem that he overtly claims as his own, he deliberately rearranged the lines that he attributes to Lydgate from a series of attempts at the translation of the *Secretum* left in a disordered state by his predecessor at his death.[17] Some justification for Pearsall's and Steele's hypotheses may be drawn from the observation that the passage on the four seasons would seem most often to have been included in the section of the *Secretum Secretorum* devoted to the king's health (the continuator begins his portion of the work with this section, at l. 1590 in the Sloane 2464 text).[18] Further historical corroboration for Pearsall's and Steele's suggestion is provided by the traditional attribution of the continuation of the *Secrees* to the poet Benedict Burgh (d. 1483), who is identified as the author of the second portion of the poem in an extension added to the author's death rubric ("per Benedictum Burgh") that occurs in three of the extant copies of the text written by the so-called Hammond scribe (more on whom below; compare notes for witnesses 12, 15, and 16 in the appendix).[19] In a manuscript largely written in the hand of the early modern antiquarian John Stow, Burgh is also identified as the author of a verse epistle directed to Lydgate in which he praises the older poet's achievements and begs to be received as his disciple;[20] the reconstructed itineraries of Burgh and Lydgate indicate a possible meeting between the two poets, perhaps in the early 1430s;[21] and the two men were connected by a complex and ramifying network of patronal relationships to the Bourchier family in Essex.[22] In short, we might argue in favor of the likelihood that the continuator of the *Secrees* knew Lydgate personally and that he accordingly enjoyed the intimate access to the dead poet's papers that Steele's and Pearsall's models for the completion of the poem presuppose. A parallel case has recently been put forward regarding the polishing of the Ellesmere text of Chaucer's *Canterbury Tales*, which Simon Horobin attributes to Thomas Hoccleve, a self-confessed devotee of Chaucer.[23]

Lydgate might have attempted to translate the *Secretum Secretorum* at some point in his career—not necessarily at its end—and the continuator, who never names himself, might have been Benedict Burgh, who might have known Lydgate personally. In reality, however, the poet who presents himself as the continuator of the work required no direct access to Lydgate or his papers in order to produce the final version of the *Secrees*. Indeed, Lydgate need not have penned a word of the text attributed to him by the continuator in order for the poem to work as a calculated tribute to Lydgate's achievements: this, I am suggesting, is how we might best approach it. It is the act of attribution that matters. What is at issue here is a phenomenon that shares some features of the "author-function" that Michel Foucault sees as the principle by which the modern reader "limits, excludes, and chooses" among the multiplicity of meanings available in any given cultural text and by which he or she thus "impedes the free circulation, the free manipulation, the free composition, decomposition, and recomposition of fiction."[24] But whereas for Foucault the author-function is something that we bring to the text, something that, "at least in appearance, is outside it and antecedes it,"[25] in the Middle Ages, as Alexandra Gillespie points out, the idea of the author could both function as a limit to the endless play of textual meaning and be a part of a literary game.[26] Thus while Lydgate is identified as the maker of the first portion of the poem in thirteen of the sixteen extant versions of the author's death rubric listed in the appendix, as we have seen, Lydgate's name is not mentioned in that paratext in Sloane 2464. In Sloane 2464, and in two other copies of the work listed as containing the anonymous rubric, the attribution of the poem to Lydgate comes solely from within the continuator's portion of the work: it is a part of his text, not external to it (compare notes for witnesses 1 and 4 in the appendix).

The appendix also compiles data demonstrating some of the variations to which the continuator's prologue was subject that have a notable effect on the reader's apprehension of the work's authorship and the process of its continuation. The passage cited above from lines 1492–1497 of the Sloane 2464 text (Steele's stanza 214), in which the completed text of the *Secrees* is presented as a tardy production, is to be found only in a minority of the extant witnesses, for instance (compare notes for witnesses 1, 4, and 19 in the appendix); the other copies of the work give less information regarding the continuator's motivation, and in at least two apparently undamaged witnesses the entire continuator's prologue is absent: in one of these, Cambridge, Gonville and Caius College MS 366/725, the author's death rubric is also missing; in the other, Oxford, Balliol College MS 329, the rubric has apparently been rewritten in order to elide the agency of the continuator in the completion of the work, reading simply "Her endyth John lydgate translator of þis be for seyde her arystotyll wrytyth a pystyll to alyzaundre how he scholde conserve naturall helth of þe body" (fol. 107r).[27] While Lydgate's conceptualized responsibility for the portion of the text attributed to him is clearly intended to be appreciated and to add value to the *Secrees*, the nature of his involvement in the work and the continuator's own motivations are presented with varying degrees of clarity and insistence from witness to witness.

The difference between Gillespie's understanding of the author function and that of Foucault as she outlines it is between "a reductive category—one that manages, controls, and answers—and a category that is *also* productive, that proliferates, energizes, and changes."[28] In the case of the *Secrees*, the energizing effects of the attribution of the first portion of the text to Lydgate are significant because it encourages readers to interpret the poem's various infelicities as a meaningful reflection of its author's failing powers. As will soon become clear, some part of the popularity of the *Secrees* clearly derived from the work's thematic engagements; interest in the *Secretum* itself was also already high in later medieval England: the *Secrees* is just one of several Middle English translations of the work that have survived from the period.[29] Alongside the appeal that these factors generated, the continuator's reconstruction of Lydgate's final moments might also be viewed as one of the causes of its undeniable popularity among late-medieval readers.

At the outset of this paper I noted that the rubric announcing Lydgate's death is written in the third person. Bridges and others have sensibly argued that the regular reproduction of this rubric across the total corpus of the extant manuscripts suggests that the continuator himself supplied these words along with the other paratextual comments that punctuate the poem.[30] Be this as it may, it remains notable that the continuator does not assume responsibility for his rubric, either because of generic constraints (manuscript apparatuses are normally written in the third person) or as a matter of personal choice. "[H]ere deyed this *translator* and nobil poete" we are told in Sloane 2464, "and the yonge folowere gan his *prologe* on this wyse." It is as if the book's scribe, or perhaps even the book itself, were speaking to us, explaining the process whereby the fraught text that it contains came to be completed and reproduced in manuscript for our perusal. With a view to obtaining a better impression of the variety of compiling voices implicated in this rubric, I want now to survey the medieval contexts in which the poem survives and, through them, to think about the various motivations that produced the surviving medieval copies of the poem.

The Medieval Witnesses and Their Makers

The Secrees of Old Philisoffres held a range of attractions for its medieval reproducers and the readers whose interests guided them. Consideration of the texts alongside which the poem was frequently compiled suggests that it was particularly appreciated among an audience of gentry readers for its development of the themes of governance and self-rule. The poem's capacity to speak to these concerns is highlighted in the title of the work preferred among the extant witnesses, of which the appendix lists seven entitling the poem *The Book of the Governance of Kings and Princes* and four calling it a *Regimen Principum* in an explicit. The poem frequently appeared in books containing texts treating governance, conduct, and feats of arms that can be associated with particular households. Identified as the "grete boke" commissioned by Sir John Paston (d. 1479), London, British Library MS Lansdowne 285 compiles texts describing chivalric spectacles alongside the *Secrees* (fols. 152r–197v) and the Middle English translation often attributed to John Trevisa of Vegetius's *De rei militari* (fols. 84r–138r), a late antique treatise on the arts of war that enjoyed huge popularity in the late Middle Ages.[31] Portions of Lansdowne 285, including its copy of the *Secrees*, appear to have been copied directly from New York, Pierpont Morgan Library MS M775, whose execution is more sumptuous but whose origins lie in a context in which a lively interest in the arts of combat might likewise be assumed: heraldic arms added to the book early in its history link it to the household of Sir John Astley (d. 1486), a famous dueler and early recipient of the Order of the Garter from Edward IV in about 1461.[32]

Books comparable to the Lansdowne and Morgan codices include London, British Library MS Additional 14408 and Oxford, Bodleian Library MS Laud misc. 416. Written throughout by the same scribe, the Additional book compiles the *Secrees* (1r–48v) alongside the first book of the Middle English *De rei militari* (fols. 49r–66r) and a Middle English translation of the *Consilia Isidori* (fols. 66v–73r), a treatise on the vices and the virtues that is traditionally associated with Richard Rolle. It concludes with a colophon announcing that "Cest liure appertient Nycolas de Saint lo Chevalier" (fol.

73r), Nicholas St. Lo being a knight of Sutton in Somerset (d. 1486).³³ In Laud misc. 416, the *Secrees* (fols. 255r–287r) appears alongside part of Peter Idley's *Instructions to His Son* (fols. 1r–64v), an imperfect copy of the *Cursor mundi* (fols. 65r–181v), the Middle English *De rei militari* (fols. 182r–226v), an abbreviated *Siege of Thebes* (fols. 227r–254r), and an imperfect copy of *The Parliament of Fowels* (fol. 288r–289v). The presence of a colophon in this book—"scriptus Rhodo per Johannem Neuton die 25 Octobris 1459" (fol. 226v)—has allowed M. C. Seymour to locate part of the copying of Laud misc. 416 in the household of John Tiptoff, earl of Worcester (d. 1471), who had a manor at La Rode in Selling, Kent (while Seymour identifies three scribes at work in the codex, the medieval foliation of the book identifies it as a late fifteenth-century compilation).³⁴ Two further books transmitting the *Secrees* manifest similar tastes, but their provenance is less clear: Cambridge, Fitzwilliam Museum MS McClean 182, which transmits the *Secrees* (fols. 12r–49r) with an imperfect copy of Lydgate's *Serpent of Division* (fols. 1r–9v), miscellaneous Lydgatean ballads, some of which are extracts from the *Fall of Princes* (fols. 9v–11v; 49v–52v), and an imperfect copy of Hoccleve's *Regiment of Princes* (fols. 54r–138r); and London, British Library MS Sloane 2027, which sees the *Secrees* (fols. 53r–92v) rubbing shoulders with an imperfect copy of the Middle English *De rei militari* (fols. 1r–36r), John Russell's *Boke of Nurture* (fols. 37r–52r), Robert of Gloucester's *Chronicle* (fols. 97v–169v), and an imperfect *Brut* (fols. 96v–188v).

A smaller group of manuscripts transmitting the *Secrees* witnesses to an interest in the advice on diet and medical matters offered in the poem. Oxford, Balliol College MS 329 situates the *Secrees* (fols. 80r–126r) alongside works on the virtues of herbs (fols. 1r–35v) and a book of remedies (fols. 36r–79r) as well as extracts from the *Fall of Princes* (127r–71v); and Cambridge, Gonville and Caius MS 336/725 accompanies the *Secrees* (fols. 108r–128r) with a series of other medical, alchemical, and astrological texts and diagrams. Both the Balliol and the Gonville and Caius's texts of the *Secrees* are presented as integral works but they lack several of the sections reproduced in the longer versions of the poems, and those portions of the poem that they do reproduce appear in an order unlike that of the text reproduced in Steele's edition of Sloane 2464.³⁵ Their texts, which are not identical, may represent attempts to whittle down the *Secrees* to what were perceived to be its essential points; in Gonville and Caius MS 336/725 it has the title "Of the crafte of phisonomye which doth trete of the qualitees and Condicions of ich membre of man" (fol. 108r).³⁶ Alternatively, they may be the result of a different arrangement of the fragments of the Middle English translation of the *Secretum Secretorum* with which the compiler of the *Secrees* would have us believe that he was working. It seems more definite that some self-conscious extraction took place during the copying of what is now the fifth booklet of Cambridge, Trinity College MS R.3.19, which reproduces only the poem's moralized rendition of the four seasons, calling its extract "A tr*ates* of the iiij seasons of the yere" (fol. 49r).

Further reading contexts are represented by the remaining extant manuscripts. An imperfect copy of the *Secrees* survives in the Winchester Anthology, London, British Library MS Additional 60577 (fols. 24v–37v), a personal collection that has been attributed to a monk of the Benedictine priory at St. Swithuns.[37] On at least one occasion, moreover, the poem circulated alone: Oxford, Bodleian Library MS Laud misc. 673 is a small paper volume; its only contents are the *Secrees*, and the book is preserved in its fifteenth-century binding.[38] Finally, one sizable group of manuscripts remains to be discussed in which an interest in Lydgate's authorship mirroring that of the continuator of the *Secrees* might be detected. This interest is perhaps most immediately clear in Oxford, Bodleian Library Ashmole 59, the latest surviving anthology written by John Shirley, which presents toward its close the first five lines of the poem as an independent text (fol. 134r).[39] The unattributed extract from the *Secrees* appears among various verses and pen trials at the end of Shirley's book and is not in Shirley's hand; it might be interpreted as a response to the respectful attitude toward Lydgate's writing cultivated in the rubrics scattered through the book in which Shirley announces the authorship of the texts that he copies, among which works by Lydgate predominate. Thus Lydgate is referred to not only as a monk, a religious, and a clerk but also as a "poete" (fol. 16v, 20r, 21r, etc.) and, on one occasion, as a "philosofre" (fol. 41r). The positive response to Shirley's presentation of Lydgate that might be discerned in the copying of the brief extract from the opening of the *Secrees* into the back of Ashmole 59 can be viewed as a precursor to the subsequent expansion of the book in the sixteenth century, when a copy of Lydgate's *Life of Our Lady* was bound with the manuscript (now fols. 135r–182r).

The interest in developing and perhaps profiting from Lydgate's reputation that determined Shirley's presentation of the poet's writing in Ashmole 59 and throughout his poetic anthologies also seems to have been at work in the production of two scribes whose output has constituted a focus of attention for manuscript scholars interested in the commercialization of book production in the second half of the fifteenth century.[40] First, operating in the rough period from 1465 to 1485 and with some sort of access to Shirley's books, the Hammond scribe is responsible for three manuscripts containing the *Secrees*: London, British Library MSS Additional 34360 (fols. 78r–116r), Arundel 59 (fols. 90r–130v), and Harley 2251 (fols. 188v–224r).[41] In the cases of the Additional and Harley manuscripts, the Hammond scribe's aim appears to have been to collect specimens of Middle English literature from the turn of the fifteenth century; where he carries over Shirley's authenticating rubrics, he participates in the mythologization of Lydgate and Chaucer that both copyists apparently thought would appeal to their readers.[42] Like Shirley, albeit much more tentatively, the Hammond scribe can be connected with a particular household that might have provided him with an occupation and thus with the initial impetus and audience for his work; but, as is also the case with Shirley, the notion that the Hammond scribe was involved in more speculative work with a commercial goal is difficult to discount definitively.[43] In the case of Arundel 59, in which the *Secrees* follows Hoccleve's *Regiment of Princes* (fols. 1r–89v), there are two unfoliated leaves separating the texts and the mise-en-page, and decoration of the *Secrees* differs from that of the preceding work. This bibliographical evidence could reflect a gap in the copying of the works and/or the combination postproduction of two separately produced books for sale to a buyer. The Hammond scribe's stint in Cambridge, Trinity College MS R.3.21, a manuscript compiled of independently produced booklets, provides a stronger link between this copyist and the practice of manuscript compilation via the booklet method, which lent itself well to speculative production campaigns whose aims might have been commercial.[44]

Closer to Lydgate's motherhouse in Bury St. Edmunds, another copyist producing manuscripts of Lydgate's work appears to have been making books both speculatively and on a bespoke basis. The copyist of four manuscripts containing the *Secrees*—Sloane 2464 (fols. 1r–65v); Oxford, Bodleian Library MSS Ashmole 46 (fols. 97r–160v) and Laud misc. 673 (fols. 1r–73v); and London, British Library MS Harley 4826 (fols. 52r–80v)—has been identified as the Edmund-Fremund scribe, so called for his frequent copying of Lydgate's dual hagiography of that name. In a groundbreaking study on the work of this scribe, Kathleen L. Scott establishes that he led a group of illustrators and illuminators who produced a series of books in the vicinity of Lydgate's monastery in the 1460s, shortly after the poet's death.[45] Although he copied texts by various authors, the Edmund-Fremund scribe seems to have specialized in the production of books of Lydgate's works, exemplars of which might have been made available to him by Bury's monks. Where they reproduced copies of Lydgate's texts, he and his associates appear to have been responding to and promoting an interest in the recently deceased poet's writing that was current among the neighbors of and visitors to his former base at Bury.

Some of the manuscripts made by the Edmund-Fremund scribe are so sumptuous that they were almost certainly bespoke productions. Thus the copies of Lydgate's *Lives of Saints Edmund and Fremund* in London, British Library MS Yates Thompson 47 and in the Arundel Castle Manuscript described by Scott are accompanied by lavish cycles of illumination whose manufacture must have taxed not only the skill but also the time and the finances of the Edmund-Fremund scribe and his team. Others of their books are cheaper productions that might have been sold on the coattails of these more extravagant manuscripts to buyers who were sought out once the bookmaking process was complete. Thus Scott comments that "pleasantly but not extensively decorated" manuscripts such as Sloane 2464 and Ashmole 46, and the unadorned paper copy of the *Secrees* that is now Laud misc. 673, might be examples of speculative work.[46] Where the Edmund-Fremund scribe and his colleagues produced copies of Lydgate's work on spec, they most likely did so in the knowledge that the more lavish codices of the poet's work that they had produced had helped to fuel demand for books of his poetry. Like the Hammond scribe, moreover, the Edmund-Fremund scribe appears to have exploited the potentialities of booklet production: the first and the last leaves of Sloane 2464 are soiled, suggesting that they remained unbound for some time after writing, and while all the texts compiled in Harley 4826 are written in his hand, the mise-en-page of the book differs across its three main sections, which comprise the *Secrees*; *The Lives of Saints Edmund and Fremund* and *The Legend of Saint Austin at Compton* (fols. 4r–50v); and Hoccleve's *Regiment of Princes* (fols. 84r–144v). They were assembled (or reassembled) at the very latest in the seventeenth century, when a series of paper leaves was added to the book, including a pen-and-ink drawing of a kneeling pilgrim accompanied by a monk (fol. 1*) and pages giving introductory information regarding the Lydgatean and Hoccleveian works compiled and on the biographies of their authors (fols. 1–3, 51–52, 82–83). The inclusion of these biographies, which are drawn from the *De claris anglicae scriptoribus* of the Catholic scholar, John Pitts (1560–1616), provides a fascinating glimpse into the value attached to the writings of Lydgate and Hoccleve long after their deaths. Not only medieval artisans such as the Edmund-Fremund scribe and the Hammond scribe engaged in the shaping and promoting of their posthumous reputations; this was a process that occupied readers less directly associated with the mechanics of book production, and it continued well into the early modern period.

    In the final reckoning, consideration of the extant manuscripts of the *Secrees* bears out Gillespie's argument that the idea of the medieval author was one means among several by which the makers of books could "limit, mediate, and profit from the movement in vernacular books before Caxton arrived on the publishing scene."[47] If manuscripts such as Ashmole 59 and Harley 4826 encourage consideration of the ways in which this tendency developed in the early modern period, the unique extant medieval print of the *Secrees* provides a salutary reminder that the tendency toward attribution typically associated with the development of that technology was not an immediate or necessary effect of its introduction. The edition of the *Secrees* that came off the presses of Richard Pynson in 1511 appears to have been designed primarily to advertise the identities of its commissioner, Charles Somerset, Lord Herbert, later first earl of Worcester (d. 1526), and its printer, Pynson himself, and to shape and to publicize the relationships between these men and Henry VIII, to whom the work is addressed on its opening page. Here the work is announced as, "This present boke called the Gouernaunce of Kynges and pryn*ces*: Imprynted at the co*m*maundement of the good and honourable syre Charles Somerset Lorde Herbert: and Chaumberleyne vnto oure Soueraygne lorde kynge Henry the .viii." (sig. [A1]r).[48]

There follow images of the royal arms and crown supported by angels, of the Tudor rose, and of three castles. In combination, the title lines and the three images look to have been designed to frame a relationship between Somerset and his king; according to the entry for Somerset in the *Oxford Dictionary of National Biography*, the castles were a part of the commissioner's insignia from 1509, when he became Constable of the Three Castles.[49] By having these textual and visual markers added to a reproduction of the *Secrees*, Somerset encouraged readers of the book to draw comparisons between the advisory relationships between himself and the young king Henry VIII, between Alexander and his old philosopher, Aristotle, and, perhaps, between Lydgate and his king, Henry VI. At the close of the book, the manipulation of Lydgate's posthumous work and reputation takes a different turn. Here Pynson names himself as "Rycharde Prynson [sic], Prynter vnto the Kynges noble grace," adding his own visual stamp in the form of his recently acquired heraldic device (sig. [H4]v). As Gillespie points out, while Pynson's self-identification as the king's printer was a novel move, it should be viewed in the context of a broader campaign whereby Pynson attempted to elevate his trade and to secure his position at its forefront.[50]

On the one hand, the variety of uses to which Lydgate's inheritance is put by both the continuator of the *Secrees* and the makers of the medieval witnesses via which it is transmitted might seem to be at odds with the poet's own plans for his writing. As Mary C. Flannery shows, throughout his work, Lydgate expresses a profound belief in his capacity as a poet to shape and promulgate his own reputation as well as that of his patrons.[51] This appears to be the principle driving the composition of another poem typically grouped among Lydgate's later works, his *Testament*, which Sebastian Sobecki rereads as the poet's attempt to prepare his heterogeneous corpus for its reception by posterity.[52] The extant medieval witnesses to the *Secrees* demonstrate only a partial uptake of these concerns. On the other hand, consideration of what the poem can reveal about Lydgate's reception uncovers a set of creative and self-interested responses that the poet might have anticipated. As Gillespie points out, Lydgate deliberately fictionalized his historical identity when, in his *Siege of Thebes*, he depicted himself joining Chaucer's pilgrims on their return from Canterbury,[53] and alternative book-historical approaches to

Lydgate's work reveal the writer's probable awareness of some of the main material conditions of his works' transmission. Joel Fredell observes, for instance, that, as well as producing a clutch of monumentally long texts, such as his *Troy Book*, Lydgate also seems to have specialized in producing shorter works that fitted neatly within the bounds of the increasingly cheap pamphlets via which so much medieval writing once circulated.[54] If Lydgate did begin a translation of the *Secretum Secretorum* at some point in his career, he might reasonably have intended it to be transmitted in this form and thence perhaps to be compiled in the kinds of household books and medical manuals in which it currently survives.

At the very least, the foregoing analysis adds further weight to the argument that the author function was not a product of print culture, as is sometimes proposed.[55] Medieval authorship does appear to be a more local affair than in later periods, however; Lydgate's predilection for self-naming notwithstanding, authorial signatures and paratextual attributions are comparatively rare in Middle English books, perhaps reflecting a culture of manuscript transmission that still ran along the lines of personal acquaintance, which rendered self-naming redundant. Despite the efforts that he expended staging his continuation of the *Secrees*, the poet of the second half of the work does not appear to have signed his writing, and while the Edmund-Fremund scribe and his associates clearly specialized in the production of Lydgate manuscripts, many of their books contain no attributions to the author, either internally, within their texts, or externally, via paratext.[56] Under these conditions, authorship remained a fluid concept whose contours might be shaped not only by writers themselves but also by their literary followers and by the manufacturers and readers of the books that transmitted their works. In a literary and book culture that "depended on adaptability rather than adherence to prescribed ideas,"[57] it appears to have been the particular adaptability of the idea of Lydgate's authorship that shaped the final forms assumed by the *Secrees of Old Philisoffres* and ensured its subsequent success.

University of Bern

APPENDIX

The purpose of this appendix is not to provide detailed descriptions of the extant medieval witnesses to the *Secrees of Old Philisoffres*, for which readers are directed to the relevant library catalogues and to the bibliographical sources listed in the foregoing article. Instead it sets out to record variance among the titles given to the poem, the texts of the author's death rubric, and the composition of the continuator's prologue (ll. 1492–1589 and stanzas numbered 214–227 in Steele's edition of the Sloane 2464 text). Brief contextualizing notes are also provided for each witness that summarize points made or alluded to above. In the absence of a critical edition of the *Secrees*, some sense of the considerable variation to which its text was subject in other aspects can be gleaned from the collation of eleven of the extant manuscripts in Theodor Prosiegel's doctoral dissertation.[58] The appendix follows the list of the extant witnesses given in *The Digital Index of Middle English Verse*, where the *Secrees* is treated as item 1544. Where the DIMEV lists twenty-three manuscript witnesses to the *Secrees*, the total reckoning of the extant manuscript copies should be set at twenty-two: the leaf transmitting forty-one lines of the poem that is now DIMEV witness 13, London, British Library MS Additional 39922, fol. 16r–v, was once part of Cambridge, Fitzwilliam Museum MS McClean 183, DIMEV witness 8.

Manuscript Witnesses

1. Oxford, Bodleian Library MS Ashmole 46, fols. 97r–160v

Title:	n/a
Author's death rubric:	Here deyed this translatour and nobyl poete and the yonge folwere gan his prologe on this wyse (fol. 131r)
Continuator's prologue:	Has all the stanzas in Steele's edition
Context:	MS written by Edmund-Fremund scribe

2. Oxford, Bodleian Library MS Ashmole 59, fol. 134r

Title:	n/a
Author's death rubric:	n/a
Continuator's prologue:	n/a
Context:	First five lines of *Secrees* copied into Shirley anthology

3. Oxford, Bodleian Library MS Laud misc. 416, fols. 255r–287v

Title:	This is the book of the gouernaunce of kyngge and pryncis (fol. 255r)
Author's death rubric:	Here died this translator and notable poiet John lydgate monk of bury and fowler by gan his prolog in this wyse (274r)
Continuator's prologue:	Lacks stanzas 214, 223–224, and 226 of Steele's edition
Context:	Household book written in part at La Rode, Selling (Kent)

4. Oxford, Bodleian Library MS Laud misc. 673, fols. 1r–73v

Title:	This is the book of the gouernaunce of kynges and of pryncis (fol. 1r)
Author's death rubric:	Here deyde this translatour *and* nobyl Poete *and* the yong folwer*e* gan his pr*o*loge on this maner wyse (fol. 41v)
Continuator's prologue:	Has all the stanzas in Steele's edition

Context:	Written by Edmund-Fremund scribe; *Secrees* transmitted alone and book still has fifteenth-century binding

5. Oxford, Balliol College MS 329, fols. 80r–126r

Title:	Hic incipit tractus De regimine principum (fol. 80r); Her endyth þe notable tretyse callyd of Arystotyles regimen principum (fol. 126r)
Author's death rubric:	Her endyth John lydgate tr*a*nslator of þis be for seyde her arystotyll wrytyth a pystyll to alyzaundre how he scholde *con*serve naturall helth of þe body (fol. 107r)
Continuator's prologue:	n/a
Context:	Collection of medical texts including a short text of the *Secrees*

6. Cambridge, Gonville and Caius College MS 336/725, fols. 108r–128r

Title:	Of the crafte of phisonomye which doth trete of the q*ua*litees and Condicions of ich membre of man and of the Image of ypocras which Arestotele wrote to kynge Allisaunder (fol. 108r)
Author's death rubric:	n/a
Continuator's prologue:	n/a
Context:	Collection of medical texts containing a short text of the *Secrees*

7. Cambridge, Fitzwilliam Museum MS McClean 182, fols. 12r–49r

Title:	n/a
Author's death rubric:	Here died þis translatoure and noble Poete John lidgate and þe folower gan his prologe on þis wise (fol. 32v)
Continuator's prologue:	Lacks stanzas 214, 218, 223–224, and 226 of Steele's edition
Context:	Household book

8. Cambridge, Fitzwilliam Museum MS McClean 183, fols. 1r–47v

Title:	n/a
Author's death rubric:	n/a
Continuator's prologue:	Begins imperfectly in stanza 215 (at l. 1501), has stanzas 216, 217, 219–222, 225, and 227 of Steele's edition
Context:	*Secrees* transmitted alone, but MS is damaged and imperfect at beginning and end; once included witness 13

9. Cambridge UK, Trinity College MS R.3.19, fols. 49r–52r

Title:	A tr*ates* of the iiij seasons of the yere that is t[o] say ver Estas Authumnus *&* yemps (fol. 49r)
Author's death rubric:	n/a
Continuator's prologue:	n/a

Context:	Extracted text, identified as such by later hand (Stowe?), which completes the incipit: *compilyd by John Lydgate as aperyth in his boke of þe secretis to alysaunder from arystotyll* (fol. 49r)

10. Cambridge UK, Trinity College MS O.3.40, fols. 1r–44v

Title:	n/a
Author's death rubric:	Here died this translatoure and noble Poete John lidgate and the folower gan his prologe oon this wyse (fol. 31v)
Continuator's prologue:	Lacks stanzas 214, 218, 223–224 and 226 of Steele's edition
Context:	*Secrees* transmitted alone, but MS is damaged and imperfect at beginning and end

11. London, British Library MS Additional 14408, fols. 1r–48v

Title:	n/a
Author's death rubric:	Here dyed this translatoure and noble poete john lidgate and þe folower gan his prologe in this wyse (fol. 27r)
Continuator's prologue:	Lacks stanzas 214, 218, 221, 223–224, and 226 of Steele's edition
Context:	Household book of Nicholas St. Lo

12. London, British Library MS Additional 34360, fols. 78r–116r

Title:	Explicit Regimen Principum (fol. 116r)

Author's death rubric:	Here deyde the translator and noble Poete Dane John lidgagate And his folower gan his prolog in this wise Per Benedictu[m] Burgh (fol. 101r)
Continuator's prologue:	Lacks stanzas 214, 223–224 and 226 of Steele's edition
Context:	MS written by Hammond scribe

13. London, British Library MS Additional 39922, fol. 16r–16v

Title:	n/a
Author's death rubric:	n/a
Continuator's prologue:	n/a
Context:	Leaf giving ll. 1268–1309 of *Secrees*, once part of witness 8

14. London, British Library MS Additional 60577 [Winchester Anthology], fols. 24v–37v

Title:	[T]his is the boke of the gouernaunce of kynges and princes (fol. 24v)
Author's death rubric:	n/a
Continuator's prologue:	n/a
Context:	Monastic anthology

15. London, British Library MS Arundel 59, fols. 90r–130v

Title:	Explicit Regimen Principum (fol. 130v)

Author's death rubric:	Here deyde the translat*or* and noble Poete Dane John Lidgate And his folower gan his prolog in this wise p*er* Benedic*tum* Burgh (fol. 115r)
Continuator's prologue:	Lacks stanzas 214, 223–224, and 226 of Steele's edition
Context:	MS written by Hammond scribe

16. London, British Library MS Harley 2251, fols. 188v–224r

Title:	Explicit Regim*en* Principu*m* (fol. 224r)
Author's death rubric:	Here deyde the translat*or* A noble Poete dane John lydgate And his folower gan his prolog in this wise p*er* Benedictu*m* Burgh (fol. 210r)
Continuator's prologue:	Lacks stanzas 214, 223–224, and 226 of Steele's edition
Context:	MS written by Hammond scribe

17. London, British Library MS Harley 4826, fols. 52r–80v

Title:	This is the book of the goue*rna*unce of kynges and Princes (fol. 52r)
Author's death rubric:	n/a
Continuator's prologue:	Begins imperfectly, has all stanzas in Steele's edition from stanza 219
Context:	MS written by Edmund-Fremund scribe; (re-)compiled in seventeenth century

18. London, British Library MS Lansdowne 285, fols. 152r–197v

Title:	This is the book of governaunce of kynges and Prynces (fol. 152r)
Author's death rubric:	Here died this translator and noble poete John lidgate And the folower began his prolog on þis wise (fol. 176v)
Continuator's prologue:	Lacks stanzas 214, 217–218, 223–234, and 226 of Steele's edition
Context:	Sir John Paston's "grete boke"

19. London, British Library MS Sloane 2027, fol. 53r–92v

Title:	this is the booke off the gouernaunce off Kynges and Pryncis (fol. 53r); Explicit librum Aristotiles Ad Alexandrum magnum (fol. 92v)
Author's death rubric:	here deyed this translatour And noble poete and the yong Folower gan his prolog on this wise (fol. 74v); the same hand adds "lidgate" above the text of the rubric
Continuator's prologue:	Has all the stanzas in Steele's edition
Context:	Household book

20. London, British Library MS Sloane 2464, fols. 1–65v

Title:	n/a
Author's death rubric:	here deyed this translator and nobil poete and the yonge folowere gan his prologe on this wyse (fol. 36r)

Continuator's prologue:	Base text for Steele's edition
Context:	MS written by Edmund-Fremund scribe; *Secrees* transmitted alone, but soiling at the opening and close of the book suggests it remained unbound after writing

21. New York, Pierpont Morgan Library MS M775, fols. 139r–195r

Title:	n/a
Author's death rubric:	Here died this translatoure and nobill poete Ion lydgate and the folower began his prologe on this wise (fol. 169v)
Continuator's prologue:	Lacks stanzas 214, 218, 223–224, and 226 of Steele's edition
Context:	Household book belonging to John Astley; consulted by copyist of witness 18

22. Philadelphia, Philadelphia Free Library MS 15/488 [also Lewis T488], fols. 1r–2v

Title:	n/a
Author's death rubric:	Here died this translatoure and noble Poete Jon lidgate and the folower began his prologe on this wise (fol. 1r)
Continuator's prologue:	Imperfect, has stanzas 215–217 and 219 of Steele's edition
Context:	Fragments containing part of continuator's prologue and stanzas from last line of stanza 234 to stanza 240 in Steele's edition; written by copyist of *Secrees* in witness 21

THE SECREES OF OLD PHILISOFFRES 55

23. New Haven, Yale University, Beinecke Library, Takamiya Deposit MS 33, fols. 1–19v

Title:	Of the crafte of Phisonomye whiche doth trete of the qualitees and condicions of the membre of man and of the Image of ypocras whiche Arestotele wrote to kynge Alisaunder (fol. 1r) [cited from DIMEV]
Author's death rubric:	n/a (?)
Continuator's prologue:	n/a (?)
Context:	"Twin" of MS containing witness 6

Print Witness

1. STC 17017. *The Gouernance of Kynges and prynces*, Pynson, London, 1511

Title:	This present boke called the Gouernaunce of Kynges and pryn*ces*; Imprynted at the co*m*maundement of the good and honourable syre Charles Somerset Lorde Herbert: and Chaumberleyne vnto oure Soueraygne lorde kynge Henry the .viii. (sig. [A1]r)
Author's death rubric:	Here dyed this tanslatour & noble poete John lydgate & the folower gan this prologe on this wyse (sig. [D3]v)
Continuator's prologue:	Lacks stanzas 214, 218, 223–224 and 226 of Steele's edition
Context:	Also transmits the printer's self-designation as "Rycharde Prynson Prynter vnto the Kynges noble grace" (sig. [H4]v)

Acknowledgment

An early version of this article was read to members of the Swiss Association of Medieval and Early Modern English Studies (SAMEMES) at the University of Geneva in November 2015; the final version is indebted to their helpful and encouraging comments. I am grateful to my colleague at the University of Bern, Margaret Bridges, for suggesting that the *Secrees* might be a profitable topic of research and for offering generous feedback on my text. Two correspondents helped me to complete the entries in the appendix for manuscripts held in the USA. The entries for New York, Pierpont Morgan Library MS M775 come from James Staples; J. Eytan Shemtov of the Rare Book Department at the Free Library of Philadelphia kindly and speedily answered my queries about Free Library MS 15/488.

NOTES

1. See, e.g., Derek Pearsall, *John Lydgate (1371–1449): A Bio-Bibliography*, ELS Monograph Series 71 (Victoria, Canada: University of Victoria English Department, 1997), 39.
2. Cited by line number from *Lydgate and Burgh's Secrees of Old Philisoffres*, ed. Robert Steele, EETS e.s. 66 (London, 1894). Steele took Sloane 2464 as his base text, and his transcription has been checked against the manuscript. Variations among the medieval denominations of the work and among the surviving texts of the author's death rubric and of the continuator's prologue are listed in the appendix and discussed below.
3. See Alexandra Gillespie, *Print Culture and the Medieval Author: Chaucer, Lydgate, and Their Books* 1473–1557 (Oxford: Oxford University Press, 2006), 21.
4. Compare the DIMEV: An Open-Access, Digital Edition of the Index of Middle English Verse, Based on the *Index of Middle English Verse* (1943) and its *Supplement* (1965), compiled, edited, and supplemented by Linne R. Mooney, Daniel W. Mosser, and Elizabeth Solopova with Deborah Thorpe and David Hill Radcliffe, http://www.dimev.net.
5. Cited by book and line number from *Lydgate's Troy Book*, ed. Henry Bergen, EETS e.s. 97, 103, 106, 106, in 3 vols. (London: Kegan Paul, Trench and Trübner, 1906–1935).
6. See Seth Lerer, *Chaucer and His Readers: Imagining the Author in Late-Medieval England* (Princeton, NJ: Princeton University Press, 1993). The following analysis of the attribution of the *Secrees* draws on Lerer's skeptical discussion (ibid., 117–146) of John Shirley's ascription to Chaucer of the "Wordes to Adam" in the book that is now Cambridge, Trinity College Library MS R.3.20. I am also inspired by Alexandra

Gillespie's discussion of Lerer's work and by her careful reading of Shirley's presentation of the same text in Alexandra Gillespie, "Reading Chaucer's Words to Adam," *Chaucer Review* 42 (2008): 269–283.
7. See Robert J. Meyer-Lee, *Poets and Power from Chaucer to Wyatt* (Cambridge, UK: Cambridge University Press, 2007), 73.
8. Walter F. Schirmer, *John Lydgate: Ein Kulturbild aus dem 15. Jahrhundert*, Buchreihe der Anglia 1 (Tübingen, Germany: Max Niemeyer Verlag, 1952), 217 ("der beherrschende Eindruck ist der eines inhaltlichen und formalen Wirrwarrs").
9. Derek Pearsall, *John Lydgate* (London: Routledge and Kegan Paul, 1970), 296.
10. On the sources of the *Secrees*, the brief comments in *Lydgate and Burgh's Secrees*, ed. Steele, xv, and M. A. Manzalaoui, "The *Secretum Secretorum*: The Mediaeval European Version of Kitāb Sirr-ul-Asrār," *Bulletin of the Faculty of Arts, Alexandria University* 15 (1961): 83–105, at 96.
11. Margaret Bridges, "Lydgate's Last Poem," in *Trajectoires européennes du* Secretum secretorum *du Pseudo-Aristote (XIIIe–XVIe siècle)*, ed. Catherine Gaullier-Bougassas, Margaret Bridges, and Jean-Yves Tilliette, Alexander redivivus 6 (Turnhout, Belgium: Brepols, 2015), 317–336, at 327–328.
12. Compare the list of repetitious passages in ibid., 327–328 n. 43.
13. At the close of their paraphrase of the poem, Alain Renoir and C. David Benson complain that the reading of the poem "is often made somewhat irritating by frequent, inconsistent, and unannounced shifts in point of view as well as by the lack of a clear principle of organization." See J. Burke Severs and Albert E. Hartung, eds., *A Manual of the Writings in Middle English, 1050–1500*, 9 vols. (New Haven: Connecticut Academy of Arts and Sciences, 1967–1993), 6:1899.
14. Of the extant manuscripts, three have lost leaves that probably transmitted the author's death rubric: Cambridge, Fitzwilliam Museum MS 183/ London, British Library MS Additional 39922 and London, British Library MSS Additional 60577 and Harley 4826. Two manuscripts transmit brief extracts from the *Secrees* and thus do not transmit the rubric: Oxford, Bodleian Library MS Ashmole 59 and Cambridge, Trinity College MS R.3.19. Cambridge, Gonville and Caius College MS 336/725 presents a series of longer portions from the *Secrees* as an integral work; the author's death rubric is absent from its text. New Haven, Beinecke Library Takamiya Deposit MS 33, which I have not seen, also looks likely to have missed the author's death rubric: Linda Ehrsam Voigts describes Takamiya MS 33 as the "twin" of the Gonville and Caius codex in Linda Ehrsam Voigts, "The 'Sloane Group': Related

Scientific and Medical Manuscripts From the Fifteenth Century in the Sloane Collection," *British Library Journal* 16 (1990): 26–57, at 27. All these manuscripts are discussed below. The remaining medieval witnesses to the *Secrees* listed in the DIMEV each contain some form of the author's death rubric: variant forms are collected in the appendix.

15. Pearsall, *John Lydgate*, 297. In a similar vein, Schirmer, *John Lydgate*, 217, imagines the poet dying over the drafts of his unfinished work.
16. *Lydgate and Burgh's Secrees*, ed. Steele, 109.
17. Compare Pearsall, *John Lydgate*, 297.
18. Compare the account of the standard contents of the *Secretum Secretorum* in Steven J. Williams, *The Secret of Secrets: The Scholarly Career of A Pseudo-Aristotelian Text in the Latin Middle Ages* (Ann Arbor: University of Michigan Press, 2003), 10–11.
19. On Benedict Burgh, see further Max Förster, "Über Benedict Burghs Leben und Werke," *Archiv für das Studium der neueren Sprachen und Literaturen* 101 (1898): 29–64. Förster argues against the attribution of the second portion of the *Secrees* to Burgh on metrical grounds; ibid., 58–59.
20. This poem is edited from Stow's book, now London, British Library MS Additional 29729, in *English Verse between Chaucer and Surrey*, ed. Eleanor Prescott Hammond (Durham, NC: Duke University Press, 1927), 188–190.
21. See ibid., 188; and compare Pearsall, *Bio-Bibliography*, 39–40.
22. On these patronal connections, see Pearsall, *John Lydgate*, 168.
23. See Simon Horobin, "Thomas Hoccleve: Chaucer's First Editor?" *Chaucer Review* 50 (2015): 228–250.
24. Michel Foucault, "What Is an Author?," in *Textual Strategies: Perspectives in Post-Structuralist Criticism*, ed. Josué V. Harari (Ithaca, NY: Cornell University Press, 1979), 141–160, at 159.
25. Ibid., 141.
26. Gillespie, *Print Culture*, 16 n. 53.
27. Given the purportedly close relationship adduced above between the Gonville and Caius manuscript and New Haven, Beinecke Library, Takamiya Deposit MS 33, it seems likely that the Takamiya manuscript transmitted neither the continuator's prologue nor the author's death rubric. The continuator's prologue is also entirely absent from the two manuscripts transmitting extracts of the *Secrees* listed above (witnesses 2 and 9 in the appendix) and from London, British Library MS Additional 60577, from which leaves have been lost (witnesses 14).
28. Gillespie, *Print Culture*, 16 (emphasis in original).
29. Compare the texts edited in *Secretum Secretorum: Nine English Versions*, ed. M. A. Manzalaoui, EETS o.s. 276 (Oxford: Oxford University Press,

1977); and *Three Prose Versions of the Secreta Secretorum*, ed. Robert Steele, EETS e.s. 74 (London, 1898).
30. Bridges, "John Lydgate's Last Poem," 335.
31. See further G. A. Lester, *Sir John Paston's 'Grete Boke': A Descriptive Catalogue, with an Introduction, of British Library MS Lansdowne 285* (Cambridge, UK: D. S. Brewer, 1984), 9–12 (for a checklist of the manuscript's contents) and 159–163 (for commentary on Vegetius).
32. See ibid., 31–33 and 93–95. A. I. Doyle's identification of the hand of Philadelphia, Free Library of Philadelphia MS Lewis T488 as that of the scribe who copied the *Secrees* into MS M775 provides valuable contextualizing information that situates that fragmentary bifolium in the orbit of MS M775 and Lansdowne 285; reported in Lester, *Sir John Paston's 'Grete Boke,'* 29.
33. The presence of fragments of a copy of *Guy of Warwick* in the binding of Additional 14408 attracted the interest of Maldwyn Mills and Daniel Huws, who provide a useful account of the provenance of this manuscript and another book owned by Nicholas St. Lo in Maldwyn Mills and Daniel Huws, *Fragments of an Early Fourteenth-Century Guy of Warwick*, Medium Ævum Monographs n.s. 4 (Oxford: Blackwell, 1974), 1–4. Nicholas's other book, Aberystwyth, National Library of Wales MS 572, contains a series of medical recipes followed by an herbal. The interests that can thus be attributed to this man—in governance, on the one hand, and medicine, on the other—provide a useful indication of the breath of the thematic appeal of the *Secrees*.
34. See M. C. Seymour, *A Catalogue of Chaucer Manuscripts*, 2 vols. (Aldershot, UK: Scolar Press, 1995), 1:25–26. Seymour also points out that the signatures of two sisters of the Bridgettine house at Syon were written on the book's end pastedowns, "Ane Colvylle" and "Clement Trysburghe." The encounters of these female readers with Laud misc. 416 are considered in Nancy Bradley Warren, "Chaucer, the Chaucer Tradition, and Female Monastic Readers," *Chaucer Review* 51 (2016): 88–106.
35. For details, see the DIMEV (witness 6 to item 1554) and the entry for Balliol MS 329 in Roger Mynors, *Catalogue of the Manuscripts of Balliol College, Oxford* (Oxford: Clarendon Press, 1963).
36. According to the DIMEV (witness no. 23 to item 1544), the poem receives an identical title in New Haven, Beinecke Library, Takamiya Deposit MS 33 (fol. 1r). By contrast, the "craft of physiognomy" section of the poem (stanzas 353-390 in Steele's edition) is absent in several of the longer copies of the poem. Steele notes its absence from the copies of the *Secrees* preserved in London, British Library MSS Arundel 59 and Harley 2251.

37. See *The Winchester Anthology: A Facsimile of British Library Additional Manuscript 60577*, ed. Edward Wilson (Cambridge, UK: D. S. Brewer, 1981), 1–16.
38. Other manuscripts in which the *Secrees* is now preserved in isolation may once have been part of bigger books: the beginnings and ends of Cambridge, Fitzwilliam Library MS McClean 183 and Trinity College MS O.3.40 have sustained damage and it is impossible to say how much material has been lost from these books. London, British Library MS Sloane 2464 is now bound alone, but its first and last pages are dirty and worn, suggesting that it was left unbound for some time before it was committed to its current binding. The potential for the transmission of the poem in booklet and in pamphlet formats is discussed below.
39. For a transcription and discussion of the extract, see Rossell Hope Robbins, "Popular Prayers in Middle English Verse," *Modern Philology* 36 (1939): 337–350, at 341.
40. For a discussion of this topic within the context of Middle English literary book production more broadly, and for further bibliography, see Linne R. Mooney, "Vernacular Literary Manuscripts and Their Scribes," in *The Production of Books in England 1350–1500*, ed. Alexandra Gillespie and Daniel Wakelin (Cambridge, UK: Cambridge University Press, 2011), 192–211.
41. On the Hammond scribe's access to Shirley's books, see Linne R. Mooney, "John Shirley's Heirs," *Yearbook of English Studies* 33 (2003): 182–198, at 186–190; for the dates of his activity, and for further bibliography, see Daniel W. Mosser, "Dating the Manuscripts of the 'Hammond Scribe': What the Paper Evidence Tells Us," *Journal of the Early Book Society* 10 (2007): 31–70.
42. On Shirley's practices of attribution, with particular reference to Lydgate, see Margaret Connolly, *John Shirley: Book Production and the Noble Household in Fifteenth-Century England* (Aldershot, UK: Ashgate, 1998), 69–101.
43. Compare the connections drawn between the Hammond scribe and London mercantile society in Mooney, "John Shirley's Heirs," 189–190. Connolly, *John Shirley*, 190–195, presents a strong case against Shirley's involvement in commercial book production, but an alternative argument is offered in A. S. G. Edwards, "John Shirley and the Emulation of Courtly Culture," in *The Court and Cultural Diversity*, ed. Evelyn Mullally and John Thompson (Cambridge, UK: Brewer, 1997), 309–318.
44. See Linne R. Mooney, "Scribes and Booklets of Trinity College, Cambridge, Manuscripts R.3.19 and R.3.21," in *Middle English Poetry, Texts and Traditions: Essays in Honour of Derek Pearsall*, ed. A. J. Minnis (Woodbridge, UK: York Medieval Press, 2001), 241–266.

45. See Kathleen L. Scott, "Lydgate's Lives of Saints Edmund and Fremund: A Newly-Located Manuscript in Arundel Castle," *Viator* 13 (1982): 335–366. For an updated list of manuscripts attributed to this scribe, a more recent description of his script (which might reflect the work of two cooperating scribes employing similar styles), and for further bibliography, see Simon Horobin, "The Edmund-Fremund Scribe Copying Chaucer," *Journal of the Early Book Society* 12 (2009): 195–203.
46. Scott, "Lydgate's Lives," 361.
47. Gillespie, *Print Culture*, 29.
48. The print is cited by signature number from the facsimile uploaded at *Early English Books Online* (http://eebo.chadwyck.com) of the unique extant copy of the book in the Huntington Library, California; STC 17017.
49. *Oxford Dictionary of National Biography*, http://www.oxforddnb.com.
50. See Gillespie, *Print Culture*, 160–176.
51. See Mary C. Flannery, *John Lydgate and the Poetics of Fame* (Cambridge, UK: D. S. Brewer, 2012).
52. See Sebastian Sobecki, "Lydgate's Kneeling Retraction: The *Testament* as a Literary Palinode," *Chaucer Review* 49 (2015): 265–293. Sobecki also discusses the role played by Lydgate's scribes in the production of the author's reputation at Bury; ibid., 278–289.
53. See Gillespie, *Print Culture*, 19–21.
54. See Joel Fredell, "'Go litel quaier': Lydgate's Pamphlet Poetry," *Journal of the Early Book Society* 9 (2006): 51–73.
55. See, e.g., A. S. G. Edwards, "Fifteenth-Century Middle English Verse Author Collections," in *The English Medieval Book: Studies in Memory of Jeremy Griffiths*, ed. A. S. G. Edwards, Vincent Gillespie, and Ralph Hanna (London: British Library, 2000), 101–112.
56. For this observation, see Gillespie, *Print Culture*, 43.
57. Ibid., 51.
58. Theodor Prosiegel, *The Book of the Gouernaunce of Kynges and of Prynces: Die von Lydgate und einem Anonymus hinterlassene me. Bearbeitung des Secretum Secretorum* (Munich, Germany: Wolf & Sohn, 1903).
59. For this identification, see A. S. G. Edwards, "A British Museum Leaf from McClean 183," *Book Collector* 21 (1972): 127.

WORKS CITED

Editions and Facsimiles
English Verse between Chaucer and Surrey, ed. Eleanor Prescott Hammond. Durham, NC: Duke University Press, 1927.
Lydgate and Burgh's Secrees of Old Philisoffres, ed. Robert Steele. EETS e.s. 66. London, 1894.
Lydgate's Troy Book, ed. Henry Bergen. EETS e.s. 97, 103, 106, 126. In 3 vols. London: Kegan Paul, Trench and Trübner, 1906–1935.
Secretum Secretorum: Nine English Versions, ed. M. A. Manzalaoui. EETS o.s. 276. Oxford: Oxford University Press, 1977.
Three Prose Versions of the Secreta Secretorum, ed. Robert Steele. EETS e.s. 74. London, 1898.
The Winchester Anthology: A Facsimile of British Library Additional Manuscript 60577, ed. Edward Wilson. Cambridge, UK: D. S. Brewer, 1981.

Secondary Sources
Bridges, Margaret. "Lydgate's Last Poem." In *Trajectoires européennes du* Secretum secretorum *du Pseudo-Aristote (XIIIe–XVIe siècle)*, ed. Catherine Gaullier-Bougassas, Margaret Bridges, and Jean-Yves Tilliette, 317–336. Alexander redivivus 6. Turnhout, Belgium: Brepols, 2015.
Burke Severs, J., and Albert E. Hartung, eds. *A Manual of the Writings in Middle English, 1050–1500*. 9 vols. New Haven: Connecticut Academy of Arts and Sciences, 1967–1993.
Connolly, Margaret. *John Shirley: Book Production and the Noble Household in Fifteenth-Century England*. Aldershot, UK: Ashgate, 1998.
Edwards, A. S. G. "A British Museum Leaf from McClean 183." *Book Collector* 21 (1972): 127.
———. "Fifteenth-Century Middle English Verse Author Collections." In *The English Medieval Book: Studies in Memory of Jeremy Griffiths*, ed. A. S. G. Edwards, Vincent Gillespie, and Ralph Hanna, 101–112. London: British Library, 2000.
———. "John Shirley and the Emulation of Courtly Culture." In *The Court and Cultural Diversity*, ed. Evelyn Mullally and John Thompson, 309–318. Cambridge, UK: Brewer, 1997.
Flannery, Mary C. *John Lydgate and the Poetics of Fame*. Cambridge, UK: D. S. Brewer, 2012.
Förster, Max. "Über Benedict Burghs Leben und Werke." *Archiv für das Studium der neueren Sprachen und Literaturen* 101 (1898): 29–64.
Foucault, Michel. "What Is an Author?" In *Textual Strategies: Perspectives in Post-Structuralist Criticism*, ed. Josué V. Harari, 141–160. Ithaca, NY: Cornell University Press, 1979.

Fredell, Joel. "'Go litel quaier': Lydgate's Pamphlet Poetry." *Journal of the Early Book Society* 9 (2006): 51–73.

Gillespie, Alexandra. *Print Culture and the Medieval Author: Chaucer, Lydgate, and Their Books 1473–1557*. Oxford: Oxford University Press, 2006.

———. "Reading Chaucer's Words to Adam." *Chaucer Review* 42 (2008): 269–283.

Horobin, Simon. "The Edmund-Fremund Scribe Copying Chaucer." *Journal of the Early Book Society* 12 (2009): 195–203.

———. "Thomas Hoccleve: Chaucer's First Editor?" *Chaucer Review* 50 (2015): 228–250.

Lerer, Seth. *Chaucer and His Readers: Imagining the Author in Late-Medieval England*. Princeton, NJ: Princeton University Press, 1993.

Lester, G. A. *Sir John Paston's 'Grete Boke': A Descriptive Catalogue, with an Introduction, of British Library MS Lansdowne 285*. Cambridge, UK: D. S. Brewer, 1984.

Manzalaoui, M. A. "The *Secretum Secretorum*: The Mediaeval European Version of Kitāb Sirr-ul-Asrār." *Bulletin of the Faculty of Arts, Alexandria University* 15 (1961): 83–105.

Meyer-Lee, Robert J. *Poets and Power from Chaucer to Wyatt*. Cambridge, UK: Cambridge University Press, 2007.

Mills, Maldwyn, and Daniel Huws. *Fragments of an Early Fourteenth-Century Guy of Warwick*. Medium Ævum Monographs n.s. 4. Oxford: Blackwell, 1974.

Mooney, Linne R. "John Shirley's Heirs." *Yearbook of English Studies* 33 (2003): 182–198.

———. "Scribes and Booklets of Trinity College, Cambridge, Manuscripts R.3.19 and R.3.21." In *Middle English Poetry, Texts and Traditions: Essays in Honour of Derek Pearsall*, ed. A. J. Minnis, 241–266. Woodbridge, UK: York Medieval Press, 2001.

———. "Vernacular Literary Manuscripts and Their Scribes." In *The Production of Books in England 1350–1500*, ed. Alexandra Gillespie and Daniel Wakelin, 192–211. Cambridge, UK: Cambridge University Press, 2011.

Mosser, Daniel W. "Dating the Manuscripts of the 'Hammond Scribe': What the Paper Evidence Tells Us." *Journal of the Early Book Society* 10 (2007): 31–70.

Mynors, Roger. *Catalogue of the Manuscripts of Balliol College, Oxford*. Oxford: Clarendon Press, 1963.

Pearsall, Derek. *John Lydgate*. London: Routledge and Kegan Paul, 1970.

———. *John Lydgate (1371–1449): A Bio-Bibliography*. ELS Monograph Series 71. Victoria, Canada: University of Victoria English Department, 1997.

Prosiegel, Theodor. *The Book of the Gouernaunce of Kynges and of Prynces: Die von Lydgate und einem Anonymus hinterlassene me. Bearbeitung des Secretum Secretorum*. Munich, Germany: Wolf & Sohn, 1903.

Renoir, Alan, and C. David Benson. "Secrees of Old Philisoffres." In *A Manual of the Writings in Middle English, 1050–1500*, ed. J. Burke Severs and Albert E. Hartung, 6:1899. 9 vols. New Haven: Connecticut Academy of Arts and Sciences, 1967–1993.

Robbins, Rossell Hope. "Popular Prayers in Middle English Verse." *Modern Philology* 36 (1939): 337–350.

Schirmer, Walter F. *John Lydgate: Ein Kulturbild aus dem 15. Jahrhundert*. Buchreihe der Anglia 1. Tübingen, Germany: Max Niemeyer Verlag, 1952.

Scott, Kathleen L. "Lydgate's Lives of Saints Edmund and Fremund: A Newly-Located Manuscript in Arundel Castle." *Viator* 13 (1982): 335–366.

Seymour, M. C. *A Catalogue of Chaucer Manuscripts*. 2 vols. Aldershot, UK: Scolar Press, 1995.

Sobecki, Sebastian. "Lydgate's Kneeling Retraction: The *Testament* as a Literary Palinode." *Chaucer Review* 49 (2015): 265–293.

Voigts, Linda Ehrsam. "The 'Sloane Group': Related Scientific and Medical Manuscripts from the Fifteenth Century in the Sloane Collection." *British Library Journal* 16 (1990): 26–57.

Warren, Nancy Bradley. "Chaucer, the Chaucer Tradition, and Female Monastic Readers." *Chaucer Review* 51 (2016): 88–106.

Williams, Steven J. *The Secret of Secrets: The Scholarly Career of a Pseudo-Aristotelian Text in the Latin Middle Ages*. Ann Arbor: University of Michigan Press, 2003.

Dating William Forrest's *The Seconde Grisilde*

OLIVER WORT

The quite prolific Tudor poet William Forrest deserves to be better known. His major works include a biblical epic, *The History of the Patriarch Joseph* (1547, 1569, and 1571), a *Speculum Principis* in verse modeled on the pseudo-Aristotelian *Secretum secretorum* that he calls *The Pleasaunt Poesye of Princelie Practise* (1548), paraphrases of forty-nine psalms (1551), a long poem on the divorce of Henry VIII from Catherine of Aragon, *The Seconde Grisilde*, and he also wrote a large collection of Catholic devotional poems, which he compiled during the reign of Elizabeth I but may have composed over a longer period of time.[1] Forrest's shorter compositions include paeans to Queen Mary on her accession—"A New Ballade of the Marigolde," and in all likelihood the text to William Mundy's *Vox patris caelestis*—as well as English paraphrases of the *Pater Noster* and *Te Deum*.[2] What is more, Forrest is already well known among musicologists for having preserved an important collection of early Tudor masses.[3]

On its own this should have proved a varied and substantial enough corpus to draw the attention of literary scholars, but this has not proved the case. Instead Forrest has fallen afoul of the long-standing tendency in literary criticism more or less to abandon the study of the mid-Tudor period to historians and theologians.[4] In the estimation of many, the sixteenth-century literary landscape before 1580 does not extend very far beyond a handful of names, chiefly Sir Thomas Wyatt, Henry Howard, earl of Surrey, and Thomas More, scholars of literature still tending today to read what interests them rather than what may have interested people at the time.[5]

We see this most clearly, for example, in the present's near-universal disregard for the sixteenth-century metrical psalm paraphrase, despite the genre's contemporary popularity.⁶ Likewise we might look to the modern age's time-honored, wholesale, and largely complacent aversion to fourteeners and poulter's measure, those meters that were the vehicles of much Tudor poetry.⁷ Rather than wonder why we can no longer hear the music in these rhythms, scholarship has preferred to assume that all mid-sixteenth-century poets were just possessed of a tin ear and that their verse is therefore not worth reading. That is one possibility, but it is also important to be reminded that a modern aesthetic is not always the most appropriate guide to our literary past, especially when it leads us to sideline what was once mainstream.

The specialist reader's neglect of mid-Tudor literature effects a vicious circle of marginalization, since without exposure there is no demand for it, and if there is no demand for it, then there is no exposure. The truth is that an inaccessible literature will always fail to generate an audience. No doubt Forrest's poetry will long remain an unlikely candidate for a low-cost Penguin Classics or Oxford World Classics edition, but happily at least one of his poems is in the process of being edited for a twenty-first-century audience: work is underway on a new edition of Forrest's *The Seconde Grisilde*, or *The Historye of Grysilde the seconde, onlye meanynge Queene Catharyne* that will be published by the Pontifical Institute of Medieval Studies.⁸ *Sic parvis magna*, there is hope that Forrest's fortunes will experience at least a modest improvement in the coming years.

This essay is written in anticipation of just such an upturn—one for which there is already small evidence in the handful of references that the poet has drawn in recent scholarship.⁹ My objective is twofold. First, in the spirit of consciousness-raising I mean to persuade scholars that there are good reasons to read Forrest's poetry and in particular *The Seconde Grisilde*. This part of my essay does not pretend to be comprehensive, my rather more modest aim being to reflect on Forrest's potential literary and historical significance and to place him in relation to some recent debates about Reformation literature. My objective in the second part of this essay is similarly the laying of foundations for the future discussion of Forrest's work, and so I turn to the more particular question of how we date *The Seconde Grisilde*. The small number of scholars who have looked at Forrest's poem have all agreed that the work was "fynysched the / 25 daye of *Iune* / the yeare of owre // lorde / *1558*," but I argue that the poet's colophon has been read incorrectly.¹⁰ Instead of 1558, the poet writes 1556, an earlier date that helps to make sense of the poem's own historical framework. If *The Seconde Grisilde* is eventually to be the gateway to the rest of Forrest's oeuvre, it is important that we try to get such details right.

I. On Reading Forrest

Forrest's *The Seconde Grisilde* does not wear its history lightly, being at heart an early verse chronicle of the life of Catherine of Aragon and the events and consequences of Henry VIII's divorce of her. This the poet hangs upon the well-known story of Patient Grisilde, a tale that was previously told by Boccaccio, Petrarch, and Chaucer, among others.[11] Though details between the various tellings differ, the basic narrative is one of womanly fortitude and spousal tyranny, with Grisilde subject to the cruelest of treatment by her husband, Walter. Forrest makes the tale entirely his own, however, by transforming Grisilde and Walter into Catherine of Aragon and Henry VIII.[12] About this matter the poet is candid, affirming that by "this sayde *Grysilde*, playnlye to defyne; | is playnlye ment; the goode Queene *Catharyne*," and so of course, "*Walter* (her husbonde) [is] kynge *Henry* the Eight." In his prologue addressed to Queen Mary, Forrest defends the Catherine/Grisilde Henry/Walter analogy he employs, explaining that:

> Her, I heere lyken / to *Grysilde* / the goode,
> as, well I so maye / for her great patience;
> Consyderinge althingis withe her howe it stoode;
> her geauynge that name; theare is none offense,
> Your noble ffather / workinge like pretence,
> as *Walter* to *Grysilde* / by muche vnkyndenes;
> by name of *Walter* / I dooe hym expresse[.] [13]

Even in marginalia Forrest repeats the explicit identification, establishing early on in his poem that "[t]his noble woman *Catharyne* / for her meeknes / applied to *Grysilde*," and that "[b]y names of *Grysilde* and *Walter* our Queenys [Queen Mary's] *ffather* and *Mother* examplyfyed." There is no misdirection here, no vigilant allegory of the sort that often characterizes political literature, a fact to which the poet calls attention. "So clokedlye vndre darke couerture | we haue not walked / in this Historye," Forrest writes, his ambition being that "Readers / may vndrestande sure | the meane of oure mentioned memorye | not fygured / as by Alligorye."[14] If the literature of the Henrician age was a literature under threat, one that was required to tiptoe around the domineering will of the monarch, then *The Seconde Grisilde* is a poem of cultural disenthrallment, one that "playnlye" tells the "Historye" of Henry VIII's "Great Matter," and this from the queen's perspective, not the king's.[15]

Although dismissive of *The Seconde Grisilde*'s "poetical merit," its nineteenth-century editor, W. D. Macray, was at least alive to the poem's evident historical importance, believing that "it is in the illustrations of contemporary history which it affords that its chief value lies." He explains:

> Fresh in personal knowledge of the events of which he writes, and of scenes of some of which he was an eye-witness, and enabled by official position as a royal chaplain to relate some things with special certainty, William Forrest gives us here a record of the Great Divorce, which is second in date only to the eloquent protest of Cardinal Pole, contemporary with the narrative of Harpsfield, and earlier than the histories of Campian and Sanders, among those who espoused the cause, as well as maintained the faith, of the rejected Queen.[16]

Of course it therefore matters that in many instances Forrest's narrative is that of an eyewitness, or one that at least poses as such. Both the records and *The Seconde Grisilde* indicate that Forrest was a man of Oxford and of the nearby town of Thame, and his poem capitalizes on those things that he was able to observe personally.[17] The poet is able to describe the "Occasion of the Erection of *Christys Churche yn Oxforde,*" for instance, as well as the progress of Walter (Henry VIII) and Anne Boleyn "thorowe *Thame /* and other Townys," and the commons' reaction to this. Forrest's ninth chapter concerns the discussion that took place at Oxford University of Henry's case for divorce, about which the poet "somewhat saye can" since he claims to have been there present "attendynge vpon a certayne goode Man." Public responses to these discussions and events are also seen through the eyes of the witness. Forrest tells the tale of a woman who threw "[a] lumpe Of mundys" at Friar Nicholas de Burgo, one of the king's advocates, "whiche myste of his noddle / the more pytie." "I sawe it trulye," Forrest avows, before going on to note that thirty women were imprisoned in "*Buckerdo*" (Bocardo) prison in retaliation. "I was then present," he likewise maintains, to hear the "weepinges / and lamentation" and "Complaynte" of those that objected to the outcome of the Oxford discussions, the bishop John Longland having secured by deceit an apparently unanimous decision in the king's favor.[18]

Events that Forrest did not observe personally might also be said to derive from firsthand reports. In his poem Forrest stages a tearful goodbye between Catherine of Aragon and her loyal household servants that issues from what "one of her Seruauntes / to mee did tell." Whether or not there really is a historical basis for the ensuing dialogue is a matter that others may well want to pursue, but the principal point is that the poet wants us to trust that there is.[19]

By implication, perhaps, much of the rest of the direct speech in *The Seconde Grisilde* is therefore also to be taken as authoritative. In Forrest's poem we listen to the mother and daughter lament one another's fates following their forced separation; we hear Catherine of Aragon's deathbed prayers, and we also eavesdrop on Mary's private mourning of her mother.

Presumably at least some of the words spoken, perhaps even most of them, are in fact the poet's creation, but if they are, then a distinction is drawn between them and other more obvious fictions. As far as I can remember, it is only when Forrest ventriloquizes the intercessory prayers of the saints in heaven, those that helped return England to Catholicism under Queen Mary, that he admits outright to fiction-making. These, the poet writes, "Imagyne I maye."[20]

It is worth emphasizing also that Forrest expected Mary to approve the words that he put in her mouth and her mother's; *The Seconde Grisilde* exists today only in a luxurious presentation copy that he dedicated "[t]o the moste excellent and vertuous Prynces, oure moste gratious soueraigne ladye, *Marye*."[21] In addition, and though there is as yet no evidence to confirm the association, during the reign of Mary's half-sister, Elizabeth, Forrest styled himself "sometyme Chaplayne to the noble Queene Mary."[22] There may in the end be reason to suppose that Forrest's perspective on the divorce of Catherine of Aragon and Henry VIII was an unusually privileged one, and so historians will want to take note of what he has to say.

It is for reasons other than its possible veracity that literary critics are slowly rediscovering *The Seconde Grisilde*. A very modest body of scholarship has begun to explore the poem's relation to other sixteenth-century versions of the Patient Griselda story as well as to other Tudor narratives of the Henrician Reformation.[23] Of significance on both fronts is that Forrest's voice in *The Seconde Grisilde* is pro-Marian and pro-Catholic, and so in the end he proves something of an interesting outlier, given the eventual direction of travel of both literary and religious culture after Mary's death. Of course, the fact that Forrest also dedicated poems to an evangelical sympathizer such as Edward Seymour, the duke of Somerset, who was for a time Lord Protector of England, and that he survived well into Elizabeth's reign, should caution us against too quickly caricaturing him simply as a reactionary or as a flash in the pan.[24] Indeed, it will surely be on account of Forrest's apparently divided associations that he will prove so interesting to future scholars. William Forrest was a poet who was able somehow to negotiate the religious and cultural pressures of the sixteenth century while remaining a bridge between the pre-Reformation and Reformation worlds. More particularly, and as I now go on to outline, his poetry is eloquent testimony to the perpetuation beyond the rupture of Reformation of what we call "medieval literary culture," not to its dwindling, and so he is a figure around whom debates about the periodization of literature may be brought into focus.

One poem in Forrest's last manuscript, for example, one that is usually identified by the line "Rose Marye / moste of vertue vyrgynall," was once ascribed to the much earlier poet William Dunbar.[25] Though the specific attribution is today questioned, Forrest himself identifying only that the poem was penned by "a devoute Scotte" who "longe time sithen: dyd yt edyfye," the lyric may still help shed some light on the oftentimes shadowy subject of early Anglo-Scottish literary exchange.[26] More to the point, whoever its author this was a lyric that inspired a response from Forrest, the later poet writing that "so well as I maye | I shall continue: In this poore quyre, | to saye with the scotte: Salue Maria."[27] The individual case only hints at Forrest's broader debt to an earlier literature.

Like his contemporaries Alexander Barclay, John Heywood, and George Cavendish, Forrest shows a marked preference for the rhyme royal stanza, which he inherited from Chaucer and Lydgate.[28] The poet in fact gestures toward a shared cultural patrimony in his first major work, where he writes respectfully about how his own poem "hathe not the florishinge vayne | of Gowers phrase / adornde in suche sorte | other of Chawcer, that poete soverayne." "[T]o aske their cownselle," the later poet continues, "I cam far to shorte | Lydgate herein / gave me no comforte | as dothe appeare / whoe so shall it reade | I cannot reyse vpp them / so longe a go deade."[29] The deferential pose is, of course, commonplace for those writing subsequent to the great medieval triad of Gower, Chaucer, and Lydgate, but Forrest's ties to this earlier native literature also extend beyond the merely superficial. In the preface to the collection of psalms that he dedicated to Edward Seymour, the duke of Somerset, Forrest points out that he modeled his own poetic practice, indeed his search for patronage, on the prior example of John Lydgate. He observes that "the vsage of wryters alweye" was "to father their workes; | as dyd John Lidgate / to noble duke humfreye," and so he follows suit: "so, I," Forrest writes, "to yowe noble Duke / theis psalmes doe present | as vnto whome my harte of love is bent."[30] Though Forrest restricts the terms of his comparison to the earlier poet-patron dynamic alone, the gesture likely carries more charge. Though Humphrey, duke of Gloucester, was a patron of the arts, like Somerset he, too, had once been Lord Protector to an infant king—his nephew—and he also ended his life in political disgrace.[31] Forrest's appeal to Lydgate is thus more than a matter of literary courtesy; with the name of the earlier poet comes associations beyond the merely benign, both pecuniary and political.

At a rather more foundational level we see the continuing influence of medieval literary culture on the forms of poetry that Forrest chose to write, and not this culture's sixteenth-century termination. In at least one case he even sustains a genre of writing that James Simpson argues was "impossible after the 1530s," namely "para-biblical invention."[32] Forrest's *History of the Patriarch Joseph* is perfectly easygoing about its amplification of the story of Joseph given in Genesis 37 to 50, being "written / collecte / and drawne":

> not kepinge ordre secratlye
> as the Byble dothe represent
> withowte any addytament
> but to declare the mateir more
> owte of twoe warkes muche meit therfore
> the twelve Patryarkes testament
> and a Sermon full excellent
> made by Effrem / a busshopp in Greece
> is take and gathered a great peece
> patched togither so well as I can.³³

As far as Forrest is here concerned—and contrary to the opinion of many Reformation divines—scripture did not adequately speak for itself but instead required fleshing out. Rather than keep "ordre secratlye" in the manner of the Bible, his life of Joseph therefore builds upon the basic narrative in an accretive way, pressing into service the words and thoughts of a specifically pre-Reformation interpretative community. It was the thirteenth-century bishop of Lincoln, Robert Grosseteste, who first introduced *The Testaments of the Twelve Patriarchs* into Christian biblical hermeneutics, and the fact that Forrest's "patched togither" life of Joseph continued to make use of the work is thus significant in placing his affinities, textual, cultural, and religious.³⁴

Ostensibly, Forrest's *Pleasaunt Poesye of Princelie Practise* is another poem that should not have been written when it was. According to Simpson's taxonomy of the medieval and Reformation political imaginations, the earlier literature was characterized by Aristotelian ideals, the latter by Platonic. The difference, in Simpson's reckoning, is pronounced. He writes, "[t]he political imagination of the fourteenth and fifteenth centuries negotiates the needs of both the body and the head of the whole body politic, whereas the sixteenth-century models generate their politics wholly from the top down, in repression of the larger body."³⁵ Given that Forrest's poem is just one of a long line of English adaptations of the *Secretum secretorum* that include Thomas Hoccleve's *The Regiment of Princes* and John Lydgate's *Secrees of old Philisoffres*, it is unsurprising to find that his political voice might upset modern indices of the "medieval" and "Reformation." Forrest's poem does not ignore the needs of the body politic, maintaining instead that "[a] kynge cheeiflye / and aboue althinge | a Commone wealthe / owght too respecte." The relationship between king and subject that Forrest's *Pleasaunt Poesye of Princelie Practise* idealizes is reciprocal more than it is top-down. In Forrest's poem the good king is made to say to his subjects that "I wische your wealthe / withe all prosperitee | as yee doo myne / witheoute dissemblaunce," and the poet argues that:

> a kynge ought to be muche desyrowse too knowe thopynyon
> of his Commons towardys hym, by thexploration of some se-
> creat wittie seruaunte whome heedoithe beste credyte, and
> thearto accordinge to reforme hym selfe / that hee and they
> may bee in looue togithers knytt / as one head & membres[.][36]

So often the aim of secret state surveillance and intelligence gathering is the control of the populace, but in Forrest's poem its purpose is instead control of the monarch, who is expected not just to "knowe thopynyon of his Commons towardys hym" but to "reforme hym selfe" accordingly. Of course it matters that Forrest's poem was unfinished, and it will be worth asking if it was for some reason unfinishable, but this does not alter the fact that "the needs of both the body and the head of the whole body politic" were of concern to Forrest, as indeed they were to other post-Henrician poets such as John Heywood and Robert Crowley.[37]

Forrest's miscellany of devotional poems, many in defense of the Virgin Mary, is redolent of an altogether different aspect of pre-Reformation culture, a spirituality that finds its mirror in the numerous medieval lyrics that were once written in her praise.[38] Indeed, it is only the passing of time that differentiates Forrest's approach to his subject from that of his literary predecessors, their different paeans to the Virgin a reflection of their different historical moments. Specifically, Forrest's Marian devotion must take the form of lament rather than celebration, a dominant theme for him being the disgraceful neglect of the Virgin Mary in contemporary devotion. Once again he might communicate this by way of a personal anecdote, such as when he tells of "a pooare woman" who "[o]f late, to my dooare [...] theare came; | to haue Refreschinge / for Charyteis sake." This woman says her prayers, "but," Forrest notes, "withe Aue Marye: she had not to doe," and so he asks her "whie she lefte it owte":

> She answearde with woordes: right gentyle & softe,
> howe, as she walked / in that maner wise:
> she was reproved / sundrye tymes / and ofte:
> by suche, as dyd her: for the same despice,
> at whiche, my stomake: gan grevouslye rise[.]

Such dereliction of duty, Forrest later suggests, first emerged "ab anno 1532," which is to say during the time of Henry VIII's divorce. "Theis fortye yeares togeathers (excepte a fewe betweene)," he writes, "hathe theis Blaspheamyes bene vsed againste the gloryous vyrgin marye," and Forrest goes on to tell tales of a number of people who were divinely punished on account of their impiety.[39]

Forrest's commitment to pre-Reformation modes of cultural and devotional expression was plainly extensive, discernible even in his collection of forty-nine psalm paraphrases that retain traces of a specifically Cistercian religiosity.[40] In numerous ways, then, he is a poet who poses a challenge to Simpson's hypothesis that Henry VIII's Reformation brought to an end the characteristic features and forms of medieval poetry, indeed "that the institutional simplifications and centralizations of the sixteenth century provoked correlative simplifications and narrowings in literature."[41] On the contrary, Forrest continued to work within the medieval idiom identified by Simpson, his poetry lending support instead to Thomas Betteridge's sense that the Henrician moment was more of an interruption in proceedings than it was a full stop.[42]

This is not to suggest, however, that Forrest was either a cultural throwback or a displaced medievalist. I have already hinted at what was a routine concern for Forrest: the social, religious, and political ramifications in his own present of the Reformation initiated by Henry VIII. His medievalism was, in other words, modern, his voice current, and, to judge by his hoped-for patrons—who in addition to Queen Mary included William Parr, Edward Seymour, King Edward VI, and Thomas Howard—he did not believe himself an irrelevance.[43]

Moreover it is important to note that fleeting references within Forrest's corpus to "my frende [John] Heywood," to the example and wit of "a certayne wryter, Alexander Barkeley," as well as to the earl of Surrey's reputation as a poet and man of letters conjure up the possibility of a compelling and modern literary context within which to assess Forrest's work.[44] There may be strong cause in addition to associate Forrest with the mid-Tudor poet and biographer George Cavendish, who similarly conceived of Catherine of Aragon as "a perfect Grysheld."[45] Finally, at least two of the poems in Forrest's last manuscript, British Library Harley MS 1703, offer versions of poems also found in *Tottel's Miscellany* (1557), which may suggest that Forrest was once part of a coterie of poets who exchanged their work. One of these poems Forrest attributes to his friend Heywood (a poem beginning "Geve place, ye Ladyes all be gone"), while the other he gives to Thomas Vaux, second Baron Vaux of Harrowden (beginning "I loathe that I dyd loue").[46] Evidently Forrest was plugged into a contemporary literary network of some description and was not simply a relic of a former age; though his taste, like his religion, links him to the pre-Reformation world, he is not to be dismissed as hopelessly nostalgic.

Many of the concerns I have here outlined are likely to come together in the study of Forrest's *The Seconde Grisilde*. The sixteenth-century editing, repackaging, and above all else "protestantization" of medieval literature, particularly of Chaucer, has long held the attention of modern scholars, but

Forrest's *The Seconde Grisilde*, his retelling of this medieval tale, is neither Henrician nor evangelical in its attitude.[47] Rather, Forrest's stance is anti-Reformation. It is on account of Henry's divorce of Catherine of Aragon, "and other abomynations," the poet writes, that "this noble *Brytayne* / hathe beene plaged sore | withe sundrye / and manye trybulations; | I thynke, no Royalme in Christendome more."[48] William Forrest's contrary attitude sets *The Seconde Grisilde* apart from other sixteenth-century appropriations of this earlier literature, his poem representing the stirrings of a new Catholic medievalism. The fact that Forrest's poem lies for the most part unread, however, means that his alternative voice has been excluded from literary critical accounts of mid-Tudor medievalism. Forrest may always prove to have been an outlier, but this is not a reason to eliminate his voice from the critical conversation entirely.

Whether it is also the case, as Mike Rodman Jones states, that *The Seconde Grisilde* is more particularly "one of the least-read examples of extended sixteenth-century *Chaucerianism*" remains to be seen.[49] Certainly Chaucer's *The Clerk's Tale* was the most well-known English version of the tale of Grisilde, but much more work needs to be done to establish the precise relationship between Forrest's and Chaucer's poems. It is difficult to imagine that Forrest was ignorant of Chaucer's version owing to its popularity—it was frequently copied independently of the rest of *The Canterbury Tales*—but, like Chaucer, Forrest actually cites Petrarch's prior telling.[50] Whether this is an act of ultra-imitation or Petrarch's narrative really was Forrest's primary source will be worth determining.

So there is scope for future research that will broaden our understanding of both mid-Tudor literature and the relationship between pre-Reformation and Reformation literary culture, between what we tend to refer to as the medieval and the early modern. However, when faced with Forrest's *The Seconde Grisilde*, readers are at present liable to be led astray, since the work has been misdated by two years. Rather than 1558, it seems to me more plausible that Forrest's poem was "fynysched" in 1556.

II. On Dating *The Seconde Grisilde*

William Forrest's *The Seconde Grisilde* exists in a single autograph manuscript now held by the Bodleian Library in Oxford, with the shelfmark Bodleian MS Wood Empt. 2. According to its later owner Anthony Wood, the manuscript was owned in the seventeenth century by the Catholic antiquary, Ralph Sheldon, presumably after whose death in 1684 the manuscript passed into the hands of Wood and thence to Oxford University in 1692.[51] The work's earlier provenance is less clear, but it has been assumed that the surviving manuscript is the one once presented to Queen Mary.[52]

This relatively large manuscript (approx. 13 1/2 x 9 3/4 inches) on vellum is decorated throughout with illuminated capitals and rubrication, and it is today bound in black velvet. This is a comparatively modern covering, as the manuscript was rebound in 1897, according to a note on the inside front cover. W. D. Macray, whose 1875 edition of *The Seconde Grisilde* predates this rebinding, offers a sense of the manuscript's earlier condition. He describes it as "having been originally 'bound in laced satin'" but explains, "Nearly all the lace has now disappeared, and the satin is tattered and faded. It has clasps, and brass bosses with the words 'Ave Maria, gracia plēa' at each corner, as well as a centre boss."[53] These bosses and one of the clasps have survived, and they still adorn the manuscript today.

Care and attention was obviously lavished on the book, which bears both a dedication to Queen Mary and a closing "*Oration* Consolatorye, | to *Marye* / oure Queene / moste worthy of fame." The dedication, which is followed by an eighteen-stanza "*Prologe* to *the* Queenis *maiestee*," is appropriately full and contains clues as to when Forrest was working on his manuscript:

> *T*o the moste excellente and vertuous Prynces, oure moste gratious soueraigne ladye, *Marye* (by the grace of God) Queene of *E*nglande, *F*rance, *N*aples, *H*ierusalem, and *I*relande, *D*efendresse of the faith, *P*ryncesse of *S*payne, and *C*icilie, *A*rcheduchesse of Austria, Duchesse of Millayne / Burgundye / and Brabande, Countesse of Haspurge, fflaundres, & Tyrale, *Y*oure maiesties moste faithefull, louynge, & obedyent Subiecte, *W*illiam *ff*orreste, wischeth all grace and fauour from God aboue, longe life (yn good healthe) and prosperous reigne: withe (after this life) aeternall felicitee[.][54]

Though Forrest does not mention Mary's husband, Philip, the forms of address he employs clearly postdate the royal wedding in July 1554, since Mary became queen of Naples and of Jerusalem only by marriage.[55] The titles Forrest gives to Mary also predate January 1556, since this is when Philip became king of Spain and Mary his queen. It is conceivable that Forrest continued in error to style Mary "Pryncess of Spayne" for a time after January 1556, though it is perhaps less plausible that he would have persisted in doing so as late as 1558.

If the terms of Forrest's royal address are anything to go on then the poet must have written the dedication to the presentation copy of *The Seconde Grisilde* after July 1554 and likely before January 1556. He was, in other words, working on his manuscript during this period.

Over the question of precisely when Forrest finished his manuscript—or rather, when he finished the central portion of it at least, his final "*Oration* Consolatorye" beginning a new gathering that comes after his colophon—it is possible to say slightly more since he tells us, and this is commonly thought to have been on June 25, 1558. Anthony Wood in the late seventeenth century, Thomas Warton in the late eighteenth century, W. D. Macray in the late nineteenth century, and all those scholars who have benefited from the use of Macray's edition of *The Seconde Grisilde*—including Frederick G. Lee, Louise I. Guiney, Richard S. Sylvester, Joseph Keena, Edward Mehok, John Milsom, Peter Holmes, Ursula Potter, Mike Rodman Jones, Valerie Schutte, Helen Cooper and I confess, I myself, along with, no doubt, a number of others—have all repeated the claim. The consensus is absolute, the key—indeed, the only—piece of supporting evidence being Forrest's colophon to *The Seconde Grisilde*, which Macray transcribes thus: "Heere endethe the Historye of Grysilde the seconde, onlye meanynge Queene Catharyne, Mother to oure moste dread soueraigne ladye Queene Marye, fynysched the 25 daye of June the yeare of owre Lorde 1558 by the symple and vnlearned Syr Wyllyam Forrest, Preeiste, propria manu."[57] Yet it is far from clear that Forrest wrote "1558" at all, as unexpected as that will surely now seem.

As is apparent from Figure 1, what Macray and others before him have read as the number eight is at best only a very odd sort of eight. On inspection (Fig. 2) we see that this number is not actually formed from two joined bowls, an upper and a lower one, but is formed instead of a lower bowl and upper loop, the left hand ascender being particularly straight where one might expect it to pinch inward if it were an eight. Admittedly this left ascender also curls around more than would perhaps be usual for a number six, but what join there is with the lower bowl on the right has the appearance of a slip, the ink stroke there being particularly light.

Identification is clinched through comparison with some of the other numbers in Forrest's manuscript, those that can be confidently fixed as either a six or an eight because they come in sequence (5, 6, 7, 8). There is a clear difference, for example, in the way that Forrest forms the 6 and the 8 of the headings "Caput 6" and "Caput 8" (Figs. 3 and 4), over which there can be no quibble.[58] Forrest's 8 (Fig. 4) is entirely standard, being made up of lower and upper bowls that join in a pinched middle. His 6 (Fig. 3) is utterly distinct, formed from a lower bowl and upper loop that ascends in a straight line on the left. On the right this ascender curls around to join the lower bowl, but they do not quite meet. When the specific digit under consideration in *The Seconde Grisilde*'s given date is set side by side with the numerals in Forrest's "Caput 6" and "Caput 8," only one verdict presents itself: contrary to what has been said for over three hundred years, Forrest's *The Seconde Grisilde* was "fynysched the / 25 daye of *Iune* / the yeare of owre // lorde / 1556."

Owing to the sheer weight of critical comment that has stated otherwise, it is to be expected that the redating of this work will be received with some skepticism, repetition of the error having created the effect of veracity. It is

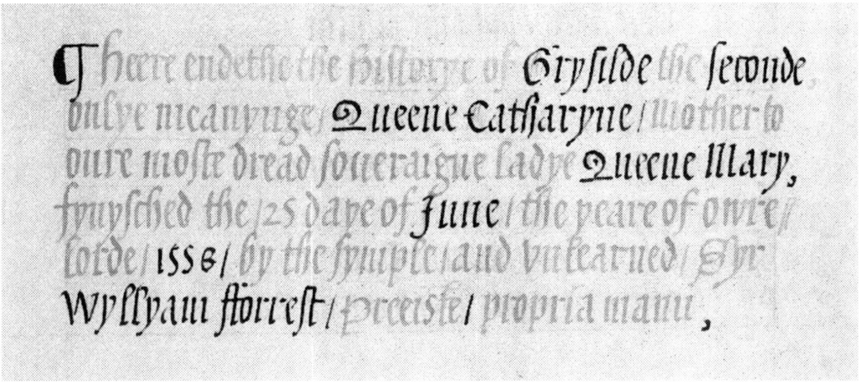

DATING WILLIAM FORREST

¶ heere endethe the hystorye of Grysilde the seconde
onlye meanynge Queene Catharyne / whother to
oure moste dread soueraigne ladye Queene Mary,
fynyshed the 25 daye of June / the yeare of owre
lorde 1556 / by the symple and vnlearned Syr
Wylliam fforrest / preeiste / propria manu,

Figure 1. William Forrest, *The Seconde Grisilde*. Bodleian Library MS Wood Empt. 2, fol. 69v. Reproduced by permission of the Bodleian Libraries, University of Oxford.

Figure 2. Detail from Figure 1.

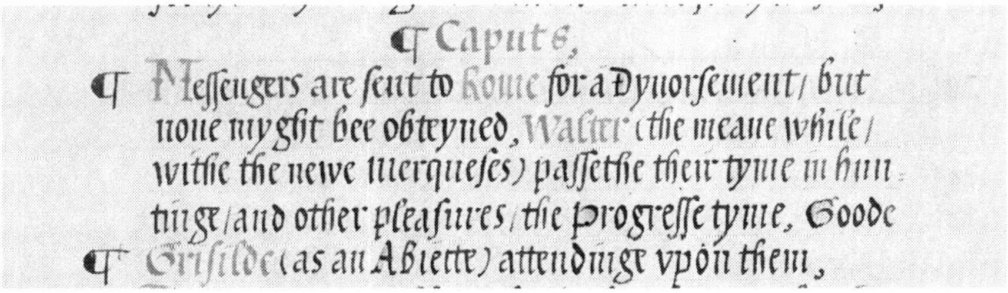

¶ Caput 6,
¶ Messengers are sent to Rome for a Dyuorsement / but
none myght bee obteyned, Wasier (the meane while /
withe the newe Inerquesies) passethe their tyme in hun
tinge / and other pleasures, the progresse tyme, Goode
¶ Grisilde (as an Abiette) attendinge vpon them,

Figure 3. William Forrest, *The Seconde Grisilde*. Bodleian Library MS Wood Empt. 2, fol. 5v. Reproduced by permission of the Bodleian Libraries, University of Oxford.

> ⁋ Caput. 8,
>
> ⁋ Walter reuertynge his progreſſe / The newe Merqueſes
> accompayneth hym thorowe Thame. goode Griſilde
> cowmynge after : at whiche / the goode People mutte=
> rethe, praymge for Griſilde / God to preſerue her.
> ⁋ What tawlke the Commons ſecreatlye had (ſynde /

Figure 4. William Forrest, *The Seconde Grisilde*. Bodleian Library MS Wood Empt. 2, fol. 6. Reproduced by permission of the Bodleian Libraries, University of Oxford.

> Here enſuithe A notable warke called the plea
> ſaunt poeſye of princelie practiſe, compoſed of late in
> meatre royall, by the ſymple and vnlearned / Willia
> forreſt preeiſte, muche parte collecte owte of A booke
> entiteled. The gouernaunce of noble men, which booke
> the Wiſe philoſopher Ariſtotele / wrote too his diſcyple
> Alexandre / the great and mightie Conqueroure.
> 1548

Figure 5. William Forrest, *The Pleasaunt Poesye of Princelie Practise*. British Library MS Royal 17 D iii, fol. 8. Reproduced by permission of the British Library Board.

> ⁋ An Excuſation: to voyde Indygnation.
> Go Joſeph gentle. depryved thye Coate,
> of thye fell Bretherne, at the begynnynge.
> whiche I haue lyued, not harmed by Moathe.
> of Anye evill thinge: to my knowledginge,
> If Anye bee, to others perceavinges,
> I, humblye ſubmytt this Operation:
> to easye the true Chriſtians caſtygation,
>   Finis, 1569. die vero Aprilis: 11,

Figure 6. William Forrest, *The History of the Patriarch Joseph*. Bodleian Library MS Eng. poet. d. 9, fol. 157. Reproduced by permission of the Bodleian Libraries, University of Oxford.

worth pointing out, then, that in Forrest's other manuscripts his 8s and 6s are similarly distinguished and just as certainly. The 8 in *The Pleasaunt Poesye of Princelie Practise*'s given date of "1548" (Fig. 5), though more oblique than one might perhaps expect, is unlikely to be confused with the 6 in *The History of the Patriarch Joseph*'s given date of "1569" (Fig. 6). The former cannot mean anything other than "1548"—it is not to be read as "1546," for example—since the poet addresses his poem to "Prynce Edwarde the Sexthe, Kynge of Engelande," Edward having assumed the throne in 1547. Also Forrest refers in his prologue to "laste yeare / the firste of his [Edward's] reigne," meaning 1547, which number the poet has helpfully written alongside this line.[59] Likewise the latter can only be read as "1569"—it certainly does not read "1589"—since Forrest's poem is dedicated to "the /right/ highe and myghtye prynce, Thomas, Duke of Northefolke," who was executed in 1572.[60] In these cases Forrest's dates are secure, and the difference between his 8s and 6s once more manifest, which provides yet another context in which to decipher the date given to *The Seconde Grisilde*. And once again, the customary year of 1558 is found wanting, with that final numeral resembling Forrest's other 6s and not his 8s (Fig. 7).

Another date in Forrest's manuscript that requires brief discussion in the light of these observations is one that appears in the body of the poem itself, alongside a stanza that describes events relating to Thomas Wolsey's 1527 diplomatic mission to France. In Macray's edition of *The Seconde Grisilde*, this date is transcribed as 1528, though on the basis of Forrest's penmanship it should instead be read as 1526, the poet being a year out in either case (Figs. 8 and 9).[61] This date appears in the fifth chapter of Forrest's poem alongside a story about "*Cardynall W*olsaye, whoe, counselinge withe Astronomyers / founde; a woman to be his vndoinge, whiche (moste wronfullye) he ymputed to goode *Grisilde*, whearfore, he went into ffraunce / and labored for the kyngis Sister theare / to matche withe *Walter* our kinge." It is Anne Boleyn, not Catherine of Aragon, who, Forrest later shows, was to prove Wolsey's undoing, but to this the cardinal was blind. Consequently Wolsey is the "wycked man" of Forrest's narrative, the "Vearye Belyall, | puffed withe Pryde" who, in an effort to protect himself, set about to secure for Walter/Henry his divorce from Grisilde/Catherine. Forrest writes:

> *Hee* [Wolsey] Counseled (men saide) withe
>   Astronomyers,
> (or what other secte, I cannot well saye)
> weare they Sothesayers / or weare they lyers.)[62]
> whyther he shoulde fall / or florysche alwaye,
> whois Answeare was; he shoulde come to decaye,
> by meanys (they fownde) of a certayne woman;

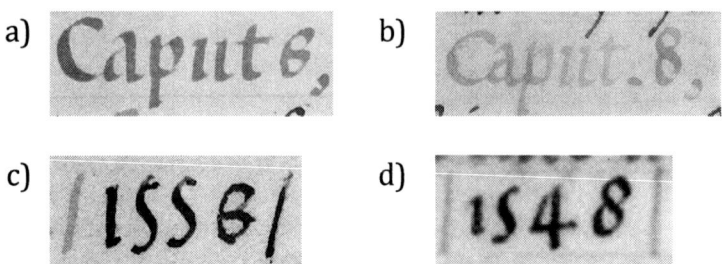

Figure 7. Details from Figures 3 [a], 4 [b], 1 [c] and 5 [d].

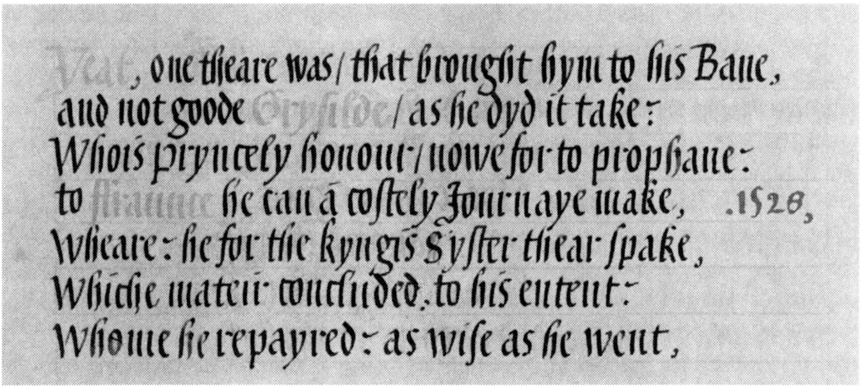

> one theare was / that brought hym to his Bane,
> and not goode / as he dyd it take:
> Whois pryncely honour / nowe for to prophane:
> to he can a costely Journaye make, .1528,
> Wheare: he for the kyngis Syster theat spake,
> Whiche mateir concluded, to his entent:
> Whome he repayred: as wise as he went,

Figure 8. William Forrest, *The Seconde Grisilde*. Bodleian Library MS Wood Empt. 2, fol. 25. Reproduced by permission of the Bodleian Libraries, University of Oxford.

Figure 9. Detail from Figure 8.

> But, what shee sholde bee; they coulde not saye than,
>
> *Vpon* whiche fonde Enygmatization,
> vnto goode Grysilde / ympute it dyd hee;
> whearefore, in his Imagynation;
> he wrought to haue her deposed to bee,
> But hee theare mystooke; it was not sure shee,
> that shoulde hym brynge / to his fynall myschaunce;
> goode Grysilde; neauer wrought anyes hynderaunce,
>
> *Yeat*, one theare was / that brought hym to his Bane,
> and not goode *Grysilde* / as he dyd it take;
> Whois Pryncely honour / nowe for to prophane;
> to *ffraunce* he can a costelye Iournaye make, .1526.
> wheare; he for the kyngis Syster thear spake,
> whiche mateir concluded, to his entent;
> whome he repayred; as wise as he went[.]⁶³

The imputation here, one repeated by George Cavendish in his *Life of Cardinal Wolsey*, by the Italian historiographer Francesco Guicciardini, and by the French Cardinal and diplomat Jean du Bellay, was that Wolsey was angling for a marriage between Henry VIII and Renée of France, daughter of Louis XII and sister-in-law of King Francis I. If these negotiations happened at all—and Peter Gwyn doubts their historicity—they are meant to have taken place at the same time that Wolsey was brokering another marriage union with the French at Amiens, one between Princess Mary and Henry, duke of Orléans.⁶⁵ In Cavendish's words, Wolsey was:

> in ffraunce [...] to conclude too mariages / theon bytwen
> the kyng our souerayn lord And madame Reygne [...]
> And an other bytwen the prynces than of England
> (Nowe beyng quene of this reallme my lady marye /
> the kynges doughter/) And the frenche kynges second
> Sonne the duke of Orlyaunce [...].⁶⁶

The latter marriage treaty was confirmed on August 18, 1527; had this taken place a year later, there would perhaps have been reason to stick with Macray's suggestion that Forrest dated these events to 1528 and, as a consequence, to reject the distinction drawn above between Forrest's 6s and 8s. As it is, we can instead assume the consistency of the poet's hand and read the marginal date as 1526, noting in addition that the proposed union of Mary and the French Henry was in fact first mooted in this year.[67]

Reconsideration of William Forrest's numerals in the manner pursued in this essay leads to the conclusion that the poet claimed to have completed the surviving manuscript of *The Seconde Grisilde* on June 25, 1556, and not two years later. Significantly, this earlier date of completion also makes sense in relation to the poem's own historical limits, since the poet seems never to refer to any event that took place after the summer of 1556. For example, in the "*Oration* Consolatorye" addressed "to *Marye /* oure Queene / moste worthy of fame" with which Forrest ends his manuscript, and which comes after his colophon, the poet glances at recent history. Therein he praises God for having appointed Mary "to set free / his *Churche* owte of bondage," before going on to celebrate his queen for having brought to an end the "moste odyous Schysmys / this Royalme dyd late perturbe," those that had infected lowborn and highborn alike—"aswell of Nobles / as the rustycall Scrubbe"—for "aboue [...] twentye yearys full." However Forrest's praise also gives way to complaint, the poet observing that there were some in recent years who had defied and disobeyed the new order and their divinely appointed queen:

> *What* goode gote *Duddeley* / defrawdynge thy Right,
> withe all that to hym / weare associat?
> what helped *Wyat* / that madde Beddelem knyght?
> to foarse his powre (by pryde) vnto *Ludgate*,
> Oather (of late) the Sorte Insanyat,
> as *Henry Peckham* / with *Danyell* his ffeeare;
> By false conspiracye / agaynste thee to steeare?[68]

Here Forrest refers in the past tense—and in chronological order—to the plot against Mary's succession by John Dudley, the duke of Northumberland, in 1553, to the younger Sir Thomas Wyatt's 1554 rebellion against his queen, and to a more recent and still pressing conspiracy to depose Mary in early 1556, which was led from abroad by another Dudley, Sir Henry Dudley.[69] Henry Peckham and John Danyell were co-conspirators in the latter Dudley's abortive uprising, and it is noteworthy that they are written about not just in terms of the past but of the recent past, their crimes explicitly "of late."

Peckham, who had formerly opposed Northumberland's attempted coup and defended Ludgate against Wyatt's rebels, and whose father and brothers were loyal supporters of Mary, was a particular disappointment to Forrest.[70] The poet asks "O *Henry Peckham* / howe happened thee; | the Dyuyll / withe suche blyndenes / thee to delude," before going on to draw attention to the rebel's divergence from the good example of his "ffather so worthye / and godlye a Man" and his "Bretherne also / bothe Catholike / and goode."[71] Peckham was arrested for his part in the Dudley conspiracy on March 18, 1556, indicted on April 29, and tried alongside Danyell on May 7. Both men's executions followed in early July 1556.

If we assume that it was not just used to fill a line, Forrest's temporal indicator—the parenthetical "of late"—insinuates that he was writing while Peckham's case was still a live issue, rather than two years later, and in contrast to the older rebellions of Dudley and Wyatt. Forrest notes that the principal consequence of Peckham's actions, which extended also to lechery, "some saithe," was that he "hathe shortened thy life," and this may suggest that at least this portion of Forrest's manuscript—the "*Oration* Consolatorye"—was written after Peckham's execution in July 1556. However this is not guaranteed. Forrest also writes, for example, that Peckham's father's "fame shall florische" even though his child "bee exiled," which may instead indicate that he was writing after Peckham had been disgraced but prior to his execution—that is to say in the wake of his arrest and trial. When Forrest asks Peckham, "why weare thowe peruerse / why weare thowe so wilde," he may still be remonstrating with a live man, not yet a dead one.[72]

There are three subsequent comments in Forrest's "*Oration* Consolatorye" that likewise make more sense if written in 1556, not 1558. Toward the end of his address to Mary, Forrest wishes his queen "yearys, longe / and manye / so to continue"; he hopes that she and Philip will by "Issuynge betweene yowe / suche worthye Issue, | this Royalme to keepe / from desolation"; and he also hopes that Philip "oure Kynge [will] bee / nomore as straunge Geste" to England.[73] It is true that Philip was more often absent from England than he was present, and the notion of his being a regrettably "straunge Geste" applied equally in mid-1556 and mid-1558. And self-evidently, an absentee king greatly limited what opportunities there were for the "Issuynge" of "Issue." What matters, however, is whether there would have been much hope for Mary's health and for the continuation of her line at the end of June 1558. By this time, Mary had suffered her second false pregnancy, news of which few had taken seriously anyway, and her health was again in decline.[74] It is always possible that Forrest was just an eternal optimist, but his aspirations for Mary's future would certainly have been more justified if written in 1556.

More to the point, Forrest links Philip's return to England and all that would follow from this—chiefly children—to his "wische" that

"Chrystyan Obedyence / in dwe sorte" will "reigne" in the realm. This is to say that he associates these happy outcomes with the resolution of the civil unrest to which he has already referred. "*Then* shall Goddys glorye; florische (as it ought)," he writes:

> then shall thy harte / bee in quyet / and reste;
> then shall weale publike / in right trade bee brought;
> then shalbe althynges / as wee can wische beste.
> Then shall oure Kynge bee / nomore as straunge
>   Geste,
> but, as behoauethe / withe thee tassociat;
> after our longinge / Issue to procreat[.][75]

Forrest's repeated adverb, "then," insists that his hoped-for future is conditional upon the satisfactory settlement of recent disturbances. The strong suggestion is that his "*Oration* Consolatorye" was written from the perspective of one looking forward from 1556, not one looking backward from 1558.

In summary, then, we can say that if the terms of his address to Queen Mary mean anything at all then William Forrest was at work on the surviving manuscript of *The Seconde Grisilde* between July 1554 and January 1556. It is to this time that his dedication seems to date. According to his own testimony he "fynysched" his manuscript on June 25, 1556, not two years later as is commonly thought, though it is also possible that his "*Oration* Consolatorye" was added at a slightly later date (though apparently not very long after if at all).

The implications of this redating are still to be worked out in full, but certain assumptions about Forrest's poem can already be corrected. Ursula Potter, for example, suggests that Forrest's criticism of Anne Boleyn in *The Seconde Grisilde*—what she terms his "slanderous comments"—would have been "politically risky" in June 1558, "given that Mary's health was poor and that her half sister, Elizabeth, was next in succession to the throne."[76] Such a hypothesis is now difficult to sustain, and a more intriguing possibility presents itself instead, one that will require further substantiation down the line. Though there is a potential question mark over the appointment, it is more likely than not that on July 1, 1556, William Forrest was made vicar of Bledlow in Buckinghamshire, which is just over the county border from Forrest's usual stomping ground of Thame in Oxfordshire.[77] According to the records, the poet's lay patron on this occasion was Anthony Lambesonne (Lamperson, Lampson or Lamson), but given that Forrest was presented to the living at Bledlow so close in time to the production of *The Seconde Grisilde*, one might wonder whether the two are related. Might the vicarage be some reward for his endeavor? As far as we can tell, Forrest remained at

Bledlow until 1576, so the appointment was certainly significant for his later church career.[78]

Greater awareness of Forrest's historical background and his movements will be necessary to establish the point, as indeed it will be to determine the shape of his literary vocation more generally, in which the search for patronage, the presentation of manuscripts, and an apparent commitment to counsel loomed large, no matter what the character of the political center.[79] But as I outlined in the first part of this article, study of Forrest's poetry will inevitably lead us also to rethink the trajectory of literature and literary history during the Marian age, however brief the period. Dating as it does to the middle years of Mary's reign and not to the last months, Forrest's *The Seconde Grisilde* must be read afresh as a literary expression of confidence in and hope for the Catholic settlement, not as an expression of regret over missed opportunities. At the very least, and though there is much work still to do to place his poem, *The Seconde Grisilde* surely gives the lie to the assumption that under Queen Mary, "[l]iterary creativity dried up."[80]

Independent Scholar

Acknowledgments

I am grateful to the Bodleian Libraries, University of Oxford, and to the British Library Board for permission to reproduce images from MS Wood Empt. 2, MS Eng. poet. d. 9, and MS Royal 17 D iii. I am also grateful to the editors and anonymous readers of the *Journal of the Early Book Society* for their helpful comments in the preparation of this work.

NOTES

1. There are eight known manuscripts of Forrest's work. *The History of the Patriarch Joseph* exists in three versions in four manuscripts: British Library Add. MS 34791 (1547); Bodleian Library MS Eng. poet. d. 9 (1569); University College MS 88 (1571, part one); and British Library Royal MS 18 C xiii (1571, part two). For Forrest's *Speculum Principis*, see British Library MS Royal 17 D iii; for his Psalms, see British Library Royal MS 17 A xxi; for *The Seconde Grisilde*, see Bodleian Library MS Wood Empt. 2; and for his later devotional verse, see British Library Harley MS 1703. Modern editions of Forrest's poems are mostly difficult to access but include Edward Eugene Mehok, "An Edition of William Forrest's *History of Joseph*" (PhD thesis, Case Western Reserve University, 1971), which edits only the poem's first part; M. A. Manzalaoui, ed., *Secretum Secretorum: Nine English Versions*, vol. 1 (Oxford: Oxford University Press, 1977), 390–534; William Forrest, *The History of Grisild the Second:*

A Narrative in Verse, of the Divorce of Queen Katharine of Aragon, ed. W. D. Macray (London: Whittingham and Wilkins, 1875); and Joseph Patrick Keena, "An Edition of the Marian Poems of the Recusant Writer, William Forrest, from MS Harleian 1703" (PhD thesis, University of Notre Dame, 1960), which edits the majority of the manuscript but not all of it. A portion of Forrest's *Speculum Principis* was also edited in S. J. Herrtage, ed., *England in the Reign of King Henry the Eighth* (London: Trübner for the Early English Text Society, 1878); and one of Forrest's later Catholic poems was edited in Franz Ludorff, "William Forest's *Theophiluslegende*," *Anglia* 7 (1884): 60–115.
2. William Forrest, "A New Ballade of the Marigolde" (1553?), repr. in Thomas Park, ed., *The Harleian Miscellany*, vol. 10 (London: John White, 1813), 253–254; John Milsom, "William Mundy's 'Vox Patris Caelestis' and the Accession of Mary Tudor," *Music & Letters* 91 (2010): 1–38; John Foxe, *The Unabridged Acts and Monuments Online (TAMO)* (1563 edition), 5:1203–1205 (Sheffield, UK: HRI Online Publications, 2011), http//www.johnfoxe.org [accessed: 02.02.16].
3. John Milsom, intro., *Oxford, Bodleian Library, MSS. Mus. Sch. E. 376–81*, Renaissance Music in Facsimile 15 (New York: Garland, 1986). Also see John D. Bergsagel, "The Date and Provenance of the Forrest-Heyther Collection of Tudor Masses," *Music & Letters* 44 (1963): 240-248.
4. Such an argument is outlined in the introduction to a collection of essays that resists the status quo, in Mike Pincombe and Cathy Shrank, "Prologue: The Travails of Tudor Literature," in *The Oxford Handbook of Tudor Literature, 1485–1603*, ed. Mike Pincombe and Cathy Shrank (Oxford: Oxford University Press, 2009), 1–17.
5. Others have argued similarly, e.g., T. A. Birrell, *The Panizzi Lectures, 1986: English Monarchs and Their Books: From Henry VII to Charles II* (London: British Library, 1987), 64.
6. On the neglect of mid-Tudor Psalms, see, among others, Beth Quitslund, *The Reformation in Rhyme: Sternhold, Hopkins and the English Metrical Psalter, 1547–1603* (Aldershot, UK: Ashgate, 2008). It should be noted that Quitslund herself fights shy of a full aesthetic defence of these; ibid., 2–5.
7. Pincombe and Shrank, "Prologue," 3.
8. William Forrest, *The Seconde Grisilde* (1558), Bodleian Library MS Wood Empt. 2, titles given on fols. 11 and 69v. Hereafter this manuscript is referred to in notes as *Seconde Grisilde*. A. S. G. Edwards and Oliver Wort are editing the new edition of this poem.
9. There are passing mentions of Forrest in a number of the essays in Mike Shrank and Cathy Pincombe, eds., *Oxford Handbook of Tudor Literature 1485–1603* (Oxford: Oxford University Press, 2009); see ibid., 16, 266,

419, 764. Scholars are, then, at least increasingly aware of the poet, if only dimly. Forrest receives slightly more extensive discussion in a handful of articles that I refer to later in the course of this essay and also in Valerie Schutte, *Mary I and the Art of Book Dedications: Royal Women, Power, and Persuasion* (New York: Palgrave Macmillan, 2015), 90–93.
10. *Seconde Grisilde*, fol. 69v. The virgule (/) is Forrest's mark of punctuation and does not indicate a line break. Throughout this essay line breaks are indicated instead by use of a single vertical line (|).
11. See Boccaccio, *Decameron*; Petrarch, *Epistolae seniles*; and Chaucer, *The Clerk's Tale*.
12. Mike Rodman Jones, "The Tragical History of the Reformation: Edwardian, Marian, Shakespearian," *Review of English Studies*, 63 (2011), 743–763, at 751; Forrest, *History of Grisild*, xx; and Schutte, *Mary I*, 91–92, all note that Mary's tutor, Juan Louis Vives, had recommended that his student read the tale of Grisilde. Jones, "Tragical History," 751, also points out that at least one manuscript copy of Chaucer's *The Clerk's Tale* can be associated with the Marian household.
13. *Seconde Grisilde*, fols 61-61v, 3.
14. *Seconde Grisilde*, fols. 11v, 3, 61. As can be seen in Fig. 8, Forrest regularly uses the punctus elevatus, which I replace with a semicolon throughout this essay.
15. Tom Betteridge, *Literature and Politics in the English Reformation* (Manchester, UK: Manchester University Press, 2012; first published 2004), 67–77; Brian Cummings, *The Literary Culture of the Reformation: Grammar and Grace* (Oxford: Oxford University Press, 2007; first published 2002), 223–232; Greg Walker, *Writing under Tyranny: English Literature and the Henrician Reformation* (Oxford: Oxford University Press, 2005), 1–4. For a study of contemporary divorce literature, see J. Christopher Warner, *Henry VIII's Divorce: Literature and the Politics of the Printing Press* (Woodbridge, UK: Boydell Press, 1998).
16. Forrest, *History of Grisild*, xi–xii. As I mention below, there is actually no firm evidence that Forrest was a royal chaplain, as noted in Milsom, "William Mundy's 'Vox,'" 5.
17. Though they disagree in certain particulars, for details of Forrest's life, see Louise I. Guiney, *Recusant Poets: With a Selection from Their Work. I: Saint Thomas More to Ben Jonson* (London: Sheed & Ward, 1938), 137–145; Peter Holmes, "Forrest, William (fl. 1530–1576)," *Oxford Dictionary of National Biography* online [accessed 2 Feb 2016] (Oxford: Oxford University Press, 2004); Frederick G. Lee,

The History, Description, and Antiquities of the Prebendal Church of the Blessed Virgin Mary of Thame (London: Mitchell and Hughes, 1883), 400–409; Forrest, History of Grisild, xi–xvii; and Milsom, "William Mundy's 'Vox,'" 2–9.

18. *Seconde Grisilde*, fols. 29, 32v, 35, 36, 36v. Forrest comments on his status as eye-witness on fol. 62v.
19. Ibid., fol. 45.
20. Ibid., fols. 40–41, 48v–50, 50v–53, 59–60v, 65v.
21. Ibid., fol. 1. I describe Forrest's manuscript in more detail below.
22. See Bodleian Library MS Eng. poet. d. 9, fol. 5; and University College MS 88, fol. 2. The point is raised in Milsom, "William Mundy's 'Vox,'" 5.
23. See Ursula Potter, "Tales of Patient Griselda and Henry VIII," *Early Theatre* 5 (2002): 11–28; and Jones, "Tragical History," 750–754. Forrest's poem merits only a single footnote in Lee Bliss, "The Renaissance Griselda: A Woman for All Seasons," *Viator* 23 (1992): 301–343.
24. Oliver Wort, "A Cuckoo in the Nest? William Forrest, the Duke of Somerset, and the *Certaigne Psalmes of Dauyd*," *Reformation* 21 (2016): 25–46.
25. British Library Harley MS 1703, fols. 79–80. For brief discussions of this poem, see Keena, "Edition," xl, lxii–lxiii; and Henry Noble MacCracken, "New Stanzas by Dunbar," *Modern Language Notes* 24 (1909): 110–111.
26. See A. A. MacDonald, "Anglo-Scottish Literary Relations: Problems and Possibilities," *Studies in Scottish Literature* 26 (1991): 172–184, at 176.
27. British Library Harley MS 1703, fols. 80v–82.
28. I mention these three poets in particular because there may be reason to connect them to Forrest, as I note below. For their use of rhyme royal see, among other works, Alexander Barclay, *The Ship of Fooles*, *The castell of laboure*, and *The Life of St George*; John Heywood, *The Spider and the Flie*; George Cavendish, *Metrical Visions*; William Forrest, *The History of the Patriarch Joseph*, *The Pleasaunt Poesye of Princelie Practise*, and *The Seconde Grisilde*; Geoffrey Chaucer, *Troilus and Criseyde* and *The Clerk's Tale*; and John Lydgate, *The Temple of Glas* and *The Lives of Ss. Edmund and Fremund*. See also Martin Stevens, "The Royal Stanza in Early English Literature," *PMLA* 94 (1979): 62–76.
29. British Library Add. MS 34791, fol. 1v.
30. British Library Royal MS 17 A xxi, fol. 2v.
31. For other mid-Tudor comparisons between Somerset and Gloucester, see Scott C. Lucas, *A Mirror for Magistrates and the Politics of the English Reformation* (Amherst: University of Massachusetts Press, 2009), 90–94.
32. James Simpson, *Reform and Cultural Revolution* (Oxford: Oxford University Press, 2004; first published 2002), 559, but see also his broader argument at 458–463, where he writes instead in terms of competing

orthodox and evangelical biblicisms, both of which are said to span the medieval and Reformation periods. Presumably Forrest would be classified as orthodox.
33. British Library Add. MS 34791, fols. 3v–4.
34. R. H. Charles, ed. and trans., *The Testaments of the Twelve Patriarchs* (London: Adam and Charles Black, 1908), xv–xviii. For a brief discussion of Forrest's sources, see Mehok, "Edition," ii, 453–466.
35. Simpson, *Reform*, 191.
36. British Library Royal MS 17 D iii, fols. 44, 44v, 72v–73.
37. See, e.g., Betteridge, *Literature and Politics*, 104–113; and James Holstun, "The Spider, the Fly, and the Commonwealth: Merrie John Heywood and Agrarian Class Struggle," *English Literary History* 71 (2004): 53–88.
38. British Library Harley MS 1703, about which see Keena, "Edition," xliv–lxviii.
39. British Library Harley MS 1703, fols. 9v–10, 27.
40. Wort, "Cuckoo," 39–40.
41. Simpson, *Reform*, 1.
42. Thomas Betteridge, "The Henrician Reformation and Mid-Tudor Culture," *Journal of Medieval and Early Modern Studies* 35 (2005): 91–109.
43. Forrest dedicated British Library Add. MS 34791 to William Parr; British Library MS Royal 17 D iii and British Library Royal MS 17 A xxi to Edward Seymour (the first of these two also bearing a second dedication to King Edward VI); Bodleian Library MS Wood Empt. 2 to Queen Mary; and Bodleian Library MS Eng. poet. d. 9, University College MS 88, and British Library Royal MS 18 C xiii to Thomas Howard. British Library Harley MS 1703 does not bear a dedication.
44. British Library Add. MS 34791, fol. 3; British Library Royal MS 18 C xiii, fols. 2–2v, and Harley MS 1703, fols. 85v–86v; British Library Royal MS 18 C xiii, fol. 2v. Some of these associations are also noted in Keena, "Edition," xx, lxv, lxxx; and A. S. G. Edwards, "Manuscripts of the Verse of Henry Howard, Earl of Surrey," *Huntington Library Quarterly* 67 (2004): 283–293, at 283.
45. Richard S. Sylvester, ed., *The Life and Death of Cardinal Wolsey by George Cavendish* (Oxford: Oxford University Press, 1959), 35, but also see ibid., 259–262, for a discussion of the Forrest-Cavendish connection. See also A. S. G. Edwards, ed., *Metrical Visions, by George Cavendish* (Columbia: University of South Carolina Press, 1980), 12, 90.
46. British Library Harley MS 1703, fols. 108–109, 100–100v. These are briefly discussed in Keena, "Edition," xxviii, xxxix–xl. For Tottel's

versions, see Amanda Holton and Tom MacFaul, eds., *Tottel's Miscellany: Songs and Sonnets of Henry Howard, Earl of Surrey, Sir Thomas Wyatt and Others* (London: Penguin, 2011), poems 168 and 182.

47. On the construction of "Protestant" and "Catholic" Chaucers in the sixteenth century, see, among numerous others, Helen Cooper, "Poetic Fame," in *Cultural Reformations: Medieval and Renaissance in Literary History*, ed. Brian Cummings and James Simpson (Oxford: Oxford University Press, 2010), 361–378; Linda Georgianna, "The Protestant Chaucer," in *Chaucer's Religious Tales*, ed. C. David Benson and Elizabeth Ann Robertson (Cambridge, UK: D. S. Brewer, 1990), 55–69; Alexandra Gillespie, *Print Culture and the Medieval Author: Chaucer, Lydgate, and Their Books, 1473–1557* (Oxford: Oxford University Press, 2006); Theresa M. Krier, ed., *Refiguring Chaucer in the Renaissance* (Gainesville: University of Florida Press, 1998); Mike Rodman Jones, "Chaucer the Puritan," in *Chaucer and Fame: Reputation and Reception*, ed. Isabel Davis and Catherine Nall (Cambridge: D. S. Brewer, 2015), 165–184; and Thomas A. Prendergast, *Chaucer's Dead Body: From Corpse to Corpus* (London: Routledge, 2004), 40–51.
48. *Seconde Grisilde*, fol. 44.
49. Jones, "Tragical History," 750 (emphasis added).
50. Helen Cooper, *The Canterbury Tales* (Oxford: Oxford University Press, 1996; first published 1989), 186; *Seconde Grisilde*, fol. 62; Geoffrey Chaucer, *The Clerk's Prologue*, in *The Riverside Chaucer*, ed. Larry D. Benson et al. (Oxford: Oxford University Press, 1988; first published 1987), l. 31.
51. Andrew Clark, ed., *The Life and Times of Anthony Wood, Antiquary of Oxford, 1632–1695 Described by Himself* (Oxford: Clarendon Press, 1892), 2:486; Edward Bernard, *Catalogi Librorum Manuscriptorum Angliae et Hiberniae in unum collecti* (Oxford, 1697), 368, no. 8563.101, 371, no. 8590.2. For brief details of Ralph Sheldon's life, see Jan Broadway, "Sheldon, Ralph (1623–1684)," *Oxford Dictionary of National Biography* online [accessed 9 Feb 2016] (Oxford: Oxford University Press, 2004).
52. See, e.g., Forrest, *History of Grisild*, xx.
53. Ibid., xxi.
54. *Seconde Grisilde*, fols. 71, 1.
55. Robert Tittler and Judith Richards, *The Reign of Mary I* (London: Routledge, 2013; first published 1983), 103–104.
56. Clark, *Life and Times*, 486; David Fairer, ed., *Thomas Warton's History of English Poetry* (London: Routledge/Thoemmes Press, 1998), 312; Forrest, *History of Grisild*, xv, 148; Lee, *History*, 404; Guiney, *Recusant Poets*, 142; Sylvester, *Life and Death*, 259; Keena, "Edition," xxiii; Mehok, "Edition," xxxix; Milsom, "William Mundy's 'Vox,'" 3; Holmes, "Forrest,

William"; Potter, "Tales of Patient Griselda," 11; Jones, "Tragical History," 750; Schutte, *Mary I*, 91; Cooper, "Poetic Fame," 374; Wort, "Cuckoo," 27.
57. Forrest, *History of Grisild*, 148.
58. Precisely the same distinction is manifest in British Library MS Royal 17 D iii, on fols. 4v ("Caput .6." and "Caput .8."), 5v ("Caput .16." and "Caput .18."), 6v ("Caput .26." and "Caput .28."), and so on.
59. Ibid., fols. 8, 3.
60. Bodleian Library MS Eng. poet. d. 9, fols. 157, 4.
61. Forrest, *History of Grisild*, 53.
62. Both closing brackets are Forrest's.
63. *Seconde Grisilde*, fols. 5, 24v–25.
64. Sylvester, *Life and Death*, 62, 220; J. S. Brewer, ed., *Letters and Papers, Foreign and Domestic, of the Reign of Henry VIII* (London: Longman & Co., 1872), 4(part 2):2020, no. 4649; Peter Gwyn, *The King's Cardinal: The Rise and Fall of Thomas Wolsey* (London: Pimlico, 2002; first published 1990), 507–508.
65. Gwyn, *King's Cardinal*, 507–508. Compare Gwyn's comments with the earlier statements in, e.g., J. D. Mackie, *The Earlier Tudors: 1485–1558* (Oxford: Clarendon Press, 1952), 324; and J. J. Scarisbrick, *Henry VIII* (New Haven, CT: Yale University Press, 1997; first published 1968), 162.
66. Sylvester, *Life and Death*, 62.
67. Brewer, *Letters and Papers*, 4(part 2):1519–1520, no. 3356; David Loades, *Mary Tudor: A Life* (Oxford: Basil Blackwell, 1989), 47–49.
68. *Seconde Grisilde*, fols. 71, 72v, 72, 74.
69. For details of these plots against Mary, see, among others, John Guy, *Tudor England* (Oxford: Oxford University Press, 1990; first published 1988), 231–232, 247, 226; D. M. Loades, *Two Tudor Conspiracies* (Cambridge, UK: Cambridge University Press, 1965); and Penry Williams, *The Later Tudors: England 1547–1603* (Oxford: Oxford University Press, 1998; first published 1995), 93–97, 107–108, 82–85. In a marginal note alongside this stanza, Forrest wrote "the Duke Duddelaye," so it is clear that in the first case it is to John Dudley that he refers by name, not Henry Dudley; *Seconde Grisilde*, fol. 74.
70. William B. Robison, "Peckham, Henry (b. in or before 1526, d. 1556)," *Oxford Dictionary of National Biography* online [accessed 13 Apr 2016] (Oxford: Oxford University Press, 2004).
71. *Seconde Grisilde*, fol. 74v.
72. Ibid., fol. 74v.
73. Ibid., fols. 77, 76v.
74. For details of Mary's pregnancies, I consulted Elizabeth Lane Furdell, *The Royal Doctors, 1485–1714: Medical Personnel at the Tudor and Stuart*

Courts (Rochester, NY: University of Rochester Press, 2001), 55–61. Also see Loades, *Mary Tudor*, 302, 305–306.
75. *Seconde Grisilde*, fol. 76v.
76. Potter, "Tales of Patient Griselda," 16.
77. In one place the appointee is apparently named William Fortescue, not Forrest, though this is not presently recorded under "Bledlow (CCEd Location ID: 7088)," in *The Clergy of the Church of England Database 1540–1835 [CCEd]*, http://www.theclergydatabase.org.uk [accessed 13 Apr 2016]. For comments, see Guiney, *Recusant Poets*, 140; Lee, *History*, 401; Forrest, *History of Grisild*, xiv–xv; and Milsom, "William Mundy's 'Vox,'" 5. About this double entry, Macray notes that he was unable to clear up the discrepancy because he did not have access to the episcopal registers for the diocese of Lincoln; see Forrest, *History of Grisild*, xiv–xv. The compilers of the *CCEd* did have access to these registers, and so presumably we are safe in giving the appointment to Forrest.
78. "Forrest, William (CCEd Record ID: 324343)," *CCEd* [accessed 13 Apr 2016].
79. Wort, "Cuckoo," 29–33.
80. John N. King, *English Reformation Literature: The Tudor Origins of the Protestant Tradition* (Princeton, NJ: Princeton University Press, 1982), 413.

WORKS CITED

Primary Sources

Forrest, William. *The Moste Famous Hystorye of Ioseph the Chaiste*. 1547. British Library Additional MS 34791.

———. *The Pleasaunt Poesye of Princelie Practise*. 1548. British Library Royal MS 17 D iii.

———. *Certaigne Psalmes of Dauyd*. 1551. British Library Royal MS 17 A xxi.

———. "A New Ballade of the Marigolde." 1553?; repr. in Thomas Park, ed. *The Harleian Miscellany*. Vol. 10. London: John White, 1813.

———. *The Seconde Grisilde*. 1558. Bodleian MS Wood Empt. 2.

———. *The moste famous Hystorye of Ioseph the chaiste*. 1569. Bodleian Library MS Eng. poet. d. 9.

———. *The moste famous Hystorye of Ioseph the chaiste*. Part One. 1571. University College MS 88.

———. *The moste famous Hystorye of Ioseph the chaiste*. Part Two. 1571. British Library Royal MS 18 C xiii.

———. British Library Harley MS 1703.

Secondary Sources

Bergsagel, John D. "The Date and Provenance of the Forrest-Heyther Collection of Tudor Masses." *Music & Letters* 44 (1963): 240-248.

Bernard, Edward. *Catalogi librorum manuscriptorum Angliae et Hiberniae in unum collecti*. Oxford, 1697.

Betteridge, Tom. *Literature and Politics in the English Reformation*. Manchester, UK: Manchester University Press, 2012; first published 2004.

———. "The Henrician Reformation and Mid-Tudor Culture." *Journal of Medieval and Early Modern Studies* 35 (2005): 91–109.

Birrell, T. A. *The Panizzi Lectures, 1986: English Monarchs and Their Books: From Henry VII to Charles II*. London: British Library, 1987.

Bliss, Lee. "The Renaissance Griselda: A Woman for All Seasons." *Viator* 23 (1992): 301–343.

Brewer, J. S., ed. *Letters and Papers, Foreign and Domestic, of the Reign of Henry VIII*. Vol. 4, part 2. London: Longman, 1872.

Broadway, Jan. "Sheldon, Ralph (1623–1684)." *Oxford Dictionary of National Biography* (online). Oxford: Oxford University Press, 2004.

Charles, R. H., ed. and trans. *The Testaments of the Twelve Patriarchs*. London: Adam and Charles Black, 1908.

Chaucer, Geoffrey. *The Riverside Chaucer*, ed. Larry D. Benson et al. Oxford: Oxford University Press, 1988; first published 1987.

Clark, Andrew, ed. *The Life and Times of Anthony Wood, Antiquary of Oxford, 1632–1695 Described by Himself*. Vol. 2. Oxford: Clarendon Press, 1892.

The Clergy of the Church of England Database 1540–1835 [CCEd]. http://www.theclergydatabase.org.uk.

Cooper, Helen. *The Canterbury Tales*. Oxford: Oxford University Press, 1996; first published 1989.

———. "Poetic Fame." In *Cultural Reformations: Medieval and Renaissance in Literary History*, ed. Brian Cummings and James Simpson, 361–378. Oxford: Oxford University Press, 2010.

Cummings, Brian. *The Literary Culture of the Reformation: Grammar and Grace*. Oxford: Oxford University Press, 2007; first published 2002.

Edwards, A. S. G., ed. *Metrical Visions, by George Cavendish*. Columbia: University of South Carolina Press, 1980.

———. "Manuscripts of the Verse of Henry Howard, Earl of Surrey." *Huntington Library Quarterly* 67 (2004): 283–293.

Fairer, David, ed. *Thomas Warton's History of English Poetry*. London: Routledge/Thoemmes Press, 1998.

Forrest, William. *The History of Grisild the Second: A Narrative, in

Verse, of the Divorce of Queen Katharine of Arragon, ed. W. D. Macray. London: Whittingham and Wilkins, 1875.

Foxe, John. *The Unabridged Acts and Monuments Online*. Sheffield, UK: HRI Online Publications, 2011. http//www.johnfoxe.org.

Furdell, Elizabeth Lane. *The Royal Doctors, 1485–1714: Medical Personnel at the Tudor and Stuart Courts*. Rochester, NY: University of Rochester Press, 2001.

Georgianna, Linda. "The Protestant Chaucer." In *Chaucer's Religious Tales*, ed. C. David Benson and Elizabeth Ann Robertson, 55–69. Cambridge, UK: D. S. Brewer, 1990.

Gillespie, Alexandra. *Print Culture and the Medieval Author: Chaucer, Lydgate, and Their Books, 1473–1557*. Oxford: Oxford University Press, 2006.

Guiney, Louise I. *Recusant Poets: With a Selection from Their Work. I: Saint Thomas More to Ben Jonson*. London: Sheed & Ward, 1938.

Guy, John, *Tudor England*. Oxford: Oxford University Press, 1990; first published 1988.

Gwyn, Peter. *The King's Cardinal: The Rise and Fall of Thomas Wolsey*. London: Pimlico, 2002; first published 1990.

Herrtage, S. J., ed. *England in the Reign of King Henry the Eighth*. London: Trübner for the Early English Text Society, 1878.

Holmes, Peter. "Forrest, William (fl. 1530–1576)." *Oxford Dictionary of National Biography* (online). Oxford: Oxford University Press, 2004.

Holstun, James. "The Spider, the Fly, and the Commonwealth: Merrie John Heywood and Agrarian Class Struggle." *English Literary History* 71 (2004): 53–88.

Holton, Amanda, and Tom MacFaul, eds. *Tottel's Miscellany: Songs and Sonnets of Henry Howard, Earl of Surrey, Sir Thomas Wyatt and Others*. London: Penguin, 2011.

Jones, Mike Rodman. "The Tragical History of the Reformation: Edwardian, Marian, Shakespearian." *Review of English Studies* 63 (2011): 743–763.

———. "Chaucer the Puritan." In *Chaucer and Fame: Reputation and Reception*, ed. Isabel Davis and Catherine Nall, 165–184. Cambridge, UK: D. S. Brewer, 2015.

Keena, Joseph Patrick. "An Edition of the Marian Poems of the Recusant Writer, William Forrest, from MS. Harleian 1703." Unpublished PhD thesis, University of Notre Dame, 1960.

King, John N. *English Reformation Literature: The Tudor Origins of the Protestant Tradition*. Princeton, NJ: Princeton University Press, 1982.

Krier, Theresa M., ed. *Refiguring Chaucer in the Renaissance*. Gainesville: University of Florida Press, 1998.

Lee, Frederick G. *The History, Description, and Antiquities of the Prebendal Church of the Blessed Virgin Mary of Thame.* London: Mitchell and Hughes, 1883.

Loades, D. M. *Two Tudor Conspiracies.* Cambridge, UK: Cambridge University Press, 1965.

———. *Mary Tudor: A Life.* Oxford: Basil Blackwell, 1989.

Lucas, Scott C. *A Mirror for Magistrates and the Politics of the English Reformation.* Amherst: University of Massachusetts Press, 2009.

Ludorff, Franz. "William Forest's *Theophiluslegende*." Anglia 7 (1884): 60–115.

MacCracken, Henry Noble. "New Stanzas by Dunbar." *Modern Language Notes* 24 (1909): 110–111.

MacDonald, A. A. "Anglo-Scottish Literary Relations: Problems and Possibilities." *Studies in Scottish Literature* 26 (1991): 172–184.

Mackie, J. D. *The Earlier Tudors: 1485–1558.* Oxford: Clarendon Press, 1952.

Manzalaoui, M. A., ed. *Secretum Secretorum: Nine English Versions.* Vol 1. Oxford: Oxford University Press, 1977.

Mehok, Edward Eugene. "An Edition of William Forrest's History of Joseph." Unpublished PhD thesis, Case Western Reserve University, 1971.

Milsom, John, intr., *Oxford, Bodleian Library, MSS. Mus. Sch. E. 376–81.* Renaissance Music in Facsimile 15. New York: Garland, 1986.

———. "William Mundy's 'Vox Patris Caelestis' and the Accession of Mary Tudor." *Music & Letters* 91 (2010): 1–38.

Pincombe, Mike, and Cathy Shrank, eds. *The Oxford Handbook of Tudor Literature, 1485–1603.* Oxford: Oxford University Press, 2009.

———. "Prologue: The Travails of Tudor Literature." In *The Oxford Handbook of Tudor Literature, 1485–1603*, ed. Mike Pincombe and Cathy Shrank, 1–17. Oxford: Oxford University Press, 2009.

Potter, Ursula. "Tales of Patient Griselda and Henry VIII." *Early Theatre* 5 (2002): 11–28.

Prendergast, Thomas A. *Chaucer's Dead Body: From Corpse to Corpus.* London: Routledge, 2004.

Quitslund, Beth. *The Reformation in Rhyme: Sternhold, Hopkins and the English Metrical Psalter, 1547–1603.* Aldershot, UK: Ashgate, 2008.

Robison, William B. "Peckham, Henry (b. in or before 1526, d. 1556)." *Oxford Dictionary of National Biography* (online). Oxford: Oxford University Press, 2004.

Scarisbrick, J. J. *Henry VIII.* New Haven, CT: Yale University Press, 1997; first published 1968.

Schutte, Valerie. *Mary I and the Art of Book Dedications: Royal Women, Power, and Persuasion.* New York: Palgrave Macmillan, 2015.

Simpson, James. *Reform and Cultural Revolution*. Oxford: Oxford University Press, 2004; first published 2002.

Stevens, Martin. "The Royal Stanza in Early English Literature." *PMLA* 94 (1979): 62–76.

Sylvester, Richard S., ed. *The Life and Death of Cardinal Wolsey by George Cavendish*. Oxford: Oxford University Press, 1959.

Tittler, Robert, and Judith Richards. *The Reign of Mary I*. London: Routledge, 2013; first published 1983.

Walker, Greg. *Writing under Tyranny: English Literature and the Henrician Reformation*. Oxford: Oxford University Press, 2005.

Warner, J. Christopher. *Henry VIII's Divorce: Literature and the Politics of the Printing Press*. Woodbridge, UK: Boydell Press, 1998.

Williams, Penry. *The Later Tudors: England 1547–1603*. Oxford: Oxford University Press, 1998; first published 1995.

Wort, Oliver. "A Cuckoo in the Nest? William Forrest, the Duke of Somerset, and the *Certaigne Psalmes of Dauyd*." *Reformation* 21 (2016): 25–46.

"Classicising Friars," Miscellaneous Transmission, and MS Royal 7 C.i

RALPH HANNA

In 1960, the great scholar of exegesis Beryl Smalley introduced a sequence of fourteenth-century English friars, mainly Oxonians, who exhibited what she took to be rather peculiar tastes. Smalley was intrigued by these figures' involvement in an occupation that she understood very well, biblical explication. But she was struck by the unusual source from which they had derived the materials they used for the task, classical and pagan history and mythography. Although she seems never to have investigated the field in any detail, Smalley argued persistently that such works had been generated to aid in the production of *sermones moderni*, with their interest in argumentative amplification and exfoliation of a text. In this pursuit, Smalley thought, productions of, in particular, Nicholas Trevet OP, John Ridewall OFM, and Robert Holcot OP addressed a different and distinctive way of going about the exegete's task.[1]

I am interested in testing Smalley's thesis and here offer, as preliminary to a more extensive study, a manuscript analysis to underpin an extensive critical study of her friars. Here, although it is a very complicated book (and testimony to the fact that *qua* books, Latinate models are often considerably more interesting and challenging than their vernacular derivatives), I consider evidence provided by British Library, MS Royal 7 C.i. I hope my analysis not only sheds light on Smalley's theory (and indicates how manuscript study might interface with some more general literary-historical concerns), but also offers an argumentative exemplification about reading complicated miscellaneous books.

The Royal MS has a fourteenth-century ex libris; it belonged to one "Dompn[us] William de Kettering," who identifies himself as a Benedictine monk of Ramsey, Huntingdonshire. I imagine that this relatively large volume could well have been Kettering's single book. It probably (given a reasonable consistency of page format shared by diverse hands) represents, not just found or collected materials, but was constructed from scratch to Kettering's specifications. The whole formed an expansible one-volume library (as added texts at the end indicate). A further testimony to the volume as a personal initiative comes from the rather shabby materials used, in some instances involving parchment that professionals would have rejected for formal purposes.

Kettering's volume presents twenty-seven texts, all in Latin. These were copied by four different individuals, one of whom (my Scribe II) I imagine to be Kettering himself. The production clearly went on piecemeal; its products are disposed in thirteen separate fascicles or booklets. These may have retained some integrity, if apparently a shifting one, at various points between copying and the manuscript we now have. Although in a modern binding, the whole survives in its fixed later-fourteenth-century form; this is indicated by a flyleaf table of contents and an accompanying foliation.

I reserve demonstration of most of these basic points to the appendix. This offers a formal description of the volume. I maintain that such an examination, whether formally presented or not, remains a primary and fundamental approach to any book. Particularly in the complicated production process that underlies the received Royal 7 C.i, much of my subsequent argument depends upon the observation and analysis of the detail reported in my description.[2]

I do, however, pause for a moment over one portion of this material, my division of the volume into booklets or fascicles. This prominently underwrites the main argument I wish here to pursue, the disposition of the volume's texts. Although recognition procedures for identifying fascicular production have long been available,[3] the variety of forms here exemplified is various and instructive. These features include most prominently:

- self-contained texts, filling more or less exactly a sequence of quires: these are ubiquitous in marking off the thirteen units among which I divide the volume.
- differing signature systems: in the Royal MS, these have largely been overridden by the imposition of late signatures in crayon, probably in the hand of the owner/potential part-producer. But surviving earlier systems certainly offer secondary evidence for the original separateness from the remainder of much of my Booklets 5 to 8, and all of Booklets 11 to 12.

- blank leaves and columns at ends of units: examples occur in Booklets 2, 4 to 10, and 12 to 13.
- filler texts, overt and otherwise, again added at the ends of units: examples occur in Booklet 8 and probably Booklet 11.
- short or long terminal quires (the Royal MS was persistently produced in twelve-leaf units): short quires conclude Booklets 1, 4, 7, 9, and 10; a long quire concludes Booklet 3 (and Booklet 13 was deliberately created as an "oversized" quire to handle possible extensions).

On the basis of these criteria, the piecemeal construction of the book is unproblematic. Every one of its units is marked as separable by some physical feature, although the full extent of this separateness only emerges from using the various criteria in combination.

In many circumstances, one might invoke a further feature marking production in booklets: changes of scribal hand (often accompanied by changes of page format). In the Royal MS, only a minority of the separate units shows the same scribal hand as appears in adjacent ones. This feature is limited to the junctures between Booklets 1 to 2, 8 to 9, and 10 to 13. However, in the Royal MS, this situation provides an insufficient demonstration of divided production. All four of the scribes here appear in multiple portions of the book. Not just those units now apparently joined by copying in the same hand could well have been produced as originally consecutive units. Rather, the form of Royal 7 C.i we receive has been ordered after completion of nearly all the copying.

This is abundantly clear, both on the basis of consecutive foliation through a large part of the book[4] and from the imposition of a set of more or less consecutive signatures in crayon across a range of quires (irrespective of whether they had been signed earlier). Copying stints that might have been undertaken consecutively have been separately disposed, and the book's order of contents, stable since the late fourteenth century, reflects decisions made to facilitate an original binding. Thus the book throws up a disparity between junctures potentially "accidental" in terms of its production but certainly "motivated" in terms of its projected use. The crayon hand plainly had some notion of the most efficacious joining of parts, the ordering that would be most useful for the book's continued consultation.

This broaches an issue that has bedevilled discussions of miscellaneous books ever since they became central objects of discussion perhaps thirty years ago. To what extent are these motivated and coherent productions? Or are they simply random products, inclusive of anything that might turn up, irrespective of relevance or similarity to other texts communicated?[5] I use the Royal MS – a congeries of twenty-seven separate items (what might be potentially more diverse?) – to examine this question in a bit more detail.

My suggestion is simply that, just as the volume itself reflects a sequence of scribal centers of production activity, one initially consider the volume's contents as a sequence of "nodes" or "cores," perhaps variously displayed. In the case of Royal 7 C.i, at least initially, I identify these generically; the cores can be further specified transmissionally, that is, through the associations created through the coherence of textual groupings across a range of manuscripts. I offer exemplification of this second point when I address my third node, the one I find of primary interest.

Considered in gross, the Royal MS would seem to combine three nodes of interest. First, there is a very healthy amount of what customarily goes under the heading of "patristics," although here written mainly by twelfth-century and later writers, rather than actual Fathers of the Church. Second, the manuscript includes an enormous amount of what one should consider *praedicabilia*, materials certainly constructed to aid preachers in their work. These include both rhetorical guides to the discipline and exemplary collections/collections of useful *exempla*, designed to facilitate the elaboration that "modern" or "university sermons" demanded. Finally, there is an unusually large swath of materials that one might – and that I do, on the basis of other manuscript contexts – associate with Beryl Smalley's Oxonian classicizing friars. I first examine each of these areas in turn.

The patristics/theology illustrates a point I make elsewhere, that within Latinate culture there is a considerably stronger sense of the "canonical" or the classic than in English or other vernaculars. Royal 7 C.i exhibits this point clearly through a sequence of unusually widely disseminated texts that are the general stock of late-medieval theological miscellanies all over Europe, customarily on some mix-and-match basis. As appears from my detailed argument about my "node 3" below, canonical lists are always suggestive, rather than proscriptive, but selections from the same materials persistently recur, in various combinations.

About one-third of Royal 7 C.i is devoted to such materials. As the book is now bound, these appear in two dispersed patches. A substantial group – indeed what appears to be the primary interest of these portions – is included in Booklets 4 to 6: Bernard (actual and suppositious) and Bonaventura in Booklet 4, the "Bonaventuran" *Stimulus amoris* in Booklet 5, and a widely disseminated (it even appears in English translation) text by Isidore of Seville in Booklet 6. Equally, the late additions to the organized original Royal MS (Booklets 11 to 13) are given over, here almost totally, to such items: Defensor, Peter of Blois, more Bernard, and another widely disseminated item, pseudo-Basil's *Monita*.

Materials certainly designed to aid preachers also form a prominent node in the book. Indeed, were one to prioritize prominence of placement as a criterion of importance, these are the most outstanding feature of the volume. As bound, these texts are concentrated at the head – most particularly the first two texts, extensive, widely disseminated, and produced as the independent units Booklets 1 and 2 by a single scribe unique to this portion. But in addition to a few examples of actual sermons, texts 13 (in Booklet 6), and 18 to 19 (filler at the end of Booklet 8), relevant items include the *exempla* and fables of Booklet 3, probably the Senecan materials of Booklet 4,[6] and all the materials of Booklets 6 to 7. Here one might draw particular attention to Robert of Basevorn's *Ars*; although not widely distributed, since its presentation by T.-M. Charland, the text has always been seen as a classic (and one might say, overly elaborate) account, the toolbox that exhibits the techniques and methods of sermon construction in a sophisticated way.[7]

This is a rich vein of commonplace, widely disseminated materials designed only to produce yet further examples of the commonplace. The number of them largely testifies, I would think, to a desire for increased flexibility of use. While many such texts overlap in content, each has its own organizational schema, facilitating a single variety of reference use (in turn, the major impulse dragging people into turning out new examples of the genre) and sense of appropriate source.[8] Thus Malachi of Ireland (text 3) is designed for a consultation predicated upon the Seven Deadly Sins and their conventional "remedial virtues"; John of Wales (text 12) for that predicated upon the classical cardinal virtues. Holcot and Odo (texts 4 to 5) provide diverting moralized tales potentially useful across a range of contexts (Odo's selected on a subject basis, beast fables). Although I have treated Defensor's *Scintillae* (text 22) as a "patristic" text (which it is), it would be equally useful in this preaching context. Defensor produced a very ancient example of a *florilegium*, arranged by topic (and within each topic, by author) – not just vices and virtues but "oratio," "confessio," and so on – and including a wealth of biblical and patristic citations.[9] I return below to similar, yet more striking examples of the polysemy or adaptability of my various nodes.

As a third node of the collection, the Royal MS includes a range of texts that I identify with the core in *miscellaneous manuscripts* largely given over to writings of Smalley's "classicising friars."[10] From a select series of manuscripts particularly rich in these materials, I identify as central portions of this component:

> Alberic of London ("The Third Vatican Mythographer"), *Scintillarium poetarum*, in **QWTB**;
> John Ridewall, *Fulgentius metaphoralis*, in **QWTB** [= **Royal text 20, Booklet 9**];
> John of Wales/Waleys, *Breviloquium de virtutibus*,

in **QWT [= Royal text 12, Booklet 6]**;
Pierre Bersuire, *Ovidius moralizatus* [+ other, less widely disseminated Ovid commentaries],
in **QTB**;
Walter Map, *Dissuasio Valerii* [+ a commentary, usually Ridewall's, sometimes Trevet's],
in **QWT**;[11]
Malachi of Ireland, *De septem venenis*, in **QT [= Royal text 3, Booklet 2]**;
Seneca the Elder, *Declamationes/Controversiae*, in **QW [= Royal text 9, Booklet 4]**.[12]

One need not necessarily be surprised in finding University-sponsored texts such as these in dispersed Benedictine houses.[13] And of course, although there is no surviving evidence of William Kettering's connection with either University, there is ample evidence for connections between Ramsey and Oxford. One tendentious example is well-known, the possible association of *Piers Plowman Z* and MS Bodley 851 with John of Wells, monk of Ramsey. Considerably more interesting is a recently published thirteenth-century trilingual glossary; since one of the languages involved is Hebrew, current scholarship would associate the production with Oxford students seeking linguistic tools to render accessible the *hebraica veritas* underlying the text of the Vulgate.[14]

At least initially, I am interested in the disposition of this material throughout Kettering's book. A substantial portion of it appears in contextually immediate juxtapositions that would utterly vindicate Smalley's view that texts of this sort are all recuperable as *praedicabilia*. For example, Malachi's *De septem venenis* occurs as an appendage to Peter of Limoges's *Oculus* in Booklet 2. Similarly, John of Wales's *Breviloquium* nestles among a clump of preaching texts following Isidore's *Synonyma* in Booklet 6. Such placements would confirm authorial statements of intent, for example Malachi's conclusion: "Therefore the things I have said about these matters, according to the weakness of my wit, should be enough. They will suffice for the instruction of simple men [*simplicium*] who are appointed to teach the people. For which may Christ grant me...," where the "*simplices*" are presumably poor Franciscan preachers like himself.[15] But, in contrast, Seneca's *Controversiae* appears tacked onto a series of straight "theological" texts in Booklet 4.

Yet I find more interesting the material in the Royal MS that might qualify such a reading of these texts as *praedicabilia*. This is most prominent in the block of texts that comprises Booklets 8 to 10 and that demonstrates a persistent "literary" or classical interest: Vegetius (text 17, Booklet 8);

Ridewall's mythography, central to my Oxonian sample (text 20, Booklet 9); and finally, Alan of Lille's *De planctu Naturae* (text 21, Booklet 10).

Vegetius is, barring the elder Seneca, the one unadulterated classical text in the Royal MS, but one with a considerable medieval use community, quite extraneous to interest in the work as a military handbook. On the one hand, Vegetius's interest in battle, for a medieval reader, is instantly recuperable as moralization of the analogous spiritual battle in which every Christian is to engage in this world. Yet, equally, the text looks directly at those behaviors that supported the greatest and most noble kingdom any medieval reader would know, Rome. *De re militari*, whatever its value for battlefield strategy, offers an unimpeachable exemplification of and a practical manual to the principles that shaped Roman discipline and statecraft. For medieval readers, these represent materials that might well shape the governance of a community, the counsel offered to kings, and (with the inevitable microcosmic extension) the behavior of the individual.[16]

Ridewall's *Fulgentius* provides unalloyed classical mythography. It is centered on a series of "*ymagines*," usually verbal "thought diagrams" but occasionally illustrated, each of which presents attributes of the classical deities. While, as in the sixth-century source that Ridewall "modernizes," these are moralized, the book is nonetheless valuable as a collection of lore on paganism.

Alan's *prosimetrum* is, of course, very well known. Its pictorialism (zoology displayed on Natura's garments) was widely admired, and it contains an extraordinary discussion of mythography and its usefulness (p4/8.115-54). But, particularly, especially in its closing movement, it shares with other works of the 1160s and 1170s, including John of Salisbury and Map's *De nugis curialium*, an interest in disciplining courtly life (perhaps particularly the courts of prelates). Alan's *De planctu Naturae* is slightly peripheral to central Oxford concerns, but is a commonplace companion to a very popular text now generally believed to have been composed by one of Smalley's friars, *Philobiblion*. Although overtly the work of "Richard Aungerville de Bury, bishop of Durham," *Philobiblion*, which at many points considers clerical life as devoted to universal (and not just Christian) study, is now usually ascribed to a member of Bury's household, Robert Holcot, OP.[17]

Thus, these works all belong, more or less securely, within the penumbra of Smalley's Oxford friars. Whether, however, they exemplify Smalley's further contention that such materials simply represent *praedicabilia* is another matter. One can instantiate the difficulties of recuperating this material as simply of preacherly use with a single example. I offer a brief discussion from John Waldeby (died ca. 1372), Augustinian friar of York's *Viridarium*, part 8. Although Waldeby was a friar – and thus a likely recipient of Smalley's Oxonian "classicising tendencies" – and a renowned preacher, this citation comes from a commented abbreviated psalter (it treats all verses that include the root miseri-). It is thus analogous to Robert Holcot's behavior in his Wisdom commentary:

> Seventh, God's mercy is the particular refuge of all those who are oppressed. There follows in the text, *My mercy and my refuge, my support and my deliverer* (Ps. 143:2). "Mercy" in pardoning sins, "refuge" in bearing up hardships. "My support" when I come to you; "my deliverer" when I call to you. Vegetius, in *On military affairs*, says that a general ought never to constrain his enemies that they not have any refuge, lest their despair about escaping give them greater strength for fighting, because despair makes men strong. Hence we read in 2 Reg 2:19ff. that Asael followed Abner closely and did not give him a place of refuge.... Thus in a moral sense, God does not abandon his enemies, that is sinners, without some kind of refuge; therefore his mercy is their refuge.[18]

I merely offer two comments on Waldeby's analysis. First of all, the biblical example is actually intrusive and logically inconsequent within the ongoing argument. In the biblical account, which Waldeby summarizes (my ellipses), Abner despairs and as a result, although defeated, can kill Asael. But Waldeby avoids stating what would seem the logical moralization of this account, that a desperate sinner kills the divine presence within himself and thus resists God. In doing so, his conclusion ("Sic moraliter...") actually segues back to the discussion *before* the introduction of any biblical materials, in fact to the dictum of the classical author, which does follow more or less smoothly – an example of a feature already noted, that of battle spiritualized – in this argument about Psalm 143:2.

Moreover, the grammar of the discussion makes it clear that Vegetius's pronouncement is primary, and the biblical material only secondary confirmation for it. "Vnde" presupposes that Abner acts in accord with, confirms the power of teaching drawn from another source, in this case the classical precept. At a certain level, this is just showing off, offering a recondite reference. But in the argument as offered, Waldeby's reference to Vegetius retains a power, as "valuable lore," if you will, quite independent of explicating the intrusive biblical text (although it addresses Psalm 143:2 directly). At the least, while it testifies to the power of learnedness, it also demonstrates the interesting and noteworthy things learnedness can turn up.

Thus, while this material in the Royal MS, perhaps especially Ridewall's Fulgentian *ymagines*, might have facilitated preaching, as Smalley argues, its use in such a context requires detailed analysis. Moreover, particularly in the case of Ridewall's text (just as with Alberic's *Scintillae*, equally prominent in an Oxonian context), there is ample evidence that sermon use virtually never occurred.[19] The absence of pulpit use raises the prospect that classical and literary materials might appear in the Royal MS for some other purpose, perhaps just "free" or informational reading. This would imply that Kettering accorded some value to the classics (and beyond them to "poetry") for itself rather than as moralizable tidbit or sermon exemplification. Thus one might see, even in fourteenth-century monastic circumstances, texts potentially subjected to some residual double use.

Moreover, one could see such "free reading" by extension as qualifying the generic distinctions I have used heretofore. One could, in fact, imagine recuperating texts like John of Wales's *Breviloquium* or Malachi's *De septem venenis* for double use. Each might well serve as both *praedicabilia* and as something simply informational, more or less interesting in its own right. Rather than being subjected to professionally motivated search procedures, the texts could offer good reading material that would open topics like the virtue of classical heroes or the wonders of the natural world (the latter not an interest inconsistent with reading Alan's *De planctu*).

In such a context, one could offer a second, competing reading of the relevant texts. Malachi constructed his tract as a way, consonant with the cursed serpent of Eden, of displaying sin as a snakebite (and the "remedies" as received medicinal cures). In his development of the topic, his first recourse was to the chapter of Isidore's *Etymologiae* where the encyclopedist explains the names of serpents.[20] But he filled out Isidore's brief accounts with more extensive "scientific" information; in addition to the expected extensive patristic citations, *De septem venenis* communicates quite a large amount of Aristotle and Pliny's natural history. The book can thus function as a compact, cheap, and more readily usable version of an earlier Franciscan preachers' tool, Bartholomaeus Anglicus's *De proprietatibus rerum*.[21] The text might then interface with the scientific interests underlying the Aristotelian zoology later in the Royal MS, although those materials here appear in a moralized form, like Malachi's suitable for sermons (item 16).

One could mount similar arguments about John of Wales's *Breviloquium*. The brief work is given over largely to lengthy sequences of examples and devoid of both biblical references and connective tissue, including instructions on its use. At one unusually explicit moment, at the end of the prologue, John points out that the work provides novelty:

> Exemplary and persuasive tales about these virtues follow below. These are useful for rulers and offer instruction to those enthroned, insofar as they appear among the deeds of powerful people or of wise men and worldly

philosophers. For plenty of holy examples appear in both
saints' lives and in the historical portions of Scripture.[22]

John here identifies a by-now-familiar user group for the work, the same worldly rulers who might be addressed by John of Salisbury, Vegetius, and Alan. But John equally suggests that this audience might profit just as well from exemplary classical models, including noninspired pagan philosophers, as from saints' lives. And the general absence of direction for users implies that rulers might benefit from reading of worldly models, and finding instruction in noble behavior of the ancients, not necessarily in concording their behavior with biblical injunction. Analogous to Malachi's Aristotelian materials, the *Breviloquium* might function as a cheap and compact entry to less accessible materials, here Valerius Maximus or derivatives of Diogenes Laertius.[23]

Such potential readings of ambiguous textual relations in the Royal manuscript may allow one to return to broader cultural issues. I think Smalley's account of her Oxonian friars and their texts is limited or limiting because of her sense that they are to be folded into a monolithic category, "exegesis." The Oxonian authors thus become only alien, when conceptualized within the subject matter of Smalley's other distinguished studies. They fit uneasily with the view enunciated by the great theoretician of exegesis, Augustine, that the classical heritage is "Egyptian gold" to be plundered.

But there is ample evidence of very long standing that reading against the grain to resuscitate the ancient world and its wisdom was very much a medieval preoccupation. For example, Augustine composed the most extensive and effective demolition of classical culture in *De civitate Dei*. In a moment more flexible than the argumentation of her book, Smalley mentions in passing that Trevet and Ridewall commented upon the Augustinian text, not because it demolished the classics, but because it communicated historical detail about the ancient world. For such figures, Augustine had inadvertently provided a handbook to classical culture, and his work stood as simply a convenient mound of informative historical material.[24]

As a much more humble analogue, one might consider the foundation of every literate's exposure to poetry, the grammar-school text *Ecloga Theoduli*. The ostensible focus of this Carolingian poem is its demonstration of the superiority of Christian biblical history to classical myth. But the book's use-value – and a perhaps unfortunately distracting interest for its poet – was in offering eight- to ten-year-olds an entrée into the commonplace mythological referents persistently displayed in the poetic culture ostensibly being debunked (and a culture that would form the subject of their subsequent study).[25]

Thus one might consider views put forward by perhaps the only modern scholar to examine Smalley's Oxonians carefully – and most especially Ridewall and his *Fulgentius*:

> The controversy over this claim [Ernst R. Curtius's of a growing "poetic theology" in the later Middle Ages] involves a number of very different problems – the problem of the classification of the arts, the problem of the nature of language and of the status of Scripture, the problem of valid tests for fact and fiction, the problem of the ethical status of the classical literary inheritance – as well as the problem of the status of the artist.

The late Judson Allen here is considering that these questions define a "Renaissance poetic sensibility," not a medieval one. The sentence following my citation runs, "The poet as creator, as prophet, as divinely inspired – these notions are touchstones of Renaissance criticism."[26] But the use evidence of the early fourteenth-century Oxonian corpus, one example of which I have examined here, would suggest that the questions Allen bruits – as well as the perhaps subpoetic issues of delight in classical history and literature – might well have been live ones for fourteenth- and fifteenth-century English medieval authors and readers.

Keble College, Oxford

APPENDIX

In the following description of Royal 7 C.i, I have routinely identified texts through short-title references to several standard bibliographical tools:

Bloomfield = Morton W. Bloomfield et al., *Incipits of Latin Works on the Virtues and Vices, 1100-1500 A.D....* (Cambridge, MA: Medieval Academy of America, 1979).
CCSL = Corpus Christianorum, series latina.
CPL = Eligius Dekkers and Emil Gaar, *Clavis patrum Latinorum...*, 3rd edn (Turnhout: Brepols, 1995).
IPMEP = R. E. Lewis et al., *Index of Printed Middle English Prose* (New York: Garland, 1985).
PL = *Patrologia Latina*
Sharpe, as below, n.7, who regularly either summarizes and refers to published manuscript-lists or constructs his own.

British Library, MS Royal 7 C.i

s. xiv med. or xiv$^{3/4}$. Parchment (after the first two booklets, of indifferent quality, both in finish and origin – a good many leaves defective at the foot, taken from the edges of the skin, and four booklet-ending quires [numbers 14, 21, 30, 32] written on waste and possibly re-used materials). Fols. ii + 444 (see further the discussion of the foliation below). Overall 310 mm x 205 mm (writing area usually 230-40 mm x 140-45 mm). About 50 lines to the page, with some variation (49-55 lines), in double columns. Written in a sequence of anglicanas and fere texturas (the most distinctive scribe I, in a fere textura of a mien no later than the 1370s, with occasional approach strokes on s-). A tentative breakdown of the stints:

scribe I copied Booklets 1-2, fols. 1-90

scribe II copied Booklets 3, 5, 10-13, and added filler texts on blank leaves at end of Booklet 8 (texts 18-19, fols. 309^v-10), fols. 91-128, 157-92, 338-end. One might suppose him to be the book's owner, William of Kettering.

scribe III copied Booklets 4 and 7, fols. 129-56, 241-82

scribe IV copied Booklets 6, 8-9, fols. 193-240, 283-337

As is customary with British Library manuscripts, the current foliation includes the original flyleaves (since they bear writing), and, at least at the start, is two ahead of an original foliation. Because it is more accurate than the Library's and corresponds to a contents table on fol. 1^v, I have followed the original medieval foliation, so far as it goes (to fol. 355). It is then succeeded by a brief second foliation (1-32, restricted to part of Booklet 11); from this point to the end (no further medieval foliation being forthcoming), I follow the Library foliation. In quire 28 (fols. 311-23, in Booklet 9), the medieval foliation was originally supplied in crayon, by a hand that has signed nearly all the quires, and then gone over in ink by the foliator of the whole, who appears likely to be the same person.

As Warner and Gilson note, the contents table to the volume (where these materials are added in a second hand) and the lapse of the contemporary foliation (at the end of Booklet 10) indicate that Booklets 11-13 were late/last additions to the book, after it had already achieved some "organized"form. This portion has a consistent and distinctive page-format, with writing area 240 mm x 145 mm, in 53 lines to the page.

Booklet 1 = fols. 1-30

[1] Fols. 1-30^v: Peter of Limoges, *De oculo morali*; for a fine recent translation, with discussion of the transmission and allusion to the large number of manuscripts, see Richard Newhauser, *The Moral Treatise on the Eye*, Medieval Sources in Translation (Toronto: Pontifical Institute, 2012).

Collation 1-2^{12} 3^6. Most quires are ordered by a hand offering leaf-signatures in crayon, irrespective of any earlier such ordering, usually in a mixture of arabic and roman leaf numbers, occasionally by letters (usually "a"-"f"). I note below only deviations from this procedure, but all quire- (rather than leaf-)ordering signs. Here quires 2-3 have (fol. 13) "2 quat< >" and (fol. 25) "3," respectively. However, the first of these units also has "f" plus numeral on all leaves in the first half. Throughout, regular catchwords, except at booklet boundaries.

The consistent signatures "f" on what is now (properly) identified as quire 2 may imply that it was originally the 6th or 7th quire (the latter, if a signature "+" preceded "a," as occurs reasonably frequently). The easiest reading of this situation is that originally Booklet 2 preceded Booklet 1 (or may have done so in Scribe 1's copying) (the "+-, a" alternative). However, "f" again appears in quire 24, and there is only an arbitrary, bifolium-ordering sign, not a quire signature.

Booklet 2 = fols. 31-90

[2] Fols. 31-76: William of Lavicea OFM, *Dieta salutis* (Bloomfield 2301), followed by a table, fols. 76rb-81vb. Bloomfield's partial list of copies, about 100 in all, includes 20-25 in British libraries.

[3] Fols. 82-90^v: **Malachi of Ireland OFM, *De septem venenis*,** only ed. Paris, 1518; for discussion of the MSS (about 45 of the 120 or so – the list is incomplete – in British collections) and ascription, see Richard Sharpe, *Titulus: Identifying Medieval Latin Texts...* (Turnhout: Brepols, 2003), 218-45. The text ends near the top of fol. 90va, and the final column is blank.

Collation 4-8^{12}. Crayon quire signatures (fol. 31)"4," (fol. 43) "q v^a (?)," (fol. 55) "6," (fol. 67) "7 q^a," (fol. 79) "8."

Booklet 3 = fols. 91-128

[4] Fols. 91-119^v: **Robert Holcot OP, *Convertimini*;** see Sharpe 554-55.
[5] Fols. 119^v-128^v: Odo of Cheriton, *Fabulae*; see Sharpe 404.

Collation 9-10^{12} 11^{14}. Crayon quire signatures (fol. 91) "9 q^a," (fol. 103) "10 q^a," (fol. 115) "11 q^a."

Booklet 4 = fols. 129-56

[6] Fols. 131-37: ps.-Bernard of Clairvaux, *Meditationes* (Bloomfield 3126), ed. *PL* 184: 485-508; Bloomfield cites numerous copies, and my half-hour search found 110 in British libraries alone.

[7] Fols. 137^v-141: Bernard of Clairvaux, *De diligendo Deo*, *S. Bernardi Opera*, ed. J. Leclercq *et al.*, 8 vols. (Rome: Editiones Cistercienses, 1957-77), 3:109-54; the editors offer a list of about 60 *twelfth-century* copies, ten of them in British collections.

[8] Fols. 141-145^v: Bonaventura, *De triplici via/Incendium amoris, Doctoris*

seraphici S. Bonaventurae...opera omnia, ed. Collegium S. Bonaventurae, 10 vols. (Quaracchi: Collegium, 1882-1902), 8:1-18; an extensive list of MSS at 8:x-xxv includes 300 copies, but only sketchily surveys British collections (18 copies noted). The edition, of course, predates M. R. James and the systematic description of British collections; my cursory search turns up another dozen (including this MS).

[9] Fols. 145^v-156: **Seneca the Elder**, *Controversiae/Declamationes*, preceded by a contents table, fol. 145^{vab} (cf. n.6 above). Ends fol. 156rb, with blank verso.

Collation 12-13^{12} 14^4. Crayon quire signatures (fol. 129) "15," (fol. 141) "16." In addition to these signatures, the crayon leaf-signatures identify the quires by arbitrary signs, "o," "+" (quire 14 unsigned).

A variety of fits and starts are evident in ordering this part of the MS. The crayon quire-numbering does not correspond to the imposed foliation: "11" at the end of Booklet 3; "12-14" in Booklet 5, "15-16" here. This probably indicates that Scribe II copied Booklets 3 and 5 to appear consecutively, a decision initially accepted by the crayon hand but rejected at the point of binding and foliation, so that the order of Booklets 4 and 5 was reversed.

Booklet 5 = fols. 157-92

[10] Fols. 157-91: James of Milan (ps.-Bonaventura), *Stimulus amoris*, 2nd edn, ed. Collegium S. Bonaventurae (Quaracchi: Collegium, 1949); for the MSS, see Falk Eisermann, *"Stimulus Amoris": Inhalt, lateinische Überlieferung, deutsche Übersetzungen, Rezeption* (Tübingen: Niemeyer, 2001), 64-209 (about 500 copies, 50-55 in British collections – and note IPMEP 46, attributed to Walter Hilton, in sixteen copies). Ends four lines down 191rb, the verso and fol. 192^{rv} blank but ruled.

Collation 15-17^{12}. Crayon quire signatures: (fol. 157) "12," (fol. 169) "13," (fol. 181) "14."

Unique to this portion of the MS, and running across the contributions of three different scribes, are signatures on leaves in the first half of quires in something resembling the text ink, in all cases the sequence roman "j"-"vj." These appear in quires 17 (the last of Booklet 5), 18 (the head of Booklet 6), 23-25 (all but the first quire of Booklet 7), and 27 (the second/last of Booklet 8). This signing would imply that this portion of the book was considered originally a distinct block (and the initial appearance of such signing implies joining Booklets 5 and 6 as consecutive). See further the discussion of Booklets 8 and 9 below.

Booklet 6 = fols. 193-240

[11] Fols. 193-205: Isidore of Seville, *Synonyma* (*CPL* 1203), ed. PL 83:826-68. There is no published list of manuscripts; a cursory ten-minute

search found fourteen copies in British collections – and note *IPMEP* 491 ("The Gadered Counseyles") in fourteen copies.

[12] Fols. 205^v-12^v: **John of Wales/Waleys OFM,** *Breviloquium de virtutibus...*; see Sharpe 337.

[13] Fols. 212^v-14^v: An unidentified sermon, inc. "Penitenciam agite appropinquauit...Matt. 4to. Scitis dilectissimi quod postquam primi parentes nostri Adam scilicet et Eua..." The text does not appear in *PL*, nor in Schneyer's *Repertorium*.

[14] Fols. 214^v-40^v: Robert of Basevorn, *Forma predicandi*; see Sharpe 524. For MSS, see Henry Caplan, *Mediaeval Artes Praedicandi: A [Supplementary] Handlist*, 2 vols. (Ithaca: Cornell University Press, 1934-36), 1:21, 2:17 (no. 116), with six copies, all in British collections. A contents table, fols. 215va-16rb, between the prologue and the text proper. Ends in the lower middle of fol. 240va, the second column blank.

Collation 1^8-21^{12}. Crayon quire signatures (fol. 193) probably "19," those at fols. 205 and 217 illegible (the second of these may be "18"), (fol. 229) "(?) d." In addition, the crayon hand has signed all leaves in the first half of quire 19 with the arbitrary sign "θ."

Booklet 7 = fols. 241-82

[15] Fols. 241-50^v: **Thomas Waleys OP,** *Moralitates super Ysaiam*; see Sharpe 686.

[16] Fols. 250^v-79: a moralized summary of Aristotle, *De animalibus*, the full Michael Scot translation presented within *Albertus Magnus de animalibus libri xxvi*, ed. Hermann Stadler, 2 vols., Beiträge zur Geschichte der Philosophie des Mittelalters 15-16 (Münster i. W.: Aschendorff, 1916-20). The text ends with three lines on fol. 279ra (this side fully ruled); fols. 279^v-82^v are blank.

Collation 22-24^{12} 25^6. The crayon leaf signatures identify the quires by arbitrary signs, "φ," quire 23 unsigned, "f," "T."

Booklet 8 = fols. 283-310

[17] Fols. 283-308^v: Vegetius, *Epitoma rei militaris*, ed. Alf Önnerfors (Stuttgart: Teubner, 1995). For manuscripts, see Charles R. Schrader, "A Handlist of Extant Manuscripts containing the *De re militari* of Flavius Vegetius Renatus," *Scriptorium* 33 (1979), 280-305, with 243 Latin copies, about 45 in British collections (and another 17 in various English translations, e.g. *The Earliest English Translation of Vegetius' De re militari*, ed. Geoffrey Lester, Middle English Texts 21 [Heidelberg: Winter, 1988]). Allmand (see n.16) at 344-56 offers a supplementary list, about twenty copies unknown to Schrader, none in British libraries.

[18-19] Fols. 308^v-310: Two sermons ascribed to Augustine, but actually

Caesarius of Arles, sermones 89 and 179 (begins fol. 309rb), *Sancti Caesarii Arelatensis Sermones*, ed. Germaine Morin, CCSL 103-4, 2 vols. (Turnhout: Brepols, 1953), 1:365-69 and 2:724-29, respectively. Filler added on blank leaves by Scribe II; fol. 310^v is blank but ruled.

Collation 26^{12} 27^{16}. Leaf signatures in roman numerals, probably by the scribe. Crayon quire signatures (fol. 283) "7," (fol. 295) "8." These may, slightly inaccurately, be the remains of a superseded initiative in which one constituent unit of the developing book began at the head of Booklet 6. Cf. the comments on Booklets 5 and 9.

Booklet 9 = fols. 311-337 [the actual 338th folio]

[20] Fols. 311-36: **John Ridewall OFM, *Fulgentius Metaphoralis*;** see Sharpe 301-2. Ends at the foot of fol. 336rb; the verso and fol. 337^{rv} are blank.

Collation 28^{14} 29^{10} 30^4. The first quire has leaf signatures in roman numerals, probably again by the scribe. A crayon quire signature (fol. 323) "24." Following the discussion of Booklets 5 and 8 above, this is a sensible continuation of the crayon-signing that began at the head of the MS. Were quire 18 to have the accurate signature "17" in this system, the current quire 28 could have been the 24th quire of the sequence. Such a view would imply that Booklet 8 was not part of this count (and might explain the aberrant signatures there as signaling a late intrusion). In any event, this variation signals the rather anomalous status of Booklets 8-10 (the last with no crayon quire notation to fix its position) within the whole.

Booklet 10 = fols. 338-55 [the actual 339-56]

[21] Fols. 338-54: **Alan of Lille, *De planctu Naturae*,** ed. N. M. Häring, *Studi Medievali* 3 ser. 19 (1978), 806-79; and see N. Häring, "Manuscripts of the *De Planctu Naturae* of Master Alan of Lille," *Cîteaux* 29 (1978), 93-115 (132 copies, about 30 in British collections). Ends near the top of fol. 354ra; the remainder of this side, the verso, and fol. 355^{rv} are blank, but all ruled.

Collation 31^{12} 32^6. The first quire has the scribe's leaf signatures, mostly a sequence of strokes.

Booklet 11 = fols. 1-32 + BL fols. 385-88 [the actual 357-92]

[22] Fols. 1-32, 385: **Defensor of Ligugé,** *Liber scintillarum* (*CPL* 1302), CCSL 117, ed. Henri-M. Rochais (Turnhout: Brepols, 1957); for the MSS, see H.-M. Rochais, "Defensoriana: Archéologie du Liber Scintillarum," *Sacris Erudiri* 9 (1957), 199-264 (360 copies, nearly 60 in British libraries).

[23] Fols. 385-88^v: a brief diatessaron, probably a supply on leaves

originally blank. The text ends about halfway down fol. 388va; it is succeeded by an added contents table, possibly in the hand of the scribe, filling the remainder of the leaf. The medieval foliation here, while in the same position as in previous portions, has been supplied in red ink.

Collation 33-35^{12}. Booklets 11-12 have a continuous signature system. This appears, uniquely in the MS, at the center of the leaf, the quire letter above the leaf number. In this system, quires 33-38 are "a"-"g" ("d" is omitted at the booklet boundary).

Booklet 12 = BL fols. 389-422, an unnumbered leaf, and 423 [the actual 393-428]

[24] Fols. 389-397: Peter of Blois, *Compendium in Job*; see Sharpe 418.

[25] Fols. 397-422: Peter of Blois, *De amicitia Christiana et de caritate Dei*, preceded by a dedicatory letter, prologue, and contents table (fols. 397ra-98va); see Sharpe 418. The text ends at the foot of fol. 422ra; the remainder of this leaf, a following unnumbered leaf, and fol. 423^{rv} are all blank, but frame-ruled.

Collation 36-38^{12}. For the signatures, see the preceding booklet.

Booklet 13 = BL fols. 424-433, five unnumbered leaves, and 434 [the actual 429-44]

[26] Fols. 424-29: Bernard of Clairvaux, *Apologia ad Guillelmum abbatum, Opera* (see item 7 above), 3:61-108; the editors' list of MSS includes sixty-odd *twelfth-century* copies, fourteen in British collections. Ends near the foot of fol. 429rb, the verso blank but ruled.

[27] Fols. 430-33^{v}: ps.-Basil of Caesarea, *Admonitio ad fratres suos* (*CPL* 1155a), ed. Paul Lehmann, *Erforschung des Mittelalters: ausgewählte Abhanglungen und Aufsätze* 5 (Stuttgart: Hiersemann, 1962), 200-45 (from selected MSS, no list of copies, but another cursory ten-minute search found 30 in British collections). The text ends at near the top of fol. 433vb, and the remainder is blank but ruled.

Collation 39^{16}, unsigned.

Pretty clearly a(n incompleted) quire designed to handle any additional texts of interest.

Binding: The Library's conventional modern Royal collection binding.

Provenance: fol. 2^{v} has the *ex libris* of Dominus William de Kettering, monk of Ramsey (Hunts., OSB), who does not appear in either of A. B. Emden's Registers of the Universities. His ownership is noted by N. R. Ker, *Medieval Libraries of Great Britain: A List of Surviving Books*, 2nd edn., RHS Guides and Handbooks 3 (London: Royal Historical Society, 1964), 294;

Andrew G. Watson, *MLGB: Supplement to the Second Edition*, RHS Guides and Handbooks 15 (London: Royal Historical Society, 1987), 107 supplies the information that Kettering was ordained subdeacon in Ely diocese in 1343. Fol. 2 has the inventory number "no. 227" from the pre-1542 Royal Library; see James P. Carley, *The Libraries of Henry VIII*, Corpus of British Medieval Library Catalogues 7 (London: The British Library for the British Academy, 2000), 51 (H2.135).

Previously described: George F. Warner and Julius P. Gilson, *Catalogue of Western Manuscripts in the Old Royal and King's Collections*, 4 vols. (London: The British Library, 1921), 1:174-76.

NOTES

1. *English Friars and Antiquity in the Early Fourteenth Century* (Oxford: Blackwell, 1960). For the only serious take-up of Smalley's views, see Judson B. Allen, *The Friar as Critic: Literary Attitudes in the Later Middle Ages* (Nashville: Vanderbilt University Press, 1971).
2. The appendix also attends to the huge dissemination of a number of Royal's texts; just as Latin books frequently involve codicological problems of greater complexity and interest than do vernacular ones, their texts often display a circulation vastly in excess of most vernacular works (where thirty-forty copies is typically a very large number).
3. A form of analysis first developed in P. R. Robinson's classic discussion, "'The Booklet': a Self-Contained Unit in Composite Manuscripts," *Codicologica* 3 (1980):46-69. See most recently and extensively, Patrick Andrist et al., *La Syntaxe du Codex: Essai de codicologie structurale*, Bibliologia 34 (Turnhout: Brepols, [2013]).
4. Its replacement (by a subsequent independent foliation) and cessation, of course, provide further evidence of separable production, here distinguishing Booklets 1-10 (an "original manuscript" later supplemented) from Booklet 11, as well as from the subsequent Booklets 12-13. These latter materials also appear as additions in the contents table to the volume.
5. See Derek Pearsall, "The Whole Book: Late Medieval English Manuscript Miscellanies and their Modern Interpreters," in *Imagining the Book*, ed. Stephen Kelly and J. J. Thompson, Medieval Texts and Cultures of Northern Europe 7 (Turnhout: Brepols, 2005), 17-29; or, broaching points to which I will turn later in this essay, my comments in a review at *Medium Ævum* 83 (2014), 329-31.
6. On one outstanding preaching use of this text, certainly of English inspiration but of only continental distribution, see Nigel F. Palmer,

"Das Exempelwerk der englischen Bettelmönchen: ein Gegenstück zu den *Gesta Romanorum*?," in *Exempel und Exempelsamlungungen*, ed. Walter Haug and Burghart Wachinger (Tübingen: Niemeyer, 1991), 137-72, at 151-55 (a reference to a book introduced in n.10, Worcester Cathedral, MS F.154, at 154). Palmer, who presents about ninety manuscripts with this material, here draws on Ruth J. Dean, "The Life and Works of Nicholas Trevet, with special reference to his Anglo-Norman Chronicle" (unpublished Oxford D.Phil. thesis, 1938) [Bodleian, MS D.Phil. d.308], 212-25. Trevet composed a commentary on this text (as well as one on all Seneca's tragedies). For other resonances of the text that render it a commonplace medieval staple (here for grammatical instruction), see Marjorie C. Woods, "Rape and the Pedagogical Rhetoric of Sexual Violence," in *Criticism and Dissent in the Middle Ages*, ed. Rita Copeland (Cambridge: Cambridge University Press, 1996), 56-86, at 67-69.
7. Although, in my experience, it was much less widely used than the text (wrongly?) ascribed to John of Wales; for it, see Richard Sharpe, *A Handlist of Latin Writers of Great Britain and Ireland before 1540*, Publications of the Journal of Medieval Latin 1 (Turnhout: Brepols, 1997), 340 (hereafter always referred to as "Sharpe"). This volume is much more basic to investigations of English manuscript culture than more widely cited tools such as the *Index of Middle English Verse*.
8. Richard Newhauser discusses a great many texts of this sort in *The Treatise on Vices and Virtues in Latin and the Vernacular*, Typologie des sources du Moyen Âge occidentale 68 (Turnhout: Brepols, 1993).
9. The possibility of such projected use, complementary to the "core" to which I next turn (Defensor provides "classical" citations from Josephus only), is enhanced by the inclusion in the same booklet of text 23, a diatessaron. This genre aids someone seeking to concord the diverse accounts of the same event in the synoptic gospels, useful for finding unique yet parallel (and potentially moralizable) detail to include in ubiquitous *sermones de tempore*.
10. I identify these in the list below by sigla: **Q** Cambridge, Queens' College, MS 10, described Montague R. James, *A Descriptive Catalogue of the Western Manuscripts in the Library of Queens' College, Cambridge* (Cambridge: Cambridge University Press, 1905), 10-12 (nine booklets, one a supersession/extension of a standing one); **D** Dublin, Trinity College, MS 115, described Marvin L. Colker, *Trinity College Library Dublin: Descriptive Catalogue of the Medieval and Renaissance Latin Manuscripts*, 2 vols. (Aldershot: Scolar, 1991), 238-44 (six booklets, one a supersession/extension of a standing one); **B** Oxford, Bodleian Library, MS Bodley 571 (no. 2019), described R. W. Hunt et al., *A Summary Catalogue of the Western Manuscripts in the Bodleian Library at Oxford*, 7

vols. in 8 (Oxford: Clarendon, 1895-1953), 2.1:166-67 (five booklets, three supersession/extension of a standing one; fols. 257-75 a separate MS); **W** Worcester Cathedral, MS F.154, described R. M. Thomson, *A Descriptive Catalogue of the Medieval Manuscripts in Worcester Cathedral Library* (Cambridge: Brewer, 2001), 104-6 (eight booklets). This last book also includes Trevet's commentary on Augustine's *De civitate Dei*. For a few more attenuated examples, see Erfurt, Wissenschaftliche Bibliothek, MS Amplonianum Q.391; Eton College, MS 117; the collected volumes (perhaps postmedieval conjunctions) Bodleian, MS Auct. F.3.5, and Cambridge University Library, MS Mm.1.8; and the lost Canterbury, St Augustine's Abbey, MSS 862 and 1492.

11. For John of Wales (although 1270s, mainly Parisian), see Smalley's discussion of him as an important precursor, *English Friars*, 51-55. Again, although he was Parisian, Smalley identifies Bersuire as an analogue or "fellow-traveler" to her Oxonians; see 261-64. Map's grand pseudo-classical parody and his Oxonian commentators (now ed. Traugott Lawler, *Jankyn's Book of Wikked Wyves* 2, The Chaucer Library [Athens: University of Georgia Press, 2014], 51-267), are largely ignored in Smalley's account, but cf. her references at 86, 149 and n.4, 155-56, 321-22. Map's text appears in at least 170 manuscripts, of which about fifty were produced in England. For a further reference to Map in an associated text I mention below, see "Richard of Bury"'s *Philobiblion*, ed. Ernest C.Thomas (London: Kegan Paul, 1888), 32/13.

12. In the Appendix description, all these texts, as well as Thomas Waleys on Isaiah (text 15), appear in bold-face. As with Holcot's international best-seller, his lections on Wisdom, extant in at least 170 copies, Waleys's customary circulation is quite apart from either miscellaneous presentation or that of the other texts I highlight here. For Waleys, see Smalley, *English Friars*, 75-108.

13. **Q** and **D** show provenances one might well expect from Smalley's account: the former a combine of three similarly trained scribes, probably Franciscans, in the 1360s; the latter a Cambridge Augustinian friar in the late 1370s. But **W**, like Royal 7 C.i, gathers Oxford materials in a Benedictine context, here Worcester Cathedral priory, s. xiv ex. **B**'s medieval provenance is uncertain.

14. See my assessment of Langland, John of Wells, and Bodley 851, "Studies in the Manuscripts of *Piers Plowman*," *Yearbook of Langland Studies* 7 (1993), 1-25, at 14-25; and Judith Olszowy-Schlanger et al., *Dictionnaire hébreu-latin-français de la Bible hébraïque de l'Abbaye de Ramsey (XIIIe s.)*, CCCM Lexica Latina medii aevi 4 (Turnhout: Brepols, 2008).

15. "Hec igitur dicta sufficient secundum mei tenuitatem ingenij de predictis ad aliqualem instruccionem simplicium qui habent populum informare.

Pro quibus sit michi Cristus..." I offer this citation, from the Paris print, with some reservation, since I have yet to find the sentence in any manuscript I have examined, e.g. not in British Library, MS Additional 46919 (William Herebert of the Hereford Franciscans, probably 1320s).

16. Cf. Christopher Allmand, *The De Re Militari of Vegetius: The Reception, Transmission and Legacy of a Roman Text in the Middle Ages* (Cambridge: Cambridge University Press, 2011). While much of Allmand's discussion seems to me hampered by his interests as military historian, he persistently notes the "politicization" of Vegetius's text. On "ghostly battle," see 64, 218; on John of Salisbury's use of Vegetius in the *Polycraticus* (probably the most important text inspiring the "classicizing friars"), see 60, 66, 84-91 (and cf. the comments on Petrarch's copy at 52). At 67-68, Allmand takes up the friars directly, but largely defers to Smalley's argumentation.

17. Although it is much more usual to find Alan's *De planctu* with other twelfith-century poetry (Geoffrey of Vinsauf, Matthew of Vendôme, Walter's *Alexandreis*, less frequently *Architrenius*) and grammar-school materials, in about one-third of the insular copies the text appears with *Philobiblion*: Cambridge, St John's College, MS E.12 (with Map + Trevet and Ridewall); and Trinity College, MS R.9.17; British Library, MSS Additional 24361, Arundel 335, Harley 492 and 3224, Royal 15 C.xvi (with Bersuire); Bodleian Library, MS Digby 147 (with Map + Ridewall; the texts in separate booklets, all separate from the astronomy that comprises most of the whole, but in the same hand and format); Oxford, St John's College, MS 172; Durham University Library, MS Cosin V.v.2. For more distant analogues, cf. Cambridge University Library, MS Ff.6.12 (with Map + Ridewall); Royal 12 E.i; Oxford, Lincoln College, MS lat. 81 (with Map + Trevet); and the lost York Augustinian friars 481.

18. "Septimo, Dei misericordia est omnium oppressorum speciale refugium. Sequitur in textu, *Misericordia mea et refugium meum, susceptor meus et liberator meus* (Ps 143:2). 'Misericordia' in remittendis peccatis, 'refugium' in pressuris [subleuandis]. 'Susceptor meus,' quando ad te venio; 'liberator meus,' quando ad te clamo. Vegecius, *De re militari*, dicit quod dux belli nunquam debet hostes sic artare quin aliquem habeant locum refugij, ne desperacio euadendi tribuat eis nimias vires dimicandi, quoniam desperacio fortes facit. Vnde 2° Regum [2:19ff.] legitur quod Asael persecutus est Abner, nec sibi dedit locum refugij... Sic moraliter Deus non relinquit hostes suos, peccatores, sine aliquali refugio; immo misericordia sua est eis pro refugio." I cite London, Westminster Diocesan Archives, MS H.38, fol. 181^v, with one emendation from the other copies. In spite of three of the four manuscripts ascribing this text to Richard Rolle, the *Viridarium* is certainly the text identified in York Augustinian booklists as Waldeby's *De misericordia Dei*. On Holcot's

ebullience in drawing in "extraneous" material, cf. Allen, *Friar as Critic*, 49 (although Allen's example manages to fuse and treat as if similar a variety of differing and easily distinguishable rhetorical devices).

19. Or so one would believe from published accounts, e.g. Siegfried Wenzel, "The Classics in Late-Medieval Preaching," in *Medieval Antiquity*, ed. Andries Welkenhuysen et al., Mediaevalia Lovaniensia 1st ser. 24 (Louvain: Louvain University Press, 1995), 127-43. But such evocations do in fact occur, if quite intermittently; cf. Wenzel's own *Preaching in the Age of Chaucer: Selected Sermons in Translation* (Washington: Catholic University of America Press, 2008), 301. Also informative is Wenzel's "Ovid from the Pulpit," in *Ovid in the Middle Ages*, ed. James G. Clark et al. (Cambridge: Cambridge University Press, 2011), 160-76 (including passing references to a variety of other authors, including Vegetius). Instructively, Wenzel's conclusion emphasizes pulpit use of Ovid not simply for structural and moral applications but for purely literary features – the preacher's "decorative" purposes, the appeal of a citation cast in witty metrical form.

20. See *Etymologiae* 12.4, *Patrologia Latina* 82:442-48.

21. It is worth noting that, although it is easy to demonstrate that Bartholomaeus selected his "scientific" detail with specific scriptural lections in mind, this predecessor text offers virtually no direction to the reader as to the application of any detail to the Bible. (Hence, Lord Berkeley's easy suggestion to John Trevisa that it might function, in English translation, as a universal compendium of human knowledge.) Bersuire's *Reductorium morale*, of which his Ovidian materials form book 15, exists precisely to "reduce," i.e. to bring Bartholomaeus's profusion of detail to a more readily consultable form.

22. "De predictis virtutibus alique narrationes exemplares et persuasorie ad vtilitatem presidentium et instructionem in thronis residentum subscribantur, prout continentur in gestis potentum siue sapientum et mundi philosophorum. Nam exempla sanctorum sufficientes patent in gestis eorum et historijs sacrarum scripturarum," cited from *Summa de regimine uite humane seu Margarita doctorum...* (Venice: G. de Arriuabenis, 30 July 1496), fol. 240ra.

23. One might compare the way in which John is resuscitated by Chaucer, e.g. at *Canterbury Tales* D 460-63, 642-49, 1165-67; see further Robert A. Pratt, "The Development of the Wife of Bath," in *Studies in Medieval Literature in Honor of Professor Albert Croll Baugh*, ed. MacEdward Leach (Philadelphia: University of Pennsylvania Press, 1961), 45-79, at 50; and "Chaucer and the Hand that Fed Him,"

Speculum 41 (1966), 619-42, at 620-23. For a "modernized" version of Diogenes, misascribed to Walter Burley, a sober Oxford logician contemporary with Nicholas Trevet, see Sharpe 727-28.
24. "John Ridewall's Commentary on *De civitate Dei*," *Medium Ævum* 25 (1956), 140-53, at 142. One might compare Bersuire's defense of his Ovidian mythographical interests (at this point, perhaps inspired by a discussion in Walter Map): "For a man is permitted, if he can, to collect grapes from thorns and suck honey out of the rock and derive oil out of the hardest stone [cf. Deut 32:13], and that he construct the Ark of the Covenant out of the treasures of the Egyptians. And Ovid says that it is morally permissible to be taught by one's enemy." ("Licitum enim est quod homo, si possit, de spinis colligat uvas et quod mel de petra suggat oleumque de saxo durissimo sibi sumat [cf. Deut 32:13], quodque de thesauris Egipciorum tabernaculum federis edificet et componat. Et Ovidius dicit [*Metamorphoses* 4:428] quod 'Fas est ab hoste doceri,'" cited from [J. Engels, ed.], *Petrus Berchorius Reductorium morale, Liber XV: Ovidius moralizatus cap. i. De formis figurisque deorum...Werkmateriaal* 3 [Utrecht: Instituut voor Laat Latijn, 1966], 2/17-22.) But, on the basis of his argumentation in *De doctrina Christiana*, one might reasonably doubt whether Augustine's program really meant what Bersuire offers, publicizing stories of the pagan gods, their misadventures, and the consequent transformations they provoked.
25. Cf. R. P. H. Green, "The Genesis of a Medieval Textbook: The Models and Sources of the Ecloga Theoduli," *Viator* 13 (1982), 49-106, who persistently notes the poet's careful reproduction of and obvious fondness for his classical sources.
26. "Commentary as Criticism: Formal Cause, Discursive Form, and the Late Medieval Accessus," in *Acta Conventus Neo-latini Louaniensis...*, ed. J. Ijsewijn and E. Keszler (Louvain: Louvain University Press; and Munich: Fink, 1973), 29-48, at 40. It's unclear to me how Allen might have explained a moment like Alan of Lille's *Anticlaudianus* 5.265-305; there the poet discards any worldly muse and claims a guiding inspiration comparable to the biblical prophets Moses and Isaiah (who required aid to perfect hampered skills merely verbal). Cf. the critique at A. J. Minnis and A. B. Scott, *Medieval Literary Theory and Criticism c.1100-c.1375: The Commentary-Tradition* (Oxford: Clarendon, 1988), 5-11, 125-26 (a volume offering immense amounts of evidence that would lay to rest much of Allen's hesitation).

WORKS CITED
(does not include material attached to the Appendix description)

Manuscripts
Cambridge, Queens' College, MS 10
Cambridge, St John's College, MS E.12
Cambridge, Trinity College, MS R.9.17
Cambridge University Library, MS Ff.6.12
—, MS Mm.1.8
olim Canterbury, St Augustine's Abbey, MSS 862 and 1492
Dublin, Trinity College, MS 115
Durham University Library, MS Cosin V.v.2
Erfurt, Wissenschaftliche Bibliothek, MS Amplonianum Q.391
Eton College, MS 117
London, Westminster Diocesan Archives, MS H.38
London, British Library, MS Additional 24361
—, MS Additional 46919
—, Arundel 335
—, MSS Harley 492 and 3224
—, MS Royal 7 C.i
—, MS Royal 12 E.i
—, MS Royal 15 C.xvi
Oxford, Bodleian Library, MS Auct. F.3.5
—, MS Bodley 571
—, MS Digby 147
Oxford, Lincoln College, MS lat. 81
Oxford, St John's College, MS 172
Worcester Cathedral, MS F.154
olim York, Augustinian friars, MS 481

Primary Texts
Isidore of Seville. *Etymologiae. Patrologia Latina* 82:72-728.
Jankyn's Book of Wikked Wyves 2..., ed. Traugott Lawler. The Chaucer Library. Athens: University of Georgia Press, 2014.
John of Wales. *Breviarium de virtutibus... In Summa de regimine uite humane seu Margarita doctorum...* Venice: G. de Arriuabenis, 30 July 1496. Fols. 239vb-59vb.
Malachi of Ireland. *Libellus, septem peccatorum mortalium venena eorumque remedia describens, qui dicitur Venena Malachiae.* Paris: Henri Estienne, 1518.

Pierre Bersuire. *Reductorium morale, Liber XV: Ovidius moralizatus cap. i. De formis figurisque deorum...Werkmateriaal 3*, [ed. J. Engels]. Utrecht: Instituut voor Laat Latijn, 1966.

"Richard of Bury" [actually Robert Holcot]. *The Philobiblion*, ed. tr. Ernest C.Thomas. London: Kegan Paul, 1888.

Secondary Discussions

Allen, Judson B. "Commentary as Criticism: Formal Cause, Discursive Form, and the Late Medieval Accessus." In *Acta Conventus Neo-latini Louaniensis...*, ed. J. Ijsewijn and E. Keszler. Louvain: Louvain University Press; and Munich: Fink, 1973. Pp. 29-48.

—. *The Friar as Critic: Literary Attitudes in the Later Middle Ages*. Nashville: Vanderbilt University Press, 1971.

Allmand, Christopher. *The* De Re Militari *of Vegetius: The Reception, Transmission and Legacy of a Roman Text in the Middle Ages*. Cambridge: Cambridge University Press, 2011.

Andrist, Patrick et al. *La Syntaxe du Codex: Essai de codicologie structurale*. Bibliologia 34. Turnhout: Brepols, [2013].

Charland, Th. M. *Artes Praedicandi: contribution à l'histoire de la rhétorique au moyen âge*. Paris: Vrin and Montreal: Institut d'études médiévales, 1936.

Colker, Marvin L. *Trinity College Library Dublin: Descriptive Catalogue of the Medieval and Renaissance Latin Manuscripts*. 2 vols. Aldershot: Scolar, 1991.

Dean, Ruth J. "The Life and Works of Nicholas Trevet, with special reference to his Anglo-Norman Chronicle." Unpublished Oxford D.Phil. thesis, 1938. [Bodleian, MS D.Phil. d.308]

Green, R. P. H. "The Genesis of a Medieval Textbook: The Models and Sources of the Ecloga Theoduli." *Viator* 13 (1982), 49-106.

Hanna, Ralph. Review of Arthur Bahr, *Fragments and Assemblages*. Medium Ævum 83 (2014), 329-31.

—. "Studies in the Manuscripts of *Piers Plowman*." *Yearbook of Langland Studies* 7 (1993), 1-25.

Hunt, R. W., et al. *A Summary Catalogue of the Western Manuscripts in the Bodleian Library at Oxford*. 7 vols in 8. Oxford: Clarendon, 1895-1953.

James, Montague R. *A Descriptive Catalogue of the Western Manuscripts in the Library of Queens' College, Cambridge*. Cambridge: Cambridge University Press, 1905.

Minnis, A. J., and A. B. Scott. *Medieval Literary Theory and Criticism c.1100-c.1375: The Commentary-Tradition*. Oxford: Clarendon, 1988.

Newhauser, Richard. *The Treatise on Vices and Virtues in Latin and the Vernacular.* Typologie des sources du Moyen Âge occidentale 68. Turnhout: Brepols, 1993.

Olszowy-Schlanger, Judith et al. *Dictionnaire hébreu-latin-français de la Bible hérbraïque de l'Abbaye de Ramsey (XIIIe s.).* CCCM Lexica Latina medii aevi 4. Turnhout: Brepols, 2008.

Palmer, Nigel F. "Das Exempelwerk der englischen Bettelmönchen: ein Gegenstück zu den *Gesta Romanorum*?" In *Exempel und Exempelsamlungungen,* ed. Walter Haug and Burghart Wachinger. Tübingen: Niemeyer, 1991. Pp. 137-72.

Pearsall, Derek. "The Whole Book: Late Medieval English Manuscript Miscellanies and their Modern Interpreters." In *Imagining the Book,* ed. Stephen Kelly and J. J. Thompson. Medieval Texts and Cultures of Northern Europe 7. Turnhout: Brepols, 2005. Pp. 17-29.

Robert A. Pratt. "Chaucer and the Hand that Fed Him." *Speculum* 41 (1966), 619-42.

—. "The Development of the Wife of Bath." In *Studies in Medieval Literature in Honor of Professor Albert Croll Baugh,* ed. MacEdward Leach. Philadelphia: University of Pennsylvania Press, 1961. Pp. 45-79.

Robinson, P. R. "'The Booklet': a Self-Contained Unit in Composite Manuscripts." *Codicologica* 3 (1980), 46-69.

Sharpe, Richard. *A Handlist of Latin Writers of Great Britain and Ireland before 1540.* Publications of the Journal of Medieval Latin 1. Turnhout: Brepols, 1997.

Smalley, Beryl. *English Friars and Antiquity in the Early Fourteenth Century.* Oxford: Blackwell, 1960.

—. "John Ridewall's Commentary on *De civitate Dei.*" *Medium Ævum* 25 (1956), 140-53.

Smith, David M., and Vera C. M. London. *The Heads of Religious Houses England and Wales II 1216-1377.* Cambridge: Cambridge University Press, 2001.

Thomson, R. M. *A Descriptive Catalogue of the Medieval Manuscripts in Worcester Cathedral Library.* Cambridge: Brewer, 2001.

Warner, George F., and Julius P. Gilson. *Catalogue of Western Manuscripts in the Old Royal and King's Collections.* 4 vols. London: The British Library, 1921.

Wenzel, Siegfried. "The Classics in Late-Medieval Preaching." In *Medieval Antiquity,* ed. Andries Welkenhuysen *et al.* Mediaevalia Lovaniensia 1st ser. 24. Louvain: Louvain University Press, 1995. Pp. 127-43.

—. "Ovid from the Pulpit." In *Ovid in the Middle Ages*, ed. James G. Clark et al. Cambridge: Cambridge University Press, 2011. Pp. 160-76.
—. *Preaching in the Age of Chaucer: Selected Sermons in Translation* Washington: Catholic University of America Press, 2008.
Woods, Marjorie C. "Rape and the Pedagogical Rhetoric of Sexual Violence." In *Criticism and Dissent in the Middle Ages*, ed. Rita Copeland. Cambridge: Cambridge University Press, 1996. Pp. 56-86.

Selling Forbidden Books: Profit and Ideology in Thomas Godfray's Printing

ALEX DA COSTA

There is a long-standing narrative about the earliest English printers of the Reformation that tells us they were as happy to print evangelical as conservative material, providing their risk (legal and financial) was minimized and a good return likely. As Charles Butterworth argued in 1947, "as soon as one such [controversial] volume had been issued with impunity, the other ... printers stood ready to join in this most welcome and profitable market, offering such material as they had at hand."[1] Or as David Loades put it a few decades later, "the appetite of Londoners for controversial ephemera was enormous, and ... most printers were men of trade first, and proselytisers second (if at all)."[2] A variation on this narrative attributed the earliest English evangelical printing to the combined effect of printers' mercantile interests and either humanists or the influence of Cromwell. In the words of James McConica, "the years immediately after Wolsey's fall from office witnessed a remarkable publication enterprise which truly deserves the name 'Erasmian.' It is sponsored by humanists committed to reform in Church and State."[3] Although this introduced an ideological motive for publication, McConica attributed it to sponsors "committed to reform" and made printers the means by which these reformers achieved their ends.

Indeed, in Andrew Pettegree's version of this tale, printers are erased entirely, becoming simply the purveyors of a medium of production, "one means by which the core messages of the reformers were brought to the reading public," and not even doing as much as that in England until the mid-1530s for fear of jeopardizing their own prosperity.[4] Conversely, when scholars do argue that "the printers who issued [controversial material] may have been motivated by a reforming religious agenda," they give little attention to how these printers went about pursuing this agenda in a commercially viable manner, from finding texts to negotiating censorship to enticing readers.[5]

What all these narratives have in common is that they take for granted the hunger of the laity for evangelical material, which writers such as William Tyndale repeatedly emphasized in their prefaces and envoys. As William Roy put it, "lett the vngodly roare and barcke never so lowde . . . the fyre which Christ cam to kyndle on erth / can nott butt burne."[6] Such claims of burning demand seem truthful to the modern reader because we know that over a single decade Tyndale's *New Testament* alone went through fifteen editions, and increasing numbers of evangelical texts were printed in English, first abroad and then within England itself. But in taking these rhetorical claims at face value, there is a tendency to see this growth in printing and reading as merely reflective of a preexistent market just waiting to be exploited and to make the printers into curiously naïve figures, functioning either as mere market agents responding mechanically to demand or as mouthpieces of God with no care for their bottom line. This is the trap that Michael Saenger suggests modern critics fall into too easily: "because paratexts are (often implicitly) read in non-literary terms," their assertions "are often read as transparent reflections of . . . truth," but "marketability not honesty, is the constant" in front matter.[7] Statements like Roy's expressed hope and belief in the laity's desire for reformation, but they were also meant to encourage new readers by presenting the tracts as desirable.

An approach that sees printers of evangelical material in English as merely responding to burning demand gives too much sway to Thomas More's claim that evangelical books were "for no lucre, caste . . . abrode by nyght" in order to spread the word.[8] Some texts were certainly given away, such as Simon Fish's pamphlet *Supplication of Beggars*, which Fox claimed was "throwen and scattered at the procession in Westminster vpon Candelmas day" in February 1529.[9] However, this distribution method would have been unsustainable for every book, especially the longer works, and the evangelicals do not seem to have had a limitless supply of funds from their supporters. The possibly apocryphal tale in *Hall's Chronicle*, published in 1548, depicts William Tyndale as grateful that Cuthbert Tunstall, the bishop of London, bought up "a heap of New Testaments and books" which he had "beggared" himself to print even though they were going to be burnt. He apparently replied to the go-between:

> I am the gladder . . . [for] I shall get money of him for
> these books, to bring myself out of debt (and the whole
> world shall cry out upon the burning of God's word). And

the overplus of the money, that shall remain to me, shall make me more studious, to correct the said new Testament, and so newly to imprint the same once again.[10]

Like any other type of printing, to produce an evangelical book abroad required money to cover the costs of the initial printing as well as some hope of recovering those costs through sales.

Thomas More was keenly aware of this despite his comment that evangelical books were given away for "no lucre." He marvels in *The Confutation of Tyndale's Answer* that though "they neyther can be ... prented [outside of the realm] without great coste, nor here solde wythout aduenture & perell: yet ceace they not with mony sent from hense, to prente them there & sende them hyther by y\e/ whole fattes full at ones."[11] Similarly, in the *Dialogue Concerning Heresies*, he emphasizes the vital role groups of sponsors had in defraying the costs of printing:

> They let not to lay theyr money togyder and make a purse amonge them for the pryntyng of an euyll made or euyll translated boke / which thoughe it happe to be forboden and burned yet some be solde ere they be spyed / and eche of them lese but theyr parte / yet I thynke there wyll no prynter lyghtly be so hote to put any byble in prynt at his owne charge / wherof the losse sholde lye hole in his owne necke.[12]

More had a clear vision of early Reformation printing as both physically *and* financially perilous, dependent on the making of a joint "purse" to spread the costs and risks across a number of backers.

The financial risk remained even after the break with Rome heralded a period in which evangelical printing was tolerated within England even if it was not officially legal. A letter from John Rastell to Cromwell in August 1534 reveals the ways in which printers might risk financial ruin by publishing controversial material. Asking for financial support, Rastell observed:

> I have spend my tyme 7 gyffyn my bysynes principally this iiij or v yers in compylyng dyuers bokes concernyng the furtherance of the kynges causis 7 opposing of the vsurpyd auctorite 7 therby gretly hyndered myn own bysynes that as I shall answer afore god I am the wors by it by a C l. 7 aboue / and beside that I haue decayd the trade of my lyffyng for where before yat I gote by the law in pledyng ... xl m\a/rks a yere that was xx nobles a terme

at the lest and printyd eu*ery* yere ij or iij C reams of papyr which was mor yerely profet to me than y\e/ gaynys y*at* I gate by y\e/ law / I assure you I get not now xls a yere by y\e/. law nor I printyd not a C. reams of papyr this ij yere.[13]

Having foregrounded the financial cost of his commitment to the king's causes and opposition to the pope, Rastell goes on to explain why he had lost rather than made money on books that modern critics assume were in hot demand. He explains that he had attempted to make such material attractive to readers by devising "certeyn p*r*ayers \in/ englissh to be put in primers of dyu*er*s sortes of small p*r*ise" and had already produced a "lytyl prim*er*" to "bryng y\e/ people ... from the beleue of y\e/ popes noughty doctri*ne*" (fol. 114r). However, he laments that far from there being great custom, "y\e/ most p*ar*t of the people be loth to bye any such bok*es* and yet yf they \be/ gyffyn to them skantly rede them" (fol. 114r). He thinks that one solution would be to put the "matt*er* in englyssh ... in pri*mers* which they vse to bryng w*ith* them to the church [so] they shal be in a man*er* com-pellyd to rede them" (fol. 114r), but is also keenly aware of the price barrier, recommending that the king print 4,000 or 5,000 and "gyff th*em* among y\e/ people." He thinks this would bring them to the right belief, "and do as much good as y\e/ prechyng do."

A similar picture emerges from the correspondence between another publisher with Lutheran leanings, William Marshall, and Thomas Cromwell. Marshall appealed to Cromwell to lend him money since his printer, Thomas Godfray, was trying to avoid making the kinds of losses that Rastell had incurred by refusing to allow Marshall "to fett ... bokes from the prynters for lacke of money."[14] In response, Cromwell lent Marshall £20, for which Marshall and his brother, Thomas Marshall, stood surety with the hope that sales of *The Defence of Peace* (STC 17817), which Robert Wyer printed for Marshall the following year, would allow the loan to be repaid. However, even though Marshall described this as "the best book in English against the usurped ... bishop of Rome," it did not sell, and Cromwell forgave the debt late in 1535.[15]

The experiences of Rastell and Marshall bring into doubt the assumption that English printers had only to take advantage of "enormous" preexisting demand for material that broke with traditional doctrine and that they did not have to continue to encourage this new market after 1534. This assumption has caused Reformation scholars to ignore the question of how the market for vernacular, evangelical writing was initially fostered and expanded. For instance, in his excellent chapter on "Reading" in *Being Protestant in Reformation Britain*, Alec Ryrie discusses the importance of reading to Protestantism and the ways in which members of this "book-religion" were trained to see reading as a fundamental part of their spiritual lives.[16] However, Ryrie takes the existence of a "Protestant reader," or would-be reader, for granted and does not address how such a reader was created in the earliest years of the Reformation, despite the book's covering 1530 to 1640. Focusing on how literacy was acquired, he avoids the question of how a reader steeped in traditional religion became a reader open to engaging with evangelical texts in the first place, especially in a period when the reading of such material was still forbidden de jure if not always de facto. This tendency, like the narratives I mentioned above, obscures the ways in which writers, printers, and publishers in the 1520s and 1530s independently and deliberately encouraged a nascent—not preexisting—market through their choice of material and the manner of its presentation.

Julia Boffey, however, offers an alternative approach in her study of John Mychell, a Canterbury printer active from the 1530s. Arguing that his "commercial shrewdness, as well as his conscience, may have prompted ... [his] overt engagement with the printing of less traditional material during a period of religious change," she explores the ways in which he exploited the potential of "older Middle English writings in a new polemical context."[17] In a similar vein, this article focuses on Thomas Godfray, who printed at least thirty-six editions between the late 1520s and 1530s, and shows the ways in which he deliberately nurtured an emerging evangelical readership, balancing his commitment to the new thinking with commercial sensitivity. A few scholars, such as Andrew Wawn, have previously suggested that Godfray was an "integral part of the Henrician propagandist organization," but in doing so, they have shifted the focus away from the printer and focused overmuch on the shaping force of Cromwell.[18] Similarly, Torrance Kirby's suggestion that Godfray's publications were part of an attempt to persuade the government erased the majority of likely readers.[19] This article argues instead that the texts that Godfray printed after 1534 were primarily aimed at assuaging the anxieties of curious readers and encouraging their demand for evangelical material, at conversion rather than political persuasion.

Godfray was "probably a Stationer" whose printing career ran "between the end of 1530 and the beginning of 1537."[20] During his career, he printed thirty-six texts and seems to have operated from two separate locations, though there are only three colophons that give a more detailed address than "London": John Stanbridge's *Sum es fui*, which was "Printed at London: in the Olde bayly," and the Exonoratorium curatorum and *The Folowyng of Christ*, which were "Prynted at London at Temple barre," though whether inside it or outside is unknown.[21] To add to the obscurity of Godfray's career, only three of the texts Godfray printed are dated: *The Workes of Geffray Chaucer* (1532), *The Forme and Maner of ... Helpyng for Pore People* (June 1535), and

Tyndale's *New Testament* (1536).[22] A further three can be fairly closely dated as a result of internal references: *A Primer in Englysshe*, which begins with the almanac for 1535,[23] *The Boke of Marchauntes*, which says it was translated in August 1534, and *A Panegyric of Henry VIII*, which mentions Henry VIII's "most lawfull wyfe quene Jane" as if she were alive, so must have been written between her succession on May 30, 1536 and death on October 24, 1537.[24] Another work, *A Treatyse of the Donation . . . by Constantyne*, can probably be dated to early 1534 based on the letter (mentioned above) by William Marshall to Cromwell in April of that year asking for a loan to help bring "the book of Constantine . . . from the printers,"[25] and Godfray's edition of the *Exonoratorium curatorum* must have been completed before November 1534, when the Act of Supremacy, was passed since it makes mention of "thy gostly father . . . the pope."

Two more works can be dated fairly closely based on typographical evidence, since Godfray used a 73 textura with a rotated 4 in its fount for these and three other editions that can be dated (for the reasons outlined above) between 1534 and 1537, that is *A Treatyse of the Donation . . . by Constantyne*, *A Panegyric of Henry VIII*, and *A Primer in Englysshe*. According to Blayney, Godfray "ordered some correctly oriented examples, but . . . added them to his typecase without discarding the rotated ones," and these corrected 4s can be seen alongside the erroneous 4s in these three works as well as two others, *The Fountayne or Well of Lyfe* (STC 11211, 1534?) and *A Treatise Declaryng . . . That Pyctures [and] Other Ymages . . . Ar in No Wise to Be Suffred* (STC 24239, 1535?).[27] This suggests that *The Fountanye or Well of Life* and *A Treatise on Pyctures and Other Ymages* postdated the other three and should be dated 1535 or 1536. For most of the other twenty-six texts' chronological order, the *Short Title Catalogue* offers ranges that cover "up to three years on either side" of a central date.

Nevertheless, the approximate time line of Godfray's career that emerges from a combination of the dated texts and approximate ranges falls into two parts. The first part, from approximately 1530 to 1534, shows little cohesiveness, encompassing *The Workes of Geffray Chaucer*, the encyclopedic *History of Kyng Boccus*,[28] the conventional *Folowyng of Christ*[29] and *Golden Epistle*[30], and *An Introductorie for to lerne . . . Frenche*.[31] The second part seems to begin around 1534 and runs to the end of his printing career, during which texts of an evangelical or controversial nature dominate. On the controversial side are texts concerned with the relationship between Crown and Church, including two tracts by Christopher St German on the limitations of the powers of the Church, *A Treatise Concernynge Impropriations of Benefices* and *A Treatise of the Donation or Gyfte . . . by Constantyne* mentioned above. There is also Marcourt's *The Boke of Marchauntes*, which uses mercantile satire to explore questions of ecclesiastical power.[32] On the more explicitly evangelical side are translations by George Joy and William Tyndale of *The Psalter of Dauid, The Prouerbes of Solomon,* and *The New Testament,* Tyndale's *A Pathway into the Holy Scripture,* and Patrick Hamilton's *Dyuers Frutefull Gatherynges.* Only four texts—15 percent of the output—printed by Godfray in this second period are concerned with other matters: two grammatical works by John Stanbridge, a third edition of the *Golden Epistle,* and a pamphlet celebrating the Battle of Agincourt.

Godfray's concentration on printing evangelical material becomes more apparent when we consider what other printers were doing at this time. In the period from 1530 to 1537, only two other London printers put their names to works by Tyndale: James Nycolson in 1536, who printed *The Parable of the Wicked Mammon,*[33] and Robert Redman, who printed three editions of *An Exposycyon vpon... Mathewe* between approximately 1533 and 1539.[34] Two other unidentified printers published *The Prophet Jonas* and *The Obedyence of a Chrysten Man,* but neither dated them nor added an imprint, while two more unidentified printers were more cautious still and used false imprints, claiming they were produced in "Nornburg" or "Malborowe, in the lande of Hesse."[35] When other evangelical writers are taken into account, only Redman comes close to the range of material that Godfray printed. Indeed, Redman and Godfray seem to have been unusually willing to explore whether previously forbidden works by Tyndale might be printed as Henry VIII led the Church in England away from Rome. Yet Redman's experiments were against a backdrop of much higher production: of the ninety-nine works he printed between 1530 and 1537, less than 14 percent, might be considered evangelical, and they are balanced by religious material of a more traditional or explicitly sanctioned nature. Godfray stands out not only for the risks he took in exploring the boundaries of acceptability but for his near-exclusive concentration on controversial and evangelical material.

A further striking feature of this period of productivity in Godfray's career is the way in which all the evangelical texts are pitched at a readership only just becoming acquainted with the idea of justification by faith alone. There are texts that introduce readers to the fundamental ideas of Lutheran-inflected belief, such as Tyndale's *A Pathway into the Holy Scripture* and Patrick Hamilton's *Dyuers Frutefull Gatherynges,* or that make scripture more accessible by offering the reader a florilegium of quotations, such as *The Prouerbes of Solomon,* and texts that combine both translations and expansions of biblical texts, such as *The Psalter of David.* The edition of Tyndale's *New Testament* attributed to Godfray by the STC is in many ways anomalous in its relatively unmediated presentation of scripture.

Although the introductory nature of these texts in part reflects the foci of the English evangelicals, Godfray seems to have done more than simply print what he "had to hand." Judging from extant editions—admittedly an imperfect guide—he avoided competing with other printers by eschewing further editions of Tyndale's most popular works, such as *The Parable of the Wicked Mammon* and *The Obedyence of a Chrysten Man*. Instead he printed the only English editions of Tyndale's *A Pathway into the Holy Scripture* and was the first English printer to print Tyndale's *New Testament*. He also avoided lengthier texts, such as Tyndale's *An Answere vnto Sir Thomas More*, printing almost entirely in octavo format with between twenty-four and sixty-eight folios, making his texts less expensive to produce and more easily purchasable. (In this practice perhaps he learned from William Marshall's experience of failing to sell the folio *Defence of the Peace*, with its 140 leaves, despite its being the "best book" against Rome.) Reading Godfray's entire print run also reveals a repetitiveness and simplicity in the messages conveyed.

It is the cheapness and basic nature of these works that brings into question Torrance Kirby's assertion that Godfray was a member of a "Tudor evangelical avant-garde whose *main* object was to prod the government to move toward a radical political break with the Roman hierarchy and to a theological break with the old religion."[36] Godfray's publications seem directed more at the common reader than at the more informed members of the king's circle. Though I argue elsewhere that Godfray was one of the first printers to test where the new boundaries of acceptable publication lay after 1534 by repositioning evangelical texts "as part of the royally sanctioned criticism of traditional Church power and practice," I am now beginning to think that the way in which Godfray chose, presented, and adapted his earliest evangelical texts was as much about fostering a market for this material as it was about negotiating censorship.[37] It seems likely that by propagating the anticlerical discussions of people such as St. German, which fitted a homegrown and monarch-led opposition to papal and clerical power, he helped to make common readers receptive to departures from traditional doctrine, while—as shown below—combining this kind of material with evangelical material made the latter further familiar and acceptable.

Two letters sent to Cromwell in 1535 illustrate how necessary it was to warm readers slowly to evangelical doctrines in the early years of the English Reformation and the risks of imprudent printing. These letters were sent following Thomas Godfray's anonymous printing for William Marshall of *A Treatise on Pyctures and Other Ymages* (STC 24238, 1535).[38] On September 11, 1535, Thomas Broke reported that "the people gretly murmureth" about the book "for that it enveith gretly ageynst worshipping of images . . . but most specially ageynst the masse wheryn the sacrament of the awter is consecrate." He specifically drew attention to the way this topic was presented "playnely" "within iiij or v. leves of the latter ende," the point at which the marginalia states that "The supper of our lord was comen to mani men celebrated at his table / 7 nat a priuate eatyng and drinkinge of one alone at the auter."[39] Lord Chancellor Thomas Audeley again marked the book's disruptive potential two days later:

> in the parts where he [Marshall] has been there has been some discord and diversity of opinion touching worshipping of saints and images, creeping at cross, and such ceremonies, which discord it were well to put to silence. This book will make much business if it should go forth. Intends to send for the printer to stop them. It were good that preachers and people abstained from opinions of such things until the King has put a final order by the report of those appointed for searching and ordering the laws of the Church. A proclamation to abstain until that time would do much good.[40]

Both Broke and Audeley saw the political consequences of not persuading readers, and it is perhaps suggestive of Godfray's cautious approach and ability to anticipate trouble that he took the unusual step of omitting his name as printer from both the first and second edition, choosing instead to clearly state that they were "Printed for W. Marshall."[41] William Marshall, by contrast, was far from careful in either anticipating or responding to such murmurs, putting into print a second edition with a truculent note at the bottom of the title page anticipating that "some popish doctor or peuish proctor" would "grunt at this treatise" but admonishing the reader to "fyrst rede and then iuge." He followed this with final envoy "to the indyfferent reder" (sig. G1r), described as a defensive "buckler" (sig. G3r), objecting that he had been "mystaken and misreported" (sig. G2r) as having "dispysed the masse or the supper of the lorde" rather than having spoken "agaynst the abuses therof . . . by the byshopps of Rome / their popysshe complyces and counsellours" (sig. G3r).

William Underwood suspects that Cromwell's protection allowed Marshall not only to continue with the issuing of the first edition but to follow it with a second edition.[42] Yet this protection eventually ran out, and in Underwood's view, this book may well have supplied evidence for the act of attainder against Cromwell in 1540, which argued that he had "secretly set forth and dispersed into all shires . . . great number of false erroneous books" including one that "hath expressly been against the said most blessed and holy sacrament."[43] Imprudent printing that failed to persuade readers and caused "public discord" by stirring up a "diversity of opinions" could have disastrous consequences. The commercial decisions that Godfray made were shaped by that awareness.

In this, Godfray's printing practices were in line with the careful tactics of evangelical writers, printers, and publishers abroad who had begun to foster the market he sought to enter. Before More's fall from power and Cromwell's ascendency made it possible for printers to experiment with printing evangelical texts in England, the Crown and Church had made it clear to printers, booksellers, and readers alike that books that strayed from accepted faith were forbidden.[44] In March 1529, a royal proclamation enforced general statutes against heresy and prohibited unlicensed and heretical books, providing a list of fifteen forbidden works. A second proclamation, issued three months later, focused more directly on the book trade and added six more books to the prohibited list. These royal proclamations were supported and strengthened by William Warham's *Public Instrument*, published in May that year, which included the judgments of university scholars on such works as *The Wicked Mammon, The Obedience of a Christian Man,* and *The Supplication of Beggars*. It also provided a sermon to be read by all parish priests to reassure the laity that these named works were full of "detestable and abominable heresies."[45] Nor were these idle words. In the persecution of heretics, ownership of banned books was used as significant evidence of heresy.

Under these circumstances, obtaining texts by writers such as Tyndale or Simon Fish before 1534 was not only difficult but dangerous, so writers and printers of evangelical texts had to find ways to persuade potential readers to take the risk of purchasing their smuggled work. These books were designed not only to bolster the faith of believers but to reach and convert new, tentative readers within a hostile environment. Andrew Pettegree observes that published under similar circumstances, "the evangelical book in France and the Netherlands eschewed the confident, self-advertising quarto format of the *Flugschriften*," which tended to have title pages containing "virtually no visual embellishments . . . made up almost wholly of text," and "very often concealed their content behind an uncontroversial anodyne title."[46]

In like fashion, the title pages of English evangelical texts seem remarkably bland to a modern reader used to thinking of writers like Tyndale as subversive firebrands. The vast majority avoided the unbridled heretical tone of the title page to Tyndale's *An Exposicion vppon . . . Mathew*,[47] which placed in opposition those who aim to restore "Moses lawe" and the "Scrybes and Pharises," who were explicitly described as "papistes." Instead, biblical translations and cribs were presented without fanfare and without any initial acknowledgment of the debate over vernacular translation, relying on the potential reader's desire for access to these texts and avoiding emphasizing the forbidden nature of that desire.

Thus there are title pages that carry no more than the titles, such as *The Newe Testamente, The Fyrst Boke of Moses Called Genesis, A Compendious Introduccion . . . vnto the Pistle off Paul to the Romayns*, and *The Exposition of the Fyrste Epistle of Seynt Ihon with a Prologge before it*.[48] Of Tyndale's works, only *The Prophete Jonas* has a more fulsome title page, and even then, it is a title page that frames the text within more acceptable humanist approaches to the scriptures. The title pages of these imported and forbidden works also emphasized the interest of the text to all Christian readers, denying any sectarian specificity. In this way, Fish's *The Summe of the Holy Scripture* is described as "the true Christen faithe / by the which we be *all* iustified . . . with an informacyon howe *all* estates shulde lyve."[49] Likewise, John Frith's *The Souper of the Lorde* recommends the text to the reader in the intimate—but nonspecific—third person: "that thou mayst be the better prepared and suerlyer enstructed."[50]

But if these texts needed to appeal to new, tentative readers, they also needed to signal to more radical readers that they would find the tract satisfyingly challenging of the old order. Often they achieved this through using marked or loaded vocabulary. We can see this particularly clearly in two of Tyndale's earliest and most influential tracts: *The Obedience of a Christian Man* and *The Parable of the Wicked Mammon*. The sparse title page of *The Obedience of a Christen Man and How Christen Rulers Ought to Governe*[51] advertises the book as being about the duties of both Christian men and their rulers, but also promises rather mysteriously that if the readers "marke diligently" they shall also "fynde eyes to perceave the crafty conveyaunce of all iugglers." Since the late fourteenth century, the term "iuggler" could mean "a parasite, deceiver, rascal" and in Lollard tracts had begun to be used as a derogatory term for religious. In *Piers the Ploughman's Creed*, for instance, the narrator calls the Carmelites "jugulers and iapers," who deceive "the folke with gestes of Rome," marking the kinship between Carmelite preacher and wandering minstrel.[52] On this title page, then, the word functions as a code for those familiar with the idiom of radical religious critique signaling the likely evangelical nature of the tract. For less informed readers, there is simply the promise of an additional bonus: learning the tricks of would-be deceivers, not necessarily religious ones.

The title page of the tract now known as *The Parable of the Wicked Mammon*[53] is much more verbose but makes similar maneuvers. The book has an unusual title page that not only presents the title of the text but gives a précis through a homely analogy, "That fayth the mother of all workes iustifieth vs / before we can bringe forth anye good worke: as the husbonde maryeth his wife before he can have any lawefull chyldrene by her." The way this title page functions is suggested in the next extant edition, when this material is left to the final pages and renamed "A shorte rehearsall or summe of thys present treatyse of iustifycation by faith."[54] The first three lines of the title page are laden with words that had become heavily freighted by this point—"faith," "iustifieth," "good worke"—and would appeal to sympathetic readers while piquing the curiosity of others only vaguely aware of the debate. However, the argument presented in brief does much to present the text not as an evangelical diatribe against and wholesale rejection of good works but as a careful explanation of how faith and good works interrelate, making the work seem less a matter of controversy and more a matter of common sense.

Like later Renaissance texts that, in Roger Pooley's words, use "apparently contradictory gestures"[55] to attract different types of reader, it seems that the function of most early evangelical title pages was to appeal to multiple readers, an aim that is sometimes developed in accompanying tabula and notes. Just as other types of book might be "demonstrably multifaceted [and] aimed at several social classes simultaneously,"[56] these early evangelical title pages are deliberately pitched at a spectrum of readers, from those already committed to heterodox ideas to those as yet still committed to the practices and beliefs of the Catholic Church but who might, with care, be encouraged to engage with a different type of thinking. There is not space here to illuminate the ways in which other paratextual elements of these evangelical tracts were exploited to simultaneously encourage tentative readers and catch the eye of the converted. However, even this brief discussion places Godfray's printing in context and reveals the extent to which he had absorbed the lessons of these earlier tracts.

This is immediately apparent in the type of evangelical material Godfray printed and the ways in which he presented it. With three exceptions, which are discussed below, he focused primarily on publishing translations that revealed their evangelical nature through the translator's linguistic choices rather than outright engagement with doctrinal debate. Moreover, Godfray's editions tended to downplay their controversial nature. For instance, the only text that the STC attributes to Godfray which named a heretical author and was explicitly listed among forbidden books by state and ecclesiastical proclamation was *The New Testament*, and it is notable that—like the edition of *A Treatise on Pyctures and Ymages*—Godfray omitted his name from its colophon. More often, he chose to omit the name of the author, as with his edition of *Diuerse Fruitfuall Gatherings* discussed below, or to further obscure it, as with his edition of George Joye's *The Psalter of Dauid*. The first edition of this text had been printed in 1530 by Martin de Keyser, who had already taken steps with Joye to anonymize its production. It was originally presented as a faithful translation "aftir the texte of Feline" (STC 2370), a pseudonym for Martin Bucer, with a prologue by Johan Aleph, a pseudonym for George Joye, and the false imprint attributing its production to "Francis foxe" in "Argentine" rather than to de Keyser.[57] When Godfray printed his edition, he kept the reference to "Felyne," clearly trusting in its pretense, but omitted the greeting by Johan Aleph, which marked the translation as the product of a foreign pen addressing "the Englishe nacion" and explicitly placed it within the freighted environment of exiled writers and translators.

Another way in which Godfray tailored his evangelical printing to the uncertain reception of the mid-1530s was to choose his material carefully so that its nature was not immediately obvious. *The Psalter* is characteristic of such a choice. Although it offered vernacular scriptural translation, which was technically forbidden, the "interest in possessing such [texts] extended far beyond the circles of those who fully endorsed the Protestant agenda."[58] Moreover, in writing *The Psalter*, Joye had emphasized the importance of obedience to the Crown—exhorting that "no man resyste his kinge" in his gloss of Psalm 75—and only intermittently ventured onto controversial matters. For instance, the argument for Psalm 16 ventures into the debate on faith and works in arguing that "god hath no nede of... goodes," that all "goodes oughte to serue ... poore neighbours," and that "they that bestowe their goodes of any other thyng than profyteth these sayntes [i.e., poor neighbors] / make Idols with them." This critique is then extended in the argument for Psalm 50, which states the importance of the gospel and faith over good works:

> Asaph declareth howe mightely god wolde call vnto him / all natyons of the worlde by the gospell / delyuerynge by his mightye power his chosen: also howe that he wolde than requyre of his / rather faythe 7 knowlege and declaringe of his goodnesse / than sacrifyces or workes / and howe greuously he wyll curse 7 entreat them that boste them of his relygyon without the pure study of his true worship.

However, these Lutheran notes were not the focus of the volume. Instead, the principal effect of *The Psalter* was to encourage the reader to trust in God through the example of David. As the argument for Psalm 27 puts it, David "remembringe the promyse of god / dyd animate himself strongly agaynst so presente 7 stormy tempestes... [and] excyteth humselfe to truste strongly in god." Joye's *Psalter* was designed to appeal to potential readers' desire for scriptural translation and, having taken advantage of that desire, to begin to teach them to value faith over works through the explanations of the Psalms. For those already committed to the principle of *sola fide* but aware of the continued risk of persecution, it also subtly offered consolation. It was not, however, an overtly evangelical volume.

Godfray's edition of the anonymous *The Fountayne or Well of Lyfe*—a translation of the biblical compilation *Fons vitae* published by Martin de Keyser in 1533—would have appeared similarly conservative and acceptable to adherents of traditional religion at first reading.[59] Although it expresses the hope that the reader "parauenture ... mightest seke" the quotations "after in the Bible," it does not offer a full biblical translation. It also presents the quotations as "consolation or comfort" not in opposition to what the traditional Church offered but to the physical help given by "parentes 7 frendes" who could provide only "bodyly helth / 7... hope of lenger lyfe" (sig. A2r). The prefatory letter "to the christen reder" even seems to suggest it was a conservative text, one aligned against those the traditional Church labeled heretics, which would help the reader leave "all co<i>n</i>tagions 7 pudels / that may infecte thy minde with errour / heresye / and sedycio<i>n</i>" (sig. A3v).

Yet the title, the metaphor of contagious puddles, and the prominent use of Jeremiah 2:13 to conclude the preface—"My people have commited two euyls / they haue forsaken me / that am wel of the water of life / and haue dygged out broken cisterns that can hold no water" (sig. A3r)—connected it to recently published humanist and evangelical tracts that presented the traditional Church, not evangelicals, as having poisoned the waters of God's teachings. For instance, in the translation of the *Enchirdion militis christiani* printed by Wynkyn de Worde for John Byddell in 1533, Erasmus laments that "we haue phylistyans whiche do preferre y\e/ naughty erthe to the lyuely fountaynes" and:

> caste in naughty erthe / and with a corrupte interpretacyon they stop vp the vaune / and driue away y\e/ dygger: or at the leste they make it so muddy with claye 7 fylthynesse / that who so euer drinketh therof shall drawe vnto hym more slyme 7 naughtynesse than he shall good lycour.[60]

Similarly, Tyndale promises in the *Parable of the Wicked Mammon* to "bri<i>n</i>ge the scripture vnto the right sense 7 to digge againe y\e/ welles of Abraha<i>m</i> 7 to purge 7 cle<i>n</i>se the<i>m</i> of the erth of wordly wisdo<i>m</i>e / where with these philistenes have stopped the<i>m</i>."[61] He also describes Christ in the *Exposition vnto the V, VI, and VII Chapters of Matthew* as "oure spiritual Isaac," who "diggeth agayne the welles of Abraham: whiche welles the scribes and phareses... had stopped and filled vp with the erth of their false exposicions."[62]

It is, however, the final "oryso<i>n</i>s / prayers / 7 exhortacyons" added at the end of the *The Fountayne or Well of Lyfe* that shift the tone of the volume subtly. In Merten de Keyser's version of *The Fountayne or Well of Lyfe* these prayers were added "*ne charta maneret uacua*" (sig. H4v) and were used as a practical and meaningful means of filling the last four blank folios of an eight-leaf quire. However, in Godfray's version of *The Fountayne*, there was no need to do this, since the text proper concluded on the penultimate page of an eight-leaf quire, so the decision to include the prayers and the addition of a four-leaf quire to accommodate them suggests their significance in the conception of this English translation. They are explicitly martial in tone and seem chosen to bolster the faith of the persecuted with headings such as "A blame of them that mistrust in batayle" (sig. G8r), "The exortation of

Asarye son to Obed in warre 7 tyme of vexation" (sig. H1r), "The prayer of Josaphat against his enemyes" (sig. H2r), and "The prayer of Judas redy to fight with his enemys" (sig. H3r). Indeed, the final page of print is taken up with "The prayer of Judas to the people," set in eye-catching hourglass fashion, which exhorts, "although our tyme draw nere yet let vs dye with ma[n] hode / for the loue of our brethren / and let vs nat brynge our honour to rebuke" (sig. H4r).

The effect of these prayers is to cast *The Fountayne* subtly as a text of consolation in a period of spiritual persecution. As Susan Felch puts it, "*The Fountayne*'s conservative rhetoric ... is pressed into a reformist narrative that highlights the moral responsibilities of the Christian life, set within a context of spiritual warfare."[63] In this context, the explanation that the prayers were added "to the entent that the boke shuld be replenished" (sig. G8r) suggests not the filling of blank space but the encouragement of resistance to spiritual persecution and the continued pursuit of biblical truth to bring about the replenishment of the wells of Abraham. In this way, readers already open to evangelical thought might be encouraged to buy the volume, recognizing its place within a larger discourse, while others of a more neutral bent might be brought to greater scriptural understanding without being frightened away.

In addition to carefully selecting the material he printed, Godfray adapted other volumes to make them more politic. One example of this is his edition of *Dyuers Frutefull Gatherynges*, also known as *Patrick's Places*, which was first printed by S. Cock in Antwerp between 1528 and 1532 and originally consisted of a set of theses by the evangelical Patrick Hamilton (1504?–1528) translated into English and prefaced by John Frith, who would later be burned for his heterodoxy.[64] In his preface to the first edition, Frith refers explicitly to Hamilton's execution for heresy in February 1528: "because he wolde not denye his savioure christ at their instance they burnte him to ashes" (fol. 1r). It was Frith's outrage at this that prompted him "to pub[l]ish vnto the hole worlde / what a man the monsters haue murthered" through the printing of this "litle treatise." Not only were the author and translator known evangelicals, the text itself was markedly unorthodox in the distinction it drew between the law and the gospel—"The lawe sayeth / paye the dette | The gospell sayeth Christ hath payed it" (fol. 3r)—and the emphasis on justification through faith alone—"No man is iustefyed by the dedes of the lawe / but by the faith of Iesu Christ" (fol. 6v). The combination of this text's author, translator, theology, and place of publication can have left a contemporary English reader in little doubt about its controversial nature.

Indeed, the first English printer of this text, Robert Redman, seems to have simultaneously acknowledged this and tried to play it down.[65] On the one hand, he entitled his edition (1534?, STC 12731.8) *Dyuers Frutful Gatherynges of Scripture and Declarynge of Fayth and Works* rather than "Patrikes

*Places."*⁶⁶ By doing so, he alerted readers to the tract's relevance to contemporary religious debate and where they could find additional copies. On the other hand, he carefully removed the preface by the infamous John Frith, with its identification of the author as the condemned Patrick Hamilton. It seems that Redman wanted to take commercial advantage of the interest in this topic but was ambivalent about whether it was safe to do so.

When Godfray printed the next edition in about 1532, he, too, seems to have been persuaded of the commercial potential of printing the text, retaining the title, and adding his own imprint. However, he also added three folios of criticism—in the St. German stamp—focused on ecclesiastical corruption and late-medieval devotional practice. The text that follows shifts the emphasis away from a complete denial of the efficacy of good works to a rejection of particular late-medieval practices such as "fastyng / keping of holy dayes / watchyng / prayeng / 7 syngynge longe prayers / dayly / 7 all day heryng of masses / settyng vp of candels / ronnyng on pylgrymages" (sig. B8r). This material was taken, without acknowledgment, from chapter twelve of *The Summe of the Holye Scripture*, translated by the evangelical Simon Fish and first printed in Antwerp in 1529.

One way of interpreting this addition is to see it as evidence that Godfray was unconvinced that Redman had done enough to alleviate risk and so presented the text as part of the royally sanctioned criticism of traditional Church power and practice, obscuring its doctrinal focus. The fact that Godfray repositioned *Patrick's Places* by selecting a section from another banned evangelical tract suggests his familiarity with such material as well as a finely attuned—and somewhat wry—sense of what was and what was not considered acceptable. However, these changes also seem designed to entice resistant readers steeped in traditional religion into reading material that was both still forbidden and probably uncomfortably challenging. Godfray's edition of *Patrick's Places* surrounds evangelical ideas with innocuous material, beginning with an unremarkable discussion of the Ten Commandments and ending with the increasingly familiar critique of the excesses of religious works. It turns a clearly heretical work into one that, like Joye's *Psalter of David,* any reader might comfortably pick up as a basic work of catechetical instruction and be gently introduced into the fundamentals of evangelical teaching.

Godfray's two editions of *A Pathway unto Scripture*—published around the same time as *Patrick's Places* ⁶⁷—adopt a similar tactic for enticing a reader by broadening the text's appeal through adaptation. The majority of each edition is taken up by Tyndale's reworking of the preface to his 1525 Cologne *New Testament*, which he probably composed around 1530.⁶⁸ Godfray's editions, however, append two further texts to Tyndale's *Pathway*: "A letter sent vnto a certayn frende / to enstructe him in the vnderstandynge of the scripture / translated out of French into Englysshe" (sigs. D5r–G6r) and "Of gouernours / as Iudges / baylyfes / 7 other lyke / An information after the gospel" (sigs. G6r–H4v). (Michael Whiting does not believe either to be "Tyndale originals," though there are echoes of his language throughout.)[69]

While *A Pathway* offers readers an introduction to key terms so that they could understand the *New Testament* according to evangelical belief, the letter suggests how the reader might build biblical reading into his or her life. The writer encourages readers to bear with them constantly the remembrance of scriptural quotation with such admonitions as "studye in that daye 7 nyght / and in all places goynge and commynge / let that neuer slyde out of your hert nor mynd all your studye to rede 7 vnderstande these holy wordes in all humylytie of hert" (sig. G4r).

The tract "Of gouernours" complements this by further demonstrating the relevance of the bible to everyday life, stating at its outset that, "the gospell is written for all persones / 7 for all estates of the worlde. And there is none estate in the worlde / but that he may fynde in the gospell howe that he shuld lyue if that he wyll folowe it" (sig. G6r–v). It then goes on to suggest better ways in which the commonwealth might be secured, including provision for the poor, and concludes with biblical quotations relevant to the good living of "husbandes," "wyues," "fathers 7 moders," "children," "maisters," "seruauntes," and "wydowes." For instance, "fathers 7 moders" are advised according to Ephesians 6, "Ye fathers / moue nat your chyldren to wrath / but bringe them vp with the nurter 7 information of the lord."

In this way, Godfray's editions of *A Pathway* widens the appeal of Tyndale's tract, helping potential readers to see how such a knowledge of scriptural basics might inform their way of living. It gives a practical slant to a text otherwise concerned solely with the theology and salvation of the reader. We might think of this as analogous to adaptations of more conservative religious tracts such as Richard Whitford's *A Work for Householders,* which had the economic guide *A Policy for Householders* appended to it in order to extend its appeal to the perhaps less religiously concerned, more pragmatic layman.[70] Since the first Continental editions do not survive, we cannot be certain that the addition of these two texts to *A Pathway* was Godfray's innovation. Nevertheless, it is in keeping with his adaptation of *Patrick's Places* and—even if not his innovation—shows a continuing interest in printing texts with a wider appeal.

The kinds of texts that Godfray printed, the formats he preferred, and the adaptations he made highlight the need to think about the ways in which early printers sought to sell previously forbidden material and the ways in which they whetted what Loades calls the enormous "appetite of Londoners for controversial ephemera." The "contradictory gestures" of Godfray's evangelical editions seem prompted by a keen consciousness that religious identity was fluid in this period. As Alec Ryrie and Peter Marshall remind us, "in earlier decades [of the Reformation], there was no agreed terminology at all. Reformers spoke of themselves as brethren, as gospellers or evangelicals, or simply as true Christians. They were also unwilling to let go of the term 'Catholic.'"[71] In a world where even Luther saw himself as a loyal son of the Church, marketing a forbidden book to readers meant appealing to a range of religious sensibilities from the radical to the wavering or curious traditionalist. Godfray seems to have recognized that an ideological commitment to spreading the good news could be furthered better by a canny negotiation of censorship and readers' anxieties than by intransigent printing.

Cambridge University

NOTES

1. Charles C. Butterworth, "How Early Could English Scripture Be Printed in England?" *University of Pennsylvania Library Chronicle* 14 (1947): 1–12, 10.
2. David M. Loades, "Illicit Presses and Clandestine Printing in England, 1520–1580," in *Too Mighty to Be Free: Censorship and the Press in Britain and the Netherlands*, ed. A. C. Duke and C. A. Tamse (Zutphen, Netherlands: Walburg Pers, 1988), 9–28.
3. James Kelsey McConica, *English Humanists and Reformation Politics under Henry VIII and Edward VI* (Oxford: Oxford University Press, 1965), 124. See also, e.g., David Loades's argument that "the main driving force behind this campaign was probably Thomas Cranmer, the Archbishop of Canterbury, but it was also consistent with Thomas Cromwell's plans for the promotion of the religious settlement which he had helped to engineer." David Loades, "Books and the English Reformation Prior to 1558," in *The Reformation and the Book*, ed. Karin Maag and Jean-Francois Gilmont (Aldershot, UK: Ashgate, 1998), 264–291, 280.
4. Andrew Pettegree, "Printing and the Reformation: The English Exception," in *The Beginnings of English Protestantism*, ed. Peter Marshall and Alec Ryrie (Cambridge, UK: Cambridge University Press, 2002), 157-180. 157.
5. Brad C. Pardue, *Printing, Power, and Piety: Appeals to the Public during the Early Years of the English Reformation* (Leiden, Netherlands: Brill, 2012), 85.
6. William Roy, *Rede Me and Be Nott Wrothe* (1462.7, 1528), sig. a4v.
7. Michael Saenger, *The Commodification of Textual Engagements in the English Renaissance* (Aldershot, UK: Ashgate, 2006), 31, 21.
8. Louis A. Schuster, Richard C. Marius, James P. Lusardi, and Richard

Schoeck, eds., *The Complete Works of St. Thomas More: The Confutation of Tyndale's Answer*, vol. 8 (New Haven, CT, and London: Yale University Press, 1973), 12.
9. John Foxe, *The Unabridged Acts and Monuments Online* (TAMO) (1576 edition) (HRI Online Publications, Sheffield, UK, 2011), http://www.johnfoxe.org, 3.497.
10. Edward Hall, *Hall's Chronicle: Containing the History of England during the Reign of Henry the Fourth, and the Succeeding Monarchs, to the End of the Reign of Henry the Eighth, in Which Are Particularly Described the Manners and Customs of Those Periods* (London: Printed for J. Johnson, et al., 1809), 762–763.
11. Schuster, *Confutation of Tyndale's Answer*, 12.
12. Thomas M. C. Lawler, Germain Marc'hadour, and Richard C Marius, eds., *The Complete Works of St. Thomas More: A Dialogue Concerning Heresies*, vol. 6 (London: Yale University Press, 1981), 331.
13. PRO SP 1/85, fol. 113v. Summary in J. S. Brewer, ed., *Letters and Papers, Foreign and Domestic, Henry VIII, Volume 7, 1534* (London: His Majesty's Stationery Office, 1920), http://www.british-history.ac.uk/letters-papers-hen8/vol7 1073. All other references to Letters and Papers (LP) are to this online edition.
14. *LP* VII, 423, PRO SP 1/83, fol. 52r.
15. *LP* XI, 1355.
16. Alec Ryrie, *Being Protestant in Reformation Britain* (Oxford: Oxford University Press, 2014), 259.
17. Julia Boffey, "John Mychell and the Printing of Lydgate in the 1530s," *Huntington Library Quarterly* 67 (2004): 251–260, 258.
18. Andrew N. Wawn, "Chaucer, the Plowman's Tale and Reformation Propaganda: The Testimonies of Thomas Godfray and *I Playne Piers*," *Bulletin of the John Rylands Library* 56 (1973): 174–192, 177.
19. Torrance Kirby, "Emerging Publics of Religious Reform in the 1530s: The Affair of the Placards and the Publication of Antoine De Marcourt's Livre Des Marchans," in *Making Publics in Early Modern Europe: People, Things, Forms of Knowledge*, ed. Bronwen Wilson and Paul Yachnin, Routledge Studies in Renaissance Literature and Culture 13 (New York and London: Routledge, 2010), 37–52.
20. Peter W. M. Blayney, *The Stationers' Company and the Printers of London 1501–1557*, 2 vols., vol. 1 (Cambridge, UK: Cambridge University Press, 2013), 277. He offers no explanation for these precise dates.
21. Ibid., 278. STC 23163.2, 1534?; STC 10634, pre-1534; STC 23963, 1531?
22. STC 5068, STC 26119, STC 2831.
23. Charles C. Butterworth, *The English Primers (1529–1545): Their*

Publication and Connection with the English Bible and the Reformation in England (New York: Octagon Books, 1971), 74.

24. STC 15988a, STC 17313.3, STC 13089a.
25. STC 5641. William A. Clebsch, *England's Earliest Protestants 1520–1535* (London: Yale University Press, 1964), 255. *LP* VII, 422–423.
26. Wawn also offers some help in dating a fourth text, *The Prayer and Complaynt of the Ploweman* (STC 20036), but only to a "date of c. 1536" based on "clear indications that a curious anti-monastic poem called the *Pilgrim's Tale*, written almost certainly between late 1536 and 1538, borrowed lines from [it]." Wawn, "Chaucer," 175.
27. Blayney, *Stationers' Company*, 1:356. STC 24239 is referred to hereafter as *A Treatise on Pyctures and Other Ymages*.
28. STC 3187, 1530?
29. STC 23963, 1531?
30. STC 1915, 1531?
31. STC 7377, 1533?
32. For a full discussion of *The Boke of Marchauntes*, see Kirby, "Emerging Publics."
33. STC 24455.
34. STC 24441, 24441.3, 24441.7.
35. STC 2788.5, 1537? and STC 24455.5, 1537?; STC 24468, 1533 and STC 24455.5, 1537?
36. Kirby, "Emerging Publics," 41.
37. Alex da Costa, "'Functional Ambiguity': Negotiating Censorship in the 1530s," *The Library*, 7th ser., 15 (2014): 410–423, 420.
38. Neither the first nor second edition of this work names Godfray as printer; both colophons simply state that it was "Printed for W. Marshall." However, as Rhodes observes, the type and ornaments used betray his involvement; Dennis Rhodes, "William Marshall and His Books, 1533–1537," *Papers of the Bibliographical Society of America* 58 (1964): 219–231, 227.
39. *LP* IX, 345. PRO SP 1/96 fol. 134r. Also partially quoted in William Underwood, "Thomas Cromwell and William Marshall's Protestant Books," *Historical Journal* 47 (2004): 517–539, 528.
40. *LP* IX, 358.
41. The only other volumes attributed to Godfray by the STC without his name in the imprint are *The Newe Testament* (STC 2831) and *Collyn Clout* (STC 22600.5). Two other texts exist only in fragmentary condition and may or may not have had imprints naming Godfray: *The History of Kyng Boccus and Sydracke* (STC 3187) and *A Panegyric of Henry VIII* (STC 13089a).

42. Underwood, "Thomas Cromwell," 528.
43. Ibid., 537.
44. For a more extensive analysis of censorship's effect during the early English Reformation see da Costa, "Functional Ambiguity." Other comprehensive surveys of early print censorship in England are John B. Gleason, "The Earliest Evidence for Ecclesiastical Censorship of Printed Books in England," *The Library*, 6th ser., 4 (1982): 135–141; Rudolf Hirsch, "Pre-Reformation Censorship of Printed Books," *Library Chronicle* 21 (1955): 100–105; Loades, "Books"; Fredrick Seaton Siebert, *Freedom of the Press in England 1476–1776* (Urbana: University of Illinois, 1952).
45. David Wilkins, ed. *Concilia Magnae Britanniae et Hiberniae, a Synodo Verolamiensi, A.D. 446 Ad Londinensem, A.D. 1717.*, vol. 3 (London: 1737), 727–737.
46. Andrew Pettegree, *Reformation and the Culture of Persuasion* (Cambridge, UK: Cambridge University Press, 2005), 173.
47. J. Grapheus, STC 24440, 1533?.
48. *The Newe Testamente* (STC 2823, 1526, P. Schöffer), *The Fyrst Boke of Moses Called Genesis* (STC 2350, 1530, J. Hoochstraten), *A Compendious Introduccion / Prologe or Preface vnto the Pistle off Paul to the Romayns* (STC 24438, 1526, P. Shoeffer), *The Exposition of the Fyrste Epistle of Seynt Ihon with a Prologge before It: by W.T.* (STC 24443, 1531).
49. STC 3036, 1529.
50. STC 24468, 1533.
51. J. Hoochstraten, STC 24446, 1528.
52. *Middle English Dictionary*, s.v. "jogelour," http://quod.lib.umich.edu/cgi/m/mec/med-idx?type=id&id=MED23872.
53. J. Hoochstraten, STC 24454, 1528.
54. James Nycolson, STC 24455, 1536.
55. Quoted in Saenger, "Commodification," 37.
56. Ibid., 45.
57. Bucer himself had adopted the pseudonym of Aretius Felinus in 1529 for his Latin commentary on the Psalms so that French and Lower German booksellers might buy it without fear since, as he explained to Ulrich Zwingli, "it is a capital crime to import into these countries books which bear our names." Constantin Hopf, *Martin Bucer and the English Reformation* (New York: Macmillan, 1946), 208.
58. Pettegree, *Reformation*, 174.
59. STC 11211, 1534?; USTC 437659.
60. STC 10479, sig. a8v.
61. STC 24454, 1528, fol. 1v.

62. STC 24440, 1533, fol. 2r.
63. Susan Felch, *Elizabeth Tyrwhit's Morning and Evening Prayers* (Aldershot, UK: Ashgate, 2008), 44–45.
64. Since Frith refers to Hamilton's death, it can only have been printed after February 1528, and as Frith returned to England in October 1532, he most likely gave the manuscript to Cook before this and certainly before July 1533, when he was also burned for heresy. There is no evidence of other Continental editions. The discussion of *Patrick's Places* draws on work previously published in the *Library*, see da Costa "Functional Ambiguity."
65. Full collation of the three editions suggests that Cook's was the first edition of *Patrick's Places* to be printed anywhere and that Redman's edition was the first surviving edition to be printed in England.
66. Cook's edition has no title page and uses the alternative title "Patrikes Places" only once, in the running title on fol. 1v.
67. STC 24462, 24463. The STC gives a date of "1536?" for Godfray's two editions of *A Pathway unto Scripture*, which translates to a range of "up to three years on either side" of 1536, so between 1533 and 1539.
68. The *Pathway* was in circulation by 1532, since More refers to the text in a *Confutation of Tyndale's Answer*, complaining that "after the Psalte ...children were wont to go to their Donate and their accidence but now they go straight to Scripture. And thereto have we as a Donate the book of the Pathway to Scripture." Quoted in J. W. Adamson, "The Extent of Literacy in England in the Fifteenth and Sixteenth Centuries: Notes and Conjectures," *Library*, 4th ser., 10 (1929–1930): 163–193, 180.
69. Michael S. Whiting, *Luther in English: The Influence of His Theology of Law and Gospel on the Early English Evangelicals (1525–35)* (Eugene, OR: Pickwick Publications, 2010), 239.
70. STC 25422, 1530.
71. Peter Marshall, "(Re)Defining the English Reformation," *Journal of British Studies* 48 (2009): 564–586, 574.

WORKS CITED

Adamson, J. W. "The Extent of Literacy in England in the Fifteenth and Sixteenth Centuries: Notes and Conjectures." *The Library* 4th ser., 10 (1929–1930): 163–193.

Blayney, Peter W. M. *The Stationers' Company and the Printers of London 1501–1557.* 2 vols. Vol. 1. Cambridge, UK: Cambridge University Press, 2013.

Boffey, Julia. "John Mychell and the Printing of Lydgate in the 1530s." *Huntington Library Quarterly* 67 (2004): 251–260.

Brewer J. S., ed. *Letters and Papers, Foreign and Domestic, Henry VIII, Volume 1, 1509–1514*. London: His Majesty's Stationery Office, 1920.
Butterworth, Charles C. *The English Primers (1529–1545): Their Publication and Connection with the English Bible and the Reformation in England*. New York: Octagon Books, 1971.
———. "How Early Could English Scripture Be Printed in England?" *University of Pennsylvania Library Chronicle* 14 (1947): 1–12.
Clebsch, William A. *England's Earliest Protestants 1520–1535*. London: Yale University Press, 1964.
da Costa, Alex. "'Functional Ambiguity': Negotiating Censorship in the 1530s." *The Library* 7th ser., 15 (2014): 410–423.
Felch, Susan. *Elizabeth Tyrwhit's Morning and Evening Prayers*. Aldershot, UK: Ashgate, 2008.
Gleason, John B. "The Earliest Evidence for Ecclesiastical Censorship of Printed Books in England." *The Library* 6th ser., 4 (1982): 135–141.
Hall, Edward. *Hall's Chronicle: Containing the History of England during the Reign of Henry the Fourth, and the Succeeding Monarchs, to the End of the Reign of Henry the Eighth, in Which Are Particularly Described the Manners and Customs of Those Periods*. London: Printed for J. Johnson, et al., 1809.
Hirsch, Rudolf. "Pre-Reformation Censorship of Printed Books." *Library Chronicle* 21 (1955): 100–105.
Hopf, Constantin. *Martin Bucer and the English Reformation*. New York: Macmillan, 1946.
Kirby, Torrance. "Emerging Publics of Religious Reform in the 1530s: The Affair of the Placards and the Publication of Antoine De Marcourt's Livre Des Marchans." In *Making Publics in Early Modern Europe: People, Things, Forms of Knowledge*, ed. Bronwen Wilson and Paul Yachnin, 37–52. Routledge Studies in Renaissance Literature and Culture 13. New York and London: Routledge, 2010.
Kirby, W. J. T. *Persuasion and Conversion: Essays on Religion, Politics and the Public*. Leiden, Netherlands: Brill, 2013.
Lawler, Thomas M. C., Germain Marc'hadour, and Richard C. Marius, eds. *The Complete Works of St. Thomas More: A Dialogue Concerning Heresies*. Vol. 6. New Haven, CT, and London: Yale University Press, 1981.
Loades, David. "Books and the English Reformation Prior to 1558." In *The Reformation and the Book*, ed. Karin Maag and Jean-Francois Gilmont, 264–291. Aldershot, UK: Ashgate, 1998.
Loades, David M. "Illicit Presses and Clandestine Printing in England, 1520–1580." In *Too Mighty to Be Free: Censorship and the Press in Britain and the Netherlands*, ed. A. C. Duke and C. A. Tamse, 9–28. Zutphen, Netherlands: Walburg Pers, 1988.

Marshall, Peter. "(Re)Defining the English Reformation." *Journal of British Studies* 48 (2009): 564–586.
———, and Alec Ryrie, eds. *The Beginnings of English Protestantism.* Cambridge, UK: Cambridge University Press, 2002.
McConica, James Kelsey. *English Humanists and Reformation Politics under Henry VIII and Edward VI.* Oxford: Oxford University Press, 1965.
Pardue, Brad C. *Printing, Power, and Piety: Appeals to the Public during the Early Years of the English Reformation.* Leiden, Netherlands: Brill, 2012.
Pettegree, Andrew. *Reformation and the Culture of Persuasion.* Cambridge, UK: Cambridge University Press, 2005.
———. "Printing and the Reformation: The English Exception." In *The Beginnings of English Protestantism*, ed. Peter Marshall and Alec Ryrie, 157-180. Cambridge, UK: Cambridge University Press, 2002.
Pollard, Arthur W. "The Regulation of the Book Trade in the Sixteenth Century." *The Library*, 3rd ser., 7 (1916): 18–43.
Reed, A. W. "The Regulation of the Book Trade before the Proclamation of 1538." *Transactions of the Bibliographical Society* 15 (1917-1919): 157-184.
Rhodes, Dennis. "William Marshall and His Books, 1533-1537." *Papers of the Bibliographical Society of America* 58 (1964): 219-231.
Ryrie, Alec. *Being Protestant in Reformation Britain.* Oxford: Oxford University Press, 2014.
Saenger, Michael. *The Commodification of Textual Engagements in the English Renaissance.* Aldershot, UK: Ashgate, 2006.
Schuster, Louis A., Richard C. Marius, James P. Lusardi, and Richard Schoeck, eds. *The Complete Works of St. Thomas More: The Confutation of Tyndale's Answer.* Vol. 8. New Haven, CT, and London: Yale University Press, 1973.
Siebert, Fredrick Seaton. *Freedom of the Press in England 1476-1776.* Urbana: University of Illinois, 1952.
Underwood, William. "Thomas Cromwell and William Marshall's Protestant Books." *Historical Journal* 47 (2004): 517-539.
Wawn, Andrew N. "Chaucer, the Plowman's Tale and Reformation Propaganda: The Testimonies of Thomas Godfray and *I Playne Piers.*" *Bulletin of the John Rylands Library* 56 (1973): 174-192.
Whiting, Michael S. *Luther in English: The Influence of His Theology of Law and Gospel on the Early English Evangelicals (1525–35).* Eugene, OR: Pickwick Publications, 2010.
Wilkins, David, ed. *Concilia Magnae Britanniae et Hiberniae, a Synodo Verolamiensi, A.D. 446 Ad Londinensem, A.D. 1717.* Vol. 3. London, 1737.

The Politics of Dedicating Printed Books and Manuscripts to King Henry VII

VALERIE SCHUTTE

In the last two decades, much work has been done on the analysis of the books and manuscripts of King Henry VII and his contributions to the Royal Library. Scholars have examined the types of books he collected and why.[1] My own work seeks to fill a gap in all of this very interesting and useful historiography. This essay examines a very specific portion of Henry VII's library: the printed books and manuscripts that were dedicated to him. These are texts not necessarily that Henry chose but that were often chosen for him. Texts dedicated to Henry VII generally came from two types of gifters, those who knew his interests and authors who may not have known his interests yet suggested texts that they thought Henry should read and support. More specifically, I am interested only in books and manuscripts that have textual dedications, not just armorials or miniatures directed to the king. Examining texts dedicated to Henry VII offers another point of view of the intersection of print and manuscript at the turn of the sixteenth century.

Recently, Julia Boffey suggests that early sixteenth century readers saw no distinct difference between manuscripts and printed books, as evidence exists that readers stored them together, bound them together, and read them together.[2] Printed books and manuscripts could be purchased from the same vendors, and print most likely offered only the increased availability of books.[3] For royalty, print presented a new medium for exerting political power, by which monarchs and their governments claimed authority and distributed information.[4] In 1490, King Henry VII became the first monarch to have the statutes of Parliament translated into English and printed so that all citizens could be informed of laws.⁵ One year earlier, he had used print to prepare his people for an upcoming military campaign in France. Henry had the earl of Oxford give William Caxton a French manuscript version of Christine de Pisan's *Faits d'armes et de chevalerie* for Caxton to translate into English and print.⁶ The prologue of Caxton's translation explains that the text was meant to instruct men how to behave in battle.⁷

Besides being a proponent of the printing press, it is well known that Henry VII was a collector of books and a contributor to the Royal Library. Janet Backhouse shows that Henry was very interested in acquiring printed books, unlike his predecessor, Edward IV, who was interested in collecting deluxe manuscripts. Yet she categorizes Henry more as a librarian rather than as a collector, because Henry focused on purchasing printed books and using them for reference instead of displaying them as desirable objects.⁸ The only books that Henry showed any interest in collecting were those printed by the Parisian printer Antoine Vérard, probably because of Henry's interest in French culture, as he had spent time in exile in France.⁹ As for Henry VII's manuscripts, those were primarily given to him as gifts by men who expected something in return, except for a few devotional manuscripts that were cherished family possessions and meant to be kept within the family.¹⁰ James Carley, in his works on the libraries of King Henry VIII, also demonstrates how Henry VII's collection of printed books and manuscripts was absorbed into that of his son.¹¹ I seek to add to this body of scholarship by examining specifically the printed books and manuscripts that were dedicated to Henry VII.

Henry VII probably developed his appreciation for books under the influence of his mother, Lady Margaret Beaufort.¹² Lady Margaret's name is directly associated with ten printed books. In seven books she is mentioned in the colophon as having commanded the printing or paid for a print run, or as a patron of the printer. Three other books have dedications to her. She even had her own royal printer, Wynkyn de Worde, whom she appointed in 1509. While Lady Margaret was involved with printing for the sake of passing on vernacular literature and religious tracts, Henry used the press to legitimize his authority by having official documents and parliamentary statutes printed.¹³

Henry VII was also involved with print beyond commissioning official government tracts. For example, in 1508, Henry requested an English translation from French of *The Passion of Owr Lord Iesu Christe*.¹⁴ In 1504, Henry commanded that William Faques print a psalter¹⁵ and that Richard Pynson print a Sarum Missal.¹⁶ Earlier, in 1495, there is evidence that Henry was involved with or at least had knowledge of Wynkyn de Worde's printing of John Trevisa's translation of Ranulf Higden's *Policronicon*.¹⁷ The colophon simply notes this was printed by de Worde in the tenth year of Henry VII's reign and commissioned by Roger Thorney. But the prologue by de Worde offers more detail. De Worde gives the history of the text and the additions made to the text since Higden's death, and notes that this is a "werke I haue fynysshed under the noble proteccyon of my moost drad naturell and souerayne lorde and moost crysten kyng."[18] Roger Thorney was a mercer and bibliophile who paid for texts to be printed by de Worde, is known to have owned several books and manuscripts, and even lent de Worde manuscripts to make printed copies from.[19]

As for Henry's relation to this text, it can probably be assumed that Henry and de Worde had established some type of relationship by this point, although not as serious a relationship as de Worde had with Lady Margaret Beaufort, Henry VII's mother. Lady Margaret adopted de Worde as her official printer in 1509, a position which he mentioned in some of his colophons of that year.[20] In 1494, Lady Margaret had de Worde print an edition of Walter Hilton's *Scala perfectionis* for her.[21] Henry could have come to know de Worde through his mother and established his own relationship with de Worde by 1495, when the *Policronicon* was printed. It would have benefited Henry to have de Worde print this text. During the previous two centuries, the *Polycronicon* was considered a standard historical chronicle of England and existed in many manuscript copies. De Worde's printing of this text, which continues the chronicle to include the reign of Henry VII, would have legitimized Henry's own authority by adding his achievements to this important historical account of England. Yet it is strange that it was not dedicated to Henry. Perhaps this is because Thorney paid for the print run, so it would not have been right to dedicate a book to one man that a different man paid for.

It is difficult to determine the books that were dedicated to Henry. Some have probably been lost over time, and some of those that are extant exist in only fragmented copies. As for dedications to printed books, Henry received nine. Two of these are products of his well-known relationship with Antoine Vérard. Henry was given two others that were foreign printings, one from a group of men asking for a favor and the other from a man well known to Henry who was trying to save his reputation and patronage relationship with the king. The other five came from two men who were members of Henry's court.

Antoine Vérard presented to or sold to Henry forty-two books. Yet he dedicated just two books to Henry VII, and these two dedications should be considered only lightly, as both books were first dedicated to Charles VIII, and Henry's name simply replaced Charles's with no other change to the dedications.[22] In fact, Vérard added dedications to twenty-one books, and it appears as though he avoided sending Henry books with dedications so that he did not have to alter them with Henry's name.[23]

In the New York Public Library copy of Henry Suso's *Orloge de sapience*, Charles's printed name was replaced with "Henry septisme" and no other decoration specific to the English king was added.[24] The prologue to this book is a paragraph in French, generic even in its language meant for Charles. It explains the subject matter of the book, why Vérard decided to print it, and how the book adds to Christian morality. Typically, it ends with prayers for the king and readers of the book.[25] *Le grant Boèce de consolation* was printed five months later (sometime in 1494) than the *Orloge*, and its dedication is also a single French paragraph, but it is accompanied by a miniature of Henry VII receiving a book from Vérard.[26] In this prologue, the name "Charles VIII" was printed within the text but was then replaced with "Henry VII dengletre" in brown ink.[27] No other parts of the dedication were changed, and this dedication more specifically states how and why it related to Charles and his responsibilities as king. In it, Charles (and by extension Henry VII) is compared to Atlas because of his responsibilities, and he is offered this text so as to find consolation in his hardships because it emphasizes philosophy and faith.[28]

While these two books were dedicated to Henry VII, it is difficult to consider them seriously because they were not originally dedicated to him and not much effort was made to personalize them for Henry. Although Henry was clearly interested in purchasing books from Vérard, Vérard must not have been as interested in gaining patronage from Henry as he was from Charles.[29]

Henry was also the recipient of two foreign-printed book dedications, *De incliti et gloriosi protomartyris Anglie Albani* and *De vera philosophia ex qvattvor doctoribvs ecclesiae*. *De incliti* was dedicated by the abbot and monks of St. Pantaleon in Cologne to Henry VII in 1502.[30] The dedication, as well as the other twelve folios of this book, declares that part of St. Alban's relics are located in England and other parts are located at the monastery of St. Pantaleon and that the abbot and monks wish to have information on the life, miracles, and translations of St. Alban so that they can put together a complete history. The dedication asks Henry for help in gathering information and supporting their project. St. Pantaleon had a shrine to St. Alban, and the abbey had had Alban's relics since at least the tenth century.

Adriano Castellesi dedicated *De vera philosophia ex qvattvor doctoribvs ecclesiae* to Henry in 1507.[31] Castellesi was an Italian papal representative sent in 1488 to settle the civil war in Scotland who quickly found favor with Henry. Castellesi brought fellow Italian Polydore Vergil to Henry's court in 1502.[32] Castellesi received patronage and positions from Henry, becoming bishop of Hereford in 1503 and later bishop of Bath and Wells in 1504.[33] Castellesi even helped to obtain the papal dispensation that allowed for the marriage of Prince Henry to his brother's widow, Katherine of Aragon. However,

Castellesi had a dispute with another papal ambassador, Silvestro Gigli, who tried to discredit Castellesi. To prove his loyalty, Castellesi presented his palace in Rome to Henry in 1504 (currently the Palazzo Giraud-Torlonia) and even had it decorated with Henry VII's arms. In another act of loyalty, in 1507, Castellesi dedicated *De vera philosophia* to Henry. The dedication gives honor to Henry from the pope, whose office he serves.[34] Castellesi suggests that the church fathers were able to clarify scripture, but that sacred scripture cannot be understood through reading classical works like the writings of Aristotle. Finally, Castellesi says he dedicated this religious work to Henry because if Henry studies it he will find truth and salvation. Castellesi may have dedicated this work to Henry to repay him for all of his kindness and more than a decade of patronage in England, but more likely Castellesi was trying to regain favor with the king, as about this time his favor had run out.[35]

There were also two English authors who were seriously interested in gaining and keeping Henry's patronage by dedicating printed books to him. William Parron dedicated at least three printed books to Henry VII. Not much is known of Parron, apart from the fragments of biography that he mentions in his books and one entry of payment given to him in the Privy Purse expenses of King Henry VII. Parron served as an astrologer and doctor at Henry's court and by the late 1490s began producing yearly almanacs and prognostications.[36] According to Hilary Carey, Henry showed an interest in astrology as early as 1490. British Library MS Arundel 66 was presented to Henry VII in the 1490s and is a text that includes an almanac, constellations, and various prophecies. This manuscript was probably commissioned as a gift for Henry.[37] Parron served as Henry's personal astrologer, so it is not surprising that when Parron had his prognostications printed, he dedicated them to Henry.

Beginning in 1496, Parron wrote annual general prognostications that included prophecies for topics from eclipses to weather to predictions for specific monarchs.[38] Only four of these general prognostications survive: a fragment of an English translation from 1498;[39] a Latin prognostication printed on December 24, 1499 (for 1500);[40] another Latin edition printed in 1501 (for 1502);[41] and a final Latin edition printed in 1502 (for 1503).[42] The three sixteenth-century prognostications all begin with a five-line dedication to Henry VII, in which William Parron simply notes that his prognostications are dedicated to Henry and written by Parron. The first line of each dedication is now listed as the title for each of the works. For example, the dedication to the December 24, 1499, prognostication reads "*Ad serenissimum ac inuictissimum omniumque genere virtutum prestantissimum dominum henricum Anglie et Francie regem septimum dominumque Hybernie. Willielmi parroni placentini phisia de astrorum influx. Anni presentis. M.d. pronosticon libellus.*"[43] In light of these three dedications to Henry VII and Parron's court service as an astrologer, it is not unreasonable to assume that the 1498 fragment was also from an edition dedicated to Henry VII. Nothing is known of Parron after 1503, although it has been suggested that he fell from favor after his 1502 prognostications proved to contain prophesies regarding Henry VII and his family that were grossly inaccurate.[44]

Parron also dedicated two manuscripts to Henry VII. In 1499, Parron wrote "De astrorum vi fatali," now held in the Bodleian Library.[45] Like his printed dedications to Henry VII, this dedication is a brief ten lines and mentions only the title of the book, the author, and that it is dedicated to Henry VII.[46] The dedication is written in red ink to differentiate it from the body of the manuscript, which is written in black ink. The first line of the actual text begins with a historiated initial "C," inside of which is an illustration of Henry VII holding a scepter and orb and seated on a throne surrounded by members of his court. This dedicated manuscript with personal prognostication for Henry was completed on October 15, 1499, and was probably given to Henry as a New Year's gift at approximately the same time that the 1499 printed prognostication was published, so that his private and public prognostications were available at the same time.[47]

Likewise, "Liber de optimo fato," written in 1502, was meant to be a "personal gift to the king timed to coincide with the appearance of the author's public prognostication for the coming year."[48] This particular manuscript was written after the death of Arthur and was a combined horoscope for Henry VII, Elizabeth of York, and Prince Henry.[49] Not only was the manuscript meant to explicate the excellent fortune of Prince Henry; one surviving copy also has a dedication to him in addition to the letter to King Henry VII.[50] For "Libero de optimo fato," the dedication is only a few lines and, as with all of Parron's other works, is embedded within the title information.[51] It, too, begins the text with a historiated "S" in which Henry is shown seated holding an orb and scepter and surrounded by members of his court.[52] Parron did not need to dedicate these manuscripts to Henry as he was already a recipient of Henry's patronage, but he probably understood "the value of a carefully targeted presentation manuscript" and how it could be used to stroke Henry's ego.[53]

Like William Parron, Stephen Hawes also had a literary relationship with King Henry VII. According to A. S. G. Edwards, Hawes was a poet born circa 1474. In 1503, he first appears in official records as a groom in the chamber of Henry VII; all of the first editions of his printed poems mention this post.[54] All of his first editions were also printed by Wynkyn de Worde, and the two men may have established a relationship courtesy of Lady Margaret Beaufort.[55] Henry appointed many poets such as Hawes to his chamber who used "their literary talents for political ends," especially those that promoted humanism and were able to elevate his court and educate his children.[56]

Beyond serving as a royal poet, Hawes presented a masque in front of Henry on Twelfth Night in 1506 and was rewarded for his performance.[57] Of the five printed poems by Hawes, only one has a dedication to Henry VII, while the other four mention Henry either in the colophon or at the end of the poem. The first printed poem by Hawes was *Here Begynneth the Boke Called the Example of Vertu* (1504).[58] The colophon of this book indicates that this poem was compiled in the nineteenth year of Henry's reign (1503/1504) and that it was first presented to Henry VII before it was printed.[59] The poem also ends with prayers for Henry VII, Lady Margaret Beaufort, and Prince Henry.[60] Only one folio of a 1509 edition exits, and the title page of the 1530 edition mentions Hawes's relationship to Henry.[61] In 1509, Hawes published *The Conuersyon of Swerers*.[62] In the colophon of this text, it is noted that Hawes was a groom of Henry VII's and that Wynkyn de Worde was serving as the printer to Lady Margaret Beaufort. After Henry VII's death, Hawes compiled a poem celebrating the accession and coronation Henry VIII.[63] *A Joyfull Medytacyon* was not explicitly dedicated to Henry VIII as it was written in celebration of him, but it does mention Hawes's service to Henry VII and how Hawes set out to emulate Lydgate. Hawes published one final poem in 1515, although he composed it sometime in 1510 or 1511, during the second year of Henry VIII's reign. The title page of *The Comforte of Louers* indicates that Hawes was "somtyme grome of the honourable chamber of our late souerayne lorde kynge Henry the seuenth," indicating that Hawes had no position in Henry VIII's chamber or household.[64]

The only one of Hawes's printed poems that was dedicated to Henry VII was *The Pastime of Pleasure*, first printed in 1509 but compiled sometime between 1505 and 1506, while Hawes was still in favor.[65] Three copies of the 1509 edition are extant and exist only as fragments; none of these copies has a dedication page. But as the *Pastime* was reprinted in 1517, 1554, and 1555, and each of these editions has the same dedication to Henry VII by Hawes, it is safe to assume that the dedication first appeared in the 1509 edition.[66] The dedication is comprised of eight rhyming paragraphs and attempts to do three things.[67] First, and most expectedly, it begs humility: Hawes asks Henry to accept his rude text. Second, it explains why Hawes chose to create this text. Primarily Hawes hoped that through his work he would eschew idleness, but he also meant to present texts to Henry VII in the manner that the monk Lydgate presented texts to Henry V, so as to place himself within the tradition of poets offering counsel to the monarch.[68] Third, it praises Henry and reinforces his legitimacy, declaring that God has given Henry much grace. Through grace Henry has sovereignty and dignity, which "hath to vs brought/ both welthe reste and peace."[69] For Hawes, Henry VII "dyscendeth/by the ryghtfull lyne ... to succede the crowne," has "hye renowne," and "by trewe ryght/sprange of the reed rose."[70]

It is not surprising that a poet would reinforce Henry VII's legitimacy and right to the crown in his dedication, as Henry had won the crown on the battlefield, and those in search of patronage would recognize that Henry VII was the rightful king all along. But what is surprising is that readers needed reminding of Henry's legitimacy and lineage as late as 1505 or 1506, in the nineteenth year of his reign. On February 2, 1503, his consort, Elizabeth of York, delivered a baby girl, Catherine, and both mother and daughter were dead only a few days later, with Elizabeth dying on February 11. By 1505, Henry was ready to enter into marriage for a second time and sent an envoy to Valencia to consider Queen Joanna of Naples, who had recently been widowed; he also considered other brides.[71] Perhaps Hawes's reminder of Henry's lineage was not meant for Henry but for potential partners to be reminded of the legitimacy of the king (without the legitimate claim of Elizabeth of York), thereby making him a good choice for matrimony.

What is interesting about these printed book dedications is that eight out of nine of them were given to Henry by men who already had his patronage. Hawes and Parron were members of his household, Castellesi worked in Henry's court as papal liaison to England for several years, and Henry had purchased approximately forty-two books from Vérard. None of these men needed more support from Henry. Vérard probably gave Henry two dedications simply as a courtesy for the numerous books that Henry had purchased from him. Hawes and Parron most likely gave Henry dedications so as to increase the readership of their texts. Having Henry's name attached would increase the desirability and salability of the texts to a wider audience, as a courtly audience would already be aware of the men and their writings. Moreover, these two men were familiar with Henry's interest in and collection of printed books, so it would have made sense for them to dedicate printed books to him instead of manuscripts. Only the monks at St. Pantaleon blindly asked Henry for something, and even then it was information and not money. Also, in having already established relationships with Henry, each of these men most likely knew that Henry preferred the new medium of print to manuscripts, so if he was going to sustain patronage it might be because of gifts of printed books.

Manuscript dedicators, on the other hand, had much less personal knowledge of the king and his interests, which is why they gave him specific dedications. The men who gave dedicated manuscripts to Henry were largely strangers and gave Henry manuscripts with the specific intent of gaining patronage.[72] Although print was an accessible medium, these dedicators gave manuscripts because "a finely produced manuscript, especially with illumination specific to the intended recipient, was considered a unique gift, more valuable and thus more flattering and respectful to its dedicatee than any printed book could be."[73] Moreover, a presentation manuscript was able to be targeted to a specific intended audience, the king, and could better serve as an introduction between the king and the one desiring patronage.[74] So for a man seeking patronage with no previous relationship with Henry, a dedicated manuscript was a very personal gift that could elicit a response from the king.

It is very difficult to confirm all of the manuscripts that were dedicated to Henry VII, as Henry was presented with many manuscripts, and scholars cannot agree if miniatures and prologues are the same as dedications. One such manuscript is BL Royal MS 12 A IX, which Paul Kristeller identifies as an oration dedicated to Henry.[75] This manuscript, however, is really a letter written by Johannis de Cisellis, a monk, asking for money for his theological studies, which is very laudatory of Henry, as any letter asking for money from the king would be. Another is Bernard Andre's *Vita Henrici Septimi*.[76] Andre was employed by Henry as an official court poet and worked for the first two Tudor monarchs for nearly thirty-five years. Although he wrote many works about the Tudors, he did not dedicate any to Henry VII, although three have prefatory letters, such as the one in *Vita* which simply notes that he is presenting Henry with the manuscript.[77]

Claude de Seyssel's translation of Xenophon's *Anabasis* is another such manuscript.[78] It was initially dedicated to Louis XII, and the copy in the British Library also contains a prologue to Henry VII and an image of Seyssel presenting his book to Henry.[79] This manuscript is often cited for Seyssel's praise of Henry's library at Shene, as mentioned in the prologue.[80] According to Rebecca Ard Boone, Seyssel was sent by Louis XII as French ambassador to Henry's court in 1506. Louis wanted Seyssel to dissuade Henry from marrying Margaret of Austria so that the English monarch would not be tied by marriage to enemies of France. At the English court, Seyssel delivered an oration to Henry explaining the circumstances around which the engagement between the future Holy Roman Emperor Charles V and Claude of France, daughter of Louis XII, was broken and how she instead became engaged to the dauphin, the future King Francis I. The oration was immediately published in England, but Seyssel, allegedly upset with its errors, corrected the oration and had it printed in Paris.[81] Seyssel's translation of Xenophon was likely presented to Henry as a gift upon his arrival at court.[82]

While aware of the nuances and differing understandings of manuscripts related to Henry VII, I have chosen to consider only manuscripts with textual dedications as being dedicated to Henry VII; I do not consider a prologue as a dedication without a specific dedication or miniatures of the king being presented with a book, so as to offer the best comparison to printed book dedications.

King Henry VII had eleven manuscripts dedicated to him by men in varying positions and seeking various forms of patronage.[83] Two manuscripts are mentioned above, those given to Henry by William Parron. The remaining nine were given by anonymous authors, Henry's librarian, and various clergy, poets, and papal representatives. Although these manuscripts were given by a variety of men, they were clearly all given in an attempt to earn some type of patronage.

Perhaps one of the first manuscripts given to Henry, and the earliest manuscript dedication that I could find, came from Thomas Forestier in 1485, just months after Henry took the throne.[84] Although Henry's army brought victory to the battlefield, it also brought an infectious new disease, which was grouped with other diseases to become known as the "sweating sickness." Within one month of the Battle of Bosworth, the sweating sickness reached London and killed hundreds.[85] For many, the disease came to be understood as divine intervention against the Tudors, signifying God's displeasure in Henry VII as monarch.[86] In response, Forestier dedicated to Henry his *Treatise on the Plague*, outlining its causes and cures. It is bound with several other manuscripts and occupies folios 70r through 77r, with the dedication appearing on folio 70r. Forestier was a Norman doctor residing in London at the time. He adapted his treatise from an important tract on the plague written by John of Burgundy (ca. 1338–1390) at the time of the 1365 epidemic.[87] In the dedication Forestier mentioned that others posted false information about the plague on gates and church doors and that with his text he meant to give correct information.[88] In giving Henry a dedicated manuscript of his text, he probably wanted Henry to patronize his text and send it to print as the official response to the plague.[89] Such patronage did not materialize, as Henry banned discussion of and printing about the disease in an effort to control the theories of God's displeasure, yet Forestier's treatise was printed in Rouen in 1490 and 1495.[90]

John Rous's *Historia regum Anglie* was also dedicated to Henry VII.[91] It was written in Latin, dedicated to Henry 1486, and is "unornamented."[92] This historical chronicle is important as it is frequently cited as being one of the earliest Tudor chronicles to villainize Richard III after his death. According to Nicholas Orme, Rous (ca. 1420–1492) was an antiquary who studied at Oxford beginning about 1437. He entered the priesthood and became a priest at the chantry of Guy's Cliffe near Warwick, where he stayed for the remainder of his life. Although Rous was a priest by occupation, he often engaged in historical research, especially of the earls of Warwick because of the location of his parish. He produced two rolls, a so-called Lancastrian Roll and a Yorkist Roll, in which he gives the history of the earls of Warwick, including Richard III, who was reigning when he completed the Lancastrian Roll. The *Historia regum Anglie* was the last major work that Rous wrote before his death. John Seymour, one of Rous's contemporaries at Oxford and later a canon of Windsor and surveyor of works at St. George's Chapel, encouraged

Rous to undertake a chronicle of England for the benefit of Edward IV so that Edward might choose who to commemorate in St. George's Chapel. Rous did not finish the chronicle until 1486, so he chose to add a dedication to Henry VII and made derogatory comments against Richard III, even though his two rolls had originally included positive comments about Richard.[93]

Quentin Poulet dedicated a manuscript about nobility and virtue to Henry in 1496.[94] Poulet was a scribe and illuminator whom Henry hired to be the first royal librarian, in 1492. He remained in that post until 1506. In the dedication, Poulet claims to have written this manuscript for Henry, though the text was originally composed by Hugues de Lannoy.[95] In addition to adding the preface, Poulet also emended the title to *Imaginacion de vraye noblesse*. The dedication is in French and begins with an illuminated capital "A" in which is a miniature of Poulet presenting his book to the king.[96] What is interesting about this dedication is that it is often noted that Henry was a collector of printed books, especially those of Vérard, and not a lover of manuscripts, in comparison with his predecessor, Edward IV. Poulet was in the best position to know this, as he was in charge of maintaining the king's library and probably acquired books for Henry as well. If Henry preferred printed books, why did Poulet present Henry with an illuminated manuscript? A treatise on nobility would have been a good theme of a work to present to Henry, yet if Henry was truly a collector of books and intent on building up a library, then it would have made more sense to present Henry with a printed book and not a manuscript.[97] Poulet's dedication, then, shows that while Henry preferred to purchase printed books, he also valued personal manuscripts.

Two other manuscripts dedicated to Henry VII are both in the same anonymous hand and are both translations of Giovanni Pico della Mirandola. In addition to having no known author, *Douze reigles en partie excitantes et en partie addressantes lhomme en la bataille espirituelle* also has no creation date but must have been completed sometime between 1485 and 1509, based on its dedication to Henry VII.[98] Likewise, *Lexposicion du xve pseaulme* has no known date of composition but was dedicated to Henry when he was king.[99] Both manuscripts have similar quatrain verse dedications, with that of *Lexposicion* being addressed to "*a treshault et trespuissant prince et mon tresredoubte souuerain seigneur te bon roy Henry VII.*"[100] The latter manuscript has two crudely illuminated capitals, one of which has a Tudor rose within it. As the dedications to these two manuscripts are simple four-line verses, it is unlikely that the author/translator had any personal relationship with Henry and most likely gave these two manuscripts as gifts in search of patronage.

Several Italians also presented Henry with manuscripts, as Henry was well known for offering his patronage to Italians as a way to establish a relationship with the papacy in an effort to bolster his legitimacy as king.[101]

(Henry's relationships with Parron and Castellesi are discussed above.) Having papal support meant having divine support, and having divine support helped to encourage the obedience of his subjects.[102] In 1496, an Italian, Johannes Michael Nagonius, presented Henry with a Latin panegyric prognostication.[103] Nagonius was an itinerant poet sent to England by Cardinal Francesco Todeschini-Piccolomini (later Pope Pius III), from whom he carried letters of recommendation.[104] Nagonius's manuscript has a miniature on the first folio of Henry riding in a chariot, beneath which is a scroll with a poem asking that Henry enjoy a long life. Opposite the miniature is the title of the manuscript, which also serves as the dedication. "*Ad divvm Henricvm Septmvm Anglie Francieque regem serenissimum potentissimum invictissimum et Hibernie dominvm illvstissimum de sorte et eius felici contra hostes Victoria pronostichon Iohannis Michaelis Nagonii civis Romani poeteque lavreati.*"[105] This prognostication treats Henry like a hero and forecasts the great things that he will do for England, as he has already done great things by bringing peace.[106] Nagonius presented many monarchs with manuscripts, but his gift to Henry is important because it was given to Henry as part of a diplomatic mission.[107] Henry must have been pleased with the manuscript, as he wrote to the cardinal to say so.[108] Again, this shows that Henry did enjoy personal manuscripts.

Filippo Alberici was a monk who served as a papal diplomat (for Julius II) and dedicated one manuscript to Henry VII. Alberici chose a version of *Tabula Cebetis* (ca. 1505–1507), a popular moral tale in the sixteenth century that was meant to serve as an allegory for life and choosing between virtue and vice.[109] Alberici was born in Mantua about 1470 and was greatly opposed to the Reformation and to Martin Luther.[110] Although Alberici spent time in both the English and French courts at the beginning of the sixteenth century, Sandra Sider posits that Alberici sent Henry the text from France when he was serving as a papal diplomat.[111] Alberici included both a six-line dedication (which preceded the prologue) at the beginning of the manuscript and a two-page epilogue also addressed to Henry. The introductory dedication, written in red ink to distinguish it from the rest of the prologue, is simple and notes the title of the manuscript, its intended reader, and its author: "*Ad excelsvm potentissimum : que Henricvm Septimvm angliae regem: Fratris Philippi Alberici mantvani carmen in tabvlam cebetis carminibvs ac pictvris intextam.*"[112] The epilogue also begins with two lines of red text with the rest in black ink. The epilogue, however, is very specific about Henry and praises him for bringing peace to England. In particular, Henry is described as glorious and triumphant, and it is stated that his name will go down in history.[113] Scholars are not in agreement whether Henry ever actually saw this manuscript, yet its author is one of many examples of Italian humanists who entered England and attempted to gain favor with the king.[114]

Francesco Portinari dedicated two copies of the same manuscript to Henry VII.[115] *Hospitalis titulo Sanctae Mariae Noue in urbe Florentina principium, ordo et institution* explains the rules and regulations of the Hospital of Santa Maria Nuova in Florence. The hospital was well known, and Henry VII asked Portinari for a copy of the rules because he was interested in founding a similar hospital in England. Portinari was a papal proto-notary at the English court, and his family had founded the Hospital of Santa Maria Nuova.[116] Henry chose the site of John of Gaunt's palace of the Savoy on the London Strand for his hospital, and his will provided for the establishment of the Hospital of the Savoy, whose rules were based on those of Santa Maria.[117] Penn asserts that it took near ten years to build and was "the first great architectural expression of the Italian Renaissance in England."[118]

Altogether, King Henry VII received twenty book dedications over the course of twenty-four years, all during his kingship; eleven of the dedications accompanied manuscripts, while nine prefaced printed books. To put this into perspective, Queen Mary I received thirty-three printed book dedications and eighteen manuscript dedications during her lifetime,[119] and Elizabeth I received 183 printed book dedications during hers.[120] This pattern of printed book and manuscript dedications to Henry is revealing. First, as Boffey claims, there was significant overlap between print and manuscript at the turn of the sixteenth century, yet custom manuscripts remained the prevalent form of literary gift when seeking patronage. Second, there is a marked contrast between printed books and manuscripts dedicated to the first Tudor king. The printed books given to him (all but one) were given by men who had established relationships with Henry. They knew of his interest in collecting printed books and gave their king books on subjects they knew he liked. These were not given to Henry in search of patronage but to strengthen already existing relationships.

The manuscripts given to Henry, however, were largely given by strangers who were presumably seeking patronage and thought that the best way to achieve this was to give Henry books custom-made by hand. This shows these men were not as familiar with Henry's interests in their assumption that manuscripts were the best way to court the king's favor. Although Parron and Poutlet, men with relationships with Henry, each gave him manuscripts, these were given in addition to printed books. Therefore, dedications to Henry show that the perceptions of Henry's interests were not the same as the reality of his interests. Manuscript dedicators gave him manuscripts because they thought that they would be more personal and elicit patronage, yet it was the men who gave Henry printed books who had the more lasting success at court.

Independent Scholar

Acknowledgments

I would like to thank Kathleen L. Scott for reading an earlier version of this essay and providing a very helpful critique.

NOTES

1. See Gordon Kipling, "Henry VII and the Origins of Tudor Patronage," in *Patronage in the Renaissance*, ed. Guy Fitch Lytle and Stephen Orgel (Princeton, NJ: Princeton University Press, 1981), 117–164; Janet Backhouse, "Founders of the Royal Library: Edward IV and Henry VII as Collectors of Illuminated Manuscripts," in *England in the Fifteenth Century: Proceedings of the 1986 Harlaxton Symposium*, ed. David Williams (Woodbridge, UK: Boydell Press, 1987), 23–41; Kathleen Scott, "Manuscripts for Henry VII, His Household and Family," in *The Cambridge Illuminations: The Conference Papers*, ed. Stella Panayotova (London: Harvey Miller, 2007), 279–286; T. A. Birrell, *English Monarchs and Their Books: From Henry VII to Charles II. The Second Panizzi Lecture, 1986* (London: British Library, 1987).
2. Julia Boffey, *Manuscript and Print in London, c. 1475–1530* (London: British Library, 2012), 79.
3. Ibid., 128.
4. Lotte Hellinga, "Prologue: The First Years of the Tudor Monarchy and the Printing Press," in *Tudor Books and Readers: Materiality and the Construction of Meaning*, ed. John N. King (Cambridge, UK: Cambridge University Press, 2010), 15, 16, 19.
5. Ibid., 19.
6. Christine de Pisan, *Here Begynneth the Table of the Rubryshys of the Boke of the Fayt of Armes and of Chyualrye* (Westminster: William Caxton, 1489?), STC 7269. Catherine Nall suggests that the copy of Pisan's *Faits* in the Huntington Library (Huntington Library, 59139) was likely the presentation copy given by Caxton to Henry, especially as it bears an inscription "thys booke the kynge gave me / M Rychemound"; Catherine Nall, "Margaret Beaufort's Books: A New Discovery," *Journal of the Early Book Society* 16 (2013): 214.
7. Hellinga, "Prologue," 19.
8. Backhouse, "Founders," 33, 38.
9. Janet Backhouse, "The Royal Library from Edward IV to Henry VII," in *The Cambridge History of the Book in Britain, Volume III: 1400–1557*, ed. Lotte Hellinga and J. B. Trapp (Cambridge, UK: Cambridge University Press, 2009), 272.
10. Janet Backhouse, "Illuminated Manuscripts Associated with Henry

VII and Members of His Immediate Family," in *The Reign of Henry VII: Proceedings of the 1993 Harlaxton Symposium*, ed. Benjamin Thompson (Stamford, UK: Paul Watkins, 1995), 187.
11. James Carley, *The Libraries of King Henry VIII* (London: British Library, 2000), xxiv.
12. Susan Powell, "Lady Margaret Beaufort and Her Books," *The Library* 6 (1998), 197–240.
13. Douglas A. Brooks, "'This Heavenly Boke More Precious than Golde': Legitimating Print in Early Tudor England," in *Tudor Books and Readers: Materiality and the Construction of Meaning*, ed. John N. King (Cambridge, UK: Cambridge University Press, 2010), 109.
14. *The Passion of Owr Lord Iesu Christe* (Paris: for A. Vérard?, 1508?), STC 14557.
15. *Psalterium ex mandato victoriosissimi Anglie regis Henrici Septimi cum psalmorum virtue feliciter incipit* (London: William Faques, 1504), STC 16257.
16. *Sarum Missale* (London: Richard Pynson, 1504), STC 16179.
17. Ranulf Higden, *Policronicon*, trans. John Trevisa (Westminster: Wynkyn de Worde, 1495), STC 13439.
18. Ibid., aa.iii.r.
19. Julia Boffey, "From Manuscript to Print: Continuity and Change," in *A Companion to the Early Printed Book in Britain, 1476–1558*, ed. Vincent Gillespie and Susan Powell (Cambridge, UK: D. S. Brewer, 2014), 19.
20. *The P[ar]lyament of Deuylles* (London: Wynkyn de Worde, 1509), STC 19305; *Nychodemus Gospel* (London: Wynkyn de Worde, 1509), STC 18566; Stephen Hawes, *The Conuersyon of Swearers* (London: Wynkyn de Worde, 1509), STC 12943; *Longe paruula* (London: Wynkyn de Worde, 1509), STC 23164.
21. Walter Hilton, *Scala perfectionis* (Westminster: Wynkyn de Worde, 1494), STC 14042.
22. Mary Beth Winn, *Anthoine Vérard, Parisian Publisher, 1485–1512: Prologues, Poems and Presentations* (Geneva: Librairie Droz, 1997), 138–153. Winn identifies eight books by Vérard as being specifically for Henry VII, but I consider only textual dedications, not armorials or miniatures of Henry.
23. Ibid., 147.
24. Ibid., 143. Another copy is held in the British Library that does not have the name change to Henry VII but does have English royal arms included.
25. Ibid., 293. See 293, fig. 5.6e for an image of the prologue.
26. Ibid., 325, fig. 5.8c.
27. Ibid., 143.
28. Ibid., 314–321.

29. Ibid., 153.
30. *De incliti et gloriosi protomartyris Anglie Albani: quem in Germania et Gallia Albinum vocant: conversione, passione, translatione, et miraculorum choruscatione* (Cologne, Germany: Martin of Werden, 1502). The dedication is located on folio 1; BL, General Reference, G.937.
31. Adriano Castellesi, *De vera philosophia ex qvattvor doctoribvs ecclesiae* (Bologna, Italy: per Giovanni Antonio I. Benedetti, 1507).
32. Thomas Penn, *Winter King: The Dawn of Tudor England* (London: Allen Lane, 2011), 244.
33. Thomas Brian Deutscher, "Adriano Castellesi," in *Contemporaries of Erasmus: A Bibliographical Register of the Renaissance and Reformation*, vols. 1–3, ed. Peter G. Bietenholz and Thomas Brian Deutscher (Toronto: University of Toronto Press, 1985), 278.
34. The dedication appears on Castellesi, *De vera philosophia*, fols. Ai.r–Aii.v.
35. Deutscher, "Adriano Castellesi," 278.
36. Martha Carlin, "William Parron," *Oxford Dictionary of National Biography* (Oxford: Oxford University Press, 2004).
37. Hilary Carey, "Henry VII's Book of Astrology and the Tudor Renaissance," *Renaissance Quarterly* lxv (2012): 665.
38. Carlin, "William Parron."
39. William Parron, *A Prognostication for 1498* (Westminster: Wynkyn de Worde, 1498), STC 385.3.
40. William Parron, *Ad Serenissimum ac inuictissimum omniumque genere virtutum prestantissimum dominum Henricum* (London: Richard Pynson, 1499), STC 494.8.
41. William Parron, *Ad Serenissimum ac inuictissimum omniumque genere virtutum prestantissimum dominum Henricum* (London: Richard Pynson, 1501), STC 494.9.
42. William Parron, *Ad Serenissimum ac inuictissimum omniumque genere virtutum prestantissimum dominum Henricum* (London: Richard Pynson, 1502), STC 494.10. A fragment of this edition is held at Westminster Abbey. Two leaves are used as pastedowns in another book. Westminster Abbey Library CC 24.
43. STC 494.8, a.i.r. "To the most serene and invincible and all powerful lord of excellent birth King Henry VII of England and France and lord of Ireland, William Parron doctor of astrology presents this book of prognositications at [the palace of] Placentia."
44. Carlin, "William Parron."
45. William Parron, "De astrorum vi fatali," 1499, Bodleian Library, MS Selden Supra 77.
46. The dedication appears on ibid., fol. 004r.
47. C. A. J. Armstrong, "An Italian Astrologer at the Court of Henry VII," in

Italian Renaissance Studies, ed. E. F. Jacob (London: Faber and Faber, 1960), 437. Penn suggests that this manuscript was an indirect reference to Warbeck and Warwick and how they deserved their bad fates. Penn, *Winter King*, 38.

48. William Parron, "Liber de optimo fato," BL, Royal MS 12 B.vi. A second copy exists in Bibliothèque Nationale, Paris, MS latin 6276. Armstrong, "Italian Astrologer," 452. See Scot McKendrick, John Lowden, and Kathleen Doyle, eds., Royal Manuscripts: *The Genius of Illumination* (London: British Library, 2011), entry #98.
49. Armstrong, "Italian Astrologer," 451.
50. Ibid., 451. The Paris copy has the dedication to Prince Henry.
51. Parron, "Liber de optimo fato," fol. 1v.
52. Ibid., fol. 2r.
53. Boffey, *Manuscript and Print*, 1.
54. A. S. G. Edwards, "Stephen Hawes," *Oxford Dictionary of National Biography* (Oxford: Oxford University Press, 2004).
55. A. S. G. Edwards, *Stephen Hawes* (Boston: Twayne Publishers, 1983), 20.
56. Ibid., 5, 8.
57. Penn, *Winter King*, 295.
58. Stephen Hawes, *Here Begynneth the Boke Called the Example of Vertu* (London: Wynkyn de Worde, 1504?), STC 12945.
59. Ibid., aa.iii.r. I cannot find a presentation manuscript.
60. Ibid., hh.iii.r–hh.iiii.v. Penn considers the poem to be a dedication to Henry VII and that Hawes wrote it hoping to become a tutor to the royal children. Penn, *Winter King*, 184.
61. Hawes, *Here Begynneth the Boke Called the Example of Vertu* (London: Wynkyn de Worde, 1509?), STC 12946; Hawes, *Here Foloweth a Compendyous Story, and It Is Called the Example of Vertu* (London: Wynkyn de Worde, 1530). STC 12947.
62. Stephen Hawes, *The Conuersyon of Swerers* (London: Wynkyn de Worde, 1509), STC 12943.
63. Stephen Hawes, *A Joyfull Medytacyon* (London: Wynkyn de Worde, 1509).
64. Stephen Hawes, *The Comforte of Louers* (London: Wynkyn de Worde, 1515), a.i.r, STC 12942.5; Penn, *Winter King*, 296.
65. Stephen Hawes, *The Pastime of Pleasure* (London: Wynkyn de Worde, 1509), STC 12948. Edwards offers an explanation for de Worde publishing many of Hawes's texts in 1509 and not when they were initially written. Edwards, *Stephen Hawes*, 20–24.
66. I would like to thank Mrs. Agnieszka Drabek-Prime, Rare Books Superintendent at Cambridge University Library, for checking the

library's copy. I would also like to thank Christian Algar, Reference Specialist on the Rare Books and Music Reference Team at the British Library, for checking the library's copy and providing me with images.
67. I would like to thank John Bidwell, Astor Curator of Printed Books and Bindings, at the Morgan Library and Museum for providing me with snapshots of the dedication. The Morgan Library holds the only known copy of the 1517 edition. Accession number PML 20895.
68. Edwards notes how Hawes invoked Lydgate in his poems; Edwards, *Stephen Hawes*, 18–19.
69. Hawes, *Here Begynneth the Passe Tyme of Pleasure* (London: Wynkyn de Worde, 1517), a.iii.r.
70. Ibid., a.iii.r–a.iii.v.
71. S. B. Chrimes, *Henry VII* (Berkeley: University of California Press, 1972), 287–293.
72. Backhouse, "Illuminated Manuscripts," 187.
73. Boffey, *Manuscript and Print*, 57.
74. David Carlson, *English Humanist Books: Writers and Patrons, Manuscript and Print, 1475–1525* (Toronto: University of Toronto Press, 1993), 21.
75. BL, Royal MS 12 A IX. See Paul Oskar Kristeller, *Iter Italicum*, vol. 4 (Leiden, Netherlands: Brill, 1989). Here Kristeller lists many manuscripts associated with Henry.
76. BL, Cotton MS Domitian A XVIII, fols. 126–228.
77. David Carlson, "The Writings of Bernard André (c. 1450– c. 1522)," *Renaissance Studies* 12 (1998): 229–250.
78. BL, Royal MS 19 C.vi.
79. Ibid., fol. 17r. Seyssel also presented copies of his translation to Louis XII and Charles II of Savoy.
80. Janet Backhouse considers this prologue by Seyssel to be a dedication; Backhouse, "Founders," 34; Backhouse, "Illuminated Manuscripts," 179. Kathleen Scott notes only that the manuscript was presented to Henry; Kathleen L. Scott, *Later Gothic Manuscripts, 1390–1490*, 2 vols. (London: Harvey Miller, 1996), 2:365.
81. Rebecca Ard Boone, *War, Domination, and the Monarchy of France: Claude de Seyssel and the Language of Politics in the Renaissance* (Leiden, Netherlands: Brill, 2007), 39, 65, 68. BL, General Reference, 12301.bb.9. The title of the oration is "Ad serenissimum Anglie regem Henricum Septimum oratio," so it is not actually a dedication to Henry.
82. See McKendrick, Lowden, and Doyle, *Royal Manuscripts*, entry #145. In this manuscript Seyssel also made mistakes, identifying the king as Henry VI and the royal motto as "Dieu est Mon Droit," rather than "Dieu et Mon Droit."
83. There may be a twelfth manuscript dedicated to Henry VII. BL, Royal

MS 16 E XIV was written by Henry Hault and finished by Gervasius Amoenus after Hault's death in 1508. Amoenus dedicated the manuscript to King Henry, but it could have been Henry VII or Henry VIII.
84. BL, Additional MS 27582.
85. Sean Cunningham, *Henry VII* (London: Routledge, 2007), 233–234.
86. Ibid., 234.
87. Joseph P. Byrne, *Encyclopedia of the Black Death* (Santa Barbara, CA: ABC CLIO, 2012), 197.
88. George Keiser, "Two Medieval Plague Treatises and Their Afterlife in Early Modern England," *Journal of the History of Medicine and Allied Sciences* 58 (2003): 58, 319.
89. Ibid., 319. Keiser makes a similar point in this work.
90. Thomas Forestier, *Contra pestilentiam* (Rouen, France: Guillaume Le Talleur, 1490); and Thomas Forestier, *Le regime contre epidemie et pestilence* (Rouen, France: Jacques le Forestier, 1495); Cunningham, *Henry VII*, 234.
91. BL, Cotton MS Vespasian A XII.
92. Scott, "Manuscripts for Henry VII," 283, n.50.
93. Nicholas Orme, "John Rous," *Oxford Dictionary of National Biography* (Oxford: Oxford University Press, 2004).
94. BL, Royal MS 19 C.viii.
95. See McKendrick, Lowden, and Doyle, *Royal Manuscripts*, entry #69.
96. The dedication and illuminated capital are on BL, Royal MS 19 C.viii, fol. 1.
97. Backhouse, "Founders of the Royal Library," 33, 38.
98. BL, Royal MS 16 E XXV.
99. BL, Royal MS 16 E XXIV.
100. "To the very high and very powerful prince and my redoubted sovereign good lord King Henry VII."
101. Penn, *Winter King*, 115–116.
102. Cunningham, *Henry VII*, 226.
103. York Minster Library MS XVI N.2.
104. Paul Gwynne, "The Frontispiece to an Illuminated Panegyric of Henry VII: A Note on the Sources," *Journal of the Warburg and Courtauld Institutes* (1992): 55, 266–270, pl. 47a.
105. "To the blessed most serene, powerful, and invincible King Henry VII of England and France and illustrious lord of Ireland, Johannes Michael Nagonius offers you a prognostication of victory against your enemies."
106. Ibid., 267.
107. For further details, see Paul Gwynne, *Poets and Princes: The Panegyric Poetry of Johannes Michael Nagonius* (Turnhout, Belgium: Brepols, 2012).

108. Gwynne, "Frontispiece," 270.
109. BL, Arundel MS 317. BL, Royal MS 12 C. iii, also by Alberici, was most likely also intended to be a gift for Henry VII. See McKendrick, Lowden, and Doyle, *Royal Manuscripts*, entry #111.
110. Sandra Sider, "'Interwoven with Poems and Picture': A Protoemblematic Latin Translation of the Tabula Cebetis," in *The European Emblem: Selected Papers from the Glasgow Conference 11–14 August 1987*, ed. Bernard F. Scholz, Michael Bath, and David Weston (Leiden, Netherlands: Brill, 1990), 5.
111. Ibid., 5.
112. BL, Arundel MS 317, fol. 1r. "To the most excellent and powerful King Henry VII of England: Brother Filippo Alberici of Mantua offers songs and pictures from the Tabula Cebetis." The prologue is located on fols. 1r–2r.
113. BL, Arundel MS 317. The epilogue is located on fols. 24r–24v. David Carlson suggests that the epilogue may have first been read aloud in Henry's presence before being printed as the epilogue; Carlson, *English Humanist Books*, 22.
114. Sider, "Interwoven," 5. Sider claims that Henry probably saw the text because of his interest in Italian humanists. David Rundle suggests that Henry probably did not see the manuscript because it is not in the inventories of books passed down to his son, and it bears a second dedication, so Alberici may have had to try to earn patronage from a second, less notable patron; David Rundle, "Filippo Alberici, Henry VII and Richard Fox: The English Fortunes of a Little-Known Italian Humanist," *Journal of the Warburg and Courtauld Institutes* 68 (2005): 144–145. Carlson suggests that Alberici's manuscript was a "magnificent failure"; Carlson, *English Humanist Books*, 21.
115. Bodleian Library, MS Bodley 488. The second copy, though not in the same hand, may have been a copy that Portinari kept for himself, BL, Additional MS 40077. J. J. G. Alexander, "Foreign Illuminators and Illuminated Manuscripts," in *The Cambridge History of the Book in Britain, Volume III: 1400–1557*, ed. Lotte Hellinga and J. B. Trapp (Cambridge, UK: Cambridge University Press, 2009), 55. I consider this second copy to be one of the eleven manuscript dedications.
116. John Henderson, *The Renaissance Hospital: Healing the Body and Healing the Soul* (New Haven, CT: Yale University Press, 2006), xxvi, 89.
117. Penn, *Winter King*, 254.
118. Ibid., 254.
119. Valerie Schutte, *Mary I and the Art of Book Dedications: Royal Women, Power, and Persuasion* (New York: Palgrave Macmillan, 2015).

120. Tara Wood, "'To the Most Godlye, Virtuos, and Myghtye Princess Elizabeth': Identity and Gender in the Dedications to Elizabeth I" (PhD diss., Arizona State University, 2008).

WORKS CITED

Primary Sources

Bibliothèque National, Paris, MS latin 6276.
Bodleian Library, MS Bodley 488.
Bodleian Library, MS Selden Supra 77.
British Library, Additional MS 27582.
British Library, Additional MS 40077.
British Library, Arundel MS 317.
British Library, Cotton MS Domitian A XVIII.
British Library, Cotton MS Vespasian A XII.
British Library, General Reference, 12301.bb.9.
British Library, Royal MS 12 A IX.
British Library, Royal MS 12 B.vi.
British Library, Royal MS 12 C. iii.
British Library, Royal MS 16 E XIV.
British Library, Royal MS 16 E XXIV.
British Library, Royal MS 16 E XXV.
British Library, Royal MS 19 C.vi.
British Library, Royal MS 19 C.viii.
Castellesi, Adriano. *De vera philosophia ex qvattvor doctoribvs ecclesiae.* Bologna, Italy: per Giovanni Antonio I. Benedetti, 1507.
De incliti et gloriosi protomartyris Anglie Albani: quem in Germania et Gallia Albinum vocant: conversione, passione, translatione, et miraculorum choruscatione. Cologne, Germany: Martin of Werden, 1502.
Forestier, Thomas. *Contra pestilentiam.* Rouen, France: Guillaume le Talleur, 1490.
———. *Le regime contre epidemie et pestilence.* Rouen, France: Jacques le Forestier, 1495.
Hawes, Stephen. *The Comforte of Louers.* London: Wynkyn de Worde, 1515. STC 12942.5.
———. *The Conuersyon of Swearers.* London: Wynkyn de Worde, 1509. STC 12943.
———. *Here Begynneth the Boke Called the Example of Vertu.* London: Wynkyn de Worde, 1504?. STC 12945.
———. *Here Begynneth the Boke Called the Example of Vertu.* London: Wynkyn de Worde, 1509?. STC 12946.

———. *Here Begynneth the Passe Tyme of Pleasure.* London: Wynkyn de Worde, 1517.
———. *Here Foloweth a Compendyous Story, and It Is Called the Example of Vertu.* London: Wynkyn de Worde, 1530. STC 12947.
———. *A Joyfull Medytacyon.* London: Wynkyn de Worde, 1509.
———. *The Pastime of Pleasure.* London: Wynkyn de Worde, 1509. STC 12948.
Higden, Ranulf. *Policronicon*, trans. John Trevisa. Westminster: Wynkyn de Worde, 1495. STC 13439.
Hilton, Walter. *Scala perfectionis.* Westminster: Wynkyn de Worde, 1494. STC 14042.
Longe paruula. London: Wynkyn de Worde, 1509. STC 23164.
Nychodemus Gospel. London: Wynkyn de Worde, 1509. STC 18566.
The P[ar]lyament of Deuylles. London: Wynkyn de Worde, 1509. STC 19305.
Parron, William. *A Prognostication for 1498.* Westminster: Wynkyn de Worde, 1498. STC 385.3.
———. *Ad Serenissimum ac inuictissimum omniumque genere virtutum prestantissimum dominum Henricum.* London: Richard Pynson, 1499. STC 494.8.
———. *Ad Serenissimum ac inuictissimum omniumque genere virtutum prestantissimum dominum Henricum.* London: Richard Pynson, 1501. STC 494.9.
———. *Ad Serenissimum ac inuictissimum omniumque genere virtutum prestantissimum dominum Henricum.* London: Richard Pynson, 1502. STC 494.10.
The Passion of Owr Lord Iesu Christe. Paris: for A. Vérard?, 1508?. STC 14557.
Pisan, Christine de, *Here Begynneth the Table of the Rubryshys of the Boke of the Fayt of Armes and of Chyualrye.* Westminster: William Caxton, 1489?. STC 7269.
Psalterium ex mandato victoriosissimi Anglie regis Henrici Septimi cum psalmorum virtue feliciter incipit. London: William Faques, 1504. STC 16257.
Sarum Missale. London: Richard Pynson, 1504. STC 16179.
York Minster Library MS XVI N.2.

Secondary Sources

Alexander, J. J. G. "Foreign Illuminators and Illuminated Manuscripts." In *The Cambridge History of the Book in Britain, Volume III 1400–1557*, ed. Lotte Hellinga and J. B. Trapp, 47–64. Cambridge, UK: Cambridge University Press, 2009.

Armstrong, C. A. J. "An Italian Astrologer at the Court of Henry VII." In *Italian Renaissance Studies*, ed. E. F. Jacob, 432-54. London: Faber and Faber, 1960.

Backhouse, Janet. "Founders of the. Royal Library: Edward IV and Henry VII as Collectors of Illuminated Manuscripts." In *England in the Fifteenth Century: Proceedings of the 1986 Harlaxton Symposium*, ed. David Williams, 23–41. Woodbridge, UK: Boydell Press, 1987.

———. "Illuminated Manuscripts Associated with Henry VII and Members of His Immediate Family." In *The Reign of Henry VII: Proceedings of the 1993 Harlaxton Symposium*, ed. Benjamin Thompson, 175–187. Stamford, UK: Paul Watkins, 1995.

———. "The Royal Library from Edward IV to Henry VII." In *The Cambridge History of the Book in Britain, Volume III: 1400–1557*, ed. Lotte Hellinga and J. B. Trapp, 267–273. Cambridge, UK: Cambridge University Press, 2009.

Birrell, T. A. *English Monarchs and Their Books: From Henry VII to Charles II. The Second Panizzi Lecture, 1986.* London: British Library, 1987.

———. "From Manuscript to Print: Continuity and Change." In *A Companion to the Early Printed Book in Britain, 1476–1558*, ed. Vincent Gillespie and Susan Powell, 13-26. Cambridge: D.S. Brewer, 2014.

Boffey, Julia. *Manuscript and Print in London, c. 1475–1530*. London: The British Library, 2012.

Boone, Rebecca Ard. *War, Domination, and the Monarchy of France: Claude de Seyssel and the Language of Politics in the Renaissance*. Leiden, Netherlands: Brill, 2007.

Brooks, Douglas A. "'This Heavenly Boke More Precious than Golde': Legitimating Print in Early Tudor England." In *Tudor Books and Readers: Materiality and the Construction of Meaning*, ed. John N. King, 95-115. Cambridge, UK: Cambridge University Press, 2010.

Byrne, Joseph P. *Encyclopedia of the Black Death*. Santa Barbara, CA: ABC CLIO, 2012.

Carey, Hilary. "Henry VII's Book of Astrology and the Tudor Renaissance." *Renaissance Quarterly* lxv (2012): 661–710.

Carley, James. *The Libraries of King Henry VIII*. London: British Library, 2000.

Carlin, Martha. "William Parron." In *Oxford Dictionary of National Biography*. Oxford: Oxford University Press, 2004.

Carlson, David. *English Humanist Books: Writers and Patrons, Manuscript and Print, 1475–1525*. Toronto: University of Toronto Press, 1993.

———. "The Writings of Bernard André (c. 1450–c. 1522)." *Renaissance Studies* 12 (1998): 229–250.

Chrimes, S. B. *Henry VII*. Berkeley: University of California Press, 1972.
Cunningham, Sean. *Henry VII*. London: Routledge, 2007.
Deutscher, Thomas Brian. "Adriano Castellesi." In *Contemporaries of Erasmus: A Bibliographical Register of the Renaissance and Reformation*, ed. Peter G. Bietenholz and Thomas Brian Deutscher, 278-79. Vols. 1-3. Toronto: University of Toronto Press, 1985.
Edwards, A. S. G. *Stephen Hawes*. Boston: Twayne Publishers, 1983.
———."Stephen Hawes." *Oxford Dictionary of National Biography*. Oxford: Oxford University Press, 2004.
Gwynne, Paul. "The Frontispiece to an Illuminated Panegyric of Henry VII: A Note on the Sources." *Journal of the Warburg and Courtauld Institutes* (1992): 266-270.
———. *Poets and Princes: The Panegyric Poetry of Johannes Michael Nagonius*. Turnhout, Belgium: Brepols, 2012.
Hellinga, Lotte. "Prologue: The First Years of the Tudor Monarchy and the Printing Press." In *Tudor Books and Readers: Materiality and the Construction of Meaning*, ed. John N. King, 15-22. Cambridge, UK: Cambridge University Press, 2010.
Henderson, John. *The Renaissance Hospital: Healing the Body and Healing the Soul*. New Haven, CT: Yale University Press, 2006.
Keiser, George. "Two Medieval Plague Treatises and Their Afterlife in Early Modern England." *Journal of the History of Medicine and Allied Sciences* 58 (2003): 292-324.
Kipling, Gordon. "Henry VII and the Origins of Tudor Patronage." In *Patronage in the Renaissance*, ed. Guy Fitch Lytle and Stephen Orgel, 117-164. Princeton, NJ: Princeton University Press, 1981.
Kristeller, Paul Oskar. *Iter Italicum*. Vol. 4. Leiden, Netherlands: Brill, 1989.
McKendrick, Scot, John Lowden, and Kathleen Doyle, eds. *Royal Manuscripts: The Genius of Illumination*. London: British Library, 2011.
Nall, Catherine. "Margaret Beaufort's Books: A New Discovery." *Journal of the Early Book Society* 16 (2013): 213-220.
Oxford Dictionary of National Biography. Oxford: Oxford University Press, 2004.
Penn, Thomas. *Winter King: The Dawn of Tudor England*. London: Allen Lane, 2011.
Powell, Susan. "Lady Margaret Beaufort and Her Books." *The Library* 6 (1998): 197-240.
Rundle, David. "Filippo Alberici, Henry VII and Richard Fox: The English Fortunes of a Little-Known Italian Humanist." *Journal of the Warburg and Courtauld Institutes* 68 (2005): 137-155.
Schutte, Valerie. *Mary I and the Art of Book Dedications: Royal Women, Power, and Persuasion*. New York: Palgrave Macmillan, 2015.

Scott, Kathleen L. *Later Gothic Manuscripts, 1390–1490.* 2 vols. London: Harvey Miller, 1996.

———. "Manuscripts for Henry VII, His Household and Family." In *The Cambridge Illuminations: The Conference Papers,* ed. Stella Panayotova, 279–286. London: Harvey Miller, 2007.

Sider, Sandra. "'Interwoven with Poems and Picture': A Protoemblematic Latin Translation of the Tabula Cebetis." In *The European Emblem: Selected Papers from the Glasgow Conference 11–14 August 1987,* ed. Bernard F. Scholz, Michael Bath, and David Weston, 1-18. Leiden, Netherlands: Brill, 1990.

Winn, Mary Beth. *Anthoine Vérard, Parisian Publisher, 1485–1512: Prologues, Poems and Presentations.* Geneva: Librairie Droz, 1997.

Wood, Tara. "'To the Most Godlye, Virtuos, and Myghtye Princess Elizabeth': Identity and Gender in the Dedications to Elizabeth I." PhD dissertation, Arizona State University, 2008.

Nota Bene: Brief Notes on Manuscripts and Early Printed Books

Highlighting Little-Known or Recently Uncovered Items or Related Issues

"ȝet þer is a streinant witȝ two longe tailes": English Musical Terminology in the "Chorister's Lament"

REBECCA WEST

The "Chorister's Lament," a rhymed and semialliterative English poem from the late fourteenth century,[1] offers humorous insight into the practice of learning to sing in a northeast Midlands monastery and details the woes of two inexpert choristers, Wa(l)ter and William. This English-language poem was written onto a blank leaf in Arundel MS 292, a trilingual miscellany produced at Norwich Cathedral Priory or at least acquired by its library by about 1325.[2] The basic outlines of the narrative are easy enough to follow: the narrator describes Walter's complaint; Walter commiserates with his fellow chorister William, and the disappointed words of their French singing master—"*que vos ren ne vawt*" [that you are worthless]—end the piece.[3] The highly technical musical content and vocabulary of the poem, on the other hand, are hard to grasp, and it is perhaps due to this impenetrability that the "Chorister's Lament" has been infrequently edited and seldom anthologized. But these difficult words make the poem a meaningful addition to Arundel 292. Providing explanation and reinterpretation of some of the more problematic of these terms and concepts and using recently uncovered evidence from a Latin musical treatise to define the particularly rare *streinant*—a note that has hitherto evaded positive identification—makes apparent how the form, use, and context of the musical terms in the "Chorister's Lament" point to the emergence of a decidedly English musical vocabulary from a trilingual context.

Although the poem purportedly details William and Walter's lack of learning and ability, the singers' incompetence ultimately serves to show the musical sophistication of the author, if not of the choristers themselves.[5] The author's level of musical erudition might have been expected of an English choir monk of his day,[6] but to be part of what Kathryn Kerby-Fulton considers the poet's "*preferred* audience . . . those who have enough parallel training to follow the allusions and terminology with agility,"[7] a modern reader needs grounding in historical background, explanation, and identification—aids that do more for the comprehensibility of the text than any translation can.[8]

Walter frequently refers to musical notes by their names according to the hexachord system attributed to Guido of Arezzo (ca. 991–post-1033).[9] In the variation of the Guidonian system used by this time in England,[10] hexachords—six-note rows of pitches with a fixed pattern of whole and half steps—are mapped onto the notes of the staff. Through a process called mutation, or modulation, a singer moves across this mental grid of half and whole steps from one hexachord to the next, passing through a wide vocal range. Each of the notes in the hexachord has a name based on its position in the hexachord (*ut, re, mi, fa, sol*, and *la*), and can also be more precisely referred to by the several names it has through the overlapping of hexachords (e.g., *effaut* is the F, which is *fa* in the second hexachord and *ut* in the third).[11] Medieval musicians employed these note names—predecessors to the modern system of solmization—as a mnemonic device for the relationship between pitches notated on the staff. The performer first sight-sings the solfege syllables to learn the pitches of a new piece before complicating matters by adding the text. When Walter complains that he cannot learn his music despite the fact that he "sol-fas" and then sings afterwards ("I solfe and singge after, and is me neuere the nerre"), he means that despite following this process of first singing the notes by their names and then singing the tune together with the text, he meets with little success.[12]

That Walter knows the notes of the hexachord system, to which he seems to apply the name *cesolfa* when he complains of how disheartening he finds the method ("þe song of þe cesolfa dos me syken sare"),[13] is apparent through the liberal use he makes of the note names throughout the poem. He mentions *elami, sol, ut, la, fa,* and *are* in tandem with *effauȝ, bemol,* and *bequarre*—three note names worth special consideration:

> Of bemol and of bequarre, of boþe i was wol bare,
> Qwan i wente out of this word and liste til mi lare
> Of effauȝ and elami; ne coudy neuer are.
> I fayle faste in þe fa, it files al mi fare.
> ȝet ther ben oþer notes, sol and vt and la,
> and that froward file[14] þat men clipis fa,

> Often he dos me liken ille, and werkes me ful wa,
> Miȝti him neuere hitten in ton for to ta.[15]
>
> Of *bemol* and *bequarre*, of both I was well unaware
> When I went out of this world and listened to my lesson
> Of *ef-fa-ut* and *e-la-mi*; nor could I ever *a-re*.[16]
> I fail fast in the *fa*; it spoils all my dealings.
> Yet there are other notes—*sol* and *ut* and *la*,
> And that harsh chastiser that men call *fa*.
> Often he ill pleases and works me full woe–
> Never can I hit him in tune.[17]

It comes as no surprise that Walter has trouble with *fa*, a note he anthropomorphizes as a *froward file* (harsh chastiser) and mentions three times. As mentioned above, the six notes of a hexachord could not cover every note of the *gamut*, or range, of the Guidonian system, and singing notes outside the interval of a sixth required switching from one hexachord to another through the process of mutation. Similarly, singers had to mutate between hexachords if their music contained both B-flat and B-natural, as these two notes cannot occur in the same hexachord.[18] By this point in the poem, the singing master has already mentioned Walter's incompetence in singing notes in tune, especially the notes *bequarre* and *bemol*—the *fa* in the F hexachord (B-flat) and *mi* in the G hexachord (B-natural):

> Thou tones nought the note ilke by his name;
> Thou bitest asunder bequarre, for be-mol I thee blame.[19]
>
> You sing not the pitch properly by its name;
> You bite asunder *bequarre* (B-natural). I blame you for [singing] *bemol* (B-flat).

Walter "bites in half" *bequarre*, the note more commonly referred to in musical treatises of the period as *b-quadratum* or *b durum* (B-natural in modern terminology); the master accuses him of singing *bemol* or *b mollem* (B-flat) instead.

If Walter's difficulty in distinguishing between B-flat and B-natural is less than surprising, the name by which he calls B-flat—*quarre*—is certainly noteworthy. This use of the French word *quarre* for the more common *quadratum* is an English convention also used in two manuscripts of the *Metrologus*,[20] a thirteenth-century treatise and commentary on Guido of Arezzo's *Micrologus*, the definitive medieval treatment of music theory. Both the "Chorister's" poet and the author of the Metrologus share this English turn of musical diction; as I will show below, they also employ in common another rare word that supports a decidedly English musical vocabulary, *streinant*:

> ȝet þer is a streinant witȝ two longe tailes;
> þerfore has oure maister ofte horled mi kailes.
>
> Also there is a streinant with two long tails;
> On its account our master has often lashed me.[21]

This term, a hapax in English, has proved most obscure and resistant to satisfactory glossing for scholars of "Choristers" and writers of dictionaries both English and French. The Oxford English Dictionary defines *streinant* as "a musical note written with two stems; a breve" and suggests that the word may be related to the equally obscure Old French word *estraignant*, while the Middle English Dictionary, also noting the estraignant connection, less boldly calls the *streinant* a "musical note of some kind." These dictionary entries cite only one occurrence of the word in English—this "Chorister's" passage—and their definitions are guesswork at best. Likewise, the definition for the French *estraignant* as a "*terme de musique … désignant les sons poussés avec force, ou éclatants, opposés aux sons bas, creux*,"[22] [a musical term designating sounds pressed with force, or brilliant, as opposed to quiet or hollow sounds] provided in the *Lexique de l'ancient français* is based on a single known use of the term *estraignant* in Old French—a poetic usage without enough context for a secure definition—from a thirteenth-century French version of Ovid's *De arte amandi*.[23] Noting that the "French and English [uses of this term] have been recorded once only,"[24] Francis Lee Utley turns from literature to the history of music theory and systematically considers and dismisses the possibilities of the streinant being a *breve*,[25] a *plica*,[26] or *strene*[27] note. Making no successful identification, Utley ultimately despairs of finding a definition for the word. The modernization of the poem in Edith Rickert's *Chaucer's World* renders the *streinant* as a "double note" but provides no comment on this intriguing suggestion.[28] Bruce Holsinger tentatively identifies the *streinant* as the *larga plicata*,[29] basing his suggestion largely on the fact that the *larga plicata*, like the *streinant*, has two tails.[30] Ultimately, the two poetic uses of *streinant/estraignant* do not provide enough context to make a definitive statement of what the word means.

A positive identification of this word requires recourse to Latin—the third of the trilingual elements in "Chorister's," Arundel, and fourteenth-century English literature in general. The *streinant* has been hiding in plain sight, thoroughly defined and illustrated, in the *Metrologus*, a thirteenth-century Latin treatise with a likely English background. Perhaps the most compelling support for the treatise's English roots is its use of the same kind of unusual musical vocabulary found in "Chorister's." For instance, Jos. Smits van Waesberghe points to the use of the terms *quarre* and *properchant* in the *Metrologus* MSS London Lansdowne 763 and Oxford Bodleian 515 as a mark of English descent;[31] as mentioned above, *bequarre* was the note Walter "bit asunder." The *Metrologus* manuscript most remarkable for the connection between "Chorister's" and the treatise is MS Rome, Bib. Vat. Reg. Lat. 1146, 67r–70v.[32] Both the English cursive hand and now-familiar English vocabulary link this manuscript to England and, as it turns out, to the *streinant*.

Reg. Lat. 1146, mentions the *streinant* three times, defining the note and its use. The treatise also gives the only known example of how the *streinant* looks on the staff (*et figuratur sic*) and contrasts the appearance of the *streinant* with a near lookalike, which the scribe illustrates below the *streinant* lest musicians confuse the two: "*Item est alia nota quae vocatur streinant et ponimus super istis videlicet mon. ton. an. in. cum. num. et super consimiles et continet in se duas breves in cantando et figuratur sic. Aliquando sequatur alia nota inferior se tunc non est streinant sed due note ut hic*" [Also there is another note which is called *streinant* and which we put above these, namely, *mon. ton. an. in. cum. num.*, and above like things and contains in itself two breves in singing and is shaped like this. When another note follows below it, then it is not a *streinant* but two notes, as here.]:

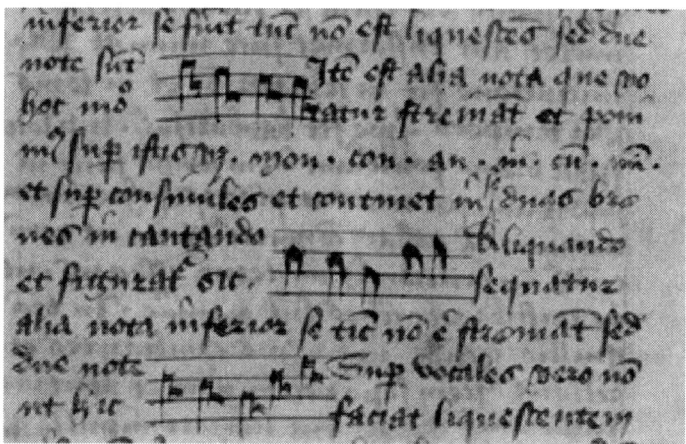

Detail from Rome, Bib. Vat. Reg. Lat. 1146, 69v. © 2016 Biblioteca Apostolica Vaticana. Used by permission of Biblioteca Apostolica Vaticana, all rights reserved The *streinant* is illustrated in the center and differentiated from the figure below it, which represents two consecutive notes instead of a single metrical quantity.

Earlier in the text of the treatise, the *streinant* is said to be an ornament with metrical value equal to a note called a *molosus*:[33] "*streinant et molosus equaliter cantentur sicut inferius patebit*" [the *streinant* and *molosus* are sung equally, as will be shown below].[34] According to these definitions provided by the text of the treatise, the *streinant* is used as a mensural quantity—one *streinant* has the same metrical value as two breves. The illustration of the *streinant* shows the "*two longe tailes*" from "Chorister's," and its juxtaposition with its look-alike in the *Metrologus* shows how easily it might be mistaken for another kind of note (or two). As with the hard-to-tune *fa*, Walter's difficulty with the *streinant* is easy to understand once the note is identified.

Holsinger suggests that the "Chorister's Lament" may have been written under the influence of *Piers Plowman* as a "stylized vernacular response to institutional and cultural transformations."[35] Extending Holsinger's argument, Schrader notes that this type of overarching "vernacular response" has a parallel in its specialized vernacular vocabulary. As he says, "a number of Latin musical terms are first recorded in English [in "Chorister's"], forcefully competing in their sudden vernacularization with ordinary language and some baffling colloquialisms."[36] This idea of vernacularization can be taken a step further. Walter's music was Latin, his teacher speaking French. His vocabulary, *bequarre, bemol, streinant* and the rest, developed from these two languages. But the end result is English—an English poem and an English vocabulary. The *Metrologus* utilizes the marked vocabulary found in "Chorister's," but its finished product is a Latin one. The two texts work from different directions to hammer out a shared vocabulary forged in a trilingual context.

"Chorister's" and the *Metrologus* share musical concerns especially pertinent to fourteenth-century English choristers; the close temporal and physical proximity of the composition of the two texts and their shared use of certain words, especially the rare *streinant*, reveal common participation in the transitional process of English vernacularization. Considering the two texts together clarifies the meaning and background of the technical terminology in the poem, making more intelligible the struggles of the choristers. More importantly, understanding these terms and their context reveals the manner in which both poem and treatise relate to the broader development of new English vocabulary.

University of Notre Dame

NOTES

1. Kathryn Kerby-Fulton suggests a date of ca. 1350 for the insertion of "Chorister's" into Arundel 292, a ca. 1275–1300 manuscript; Kathryn Kerby-Fulton, Maidie Hilmo, and Linda Olson, *Opening Up Middle*

English Manuscripts: Literary and Visual Approaches (Ithaca, NY: Cornell University Press, 2012), 40. This dates the insertion slightly earlier than J. P. Oakden's suggestion of 1375–1390 (composition 1350–1380). See J. P. Oakden, *Alliterative Poetry in Middle English: the Dialectical and Metrical Survey* (Manchester, UK: Manchester University Press, 1930), 108. For other manuscript descriptions of Arundel 292, see H. L. D. Ward, *Catalogue of Romances in the Department of Manuscripts in the British Museum* (London: British Museum Department of Manuscripts, 1803–1910), 2: 452; Hanneke Wirtjes, ed., *The Middle English Physiologus*, Early English Text Society 291 (Oxford: Oxford University Press, 1991), ix–xv; and Bruce Holsinger, "Langland's Musical Reader: Liturgy, Law, and the Constraints of Performance," *Studies in the Age of Chaucer* 21 (1999): 135–141.

2. See Kerby-Fulton, *Opening Up*, 40. Ralph Hanna writes that the "Chorister's" poet's language and subject matter suggest an author from "no further south than the minster at Beverly or York"; Ralph Hanna, "Alliterative Poetry," in *The Cambridge History of Medieval English Literature*, ed. David Wallace (Cambridge, UK: Cambridge University Press, 1999), 488–512, 510. Citing the spelling conventions of the poem, Kathryn Kerby-Fulton suggests that the "Chorister's" scribe trained in the area of King's Lynn. Kerby-Fulton, *Opening Up*, 45. The author's affiliation with the priory and his apparent familiarity with musical practice and theory identify him as a choir monk or clerk.

3. Some confusion does exist as to even this outline. Schrader notes the difficulties editors have experienced in glossing and punctuating the text and refers, it seems, to confusion over which voice is speaking at what point. See Richard J. Schrader, "The Inharmonious Choristers and Blacksmiths of MS Arundel 292," *Studies in Philology* 104 (2007): 2.

4. For twentieth-century editions of the lament, see Francis Lee Utley, "The Choristers' Lament," *Speculum* 21 (1946): 194–202; Celia and Kenneth Sisam, eds., *The Oxford Book of Medieval English Verse* (Oxford: Clarendon Press, 1970), 184–187; and Holsinger, "Langland's Musical Reader." The poem has been rendered into modern English in Utley's article and in Edith Rickert, comp., *Chaucer's World* (New York: Columbia University Press, 1948), 126–128. Due to errors in transcription and confusing or incomplete explanatory notes in the available editions, the poem is due for fresh editing and a full set of notes and diagrams on its musical terminology. I expect to undertake this project at a later date.

5. In passing, Elizabeth Salter refers to "Chorister's" as a "wry and technically expert satirisation of the rigorous training imposed in monastic or cathedral song-schools." Elizabeth Salter, *English and International Studies in the Literature, Art and Patronage of Medieval England*, ed. Derek

Pearsall and Nicolette Zeeman (Cambridge, UK: Cambridge University Press, 1988), 200. Kathryn Kerby-Fulton agrees that "the only possible author for a text such as this is someone with real chorister training." Kathryn Kerby-Fulton, *The Clerical Proletariat and the Rise of English* (Philadelphia: University of Pennsylvania Press, forthcoming 2017).

6. Schrader suggests that difficulty in understand the poem may not be only a modern problem, writing that the poem "requires so much knowledge of musical terminology that it may have been incomprehensible even to many in the monastic audience of the manuscript." Schrader, "Inharmonious Choristers," 1.
7. Kerby-Fulton, *Clerical Proletariat*.
8. In this article I provide explanation only of the terms and concepts pertinent to the excerpts presented.
9. The hexachord system and other elements referred to in this paper as Guidonian are not preserved in Guido's extant writings but are traditionally attributed to him. See Margot Fassler, *Music in the Medieval West: Western Music in Context* (New York: W. W. Norton and Co., 2014), 95–97 and 100–102.
10. Over the three hundred years between Guido's death and the writing of "Chorister's," there had been many major developments of and additions to Guido's system, some of which are discussed briefly below.
11. The following table illustrates how the first, second, and third hexachord overlap with one another. *Effaut* is bolded.

						ut	re	mi	fa	sol	la
						F	G	A	B♭	C	D
			ut	re	mi	**fa**	sol	la			
			C	D	E	**F**	G	A			
ut	re	mi	fa	sol	la						
G	A	B	C	D	E						

12. "Chorister's," line 34.
13. "Chorister's," 3. *Cesolfa* is the note corresponding to the modern C—the C above middle C—one of the highest notes in the Guidonian system. Since the *gamut*, or *gamma ut*—the lowest of the notes—can represent the whole range, it seems plausible that one of the highest notes might serve the same function.
14. *File* can mean a wretch or rascal, but I have taken it as a figurative use of the word that is our modern file (a rasp), an agent of castigation or

15. "Chorister's," 37–44. The modernization is my own.
16. Here I depart significantly from the punctuation and translation proposed by Utley, who construes this line as, "Before that I knew nothing of F-fa-ut and E-la-mi"; Utley, "Choristers' Lament," 187. *Effauȝ* is f, the F below middle C (fa in the second hexachord) and *elami* the E just below that (mi in the second hexachord). *Sol, ut, la,* and *fa* are the simple names for the fifth, first, sixth, and fourth positions in each hexachord, regardless of the mutation. In Utley's translation of the poem, the only note left unmentioned, since the third position is represented by the note *elami*, is *re*, or the second position of the hexachord. But if *are* refers not to the copula but to the note *a-re*, the A below middle C and the second note of the first hexachord, then these lines become much simpler to punctuate and construe. In this case, Walter has mentioned *ut, (a)re, (ela)mi, fa, sol,* and *la*—all of the notes in a hexachord.
17. Unless otherwise noted, all translations and transcriptions are my own.
18. This diagram of the overlapping of the second, third, and first hexachord shows the tricky spot where B♭ and B♮ cause trouble. Whole steps allow all the other notes to stack neatly one over the other, but the half-step between mi and fa forces askew this tidy system:

				ut G	re A		mi B♮	fa C	sol D	la E
			ut F	re G	mi A	fa B♭		sol C	la D	
ut C	re D	mi E	fa F	sol G	la A					

19. "Chorister's," 19–20.
20. London MS Lansdowne 763 and Oxford MS Bodleian 515. *Bemol* is also a French spelling.
21. *Horled mi kailes*: "rushed strokes upon me," or perhaps, as Utley suggests, "played ninepins with my head"; Utley, "Choristers' Lament," 197–198.
22. Jean Frédéric Godefroy Bonnard and Amédée Salmon, *Lexique de l'ancient français, s.v. estraignant* (Paris: H. Welter, 1901).
23. "D'avalees, ne d'estraignanz, / Ne de faire beaus moz plaisanz, / Ne sont onques envers lui rien: / Meloudie qui chante bien, / Ne la muse qui les lais fist, / Onques nu mot si lien n'asist, / Ma douce amie, con vos faites."

Maître Elie's Ovide, De arte, Richelieu 19152, fol. 97a. For a description of Richelieu 19152, see the Bibliothèque Nationale, Département des Manuscrits, *Catalogue général des manuscrits français: Ancien St. Germain français,* vol. 3, nos. 18677–20064, ed. Henri Omont, Camille Couderc, Lucien Auvray, and Charles de la Roncière (Paris: E. Leroux, 1900), 247–251.

24. Utley, "Choristers' Lament," 201.
25. In mensural notation, a *brevis* is a short, small syllable or note. See Michael Bernhard and Bernhold Schmid, *Lexicon musicum latinum Medii Aevi. Wörterbuch der lateinischen Musikterminologie des Mittelalters bis zum Ausgang des 15. Jahrhunderts* (Munich, Germany: Verlag der Bayerischen Akademie der Wissenschaften in Kommission bei der C.H. Beck'schen Verlagsbuchhandlung, 1992–), s.v. brevis.
26. *Plica* designates a descending neume with two pitches. *Lexicon musicum latinum,* s.v. plica.
27. Utley may have been closer than he thought in considering the *strene* note. As he mentions, John Merbecke's 1550 preface to the *The Booke of Common Praier Noted* (BCPN) presents four note shapes: *strene note, square note, pycke,* and *close* and states that the *strene note* is a *breve*. Utley, informed by his musicologist correspondents that the *streinant* "can hardly be a breve," drops the thought of identifying the *strene* with the *streinant;* Utley, "Choristers' Lament," 201. But as Hyun-Ah Kim notes, the BCPN preface consistently "conveys a reduction of the normal note values and the proportional relationship between the notes." Typically, the square note is a breve, the diamond shaped note a semibreve, etc. If these common note shapes are considered with their these typical values (square as breve, diamond as semibreve) but kept proportional to the *strene*, the *strene* would have the value of two breves, a definition we meet below applied to the streinant. Hyun-Ah Kim, *Humanism and the Reform of Sacred Music in Early Modern England: John Merbecke the Orator and* The Booke of Common Praier Noted *(1550)* (Aldershot, England, and Burlington, VT: Ashgate, 2008), 160–161. For more on the *strene* note, see Hugh Benham, "'Stroke' and 'Strene' Notation in Fifteenth- and Sixteenth-Century Equal-Note Cantus Firmi," *Plainsong and Medieval Music* 2 (1993): 163.
28. Rickert, *Chaucer's World,* 128.
29. A *larga plicata* is a mensural note with both ascending and descending forms and has the value of two or three longs, depending on the mensuration. *Lexicon Musicum Latinum,* s.v. larga.
30. Holsinger, "Langland's Musical Reader," 119.
31. For arguments supporting the English provenance of the treatise, see Van Waesberghe, who cites the manuscript tradition of the *Metrologus*

and the facts that with one exception, MS Siena L.V. 30, the only extant complete copies of the treatise are found in England and that the text refers to Guido of Arezzo as "Guido de Santa Mauro;" Jos. Smits van Waesberghe, ed., *Expositiones in Micrologum Guidonis Aretini: Musicologica Medii Aevi* (Amsterdam: North-Holland Publishing Company, 1957), 61–62.

32. All quotations from the text of the Metrologus are from this fourteenth-century manuscript, which I have examined in digital facsimile.
33. *Molosus* is not a common note name and requires more study.
34. This statement is in the context of differentiating the length of *longas* and *breves*, not, as the treatise points out, in the context of plainchant, but rather *organum: "Licet enim longas et breues nominemus non sic tenentur in plana musica. sicut et in organo"* [For we can call them longs and breves not as they are held in plainchant but as in organum.] *Metrologus*, 69v.
35. Holsinger, "Langland's Musical Reader," 134–135. It is also possible that "Chorister's" was written before *Piers Plowman*.
36. Schrader, "Inharmonious Choristers," 4.

Loose Leaves, Lost Leaves, and the Text of *Piers Plowman*

RALPH HANNA

For more than a century, leaves mishandled in or lost from various archetypes/exemplars of *Piers Plowman* have played a disruptive role in studies of the poem. The only begetter of this critical strain was John M. Manly, and his intervention eventually underwrote an enormous controversy over the poem's authorship that exhausted scholars for some forty years.[1] Yet it is worth examining the genesis of Manly's intervention; he could not believe that a committed teacher like he imagined the poet of the A Version would deliberately have omitted from his confession of the deadly sins any account of Wrath.

Like virtually all his successors, Manly simply objected to the text as received and thought he might imagine a better, and a more coherent one.[2] Almost invariably (only Robert Adams addresses a problem that might be construed exclusively textual) later efforts have followed this lead and build upon a literary-critical response to some perceived discontinuity; the shifting arguments of B Version passus 15 (perhaps a way of characterizing a figure who claims to be an amalgam of many faculties?) have proved an irresistible site for such interventions. But invariably critics join to this belief that they are in touch with and recognize a poet who should not have perpetrated such a thing, the assumption that their perceived incoherence must reflect the defectiveness of an underlying manuscript state.

Merely as explanatory gestures, such arguments should be seen as particularly uncompelling in logical terms. They represent what Chaucer's Canon's Yeoman would call "ignotum per ignocius" (*Canterbury Tales* G

1457). In these arguments, a mystery, a failure to communicate construed as a lacuna, is resolved by invoking a situation in which there was no such disruption – but indeed, only a deeper mystery. Discontinuity gets "explained" by a thoroughly hypothetical invention, the lost leaf, for whose explanatory power no evidence can be forthcoming. Alternatively, these proposals might be perceived as analogous to the "saving the appearances" of Ptolemaic astronomy, the invention of an entity whose existence depends entirely on a prior logical construction. Once posited, such an entity restores comprehensive form to what remains otherwise fragmented, and thus inexplicable. (In Ptolemaic terms, this function is fulfilled by the epicycle, appropriately enough a circle that is going around a circle that is going around....)

But leaving aside the susceptibility of such arguments to Ockham's razor, these proposals–as most of their perpetrators have failed to recognize –involve paleographical difficulties as well. In most instances of this argument–Manly's leaf had simply vanished (along with any single author)–lost or loose leaves have regularly been invoked to explain local textual peculiarities. These especially include attestational difficulties associated with Langland's revisions, whether putative or overt; from them advocates have generated hypotheses as to what Langland's authorial manuscript should have resembled. But following in the footsteps of the poem's greatest editor, George Kane, who quite unabashedly viewed manuscripts as merely inert skins bearing important inky squiggles, these investigators seem never to have considered the huge amount of codicological evidence that might query their contentions.

In fact, from the broadest paleographical perspective, the notion of lost single inserted leaves is inherently implausible. Any competent medieval book-producer–and there is no sign that Langland was not such–knew that inserting single leaves into manuscripts is asking for trouble. This is because the physical integrity of a manuscript depends upon its sewing–which universally requires anchoring full bifolia through stitching down their centers. This work, customarily joining to one another eight, ten, or twelve leaves, was conceived as stable–and the many thousands of intact surviving medieval quires so sewn would indicate that this was a reasonable expectation. Intruding into this fixed format an odd leaf or two–although there are ways of mitigating the effect (see n.3 below)–generally risks loss, the leaf effectively being anchored to nothing. As a consequence, all book-producers who care about their texts, among whom one would surely count the meticulously revising poet of *Piers Plowman*, try to avoid such dangers.

Second, the evidence of extant *Piers Plowman* manuscripts suggests that, with the exception of one notable and apparently cash-beleaguered individual, everyone who worked with the poem knew this basic practice. As a result, both intruded single leaves and indeed lost leaves of any sort, are generally alien to the poem's circulation. In any such survey, one must make certain predictable exclusions: opening leaves (because frequently decorated) have always been the target of souvenir seekers; given that board-bindings were always supererogatory in the Middle Ages, opening and concluding quires are regularly subject to damage; blank leaves at the ends of books or their subsidiary units are regularly cut out for some informal use. But, merely to take the most persuasive example, in the B Version manuscripts, even after six centuries of (ab)use, lost individual leaves are in decidedly short supply, a mere seven examples in books totaling well over 1400 folios in total. The lost-leaf hypothesis comes nowhere near describing anything like the normal case.[3]

Finally, these arguments assume what I would describe as a "worst-case" scenario. They generally assume (largely on the basis of Kane and Donaldson's presentation of Langland's C archetypal copy) that the poet revised on a scribal manuscript of his standing text and then passed a necessarily messy corrected copy to the scribe responsible for textual promulgation.[4] The transitions A Version to B Version and B Version to C Version necessitated a considerable number of sweeping changes, and lost leaves have been invoked wherever perceived anomalies in either coherent sense or in coherent transmission appear to demand it.

But such a scenario runs afoul of evidence provided by comparable examples elsewhere. I would offer as one analogous instance the complicated presentation of Rolle's *Incendium amoris* in Cambridge, Emmanuel College, MS 35.[5] This book, copied c. 1460, offers, *inter alia*, a full "short version" of *Incendium*; this is a truncated nonauthorial rendition of the original text. However, the book's apparent owner, one John Neuton, had access to what he believed was Rolle's autograph copy of the authorial "long version" and set about bringing his received "short version" text into accord with it. The manuscript is thus useful as showing the procedures by which differing versions of the same text, one of them subject to radical expansions (as is *Piers Plowman*, which in its iterations rarely gets any shorter), might be brought into accord. Neuton's activity here could be seen as analogous to Langland's conversion of the briefer A Version into B, with the understanding that Neuton is a collator, comparing two versions not of his own manufacture rather than an author inventing his insertions.

For a medieval corrector, Neuton, no doubt driven by his access to "authorial papers," is unusually thorough and fastidious.[6] But importantly in this context, his conversion of "short" into "long" *Incendium*, so far as it possibly can do so, respects the form of the book he had received. That is, so much as possible, Neuton corrects on the standing leaves, using well-attested methods to replace discordant readings and insert ones overlooked. Most of his work is accomplished by interlineation and marginal notes (for short omissions), alternatively by expunction and accompanying interlineation for rejected short readings. He added a large proportion of the protracted "short version" omissions at the page foot, with *signes de renvoi* and with the onsets and terminations of material to be inserted carefully marked. Only in a restricted number of major additions did Neuton feel the need to intrude extra leaves (e.g., the table of chapters, necessary to negotiate the complicated whole, on the inserted fol. 59).[7]

The evidence offered by most *Piers Plowman* manuscripts would suggest that page-foot additions might well be sufficient to accommodate most examples of materials added in revision. In a normal medieval manuscript (as in its imitator, the modern print book), lower margins are considerably deeper than upper ones. Even in their cut-down form (the product of six centuries of rebindings), most manuscripts of *Piers* B and C show at least 50 mm of blank space at page feet, probably enough – especially if the insertions were written as carefully punctuated prose – to handle something like the addition at C 19.234-48a.

On the other hand, Emmanuel 35 suggests scenarios alternative to the provision of missing leaves, ones provocative in considering such matters as the C Version "frontloading" of substantial pieces of the text from much later positions in the B Version. In lost-leaf theories, this might possibly have involved excision of leaves from a reworked B manuscript and their movement (if consecutive, most probably as loose singletons) to earlier positions in a developing draft.[8]

But the Emmanuel manuscript implies, perhaps more probably, different procedures. The book ultimately provides a complete *Incendium amoris* without a large number of loose insertions. But this is presented in the volume through three dispersed texts: a copy of "the compilation," a sequence of Rolle excerpts designed to supplement the "short version"; an excerpted "long version," generally ignoring materials copied elsewhere; and the "short version" corrected by Neuton.

In the manuscript, the presentation of these as a single whole relies upon careful marginal notes, sometimes accompanied by *signes de renvoi*; these direct the reader to the book's other presentations of the text. For example, the classic *Incendium* ch. 15 is ignored in both Emmanuel's copies of the standing "long" and "short versions" of the text. (In the first instance, this is deliberate, the scribes' economies of never copying anything twice; but ch. 15 is simply absent from all copies of the "short version.") Instead this material is present elsewhere in the book–and signaled for insertion from this locus in the other two formal versions of the text. In Emmanuel, ch. 15 is presented within the "compilation;" this appears about sixty folios (!) earlier than the signal for its placement as a correction to the "short version" (on fols. 17-18^v, its "short version" placement being at fol. 76).

The original Emmanuel scribes practice efficiency here: they strive never to repeat a portion of the text already copied elsewhere. But their ability, as well as that of both Neuton and his putative readers, to negotiate substantial textual displacements, implies an expectation of consultative skill, as does a further example. Oxford, St. John's College, MS 57, fols. 135-37 (here the final leaves of a booklet-ending regular quire), have a "supplementum defectus libri precedentis." The leaves provide a series of verses omitted in the preceding copy of *The Prick of Conscience*, some with *signes de renvoi*. These marks that would have facilitated ready consultation were not, however, added to the text. In some cases, the corrections refer to materials to be inserted twenty or so folios earlier.[9] "Lost-leavers" (to coin a phrase) have been reluctant to attribute any comparable skill to a vastly more intelligent poet and to the archetypal scribes who may have worked directly with him and his materials. It is perfectly plausible to imagine that Langland might similarly have used full, normally constructed quires to hold (sequences of ?) more lengthy insertions into standing copy and might have marked their places for insertion by means analogous to those used in Emmanuel 35 and St. John's 57.

If John Neuton's behavior might offer a template for considering Langland's archetypes, it is nonetheless possible to point to the number of passages across all the revisions *Piers Plowman* received that could have required any insertion of leaves. On Neuton's model, all these should have involved substantial augmentation of what had been the standing text. There are relatively few of these, considering the nearly 18,000 verse lines of the poem's three versions: nine associated with the revision that converted A into B, eight or nine with that converting B into C.[10]

The length of these insertions rather interestingly shows some bunching. Taken in the aggregate, these insertions are suggestive of composition in modules of about twenty-five to twenty-eight lines of edited text. The largest examples might constitute filled bifolia; the shortest, one side of a single leaf. But they need not have been such detachable segments; rather, they might have been consecutively written yet spaced apart as separate in added normal quires. But I would suggest that this seems an inexpansible maximum of possible intruded leaves – and the fact that such leaves may have occurred should be subject to the constraints of Ockham's razor, to paraphrase H. Marshall Leicester Jr., "Folia dispersa non multiplicanda sunt."[11]

But I think that the persistence of "lost-leaf" arguments represents more than logical error and an absence of paleographical nous. Insofar as it has a constructive dimension, the persistent recourse to lost materials in discussions of the poem shrouds a considerably more global issue. For the real difficulty with *Piers Plowman* that these theories strive to address is simply that of the text itself – that some statements do not for some readers appear to follow from their context–and, beyond these perceived discontinuities, a variety of problems inherent in the text's transmission.[12] The Athlone editions, whatever their commendable scrutiny of variation, had–almost by postulate–to ignore these issues: the two ancient bugbears that haunt all editors, accidentally convergent variation and conflation.

George Kane remains the greatest editor of the late twentieth century, and his editorial theory remains the only workable method for constructing a text of anything. But it may have been, as I have remarked elsewhere, a theory uniquely unsuited to editing *Piers Plowman*.[13] Put simply, Kane's theory postulates that certain kinds of scribal errors are very apt to occur in certain circumstances. But what happens when–as with *Piers Plowman*– one is frequently faced, for long stretches, with reiterations of much the same text? If Kane is correct (as I think he is), it must follow that the same confused heap of variants will repeat itself across all versions–and not always with neatly resoluble results. A simple example, in this case a reading that is thoroughly "indifferent" (i.e., not involving any substantial change of meaning and not capable of resolution on the basis of editorial judgement) will illustrate the difficulty.

At A Prol.21 (B Prol.21, C Prol.23), the text reads, "In settyng and sowyng swonke ful harde." On the basis of the collated manuscripts, this is surely the reading of A (two copies only have "and **in**"). However, although the C editors print the same line, the C manuscript evidence implies that the original C read "and **in** sowyng." In B, the evidence is less clear ("and **in**" occurs in HmGYCL). Following "the rule of copy-text," in which the base manuscript determines the text in indifferent readings, one might have equally authoritative but differing editions of B; Kane and Donaldson's, predicated on W, would read simply "and," but Walter Skeat's and the recent online edition of the B archetype, both predicated on L, would read "and in."[14] Yet it seems highly unlikely that this is the kind of detail that Langland should have fussed over in revision, and a fair likelihood that all authorial versions of the poem read identically (as all three Athlone editions and Skeat's do, if variously). But agreements of this sort across all three versions offer substantial challenges to the value of manuscript attestation of readings.

The second problem is much more acute–and has implicitly been the site where most lost leaves have recently been invoked. If we believe that Langland promulgated his poem three times, he can only have imagined an audience of individuals who would recognize new initiatives and would see that older iterations of the poem were now superseded, perhaps discardable. Such an audience must have been a coterie, and very small indeed. But as a "public text" detached from this knowing audience, versions were quite indistinguishable as such; all of them were simply, as manuscript rubrics tell us, "the poem called Piers Plowman." And the number of scribes who could distinguish versions–and then only in the grossest manner–was very limited indeed.[15]

The result is that beyond their convergence in expected misreadings, manuscript versions of the poem are persistently not discrete representatives of authorial "versions." They result from massive and repeated cross-versional conflations, scribes constructing variously full renditions with materials pieced together from different stages of authorial composition. This situation is usually recognized as if it were a sport limited to "deviant" copies–for example, the widely discussed Z, F, N^2, and Ht. But this transmissional feature persists equally in small readings as well, and as a result not necessarily of actual multiple book consultation but of memorial contamination.[16]

Obviously enough, the Athlone text needs to be redone, root and branch. And it needs to be redone in a way perhaps only Carl Schmidt has attempted–as an effort engaged with all three authorial texts simultaneously, not in sequence.[17] A considerably more critical eye to the convergence of versions, both accidental (convergent variation) and motivated (conflation), is required. The results, as my example above indicates, are going to be extremely messy and will not offer the clarity that Kane always sought (and sometimes imposed on his evidence). Such detailed analysis, undertaken in the light of abundant paleographical evidence for scribal behavior, might well dispel the fascination with lost leaves that has led to many scholars surrendering to the implausible lure of the textual epicycle.

Keble College, Oxford University

NOTES

1. See Manly, "The Lost Leaf of 'Piers the Plowman,'" *Modern Philology* 3 (1906):359-66; and "The Authorship of 'Piers Plowman,'" *Modern Philology* 7 (1909):83-144. More recent avatars of similar arguments include George Kane and E. Talbot Donaldson, in their edition, *Piers Plowman: The B Version* (London: Athlone, 1975), 176-79 (a misfolded bifolium); Wendy Scase, "Two *Piers Plowman* C-Text Interpolations: Evidence for a Second Textual Tradition," *Notes and Queries* 232 (1987):456-63 (loose leaves with extra materials); Robert M. Adams, "The R/F MSS of *Piers Plowman* and the Pattern of Alpha/Beta Complementary Omissions: Implications for Critical Editing," TEXT 14 (2000):109-37 (lost leaves); Lawrence Warner, *The Lost History of Piers Plowman: The Earliest Transmission of Langland's Work* (Philadelphia: University of Pennsylvania Press,

2011), passim. All citations of the poem are drawn from William Langland, *Piers Plowman*, George Kane, gen. ed., 3 vols. (London: Athlone, 1960-97).
2. Cf. Kane and Donaldson, *The B Version*, 178: "However prone to digression [Langland] may have been, he was not given to incoherent or otherwise feeble argument." Merely to indicate the overtly *parti pris* nature of Manly's intervention (an argument that, *mutatis mutandis*, might be mounted against most of the other studies mentioned here): Manly might have noticed the omission of Wrath in the sin-catalogue at A 2.60 (cf. B 2.84, C 2.88). Moreover, Langland frequently considers Envy and Wrath capable of fusion. Perhaps typical is the revision of A 2.60 into "The Erldom of enuye and yre [togideres, B only]" in C 2.91 (B 2.84). Similarly, the two sins are joined at B 13.320-41, indeed mostly about Envy; at B 14.224 Envy is omitted in favor of a Wrath description, and both are ignored altogether in the assault of the sins in C 22/B 20.114-82.
3. I have obviously chosen the most emphatic evidence; that from A and C is much less conclusive, but much of it explicable. My totals are derived from the *Piers* portions only of BmBoCC2CotFGHmHtLMORWY; R lacks two quires, one the opening (and partially preserved apart from the remainder). The individual to whom I refer early in the paragraph is the scribe of F; although a professional (and his book including the one bit of integral B Version illumination), he worked with substandard scrap parchment, so thin that it routinely has "show-through," and he saved bits and bobs of the wretched stuff for book-use (as well as excising a few leaves in F itself to add to his stock). But in every instance where he inserted a leaf, although it is technically "single," it actually represents half a normal bifolium (with a matching partner) and these paired examples may at some earlier point have actually been fixed to form such.
4. See Kane and Donaldson's discussion of "The C Reviser's B Manuscript" at *The B Version*, 98-127.
5. For descriptions and discussions, see Margaret Deanesly, ed., *The Incendium Amoris of Richard Rolle of Hampole* (Manchester: Manchester University Press, 1915), 12-15; Michael G. Sargent, *James Grenehalgh as Textual Critic*, 2 vols., Analecta Cartusiana 85 (Salzburg: Universität Salzburg, 1984), 2:478-487. One should ignore Deanesly's later discussions of the book, predicated on her belief that it had been copied before 1414.
6. On corrections and the customary forms these take, including in *Piers Plowman* manuscripts, see the sound basic introduction, Daniel Wakelin, *Scribal Correction and Literary Craft: English Manuscripts 1375-1510* (Cambridge: Cambridge University Press, 2014), 101-83. I have checked

Neuton over about 10 per cent of the text, where he appropriately corrected just about half the "short version" variants that my collation uncovers. I would say that his work was more accurate than the modern editor Deanesly's; see "Richard Rolle's *Incendium Amoris*: A Prospectus for a Future Editor," *Journal of Medieval Latin* 26 (2016), 227-61.

7. The book, on paper, has been subjected to radical oversewing, and there is no published collation (cf. Sargent, *James Grenehalgh*). Quite accidentally, I last examined the book on a very bright day; I could at least ascertain where watermarks were present, but not, given the sewing, identify them. Their sequence, however, revealed a book totally in eight-leaf quires, except for inserted leaves (generally recognizable as being in Neuton's hand rather than that of either original scribe).

8. One might note that such an extension of lost-leaf theory to include these examples would undermine the theory altogether. This C revision material, including largescale movement of chunks and a fair amount of local rewriting, fails to show any disruption across the manuscripts.

9. A similar situation might offer an explanation of lines unique to the B manuscripts RF more plausible than Adams's postulated lost leaves: that excepting the individual behind RF, archetypal B Version scribes failed to respond to signals for insertion of material.

10. The B examples include: after A Prol.95, B Prol.100-210 (111 manuscript lines); after A 3.276, B 3.301-353 (54 lines); after A 5.106, B 5.135-187 (53 lines); after A 5.145, B 5.230-295 (72 lines); after A 5.212, B 5.385-440a (57 lines); after A 5.250, B 5.477-509 (33 lines); after A 11.59, B 10.74-116a (44 lines, some of A retained); A 11.182-203 replaced with B 10.235-96 (72 lines); after A 11.214, B 10.313-335 (26 lines); after A 11.278, B 10.395-419 (25 lines) – all of these retained in C. The C examples include: after B Prol.96, C Prol.95-124 (30 lines); after B 3.86, C 3.86-114 (29 lines); after B 3.258, C 3.315-412 (103 lines); after B 4.195, C 5.1-104 (110 lines); after B 7.75 (roughly), C 9.71-159 (93 lines); after B 7.106, C 9.187-280 (96 lines); after B 11.269a, C 12.156-247 and 13.1-100 (97 and 105 lines, perhaps to be construed a single insertion); after B 15.390, C 17.125-164 (43 lines).

11. "The Art of Impersonation: A General Prologue to *The Canterbury Tales*," PMLA 95 (1980):213-24, at 215.

12. Here two of the studies mentioned in note 1, those of Scase and Warner, are particularly challenged, through the authors' inability to distinguish readings that might be ascribed to an author and those produced by scribes (the latter enthusiastic representatives of "The *Piers Plowman* Tradition").

13. On the necessity for and the power of Kane's techniques, see *Editing Medieval Texts...*, Exeter Medieval Texts and Studies (Liverpool:

Liverpool University Press, 2015), 46-53; and for my earlier comment on method and the text of Piers, "George Kane and the Invention of Textual Thought: Retrospect and Prospect," *Yearbook of Langland Studies* 24 (2010), 1-20, at 19.
14. I am grateful to John Burrow and Thorlac Turville-Petre, and their edition of the B archetype, available in The *Piers Plowman* Electronic Archive at http://piers.iath.virginia.edu/texts/html, for drawing this example to my attention.
15. These are the individuals who recognized the "incomplete" status of the A Version and affixed a C Version conclusion. The difficulty of distinguishing the poem's states is evident from a scribe who filled out a headless B Version copy with materials from both other Versions. The attestation is much narrower than appears from the number of survivors, e.g. the manuscripts TH²Ch of A+C and BmBoCot of CA+B depend on decisions taken by only a single scribe.
16. One might note a variety of B Version readings present in one or another of the A copies EAMH³, but suggested for inclusion in A by Kane, *The A Version*, rev. edn. (London: Athlone, 1988), 461-62 *passim*; see Simon Horobin's discussion, "Harley 3954 and the Audience of *Piers Plowman*," in *Medieval Texts in Context*, ed. Graham D. Caie and Denis Renevey, (London: Routledge, 2008), 68-84. As Kane trenchantly pointed out, Z is certainly a memorial mixture of different versions; see "The 'Z Version' of *Piers Plowman*," *Speculum* 60 (1985): 910-30.
17. A. V. C. Schmidt, ed., *William Langland Piers Plowman: A Parallel-Text Edition of the A, B, C and Z Versions*, rev. edn., 2 vols. in 3 (Kalamazoo: Medieval Institute, 2011).

A Trilingual Version of "Erthe upon Erthe" in The National Archives of the United Kingdom, E 175/11/16

MARJORIE HARRINGTON

The very common Middle English poems referred to collectively as "Erthe upon Erthe" are structured around the paradox that man who was made from earth dwells on earth and will return to earth. One medieval version of the poem is intriguingly accompanied by translations of it in Latin and Anglo-Norman French, but until now the manuscript containing this version has been unlocatable and presumed lost. The "loss" was due, however, to a simple mislabeling of the manuscript. Here, I relocate the trilingual version of "Erthe upon Erthe" on the dorse of a fourteenth-century Exchequer roll, National Archives of the United Kingdom E 175/11/16, and I propose that the Latin and Anglo-Norman translations were produced as a rhetorical exercise by a member of the clerical proletariat.

The trilingual "Erthe upon Erthe" was first observed in the modern era by the antiquary Joseph Hunter (1783–1861), who became one of the first assistant keepers at the newly established Public Record Office in 1840. Under his direction, it was transcribed from the Exchequer roll into a volume of miscellaneous poetry from manuscript sources.[1] After his death, Hunter's library was acquired by the British Museum, and the volume of poetic transcriptions was given the shelfmark Additional 25478.[2] Helen Sandison located the transcription in Additional 25478, folios 1r to 3v, as Hilda Murray was completing her 1911 EETS edition of two dozen versions of "Erthe upon Erthe." Together, they were able to identify the medieval copy of the trilingual version, then in the Public Record Office, and Murray published an edition of it as an appendix in the EETS volume.³ At the time that Sandison and Murray located the roll containing the trilingual "Erthe upon Erthe," it was in a bundle awaiting rearrangement and Murray gave it the temporary shelfmark "Public Record Office, Exchequer Roll, King's Remembrancer Proceedings bundle 1." Further references to the poem do not look beyond Murray's edition and simply repeat this shelfmark. Because this was never intended as more than a temporary label, and because the nomenclature used by the Public Record Office (and later, by The National Archives) has since been updated, the link between Murray's shelfmark and the physical artifact containing the poem was entirely lost until now.⁴

The main text of E 175/11/16, which is composed of four membranes sewn head to foot, is a copy of the Ordinances of 1311. This is a series of forty-one articles limiting the power of Edward II, removing Piers Gaveston and other "malveis conseilers," and reforming the royal finances.⁵ The hand responsible for copying the Ordinances is typical of the second quarter of the fourteenth century, some decades after the articles were first published.⁶ Articles 1 to 31 of the Ordinances are copied on the recto of the roll. Passing over the dorse of the first membrane, which was on the outside when the manuscript was rolled for storage, the scribe copied articles 32 to 37, 40, and the beginning of 39 on membrane 2d. On membrane 3d, he copied the remainder of article 39 and the entirety of articles 38 and 41 *twice*, at the head and foot of the membrane, which has been flipped 180 degrees between the two copies. This suggests that the membranes were not sewn together until after the text had been copied and that the scribe accidentally rotated membrane 3 after completing the recto, resulting in misaligned text on the dorse. Rather than erasing the upside-down text, he recopied it in the space remaining at what became the head of the membrane and added "ici sont les ordeynauntes finys" to mark the correct ending.

A second hand, at least a generation later than the first, filled in the blank spaces on the roll with texts unrelated to the Ordinances. This hand uses anglicana forms exclusively, with no sign of secretary variants, but has stylistic features typical of the latter half of the fourteenth century and even the early fifteenth century.⁷ Texts in this hand fill membrane 1d, left blank by the first scribe as a protective covering for the roll and now rather stained and worn; the space between the mirrored copies of the end of Ordinances on membrane 3d; and the entirety of membrane 4d. On membrane 1d and the middle portion of membrane 3d, he copies medical recipes in Anglo-Norman, Middle English, and Latin (e.g., "p*ur* maladie maleursement garrie," mem. 1d; "ffor stinge aboute þe he*r*te," mem. 1d; "ut cadit dens put*r*id*us*," mem. 3d). The scribe copies the trilingual "Erthe upon Erthe" on the top of membrane 4d and another series of medical recipes below it, beginning "P*ur* mal de foye. de pulmo*n*. de splen."

The copy of "Erthe upon Erthe" is written in two unruled, uneven columns at the head of membrane 4d. The Latin text is copied in the slightly narrower column A and the Anglo-Norman text in the slightly wider column B, with a horizontal line drawn under the final line of each. The Middle English text begins in column A, with five stanzas (ll. 1–20) copied under the Latin text, and concludes in column B, with four stanzas (ll. 21–36) under the Anglo-Norman text. The scribe uses the same verse layout throughout, with a paraph in the left margin at the head of each stanza and rhyme brackets in the right margin connecting the first and last lines of each stanza. The Latin version uses a medial *punctus* consistently in the first stanza but only once thereafter.

Errors in copying all three versions of the poem in E 175/11/16, some of which were corrected in the same hand, show that the scribe was not their author. For example, the Latin text as written reads "aterreis" (l. 4) and "terram" (l. 14) for "a terrenis" and "terras." Both errors occur in the densely repeated words related to "terra," where it would be particularly easy for a scribe to lose track of his position. In the Anglo-Norman text, the scribe writes "couent" (l. 30) for "coment," omitting a minim. The word "en" is inserted above the first line, and likewise, in line 24, the first occurrence of "tere" was at first omitted, then added in the left margin. The third and fourth stanzas of the Middle English text show a great deal of corrections, including words inserted above the line, between words, and over erasures. Taken as a whole, the evidence suggests that the scribe was copying from an exemplar that already included all three languages, as it is unlikely that he would make these mistakes if he were copying from his own draft translations.

Although the text of "Erthe upon Erthe" in E 175/11/16 is most distinctive because of its tripartite nature, even the Middle English text in isolation is unlike the vast majority of poems in the tradition. Murray divides the "Erthe upon Erthe" tradition into two distinct strands. Her A version is represented by two copies from the first half of the fourteenth century: the single quatrain in British Library MS Harley 2253 and the fourteen-stanza bilingual Middle English and Latin poem in British Library MS Harley 913. The B version has far more representatives, largely in fifteenth-century manuscripts.[8] Murray regarded the Middle English portion of the trilingual text in E 175/11/16 text as an anomaly related only loosely to the larger tradition, distant from both the A and B versions. Max Förster revisited the question of "Erthe upon Erthe" taxonomy in 1919, revising Murray's groupings from two strands to three.[9] Förster's first strand corresponds to Murray's B version and his third strand to Murray's A version, but he reassesses the Middle English text of E 175/11/16 as a member of an independent second strand of the tradition ("ein zweites Gedicht") rather than as an isolated anomalous text.[10]

Following Förster's three-strand taxonomy, the closest parallel to the

Middle English text of E 175/11/16 is in Cambridge, St. John's College (SJC) E.24, folios 44r to 45r. This version, in fourteen stanzas and an introductory couplet, has been indexed as if it were a member of Förster's first strand (Murray's B version; DIMEV 6369 no. 3), but this placement is only half accurate. In fact, this text conflates material from two different strands, splicing together five stanzas from the first strand with eight stanzas from the second strand, along with one stanza (ll. 51–54) with no clear parallels in other manuscripts. The eight stanzas from the second strand in SJC E.24 closely correspond to all but one of the Middle English stanzas in E 175/11/16 (ll. 17–20).[11] Because of the similarities between these two instances of the second strand, parallel texts in SJC E.24 can be used to clarify some of the more difficult passages in the Middle English text of E 175/11/16.

Murray suggests that the production of the parallel Anglo-Norman and Latin texts in E 175/11/16 may have been inspired by the bilingual Middle English and Latin "Erþ" in Harley 913, but the poems have little in common.[12] The two poems resemble each other superficially, if only in that both incorporate translations, but where the E 175/11/16 text is laid out as three separate poems of unequal length, the Harley 913 version alternates between Middle English and closely translated Latin stanzas.[13] There are, moreover, almost no verbal correspondences between the Harley 913 text, which is a member of Förster's third strand, and the E 175/11/16 text, which is in the second strand. Compared with Harley 913, the translation in E 175/11/16 is much freer; while the translator occasionally preserves both the structure and argument of a Middle English stanza in his Anglo-Norman and Latin renditions, he also frequently translates by producing a new stanza on a similar theme. As with Harley 913, however, it seems clear that the Middle English text in E 175/11/16 is the original, considering its close parallels with versions in other manuscripts, particularly that in SJC E.24.

Comparing the three versions of "Erthe upon Erthe" in E 175/11/16 reveals some of the translator's practices. The Latin and Anglo-Norman translations are most closely related to the Middle English source text at the outset. The first two stanzas are roughly parallel in all three languages, though the Latin version sometimes compresses the Middle English material and fills the resulting space with new material (e.g., "*terram* dat et vendit," l. 7). Each version closes the second stanza with a description of earth's deathbed repentance, but they employ different images to do so: in Middle English, earth cries out toward heaven (l. 8); in Latin, earth stretches its hand toward "*terram* viuencium" (l. 8); and in Anglo-Norman, earth requests healing from "haute tere" (l. 8). By replacing the Middle English "heuene" with a metaphor interpreting heaven as a kind of earth, both translations add to the overall repetition and wordplay in the poem.

The Anglo-Norman diverges entirely in the third stanza, while the Middle English and Latin versions continue roughly in parallel. Various erasures and insertions in the Middle English stanza obscure its relationship with the Latin translation; for example, the Latin text reads "Terra terre serviens wlt refrigerari" (l. 11), for which the corresponding line in Middle English is the apparently unrelated "*And* eorthe on eorthe sone bigenneþ for to elden" (l. 11). The second half of that line, "bigenneþ for to elden," is written over an erasure, however, and the version in SJC E.24 reads "*And* erþe in erþe sone so a colde" (l. 29) instead. Taking rhyme into account, I propose that the exemplar for E 175/11/16 read "*And* eorthe on eorthe sone so achelden"—a reading that would account for the use of "refrigerari" in the Latin. That is, the E 175/11/16 scribe copied a text that had already been translated into Latin and Anglo-Norman, but either he or an earlier copyist had garbled the text at this point, and the E 175/11/16 scribe attempted to recover the sense by creating a line in which earth grows old on earth, rather than cold. This in turn could have triggered the corrections in the preceding line, which now reads "*And* eorthe on þat eorthe allewey bi helden" (l. 10), but "þat" and "bi h-" are later additions, and there is a gap after "alleway" with space for five or six letters. The corresponding line in SJC E.24 is "And erþe on þis erþe eche day schal elde" (l. 28); supposing that the exemplar for E 175/11/16 had a similar line, when the E 175/11/16 scribe altered "achelden" to "elden" in l. 11, he may have wanted to avoid repeating a rhyme word and so changed "elden" to "bi helden" in l. 10. As evidence against this, however, the Latin "Et ad terre terminum terram inclinari" (l. 10) has the image of earth falling to earth conveyed by "bi helden" and no similarity to a hypothetical line reading "elden," suggesting that the correction in the Middle English may have instead restored an earlier reading.[14]

In the final line of the stanza, the Middle English text in E 175/11/16, "Hou may þat eorthe on eorthe wo belden" (l. 12), again can be linked both to the Latin and to the SJC E.24 text. Both "þat" and "wo" are later insertions, presumably intended to correct the meter, and "wo" should be understood as an interjection. When read against the line in SJC E.24, "How may erþe in erþe be bolde" (l. 30), the line in E 175/11/16 could be interpreted as "How may that earth (alas!) be confident on earth?," while if read against the Latin "Et terra terribilis in terra locari" (l. 12), the same line in Middle English would become "How may that earth (alas!) dwell on earth?"[15] The Anglo-Norman text provides no evidence to resolve these cruces, since the corresponding stanza is not a translation of the Middle English but a general injunction against succumbing to temptation because earthly life is fleeting.

The fourth stanza, which argues that there is nothing but sorrow on earth and that all people must inevitably return to earth, brings the Anglo-Norman version back in parallel with the Middle English and Latin versions, but the close relationship between all three versions does not last long. The fifth through seventh stanzas, lines 17 to 28, address the same themes in each version, but with differing structures and arguments. In the fifth stanza, each version states that earth fails to remember its earthly origins and asserts the necessity of salvation, but the Middle English is a lament to an unknown listener ("Alas, why does earth on earth not think?"); the Anglo-Norman is an injunction to earth ("Remember, o thou wretched earth on earth!"); and the Latin is a simple third-person description ("Earth does not consider earth with a strong mind"). The sixth stanza considers earth's response to seeing its end approaching, but that response varies in each of the languages. Similarly, the seventh stanza addresses the Last Judgment, but the description of what will happen on that day differs; in particular, the Latin version omits the word "judgment" itself, instead referring to the day when "earth must arise from earth and possess what earth earned on earth" (ll. 25–26).

After this point, the three versions diverge further, with a handful of stanzas that are present in only one or two of the three languages and that thereby account for the difference in overall length between the three versions. First of these is a stanza depicting earth quarreling with earth because of a broken promise (ll. 29–32 in Latin and Middle English, omitted in Anglo-Norman). The Latin version alone follows this with a stanza (ll. 33–36) that anticipates the themes of the closing prayer. The next stanza describes how angels will awaken the dead to come before God (ll. 37–40 in Latin, ll. 29–32 in Anglo-Norman, omitted in Middle English). The details of the Latin and Anglo-Norman stanzas do not correspond exactly (e.g., alliterative trumpets sound in Latin but not in Anglo-Norman: "In terra terribiles tube resonabunt," l. 38), but the two versions are close enough to suggest that they are both translations of a lost Middle English stanza, perhaps skipped over by the E 175/11/16 scribe himself.[16]

The three languages come back together in a closing prayer (ll. 41–44 in Latin, ll. 33–36 and 40 in Anglo-Norman, ll. 33–36 in Middle English). All three versions begin by appealing to Christ through his connections to earth, addressing him as "terre domine" (l. 41), "Jesu qe *pour* la tere en tere fuist ne" (l. 33), and "Houre louerd þat on eorthe for eorthe was iboren" (l. 33), respectively. Likewise, they conclude with the desire that he bring earth to heaven, which is described in all three versions as a celestial earth: "terra glorie" (l. 44), "tere de viuauns" (l. 40), "þat eorthe þer beþ his icoren" (l. 36). In between, however, the Anglo-Norman takes three lines to ask Christ to protect earth, which the other versions accomplish in two. As a result, in order to bring the poem to a close at the end of a stanza, the Anglo-Norman translator inserts three unrelated lines into the middle of the prayer, including the self-referential "Pluis ne voil en tere ore de tere chaunter" (l. 39), before concluding with the plea that earth be allowed to dwell in the "earth of the living." Considering the three versions as a whole, it seems that the Latin and Anglo-Norman translations are most similar to the Middle English at the beginning of the poem, diverging more and more as they progress, perhaps as the translator found it difficult to render the rhetorical flourishes of the densely alliterative and multivalent Middle English poem in another language, and finally coming back into alignment with the source text in the last stanza.

Why would someone wish to produce versions of "Erthe upon Erthe" in three languages? In the case of the bilingual Harley 913 version, I looked to the manuscript's Franciscan contexts, arguing that the Latin text might have been incorporated into sermons delivered to the clergy, just as the English text was used in sermons addressed to the laity.[17] However, a scribe copying medical recipes and a poem on the reverse of an Exchequer roll like E 175/11/16 is unlikely to have shared these homiletic aspirations. More plausibly, he may have been (like Thomas Hoccleve) an unbeneficed member of the clergy working in the public service: a member of the "clerical proletariat."[18] Producing Latin translations of English sentences was a common classroom exercise, one any educated person would be acquainted with, since Latin was effectively the native language of literacy.[19] The Anglo-Norman translation in E 175/11/16 is more surprising but suggests that the translator, like the scribe, worked with Anglo-Norman government records. The fact that these rhetorically sophisticated translations of "Erthe upon Erthe" were both produced and preserved in a secular context implies that these clerical proletarians continued to be interested in wrestling with theological issues despite being employed by the government.

University of Notre Dame

APPENDIX: TEXTS AND TRANSLATIONS

Each version of the poem is transcribed individually, followed by a prose translation keyed to the line numbers in the edition.[20] Expanded abbreviations are italicized and emendations are marked in square brackets. Substantial differences between this text and the nineteenth-century copy in Additional 25478 are indicated in the notes, as are places where this edition diverges from Murray's. Minor differences in orthography between the roll text and Additional 25478 (e.g., "couetise" versus "coueytise" in l.6 of the Middle English text) are not marked. In the Middle English text, corresponding stanzas from the text in SJC E.24 are also given in the notes.

The Latin Version

mem. 4d col. a ⁋ In terra cum terra sit . fraude perquisita
Terra terre vermibus sic . putressit trita
Terra terram deseret . erit et finita
Terra tunc a terre[n]is[21]. mox erit oblita

5 ⁋ Terra per superbiam terram cum ascendit
Terra tunc cupidine terram comprehendit
Terra morti proximans . terram dat et vendit
Ad terram viuencium terra manus tendit

⁋ Terra terram speculans non iustificari
10 Et ad terre terminum terram inclinari
Terra terre serviens wlt refrigerari
Et terra terribilis in terra locari

⁋ In terra quid possidet terra nisi penas
Quando terra respicit terra[s][22] lite plenas
15 Et terram deficere tanquam terre tenas
Sic terra puterdinis [intrat][23] terre venas

⁋ Terra non considerat terram firma mente
Atque terra labitur in terra[24] repente
Terram suo sanguine terra redimente
20 Terram potens eruit[25] de terra dolente

⁋ Terra quando respicit terram terminare
Terra terram debuit sese castigare
Terra terram valeat ut humiliare
Terra terram faciat flere ieiunare

25 ⁋ De terra resurgere terra debet vere[26]
Et quod terra meruit terra possidere
Hic dum terra vixerit terra valet flere
Ut in terra valeat terra post gaudere

⁋ Aduersus terrigenas quando terra stabit
30 Et terram interrogans terra tunc culpabit
Terra finem capiat terram [obiur]gabit[27]
Quod terra promiserat terra tunc negabit

          ¶ In terra *qui* mortuus *et* in terra natus
          Ffuit terram protegat sic *et* terre gratus
35   Ut in terra quilibet de terra formatus
          Terre ponat terminum terre commendatus

          ¶ In terra cum Angeli terram suscitabunt
          In terra terribiles tube resonabunt
          De terra terrigene corpora levabunt
40   Et ad terre judicem terre tunc clamabunt

          ¶ O tu terre domine terre miserere
          Et terra respiciens terenos tuere
          In terra deficimus terra sumus vere
          Nos in terra glorie terram fac videre.

[1–4] When earth is falsely sought in earth, trodden earth decays with the worms of the earth. Earth forfeits earth, and when earth will be brought to an end, then earth will soon be forgotten by those on earth.
[5–8] When through pride earth climbs earth, then earth seizes earth because of greed. Approaching death, earth gives and sells earth. Earth stretches a hand toward the earth of the living.
[9–12] When earth sees that earth is not justified and that earth is bent toward the end of earth, earth in service to earth wants to grow cold and frightful earth wants to be placed in earth.
[13–16] What does earth possess on earth but trials, when earth sees that earth is filled with quarrels and that earth is wanting? As long as you cling to earth, the earth of putrefaction thus enters earth's veins.
[17–20] Earth does not consider earth with a strong mind and earth falls suddenly into earth. By means of its blood that redeems earth, powerful earth plucked earth from sorrowing earth.
[21–24] When earth sees that earth is ending, earth ought to have chastised itself, which is earth. Earth would do well to humble earth. Would that earth made earth weep and fast!
[25–28] Truly, earth must arise from earth and possess what earth earned on earth. Here, while earth has lived, earth can weep so that earth may later be able to rejoice on earth.
[29–32] When earth will stand as an enemy to those who dwell on earth, then earth, questioning earth, will reproach [it]. Earth will scold earth so that it may reach an end. What earth promised on earth, it will then deny.
[33–36] May he who died on earth and who was born on earth thus protect earth and be pleasing to earth, so that whoever is formed from earth on earth may place an end to earth entrusted to earth.

[37–40] When angels on earth awaken the earth, terrible trumpets will sound on earth. Those who dwell on earth will raise their bodies from earth and then the earths will cry out to the judge of earth.

[41–44] Oh Lord of earth, have mercy on earth! Gazing on earth, protect us on earth. We are extinguished on earth; we are truly earth. Make us see earth in the earth of glory.

The Anglo-Norman Version

mem. 4d col. b

¶ Quant terre auera en[28] terre large terre gayne
E terre serra en terre a la mort liuere
Puis ert tere en tere de vermyne mange
Dount[29] vendra tere en tere et toust ert oblie

5 ¶ Quant tere sour terre de orgoyl ne[30] descline
E tere uers[31] tere par coueitise encline
Dount tere uers tere se treit a Ruyne
E tere a haute tere requeit medicine

¶ Quant tere ne peot de terre la malueste sourueyndre
10 Par force deit tere de terre temptaciouns esteyndre
Encontre la frele tere sa tere deit refreyndre
Quant tere leue en tere face sa tere moyndre

¶ Quey ad tere de tere forqe dolour et peygne
Quant tere veyt en terre soun enemi demeygne
15 E tere court[33] en tere a la mort certeyne
E tere pase en tere par frelete humeyne

¶ O tu cheytiue tere de tere remembrez
Vous estes pris de tere et tere deuendrez
Pensez[35] coment en tere et par tere pecchez
20 E tere fuist en tere tant fortment[36] rechatez

¶ Quant tere veyt qe tere se treit a la mort
E tere nad en tere forque poure confort
Quant tere moert en tere ni ad nul resort
Merueille est que tere de tere nad retort

25   ¶ Quant tere[37] deit de tere leuer sodeynement
      Tere vendra en tere pour oyr jugement
      Dount[38] auera tere en tere dolour et turment
      Si tere neit fet en tere bon amendement

      ¶ Angeles vendrount en tere la tere resusciter
30   E dirrount a la tere de tere co[m]ent[39] leuer
      Deuant le Roy de tere en tere deuez aller
      Que[40] soffri en tere pour tere dolour amer.

      ¶ Jesu qe pour la tere en tere fuist ne
      Soyt eydaunt[41] a la tere qe tere soit sauue
35   Et nos meyne[42] de tere ou tere est benure
      Kar si sumes en tere par tere turmente

      ¶ Dolour est en tere par tere et par mer
      Ffaus est tere et tere desir auer
      Pluis ne voil en tere ore[43] de tere chaunter
40   Dieu deynt tere en tere de viuauns habiter.
                                                    Amen.

[1–4] When earth will have won[44] earth throughout earth, and earth will be delivered to death on earth, afterward earth on earth will be eaten by vermin. Then earth will pass into earth and it will soon be forgotten.
[5–8] When out of pride earth does not bow down to earth, and through greed earth stoops toward earth, then earth draws near to ruin toward earth and earth needs a remedy from high earth.
[9–12] When earth cannot overpower[45] the wickedness of earth, earth ought to extinguish the temptations of earth through force. Against frail earth, it ought to restrain its earth. When earth rises, it may make its earth stay behind on earth.
[13–16] What does earth have from earth except sorrow and pain, when earth sees in earth its own enemy, and earth rushes to certain death on earth, and earth passes into earth because of human frailty?
[17–20] Remember, o thou wretched earth from earth,[46] that you are taken from earth and you will become earth. Consider how you sin on earth and through earth, and how earth was so abundantly redeemed on earth.
[21–24] When earth sees that earth approaches death and that earth has only poor comfort on earth, when earth dies on earth and has no recourse, it is a marvel that earth has no reply from earth.
[25–28] When earth must rise suddenly from earth, earth will come to earth

to hear judgment. Then earth will have sorrow and torment on earth if earth has not made good amends on earth.

[29–32] Angels will come to earth to revive the earth and they will tell the earth how to rise from earth: "You must go before the king of earth on earth, who suffered bitter sorrow on earth for earth."

[33–36] Jesus, who was born on earth for the earth, help the earth so that earth may be saved and lead us from earth to where earth is blessed, for we are on earth afflicted throughout earth.

[37–40] There is sorrow on earth throughout the earth and throughout the sea. Earth is false and earthly desire is miserly. Now I do not wish to sing more on earth about earth. God grant that earth may live in the earth of the living. Amen.

The Middle English Version

mem. 4d col. a ¶ Whanne eorthe hath eorthe wiþ wrong igete
And eorthe in eorthe beginneþ to alete
And eorthe *in* eorthe wiþ wormes is afrete
Thanne eorthe is on eorthe sone forȝete[47]

5 ¶ Wanne eorthe ouer eorthe þorw prude styeþ
And eorthe toward eorth þorw coueytise wryeþ
And eorthe into eorthe toward þe deþ hyeþ
þanne eorthe aȝeyn eorthe toward heuene crieþ[48]

¶ Whan eorthe juynt[49] eorthe so luþer to awelden
10 *And* eorthe on *þat* eorthe allewey[50] bi helden
And eorthe on eorthe sone bigenneþ for to elden[51]
Hou may þat eorthe on eorthe wo[52] belden[53]

¶ What haueþ eorthe on eorthe bote þouȝt and[54] wo
Whan eorthe isoeþ eorthe his dedliche fo
15 *And* eorthe into eorthe so sone gynneþ guo[55]
And eorthe iworthe to eorthe alle we sullen so[56]

⁋ Alas why naþ eorthe in eorthe[57] is þouȝt
Hou eorthe is on eorthe wiþ sinnes of souȝt
And eorthe was in eorthe so mychfulliche ibouȝt
20 þat eorthe þorw eorthe ne foelle to nouȝt[58]

mem. 4d col. b   ⁋ Whan eorthe iseoþ eorthe to endinge drawe
And eorthe on eorthe wiþ deþ is islawe
And eorthe on eorthe wiþ wormes is ignawe
þanne eorthe may eorthe him seluen iknawe[59]

25 ⁋ Wan eorthe ssal of eorthe netfulliche aryse
And eorthe on eorthe ihere þilke assise
þer eorthe ne may eorthe noþer lere ne wise
þanne eorthe sal on eorthe grimliche agrise[60]

⁋ þanne eorthe sal to eorthe holden gret cheste
30 And eorthe asken eorthe were is hiere byheste
þat eorthe byhet eorthe allewey to leste[61]
Wanne eorthe turneþ to eorthe toward helle feste[62]

⁋ Houre louerd þat on eorthe for eorthe was iboren
On eorthe of eorthe wiþ wounden to toren
35 Wyte eorthe from eorthe þat ne be furloren
And bringe eorthe to þat eorthe þer beþ his icoren.[63]
Amen.

[1–4] When earth has gotten earth wrongfully and earth begins to disintegrate and earth is gnawed by worms in earth, then earth is soon forgotten on earth.
[5–8] When earth climbs over earth because of pride and earth turns toward earth because of greed and earth hastens into earth toward death, then earth facing earth cries toward heaven.
[9–12] When earth comes to earth, so wicked to govern, and earth collapses entirely on that earth, and earth soon begins to grow old on earth, how may that earth (alas!) dwell on earth?
[13–16] What does earth have on earth but cares and woe, when earth sees

that earth is his deadly foe, and earth so quickly begins to go into earth? And earth turns into earth: we all shall be the same.

[17–20] Alas, why does earth on earth not think about how earth is attacked on earth by sins? And earth was so dearly bought on earth in order that earth would not fall to nothing because of earth.

[21–24] When earth sees earth draw toward its end and earth on earth is slain by death and earth on earth is gnawed by worms, then earth may know himself to be earth.

[25–28] When earth shall of necessity arise from earth and earth shall hear that judgment, earth cannot either learn from or instruct earth there: then earth shall tremble sorely.

[29–32] Then earth shall have great strife with earth and earth shall ask earth where is her promise, that earth promised earth would last forever, when earth, hastening toward hell, turns to earth.

[33–36] Our Lord, who was born on earth for earth, who was rent with wounds by earth on earth, protect earth from earth so that it may not be destroyed, and bring earth to that earth where his chosen are. Amen.

NOTES

1. David Crook, "Hunter, Joseph (1783–1861)," in *Oxford Dictionary of National Biography*, vol. 28 (Oxford: Oxford University Press, 2004), 911–912.
2. The British Library catalogue records the acquisition of "biographical and historical collections of the late Joseph Hunter, partly from the Public Records, with correspondence" as Additional MSS 24436–24630, 24864–24885, 25459–25481, 25676, and 25677. In the catalogue, Additional 25478 is described as "Transcripts of miscellaneous English poetry, with a few Latin pieces, chiefly derived from manuscript sources; xivth–xixth centt." *Catalogue of Additions to the Manuscripts in the British Museum in the Years 1854–1875*, vol. 2 (London: Published by the Trustees of the British Museum, 1877), xi, 197.
3. Hilda M. R. Murray, *The Middle English Poem Erthe upon Erthe*, EETS o.s. 141 (London: Oxford University Press, 1911), 41–45.
4. The IMEV and its successors give "London (Kew), Public Record Office, Exchequer Roll, K.R. Proc. bundle 1" as the source for the Middle English portion of the trilingual poem (DIMEV 6293 no. 3); the transcript in Additional 25478 is also cited (DIMEV 6293 no. 2). The misnamed roll is listed as lost in Richard Hamer, *A Manuscript Index to the Index of Middle English Verse* (London: British Library, 1995).

5. The Ordinances of 1311 are printed in *The Statutes of the Realm*, vol. 1 (London: Record Commission, 1810), 157–168. E 175/11/16 is not listed as one of the manuscript sources for the Ordinances.
6. I am grateful to Teresa Webber for dating this hand; email message to author, February 22, 2016.
7. Ibid. As Webber observes, the second hand "lacks all but the slightest trace of the bulging horizontal and diagonal strokes characteristic of Anglicana in the later thirteenth and earlier fourteenth century, but instead there is a decorative use of hairline strokes below the baseline." The hairline strokes, the overall proportion of the hand, and the generous spacing between letters lead Webber to date this hand to no earlier than the second half of the fourteenth century and perhaps as late as the early fifteenth century.
8. Murray, *Erthe upon Erthe*, ix.
9. Förster refers to the three subgroups of the "Erthe upon Erthe" tradition as three "Gedichte." I use the term "strand" rather than "poem," since Förster's nomenclature (like Murray's "A" and "B version") tends to obscure the substantial differences between individual members of each subgroup. Within each subgroup, the manuscript witnesses fall into genealogical strands of related but distinct poems; they are not simply more-or-less miscopied instances of the same poem. Förster's first strand corresponds with Murray's B version. Förster explains the varying lengths of poems in this strand by positing that they descend from an original five-stanza version that was expanded in stages, resulting in widespread seven- and twelve-stanza versions. However, many of the individual poems also append unique stanzas not known in other manuscripts. For poems in the first strand with an introductory couplet, see DIMEV 6369; for versions without the couplet, see DIMEV 1170. Förster's third strand corresponds with Murray's A version (see DIMEV 6292). In addition to the two witnesses of this strand identified by Murray—Harley 2253 and Harley 913—Förster identifies a version in John of Grimestone's preaching notebook, Edinburgh, National Library of Scotland Advocates MS 18.7.21, as a conflation of material from the third and first strands of the poem (DIMEV 1167). Max Förster, "Die älteste Fassung des mittelenglische Gedichtes 'Earth upon Earth,'" *Archiv für das Studium der neueren Sprachen und Literaturen* 138 (1919): 39–61, 40–44.
10. See DIMEV 6293. Förster did not examine the trilingual roll text himself but uses Murray's edition and refers to the manuscript with her temporary shelfmark.
11. Förster argues that the eight stanzas held in common by SJC E.24 and E 175/11/16 represent the earliest version of the second strand, though the two manuscripts preserve the stanzas in a different order; Förster,

"Älteste Fassung," 57. Two other manuscripts not known by Förster also include versions of the second strand. New York, Pierpont Morgan Library M.957, fol. 126 (DIMEV 6293 no. 4), is damaged, but includes portions of at least 11 lines of the second strand. Oxford, Bodleian Library Holkham misc. 39, fol. 438r (DIMEV 6293 no. 1), has a version of the first stanza of the second strand, followed by a three-line Latin translation that is apparently unrelated to the Latin text in E 175/11/16: "Qwan erde hath erde wyth wo I gete / And erde ys in erde wyth erde I reke / And erde ys vnder erde with vyrmys I frete / þan chal erde on erde sone ben for ȝete // Terra tenet terram quando cum ve sibi nacta / Et tellus terra sistat cum puluere pacta / vermibus est rosa tellus cum sub quoque terra." The Latin translation in this manuscript has not previously been observed.
12. Murray, *Erthe upon Erthe*, 46.
13. For a discussion of the bilingual Middle English and Latin poem in Harley 913, with comparison to the closely related version in Harley 2253, see Marjorie Harrington, "Of Earth You Were Made: Constructing the Bilingual Poem 'Erþ' in BL MS Harley 913," *Florilegium* 31 (2014): 105-137.
14. See MED s.v. *"hēlden,"* def. 2a, "to bend, incline, obey, submit to, yield up" and def. 3, "to fall, collapse, die, fade away."
15. For the interpretation of "belden" suggested by comparison to SJC E.24, see MED s.v. *"belden."* For the interpretation suggested by the parallel Latin line, see MED s.v. *"bilden."* The form used in E 175/11/16 is consistent with either verb.
16. There is no corresponding stanza in SJC E.24, but that is insufficient evidence to claim that such a stanza was not present in the E 175/11/16 scribe's copy-text; after all, ll. 17–20 manifestly exist, and they have no parallel in SJC E.24.
17. Harrington, "Constructing the Bilingual Poem." Siegfried Wenzel identifies a sermon on *Benedictus qui venit in nomine Domini* that cites a Middle English "Erthe upon Erthe"; see Siegfried Wenzel, *Preachers, Poets, and the Early English Lyric* (Princeton, NJ: Princeton University Press, 1986), 126.
18. For a recent discussion of the vernacular literary endeavors of the clerical proletarians, see Kathryn Kerby-Fulton, "The Clerical Proletariat: The Underemployed Scribe and Vocational Crisis," *Journal of the Early Book Society* 17 (2014), 1–34, 7–8.
19. Christopher Cannon discusses the phenomenon of "making Latins" in relation to the translations of William Herebert, an early-fourteenth-century Franciscan; see Christopher Cannon, "Vernacular Latin," *Speculum* 90.3 (2015): 641–653, 651–653.

20. I am grateful to Julia Marvin for assistance in translating the Anglo-Norman text. Any remaining errors or infelicities are my own.
21. E 175/11/16 reads "aterreis," whereas Additional 25478 reads "aterrens"; I follow Murray in emending the reading to "a terrenis."
22. E 175/11/16 reads "*terram*"; I emend it to "terras" to agree with "plenas."
23. E 175/11/16 is damaged here, and Additional 25478 does not attempt to fill the lacuna. Murray supplies "intrat," writing "portions of *nt* and the second *t* can be seen." Murray, *Erthe upon Erthe*, 42.
24. Additional 25478 reads "*terram*" for "terra" (an error replicated by Murray).
25. Additional 25478 reads "erint" for "eruit."
26. Stains and holes in E 175/11/16 obscure the text of this stanza and the next; the copy in Additional 25478 leaves lacunas in the second half of ll. 25–32. My transcription here draws heavily on Murray's.
27. The text in E 175/11/16 is entirely illegible. Murray posits that the word ending "-gabit" may have been "obiurgabit," since "there is room for 2–3 letters, and possibly a trace of an r contraction." Murray, *Erthe upon Erthe*, 44.
28. The word "en" is inserted above the line.
29. Murray silently corrects the manuscript, printing "dounc" for "dount."
30. Murray's edition omits "ne."
31. Here and in the following line, Additional 25478 reads "ils" for "uers." Murray emends this to "vers" in her edition, suggesting that the abbreviation stroke for er, written over the second stroke of u, would look like il. Murray, *Erthe upon Erthe*, 43. However, examining E 175/11/16 under magnification reveals that the roll scribe *did* write "u*ers*" and that the error was not introduced until the copy in Additional 25478 was made.
32. Murray silently corrects the manuscript, printing "dounc" for "dount."
33. Additional 25478 and Murray's edition both read "coust" for "court," an error derived by the overlap of *y* in "veyt" above with the *r* in "court."
34. Additional 25478 reads "e'teyne" for "c*er*teyne."
35. Additional 25478 reads "peisez" for "pensez."
36. Additional 25478 reads "foilment" for "fortment."
37. The word "tere" is inserted in the left margin; the copy in Additional 25478 omits it entirely.
38. Murray silently corrects the manuscript, printing "dounc" for "dount."
39. Both E 175/11/16 and Additional 25478 read "couent," but "coment" makes more sense contextually.
40. Additional 25478 reads "Le" for "Que."
41. Additional 25478 reads "Sayt cydaunt" for "Soyt eydaunt."

42. Additional 25478 omits "*Et* nos m-", marking the lacuna with dashes.
43. Additional 25478 reads "ou" for "ore."
44. "Gainer" also means "plow" or "cultivate" as well as "win." This dual meaning allows this line to simultaneously refer to literal and metaphorical earthly harvests. See the *Anglo-Norman Dictionary (AND)* s.v. "gainer."
45. "Sourveyndre" is not attested in the *AND*. Julia Marvin suggests that this may be a form derived from *sur* + *veintre*; email message to author, March 19, 2016. I translate accordingly.
46. The Anglo-Norman line switches register in the middle of the line, addressing earth first as "tu" and then as "vous" for the remainder of the stanza.
47. The corresponding stanza in SJC E.24 (ll. 23–26) reads: "Whan erþe hauet erþe with woo byʒute. / And erþe in erþe bygynnyt to lete. / And erþe liþ in erþe with wormys yfrete. / þan erþe ys yn erþe sone forʒute."
48. Additional 25478 reads "bireþ" for "crieþ." The corresponding stanza in SJC E.24 (ll. 31–34) reads: "Whan erthe on erthe þorow pryde styyþ. / And erthe on thys erþe to covytise wryyþ. / And erthe in to erþe sone aʒen heyyþ. / þan erthe toward erþe to hevyn cryeþ."
49. In SJC E.24, this line reads "erþe wynt erþe" (l. 27) instead of "eorthe juynt eorthe" (l. 9). The exemplar for E 175/11/16 may have also read "wynt" but with the initial w written as three minims. If so, the copyist could have mistaken it for *iu*, thus producing "juynt."
50. "þat" is a later insertion in gray ink; there is a gap after "allewey" with space for five or six letters, and "bi h-" is written in the later gray ink.
51. "bigenneþ for to elden" is a later addition in gray ink. The ink in "bigenneþ" has bled where it was written over an erasure.
52. "þat" and "wo" are inserted above the line in gray ink.
53. The corresponding stanza in SJC E.24 (ll. 27–30) reads: "Whan erþe wynt erþe so luþur to a wylde. / And erþe on þis erþe eche day schal elde. / And erþe in erþe sone so a colde. / How may erþe in erþe be bolde."
54. "þouʒt and" is inserted above the line in gray ink.
55. "gynneþ guo" is written in gray ink on top of "go" in brown ink. Additional 25478 reads "gro" for "guo."
56. The corresponding stanza in SJC E.24 (ll. 35–38) reads: "What hauyþ erþe in erþe but woo. / Whan erþe sieþ on erþe greueliche foo. / And erþe ne may on erþe ryde ne goo. / þan erthe a curseþ erþe þis worlde fareþ soo."
57. The second instance of "eorthe" is inserted above the line in gray ink.
58. This stanza is omitted in SJC E.24.
59. The corresponding stanza in SJC E.24 (ll. 43–46) reads: "Whan erþe

syeþ erþe to endynge drawe. / And erþe is on þys erþe wiþ deþ aslawe. / And erþe lyþ on erþe wyþ wormes ygnawe / þan may erthe. erthe yknawe."

60. The corresponding stanza in SJC E.24 (ll. 47–50) reads: "Whan erþe schalle of o erþe nedeliche aryse. / And erþe yhure in erþe þe greueliche asyse. / And erþe ne may erþe lere no wyse. / þer schal erþe for erþe sorelyche agrise."
61. Ll. 30–31 are written in the opposite order in Additional 25478, with "2" and "1" in the right margin to indicate that the lines should be reversed.
62. The corresponding stanza in SJC E.24 (ll. 39–42) reads: "Whan erþe axyþ erthe whare be hur beste. / þat erþe by hete erþe þat he schulde yleste. / Whan erþe for erþe drawet to helle cheste. / þer erþe for erþe lesyt ioy wele an feste."
63. The corresponding stanza in SJC E.24 (ll. 55–58) reads: "Owre lorde þat on erþe for erþe was ybore. / And on erþe for erþe wiþ wondys totore. / Wyte erþe uppon erþe þat owre ne be forlor. / And brynge owre erþe þer boote is yfore."

An Unnoticed Fragment of the Anglo-Norman *Miroir* by Robert Gretham in Marsh's Library, Dublin

NIAMH PATTWELL

Marsh's Library, Dublin, was founded in the eighteenth century by Archbishop Narcissus Marsh (1638–1713) and currently houses over 25,000 books.[1] Collections in the library include those of Marsh, Elias Bouhéreau (1643–1719), and Edward Stillingfleet (1635–1699), all of whom were renowned book collectors in their time. The books in the collections are largely early-modern print publications that cover a wide range of topics, including theology, philosophy, medicine, science, and literature. As one might expect in a library that holds such a large collection of early printed books, one also finds a significant number of medieval manuscript fragments used as book bindings, fly leaves, or limp covers. The majority of the fragments consist of Latin liturgical and theological material, but in their midst I recently discovered a small fragment of parchment containing thirty-three lines of Anglo-Norman verse. The fragment contains four excerpts from Robert Gretham's Anglo-Norman *Miroir*, from the sermon to be preached on the Fifteenth Sunday after Trinity, based on the pericope from Matthew 6:24.[2]

Robert Gretham's *Le miroir ou les évangiles des domnées* is a collection of sixty homilies that was composed in the mid-thirteenth century. The *Miroir* offers a complete sermon cycle, written in octosyllabic rhymed couplets, based on the Sunday Gospels according to the Use of Sarum. Gretham wrote the sermons for a patroness, Aline, but references to "seigneurs" and "seigneurs, barons" suggest a wider audience was also intended.[3] The *Miroir*, which was intended for an aristocratic audience, was translated into Middle

English in the late fourteenth century, probably in response to the growing demand for vernacular religious material among the urban bourgeoisie of London.[4] According to Thomas Duncan and Margaret Connolly, the editors of the first of several volumes to contain the entire Middle English *Mirror*, none of the extant Anglo-Norman *Miroir* manuscripts "was the English translator's exemplar."[5]

There is no complete edition of the *Miroir*, although the *Anglo-Norman Literature: A Guide to Texts and Manuscripts* compiled by Ruth Dean and Maureen Boulton lists a number of partial editions, redactions, and transcriptions.[6] To Dean and Boulton's list, we can now add Duncan and Connolly's transcription of the Anglo-Norman text in their edition of the English *Mirror* for the Middle English Text series.[7] Duncan and Connolly's Anglo-Norman transcription is based on Nottingham, University Library, Mi Lm4 (W^2). The published volume, however, covers only the twelve sermons from Advent to Sexagesima and is not, therefore, a match for the Marsh's fragment, which is from a later Sunday in the liturgical year. The 1967 edition listed by Saverio Panunzio is also unhelpful in providing a means of identifying Marsh's fragment because it is limited to the sermons for the Nativity, Epiphany, Palm Sunday, Passion Sunday, Easter Sunday, and the first, second, and third Sundays after Easter.[8] If it were not for M. H. Aitken's 1922 edition, which contains a selection of sermons and a complete set of the exempla, the Marsh's fragment might have gone unidentified, but as it happens, lines 10 to 33 of Marsh's fragment correspond with sections of the thirteenth exemplum found in that edition.[9]

It is worth noting at this point that the extracts of the *Miroir* found in the Marsh's fragment are written in two columns on the verso and recto side of a single scrap of parchment and therefore are not continuous. Consequently, the Marsh's fragment offers four discreet blocks of text, each approximately eight lines long, rather than a single block of continuous text. The exempla in Aitken's collection are extracted from longer sermons, as was common practice in the Middle Ages. If the Marsh's fragment were part of a collection of exempla, lines 1 to 9 of the Marsh's fragment should have corresponded with lines from the previous (twelfth) exemplum in her collection. This is not the case; they are part of the sermon text coming shortly before the sermon.[10] We can conclude, therefore, that the Marsh's fragment is from a full sermon, possibly a complete cycle.[11] An examination of a complete cycle in Cambridge, University Library, Gg.I.i, confirmed that all thirty-three lines of the Dublin fragment correspond with sections of the *Miroir* text found on folio 240r–v of the Cambridge manuscript, thus confirming that the Marsh's fragment is a series of short extracts from the forty-fourth sermon or Fifteenth Sunday after Trinity of Robert Gretham's *Miroir*.

AN UNNOTICED FRAGMENT OF *MIROIR*

Table for Line Correspondences

Cambridge, UL, Gg.I.i (U)[12]	Marsh's	Aitken[13]	Blumreich[14]
fol. 240r, col. 1, ll. 21–27	ll. 3–9		ll. 150–153
fol. 240r, col. 2, ll. 16–23	ll. 10–17	ll. 15455–15462	ll. 166–170
fol. 240v, col. 1. ll. 12–19	ll. 18–25	ll. 15489–15496	ll. 179–184
fol. 240v, col. 2, ll. 7–14	ll. 26–33	ll. 15523–15430	ll. 192–193

 The Marsh's fragment, though removed from the original binding, looks as if it were used as a strengthener for the end leaves. The original leaf measures 40 mm by 150 mm and has been folded over along the top line of text to act as a hook around the end leaves.[15] The text is written in double columns over 130 mm on the recto side and 120 mm on the verso side of the leaf. The parchment is in relatively good condition, although there are some stains on the verso side of the fragment, possibly because it was the side that was folded outwards. The text is legible, apart from the top lines of the recto side, where the parchment was folded and is now almost cut through. On the left-hand side of the recto side, the margin and beginnings of the words have been cut away, leaving the first column of text incomplete. The remaining three columns—approximately eight lines of text each—are intact. The remaining margins measure 40 mm on the right of the recto side, and 10 mm on the right and 20 mm on the left of the verso side. The parchment has been ruled in double columns, with each horizontal line measuring 5 mm. It is impossible to be certain of the original size of each folio. It is equally impossible to calculate the precise number of lines per folio, given that the extant *Miroir* manuscripts exhibit uneven line numbers. For example, Nottingham, University Library, Mi LM 3 has 20 to 28 lines per page, with the greatest variation in line numbers occurring in San Marino, CA, Huntington Library, HM 903, with 36 to 43 lines per page.[16] That said, if we calculate the line difference between the end of the first columns and the end of the second columns of text on each side of the Marsh's fragment, we reach an average difference of thirty-five lines per page.

 The script is a late-thirteenth-century or early-fourteenth-century rotunda anglicana hand. The beginning letter of each line measures 3 mm to 4 mm, is touched with red ink, and sits towards the left margin, slightly separated from the remainder of the word.[17] The Marsh's fragment is too brief to offer a full description of the script, but some notable features include double compartment "a," often oversized in relation to the rest of the letters. The ascenders of "b," "l," and "h" are distinctly clubbed. Most letters sit on the line, including long "l," "s," "f," and "g." The minims exhibit ligatures rather than clubbing. The "i" has a notable slash above the line (equivalent of modern-day dot). There are two forms of r, regular and 2-shaped; the latter is normally used after "o." Long "s" is generally used in initial position, and 8-shaped "s" is found in medial and finial positions.

Duncan and Connolly list ten manuscripts of the Anglo-Norman *Miroir*. These are: Nottingham, University Library, Mi LM 3 (W^1); Nottingham, University Library, Mi LM 4 (W^2); Oxford, Bodleian Library, Holkham Misc. 44 (O); London, British Library, Additional 26773 (L); Cambridge, University Library, Gg.1.1 (U); San Marino, CA, Huntington Library, HM 903 (Hm); Paris, Bibliothèque Nationale, na fr. 11198 (F); Columbia, MO, University of Missouri, Ellis Library, Fragmenta Manuscripta 135 (Mo); Cambridge, Trinity College, B.14.39 (T); and York, Minster Library, XVI.K.14 (Y).[18] A brief survey of the physical features (script, written space) of the extant manuscripts suggests that the Marsh's fragment is most likely an eleventh witness to the *Miroir* cycle.[19]

According to Duncan and Connolly's "Checklist of Sermons and Additional Material" of their edition, W^1 and O are the only manuscripts to lack the sermon for the Fifteenth Sunday after Trinity.[20] A brief examination of a sample of script from W1 suggests that the Marsh's fragment is not a missing portion of the W^1 manuscripts. The minims of W^1, for example, are more distinctly clubbed; "k" is more compact; the tail of "q" descends from the side of the bowl of the letter, rather than appearing horizontal as it does in Marsh's fragment; the initial letters of W1 also lack the red "touch" found on the initial letters of each line in the Marsh's fragment. Moreover, the written space (168 x 136 mm) as described by Duncan and Connolly suggests that it is slightly larger than that found in the Marsh's fragment.[21]

The script of Bodleian Library, MS Holkham misc. 40 (O) more closely resembles the Marsh's fragment, but there are enough differences to suggest these are distinct witnesses; for example, the "m," "s" and "e" of the initial letters in O have more exaggerated extenders to the left than those found in Marsh's. Again, the description of the written space in Duncan and Connolly's description suggests that O might be larger (220 x 138) than the written space in the Marsh's fragment. The Huntington manuscript is written in a later hand than that of the Marsh's fragment, a bastard anglicana hand, and is not, therefore, a likely match for the Marsh's fragment.[22]

A brief examination of the fragments of the *Miroir* also suggests that the Marsh's fragment is a distinct fragment. T and Y are collections of sixteen and nine (respectively) exempla extracted from the sermons and are unlikely ever to have contained a full copy of the forty-fourth sermon.[23] The fragment found in F has a rounder script and other features, such as more frequent use of single-compartment "a" and long "s," that suggest it is distinct from the Marsh's fragment.[24] The script of the Missouri fragment (Mo) is also different, appearing more clubbed and compressed than the script of the Marsh's fragment.[25] The Marsh's fragment is most likely, therefore, an eleventh witness to the *Miroir* sermon cycle.

It is doubtful that such a tiny sample of thirty-three lines could provide any further information to aid the construction of a stemma that already seems elusive. Duncan and Connolly were searching for an exemplar that was closest to the English *Mirror* and chose W^2 as the base text for their transcription of the *Miroir* because it is "not only the best complete manuscript of the Miroir but also, in all probability, the best witness to the translator's copy of the Anglo-Norman text even if its readings by no means always represent those of that version."[26] Aitken could not devise a convincing stemma for the Anglo-Norman tradition, and Duncan and Connolly are dubious about Laird's conclusion, in his study of Hm, that it "was related to W^1 and U rather than to W^2 and L."[27] A successful stemma, therefore, has yet to be established for the Anglo-Norman *Miroir* manuscripts, and the Marsh's fragment will hardly provide sufficient evidence to begin to construct one, although it may provide some further clues.

In my comparison of Aitken and the Marsh's fragment, for example, I note that there are some notable points where the Marsh's fragment agrees with U (and occasionally L) instead of W^2. In lines 29 to 30 of this transcription (ll. 15526–15527 of Aitken), the Marsh's fragment has "durement" in the first line, rhyming with "tendrement" in the second line; Aitken (using W^2 as her base text) has "tendrement" in the first line, rhyming with "amerement" in the second line. The Marsh's fragment on this occasion agrees with L and U. In a second example, however, Marsh's and U disagree; notably, "faite" on line 23 of Marsh's reads "fort" in U. In such a short extract it is difficult to determine the relationship of the fragment to the extant witnesses. It is possible to claim, however, that the Marsh's fragment is another witness to the Anglo-Norman *Miroir*, representing another point in its textual history. As an eleventh witness, it is further evidence, if it were needed, of the popularity of the text in the Middle Ages.

The Anglo-Norman fragment presented here is but one of the many fragments to be found in the book bindings of Marsh's Library, though it should be noted that not all of the binding fragments are, of course, from medieval manuscripts. In a box containing fragments removed in the early twentieth century by the then-master of the library, Newport Benjamin White, there are 110 fragments. Seventy-seven of those are print fragments, and the remaining thirty-three are from manuscripts, two of which have been dated to the sixteenth century. The fragments range from letters or word fragments to whole pages; they are in Latin, Anglo-Norman, and Middle English and cover a vast array of topics. Some can be linked with the early-modern book in which they were bound; others, including the Anglo-Norman fragment discussed, can no longer be traced to their original place in the library. Work has begun digitally to reproduce the disbound fragments and make them available to interested readers on the library's Web site. There remains, however, a significant number of the fragments still in situ in the covers and bindings of the collection.

University College Dublin

APPENDIX 1

The following is a transcription of the text as it appears in the fragment. Ellipses between square brackets indicate illegible sections in the text. Abbreviations have been expanded and the expansion indicated by underlining. Square brackets indicate a reconstruction based on Dr. Duncan's understanding of Anglo-Norman language and readings in other manuscripts.[29] The numbers on the side refer to line numbers of Marsh's fragment.

Fig 1. Column a
1. [...] nt <u>a iustice</u> puse trare
2. [...................][30]
3. [E] par tant tut perist
4. [M]es cil <u>qui</u> que<u>r</u>t le regne de
5. [D]e bon <u>quor</u> <u>et</u> de ue<u>r</u>ite
6. [I]ci li e<u>r</u>t tut aiuste
7. [Quanque] ad mest<u>er</u> sa frailete
8. [A]iuste dit kar ci auerait
9. [D]el deu dun <u>quanque</u> mest<u>er</u> ait

Fig 1. Column b
10. E pur ceo suuent lui mustrot
11. Auant main ceo <u>que</u> auenir dot
12. Quant dex li out si longes fait
13. Sun <u>quo</u>r entra en un fol hait
14. D<u>un</u>t il pensa <u>que</u> ceo ert drait

AN UNNOTICED FRAGMENT OF *MIROIR*

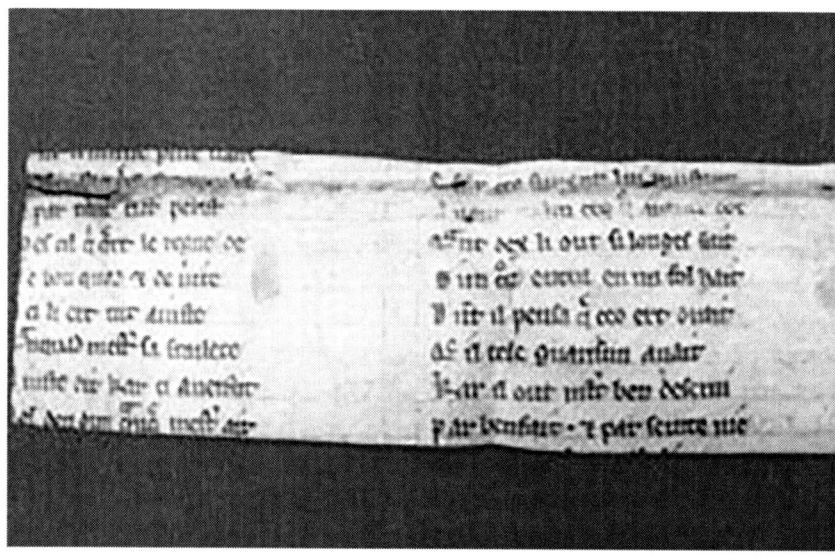

Figure 1.

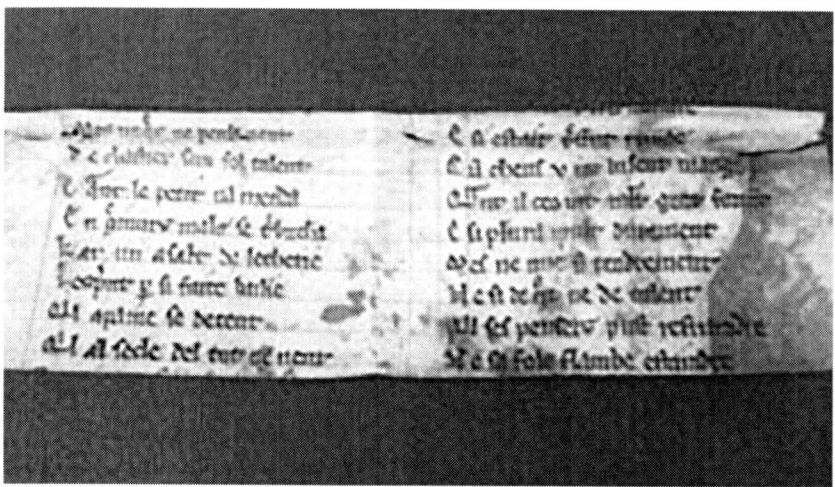

Figure 2.

15. Que il tele guarisun auait
16. Kar il out mult ben deserui
17. Par benfait et par seinte uie

Fig 2 Column a
18. Mes unques ne pensa nent
19. De chastier sun fol talent
20. E quant le petit na menda
21. En greinurs mals se tribucha
22. Kar un asalt de lecherie
23. Lesprent par si faite bailie
24. Q'il apaine se detent
25. Q'il al secle del tut ne uent

Fig 2 Column b
26. E si estait trestut runge
27. Cum chens v raz lusent mange
28. Quant il ceo uit mult gent forment
29. E si plura mult durement
30. Mes ne mie si tendrement
31. Ne si de quor ne de talent
32. Q'il ses pensers pust refraindre
33. Ne sa fole flambe estaindre

NOTES

1. For further reading on the history of Marsh's library, see Muriel McCarthy, *Marsh's Library: All Graduates and Gentlemen* (Dublin: Four Courts Press, 2003). See also the Marsh's Library Web site at http://www.marshlibrary.ie.
2. "Anglo-Norman Miroir," http://www.marshlibrary.ie/digi/items/show/124.
3. For a discussion on the identity of Gretham and of his patron, Dame Aline, see K. V. Sinclair, "The Anglo-Norman Patrons of Robert the Chaplain and Robert of Greatham," *Forum for Modern Language Studies* 27 (1992): 193–208.
4. There are also some indicators that the ME *Mirror* may have some "tentative links" with monastic production and, more specifically, the Augustinian and/or Praemonstratensian orders. See Thomas Duncan and Margaret Connolly, *The Middle English Mirror: Sermons from Advent to Sexagesima*, Middle English Text Series 34 (Heidelberg, Germany: Universitätsverlag Winter, 2003), lvii–lviii. I wish to

acknowledge here the generous assistance of Margaret Connolly and Thomas Duncan in the preparation of this article.
5. Ibid., xxxvii. For a more detailed discussion on the relationship between the Anglo-Norman *Miroir* and its Middle English translation, see ibid., xxxvi–li.
6. See Ruth Dean and Maureen Boulton, *Anglo-Norman Literature: A Guide to Texts and Manuscripts*, Anglo-Norman Text Society Occasional Publication Series 3 (London: Anglo-Norman Text Society, 1999): 325–326.
7. See Duncan and Connolly, *Middle English Mirror*.
8. Robert de Gretham, *Le miroir ou Les évangiles des domnées: Edizione di otto domeniche, Studi e testi di lettteratura francese*, 2nd ed., ed. Saverio Panunzio (Bari, Italy: Adriatica Editrice, 1974). This edition is considered derivative and inaccurate by a number of reviewers. See, e.g., L. Marshall and W. Rothwell, "The *Miroir* of Robert of Gretham," *Medium Aevum* 39 (1970): 313–321.
9. M. Y. H. Aitken, Étude sur le "Miroir" ou les "Évangiles des domnée" de Robert Gretham (Paris: Champion, 1922).
10. Thomas Duncan informs me that lines 1 to 9 begin eleven lines before the start of the exemplum and are from the sermon text that precedes the exemplum. There are two further lines of the sermon text (not in the Marsh's fragment) before the exemplum begins.
11. It is worth pointing out that all thirty-three lines also show some correspondence with the forty-fourth sermon in another Middle English edition, produced by Kathleen Blumreich in 2002. See Kathleen M Blumreich, ed., *The Middle English Mirror: An Edition Based on Bodleian Library, MS Holkham misc. 40*, Medieval and Renaissance Texts and Studies 182, Arizona Studies in the Middle Ages and the Renaissance 9 (Turnhout. Belgium: Brepols, 2002), 375–378. For corresponding line numbers, see the table below.
12. Cambridge University Digital Library, https://cudl.lib.cam.ac.uk/view/MS-GG-00001-00001/485.
13. Aitken, *Étude*, 166–168.
14. Blumreich, *Middle English* Mirror, 350–378.
15. "Book structures were commonly strengthened by incorporating strips of parchment around the endleaves"; David Pearson, "English Centre-Piece Bookbindings 1560–1640," in *Eloquent Witnesses: Bookbindings and Their History*, ed. Mirjam M. Foot (London and Delaware: Bibliographical Society of London and Oak Knoll Press, 2004), 114.
16. The line numbers per page for the remaining manuscripts are: W^1 20–28; L 29–42; U 37–40; Hm 36–43; F 38–40; Mo 39–41; T 32–34 (Duncan and Connolly, *Middle English Mirror*, xx–xxviii).

17. See Figs. 1 and 2 below.
18. Here I am following the sigla found in Duncan and Connolly, *Middle English Mirror*, x; for a list of the same manuscripts, without the sigla, see also Dean and Bolton, *Anglo-Norman Literature*, 325–326.
19. I am grateful to Margaret Connolly, who supplied and checked images from O, and to Jayne Amat, who supplied images from W^1. See also the image database of medieval and Renaissance manuscripts hosted at Berkeley: Digital Scriptorium, http://bancroft.berkeley.edu/digitalscriptorium/; see also Bibliothèque Nationale de France, Gallica, http://gallica.bnf.fr/html/manuscrits/manuscrits.
20. Duncan and Connolly, *Middle English Mirror*, 171–172.
21. Ibid., xx–xxi.
22. See images from Hm and description in the Digital Scriptorium, at http://bancroft.berkeley.edu/digitalscriptorium/.
23. According to Dean and Boulton, Trinity College, Cambridge MS, B. 14.39 (T) has two exempla not found in Aitken and lacks three found in her edition; Dean and Boulton, *Anglo-Norman Literature*, 325. They suggest that York, Minster Library, XVI.K.14 (Y) is a fragment of 880 lines, containing the first six exempla and the beginning of the seventh as they appear in T; ibid., 326. See also P. Meyers, "Les manuscrits français de Cambridge," *Romania* 32 (1903): 18–120; and Duncan and Connolly, *Middle English Mirror*, xxviii.
24. See images of the fragment and description online at *Miroir* fragment in Paris, Bibliothèque Nationale, na fr. 11198. Bibliothèque Nationale de France, Gallica.
25. For a description and images of the Missouri fragment online, see the *Miroir* fragment in Columbia, MO, University of Missouri, Ellis Library, Fragmenta Manuscripta 135. Berkeley Digital Scriptorium. (http://vm133.lib.berkeley.edu:8080/xtf22/search?rmode=digscript;smode=basic;shelfmark=135;docsPerPage=1;startDoc=3;fullview=yes)
26. Duncan and Connolly, *Middle English Mirror*, xxxvii.
27. They describe Laird's evidence as "limited and inconsistent"; ibid., xxxvii.
28. Maria O'Shea, Librarian, Marsh's Library, in correspondence, July 4, 2015.
29. I am grateful to Thomas Duncan for his help with the transcription.
30. This line is cut through and is illegible.

A New Text of the *Marvels of Merlin*

ERIC WEISKOTT

The *Marvels of Merlin* is a cross-rhymed, alliterating Middle English political prophecy in twelve quatrains, beginning "Of al þe merveilis of Merlyn how he makes his mone." Sharon Jansen made the poem the subject of an extended study in 1985, identifying seven long texts and three excerpts in five fifteenth- and sixteenth-century manuscripts.[1] In a 1991 monograph dedicated to English political prophecy in the sixteenth century, Jansen noted an eighth long text of the *Marvels* and a fourth excerpt in a sixth late manuscript.[2] The purpose of this essay is to bring to light a ninth long text of the *Marvels* in a manuscript of the late sixteenth century: London, British Library, MS Additional 24663.

The *Marvels of Merlin* has never appeared in a critical edition, and the extent of its manuscript circulation is not fully recoverable from available bibliographical reference works. Presentation of a new text of the poem therefore involves some negotiation of textual as well as bibliographical history. This essay seeks to augment the handlist of *Marvels* texts compiled by Jansen and to confirm that these various texts witness a single Middle English poem. Before turning to the new text of the *Marvels* in MS Additional 24663, I provide an overview of the textual history of the poem and of the itemization of its extant manuscript witnesses by modern bibliographers.

In her 1985 essay, Jansen included full diplomatic transcriptions of nine of the ten texts of the *Marvels* then known to her. (The tenth text, an excerpt tacked onto the end of a different verse prophecy, had been printed by V. J. Scattergood in 1972.)[3] While exhibiting signs of textual corruption or scribal revision in many cases, these texts clearly witness one and the same poem. The earliest, London, British Library, MS Harley 2382, a long text, dates to the late fifteenth century, justifying reference to the *Marvels* as a "Middle English" poem despite its appearance elsewhere only in manuscripts of the sixteenth century.⁴ The composition of the poem likely predates the copying of MS Harley 2382 by a few decades at most. Jansen, following Charles L. Kingsford, interprets certain symbols in the *Marvels* as oblique allusions to political events of the early 1460s.⁵ For example, the first quatrain mentions a lion (l. 3), a rose (l. 4), and a ragged staff (l. 4), elements in the coat of arms of Henry VI and the heraldic badges of Edward IV and the earl of Warwick, respectively. Although the symbology of late-medieval English political prophecy is obscure and polysemous by design, Kingsford's and Jansen's identifications are consistent with established conventions of this literary genre, in which heraldic devices come to life as avatars of their real-world owners.

The preponderance of postmedieval textual evidence for a medieval poem, no less than the veiled topical allusions, typifies the genre of political prophecy. Prophecies tended to be recycled and recombined from manuscript to manuscript and century to century, their symbolic imaginaries amplified, redacted, and updated in light of new developments in political and literary history. Sixteenth-century witnesses of the *Marvels* are of value both as textual reproductions of a fifteenth-century original and as cultural productions in their own right. Jansen's studies emphasize the latter perspective, detailing the ways in which sixteenth-century scribe-revisers tuned the text of the poem to new political realities and new literary prerogatives. Her monograph is entitled *Political Protest and Prophecy under Henry VIII*, though many of the prophetic texts she discusses are also extant in versions from before 1500. Jansen finds the text of the *Marvels* in large anthologies of prophecies, in the state papers of Henry VIII, and even in the mouth of a servant named Richard Swann at his 1538 trial in Kent for spreading the prophecy.⁶ In this essay I look backward as well as forward, discussing the text of the *Marvels* in MS Additional 24663 in codicological context and also locating it in the textual tradition of the fifteenth-century poem.

Modern bibliographical treatment of texts of the *Marvels* has been incomplete and inconsistent. This is hardly surprising, since the poem appears in large, multifarious anthologies on the periphery of late manuscript culture and just to either side of the boundary between the medieval and early-modern periods. At the time of Jansen's writing from 1985 to 1991, the *Supplement to the Index of Middle English Verse* recorded two texts of the *Marvels*, both long, incorrectly listing one of them as a separate poem under the third line.⁷ The volume of the *Manual of the Writings in Middle English, 1050–1500* covering "Poems Dealing with Contemporary Conditions" lists the same two texts of the *Marvels* listed in the *Supplement*, dividing them, as the Supplement does, into two separate entries.⁸ This situation has been carried over into the *New Index of Middle English Verse (NIMEV)*, which lists three long texts under the first line of the poem (*NIMEV* 2613.5) and two of these same long texts under the third line (*NIMEV* 1253.5) in a deleted entry pointing to William Ringler's *Bibliography and Index of English Verse in Manuscript 1501–1558* (TM 1260).[9]

The incomplete list of texts of the *Marvels* in the *Supplement*, the *Manual*, Ringler's *Bibliography*, and *NIMEV* is entirely understandable in light of the convoluted manner in which this poem mutated and circulated in late-medieval and early-modern literary culture. Some of the sixteenth-century texts of the *Marvels* may have been known to the editors of *NIMEV* but omitted on the grounds that they represent new, postmedieval poems rather than postmedieval copies of a Middle English poem. Such modern judgments about textual form, while defensible in advance of a critical edition or other concerted textual analysis, serve to highlight the perplexities of fifteenth- and sixteenth-century prophecies as textual objects. Late manuscript anthologies, in which older and newer texts in little-studied subgenres freely intermingle with few or no structures of textual layout to divide one from the next, pose a special challenge to the procedures of indexers. And texts like the *Marvels*, which enjoyed widespread circulation in relatively variant forms across centuries, expose the artificiality of the divisions that bibliographers must make between texts and between periods of literary production.

MS Additional 24663 contains English and Latin prophecies in prose and verse attributed to such figures as Geoffrey Chaucer, Merlin, and St. Thomas of Canterbury. Like many late manuscript collections of political prophecies, MS Additional 24663 has received scant critical and codicological attention. The British Library catalogue entry identifies only one text in the manuscript, the Latin *Vaticinium* attributed to John of Bridlington.[10] *NIMEV*, whose scope is restricted to poems known to have been composed before 1500, lists three items in the manuscript, all prophecies: the *Ireland Prophecy* (*NIMEV* 2834.3), an alliterative verse prophecy; 'When faith faileth' (*NIMEV* 3943), a short rhyming prophecy sometimes, as here, attributed to Chaucer; and the cross-rhymed, alliterating *First Scottish Prophecy* (*NIMEV* 4029).[11] Ringler's *Bibliography* lists a total of seven poems in the manuscript, but even this is an incomplete reckoning.[12]

On folios 4v to 6r of MS Additional 24663 is a previously unremarked text of the *Marvels* written in a single column in a secretary hand. The text of the *Marvels* is laid out in prose paragraphs, like many previous and subsequent English prose and verse texts in this manuscript. While prose format for verse remained an option in fifteenth- and sixteenth-century English book production, the various syntactically difficult revisions to the poem in this text lead one to question whether the scribe of MS Additional 24663 recognized the *Marvels* as verse for most of the copying process.[13] Only the penultimate quatrain (ll. 41–44), which begins a new manuscript page, is lineated as verse. Lines 20 and 21 of the text are interrupted by a long section of prosified verse laid out as prose on folios 5r to 5v, beginning "Then in the land shal be greatt warres" and ending "and be the cheeff makere of peace and vnytie." The text of the *Marvels* is punctuated with virgules, most of which coincide with line boundaries, as well as horizontal section divisions, most of which coincide with stanza boundaries. The final quatrain of the poem (ll. 45–48), thoroughly reworded as prose and now nonrhyming, appears after "ffinis" but before the next item.

In the following transcription, I omit all scribal punctuation and lineate the poem as verse in order to facilitate comparison with other manuscript copies. I include the final quatrain, although the scribe of MS Additional 24663 possibly received it and probably perceived it as prose, and although the addition of "ffinis" before line 45 locates the final quatrain outside the text proper in this copy. I make this slightly unconventional editorial decision in order to recover for inspection as complete as possible a text of the *Marvels*. Italics indicate expansion of scribal abbreviations, except that the ampersand is silently expanded to *and*. Capitalization is editorial and follows modern usage, including capitals at the beginning of each line of verse. Word division is regularized. *Y* for þ in abbreviations of particles such as "that" and "the" is printed þ. Line-initial *ff* is rendered *F*; *ff* elsewhere is rendered *ff*. At line 27, ellipses in brackets denote a line omitted in MS Additional 24663 but implied by the rhyme scheme and attested in other copies. I leave space for this phantom line in order to facilitate comparison with other texts of the *Marvels*.

The Marvels of Merlin
London, British Library, MS Additional 24663 (fols. 4v–6r)

> [4v] Above all places Merlyn makethe his mone
> Take heede to his talkinge wher he tellethe
> How a lyon shal be bannyshed and to Barwick gone
> The rose and the raggid tree followethe by frythes by felles
>
> 5   A stowt knyght in a storme a bugell shall blowe
> To rease vpp his rachettes and ryne *with* open mowthe
> And sleye hym þat never was borne the black crowe

Shal be cawse of the vengeaunce then shall in the sowthe

The whit lyon vnder the mone rampe and ryse
10   With sealles to see his own deathe to seke
The yonge bull and þe bastard shall play at þe basse
The bore and þe beare shall make þe lyon meek

[5r] The wolff shall waxe woed and wander by ffeldes
To seeke a bore that is put to greatt deryssion
15   The same bore shall whett his tuskes vppon his shelde
To brynge hym owt of baell and his ffone to connfusione

The beare and the wolff shall assemble together
And brynge wheatt into Brytten in a horsse of tree
Then shall a kinge fflee for feare and he wyst where
20   For dreade of a dragone that shall distroye a cyttie

Then in the land shal be greatt warres and every man agaynst other shall cast downe bothe wood and water...

[5v] [A passage of prosified verse, written as prose, fols. 5r–5v]

A bore shall come with a beare and a yonge bull
To brynge a foxe owt of his den that lyethe in a tower
A femall gryffen and her byrdes an auntelope shall down pull
Thorowghe the succor of a lyon redd and þe lyllye fflower

25   Flaunders and England shall fall att defyance

Becawse of falcenes of a traytor vntrewe
[...]
And Flemmyshe flece Saxsones shall rewe
The Teames shall rone bloode as redd as the rose
30 And the shyers abowt shall wepe and crye
For slaunderinge the ellyffant with the longe nose
The rose feamale with her fflowers dolfullye shall dye

A fawcon down shall ffall an eagell for fear shall ffly
And they shall come agayn to Iulyvs Seasors place
35 And a beare shall shake his cheane a false mayor to distroye
The sherryves and ther offycers shall have no grace

Then shall Kent lawghe and Essexe make sport
And other shyers moe than I can tell
In trust of a yong prynce þat shall them support
40 All landes and commons in peace shall dwell

[6r] The same prynce ffayre and ffull of famosytie
Shall call the prellattes to his presentes and prymates principallye
To sett the realme in peasse and þe churche in traunquillytie
And to geve good exsample to the greatt estates
ffinis

45 Saynt Thomas with John of Byrlington and Merlyn
Saythe that connfusion shal be in England
When the childe beattethe the mother then the father will take vengeance
Thre ffloodes fflowinge in Bryttayn shall cawse greatt connfvsion

In three respects, the text of the *Marvels* in MS Additional 24663 (henceforth **A**) closely resembles the second of the two long texts of the poem in London, British Library, MS Sloane 2578 (henceforth **S**), a copy from the mid-sixteenth century.[14] First, like the text in **A**, that in **S** appears in a longer sequence of prophetic sayings attributed to various reputed prophets. The *Marvels* is accommodated to this scheme in both manuscripts by a modified opening line (in **S**, "Also aboue all places Merlyon makethe mencion"). Second, like the text in **A**, that in **S** is formatted as prose. Finally, and most significantly, in both texts lines 20 and 21 are divided by the same passage (beginning in **S** "Then in the lande shalbe greate warr"). These three points of similarity indicate a very close textual relationship between **A** and **S** here.

A third, somewhat earlier sixteenth-century manuscript, London, British Library, MS Lansdowne 762 (henceforth **L**), contains an excerpt of the *Marvels* whose text and codicological context connect it to the **A** and **S** texts.[15] This is the excerpt printed by Scattergood. In **L**, the first eight lines of the *Marvels* appear as the last eight lines of an amalgamated cross-rhymed poem. The first of these lines (l. 127 in Scattergood's numbering: "above all places he and merlin make mone") shares the modified opening of **A** and **S**. What is more, the portion of the prophecy in **L** immediately preceding the first line of the *Marvels* (ll. 103–126 in Scattergood's numbering, beginning "A dede man shall aryse that beryed was in fight") corresponds to the item immediately preceding the *Marvels* in both **A** and **S**.[16] This verse prophecy, logged as TM 5 in Ringler's *Bibliography*, is known in only one other manuscript: Oxford, Bodleian Library, MS Arch. Selden B.8, a copy from the mid-sixteenth century. Finally, and most significantly, the text that stands between lines 20 and 21 of the *Marvels* in **A** and **S** appears, as a passage of rhyming verse, earlier in the same amalgamated poetic text in **L** (ll. 62–102 in Scattergood's numbering, beginning "Then in the londe shalbe grete warre"). This passage in **L**, in turn, immediately precedes the text of TM 5.

To summarize, **L** runs together three verse texts of special relevance to the texts of the *Marvels* in **A** and **S**. These are (1) cross-rhymed lines beginning "Then in the land shall be great war(s)" (missing from Ringler's *Bibliography*), (2) TM 5, and (3) lines 1–8 of the *Marvels of Merlin*. **L** differs from **A** and **S** in placing the text of "Then in the land shall be great war(s)" before rather than within the *Marvels*, in retaining only the first two quatrains of the *Marvels*, and in presenting all three poetic texts in verse lineation rather than as prose. Nonetheless, the disposition of materials in **L** aids in reconstructing how TM 5 and "Then in the land shall be great war(s)" came to precede and bisect the texts of the *Marvels* in **A** and **S**.

The *Marvels* has not yet appeared in a critical edition. Although Jansen's essay provides most of the necessary textual evidence for an edition, Jansen herself discussed each text individually and made no attempt to infer archetypal readings. I collate **A** with the earliest text, from MS Harley 2382 (henceforth **H**); with the excerpt in **L**; and with the second of the two long texts in **S**, which bears such a striking resemblance to **A**. Text from **H** and **S** is from Jansen's essay, with Jansen's punctuation omitted, and text from **L** is from Scattergood's book, with Scattergood's punctuation omitted and with the manuscript reading *brone* at line 7 (l. 133 in Scattergood's numbering) restored from Scattergood's correction to *borne*. In the following collation, shared readings are given in the form of the earliest witness:

> 1 Above] AL; Also aboue S; Of H places] ALS; þe merveilis of H Merlyn] AHS; he and merlin L makethe] ALS; how he makes H his mone] AH; mencion S; mone L 2 heede] AS; tent HL wher] ALS; in tales wher H 3 How] AHL; yone S 4 The] ALS; bi þe H tree] ALS; staf H followethe] AL; flowe S; *om.* H by] & by HLS felles] AL; feldes HS 5 in a storme] AL; & a sterne S; & a stour H 6 rease] AS; arre H; reve L rachettes] AS; racches HL and] ALS; to H mowthe] ALS; mouthes H 7 And] AL; to HS borne] AHS; brone L the] & eke þe H; for the LS crowe] AHL; cow S 8 Shal] AS; *om.* HL be cawse] AHL; be the cause S the^{1}] AHL; that S then shall] þat wil falle H; that shall fale LS 9 The] AS; A H rampe] shal rampe HS and ryse] AS; in a-rase H 10 sealles to see] sayles to the seye S; zelis in-to þe see H owne deathe] AS; frendes H to^{2}] AS; for to H 11 The] AS; a H þe^{1}] AS; a H þe^{2}] AS; a H 12 make þe] make a H; the S meek] AS; ful meke H 13 The] A HS waxe woed] be wude S; wax wroth H ffeldes] frith & feld H; the fielde S 14 to] AS; in H 15 bore] AS; *om.* H vppon his shelde] apon his owne sheld H; on his shielde S 16 hym] a bere H; him-self S and] AS; *om.* H ffone] fomen HS 17 The beare and the wolff] A bere a bore & a wolf H; The bore & the beare & the wulf S assemble] semble them H; sembull S 18 And] to HS into] AS; out of H in] apon H; on S 19 fflee for feare] AS; fle H where] whether HS 20 a^{1}] AH; þe S shall] AH; will S 21 bore] AS; bere H beare] bore H; brave S and a] AH; *om.* S 23 byrdes] brid HS 24 Thorowghe] AH; *om.* S the succor] a stronge socoure S; sace H redd] AH; The redd rose S þe] AS; a H fflower] AH; flowers S 25 Flaunders] AS; Then Fflaundres H att defyance] at division S; in distencion H 26 falcenes] false S; the falsnes H of a traytor] of þe Troian H; tratores S 27 *om.* A] ther-for a dragon shal be ther confusion HS (ther

confusion] confuson of S) **28** And] a kyng to were a H; the kinges tower and S Saxsones] alle Saxons H; & Saxon[s] S rewe] AS; it rewe H **29** The] & S; *om.* H bloode] AS; ful of blode H the] a HS **30** the] al þe H; all S shyers abowt] AH; streates S shall wepe] AS; wepe shal H and] AH; & shall S **31** the[1]] of an S; of þe H the[2]] AH; a S **33** for fear] AS; frosen H ffly] AS; fle H **34** And they] [b] ut they S; zet þat H to] AS; in-to H **35** And a] AS; þe H cheane] AS; cheynes H false mayor] folmer H; meyre S **36** ther offycers] her affinite HS no] AS; no maner H **37** shall Kent] Kent shal HS make sport] & make gret disport H; make disporte S **38** shyers] AH; diueres [s]hiers S **39** þat] AH; *om.* S shall them] AS; they shal H support] AH; supported S **40** landes] lordes HS in peace shall dwell] in loue & rest shal dwell H; *om.* S **41** The same prynce] AH; *om.* S ffayre] faire of face H; full fayre S and ffull] AS; ful H famosytie] AS; formosate H **42** the prellattes] AS; prelates H prymates principallye] principally ij primettes HS (ij] *om.* S) **43** realme in] AS; churche in lond & H and þe churche] AS; þe reme H **44** And] the churche H; *om.* S good] AS; *om.* H the greatt estates] pore & gret estatis H; the poore & to thestates S **45** Saynt Thomas with John of Byrlington and Merlyn] Bede Merlyon & Assheldon with Saint Thomas of Caunterbery H; St. Thomas & Marlion & John of Birlington with other S **46** Saythe that connfusion shal be in England] AS; and Bridlyngton in þer prophecie accordes in conclusio[n] H **47** beattethe] smytes HS the[2]] AH; his S then] for then S; *om.* H will take vengeance] AS; shal him destroye H **48** Thre] the HS greatt connfvsion] greate insurrection with confuson S; interdiction H

The first point to make is simply that these four manuscript texts witness the same poem. The degree of variation is comparable to that among, say, manuscripts of *Piers Plowman* B. That is, textual variation is relatively fluid but largely restricted to substitution, rewording, and rearrangement within individual lines of verse. All three long texts contain twelve quatrains; only **A** omits any of the 48 lines (l. 27). The rhyme scheme remains legible throughout (but cp. 2 *tellethe* for presumptive *tellys* as in **H**, **HS** *feldes* at l. 4 for presumptive *felles* as in **AL**, and so on). Despite signs that the *Marvels* has been worked over as prose in places in **A** and **S**, for example, **A** 45–48 and **S** 24 and 27–28, with sentence structure superseding line structure, for the most part the four texts contain the same words in the same order. And despite the integration of the *Marvels* into a longer sequence of prophecies in prose format in **A** and **S**, a reader of either manuscript can readily perceive the alliteration and quatrain structure of the poem. Indeed, the scribe of **A** or a predecessor in the same textual lineage highlighted these poetic structures (effectively, if not knowingly) through details of textual layout: with a few exceptions, virgules mark line breaks and horizontal section divisions mark stanza boundaries in **A**. As a topical vernacular poetic text, the *Marvels* was characteristically exposed to textual *mouvance* in transmission. As it happened, however, scribes remade the text within a relatively narrow scope. **A** and **S** witness the fifteenth-century poem attested in **H** rather than a new, sixteenth-century composition. **L** witnesses the first two quatrains of the same fifteenth-century poem, embedded in a larger prophetic verse amalgam.

The collation also confirms the close textual affiliation of **A** and **S**. **A** and **S** agree as against **H** more than twice as often as either **A** and **H** agree as against **S** or **H** and **S** agree as against **A**. **A** and **S** agreements as against **H** are 2 *heede*; 4 *The* and *tree*; 6 *rease, rachettes, and,* and *mowthe*; 9 *and ryse*; 10 *owne deathe*; etc. **A** and **S** are roughly contemporary productions, and one might inquire whether one text was copied directly from the other.[17] On the basis of textual evidence, copying in either direction seems highly unlikely. On the one hand, **A** was not copied from **S**, since **A** and **H** frequently agree as against **S** in ways that clearly do not reflect convergent variation, for example, 3 *How*; 7 *crowe*; 24 *Thorowghe, redd,* and *fflower*; 30 *shyers abowt*; 38 *shyers*; and 41 *The same prynce*. On the other hand, **S** was not copied from **A**, either, since **S** does not omit line 27, found in a similar form in **H**. Other significant **H** and **S** agreements as against **A** include *feldes* at line 4, *fomen* at line 16, *principally ij primettes* at line 42, and *smytes* at line 47. Barring lateral contamination, **A** and **S** must derive from a lost common ancestor codex containing the same poem in the same textual format and with "Then in the land shall be great war(s)" dividing lines 20 and 21. The possibility of lateral contamination appears remote in a manuscript subculture characterized by extreme informality and a tendency to mix and match what modern analysis can recognize as individual texts. To summarize, while the close textual and codicological similarities between **A** and **S** place them within one stemmatic subfamily, neither text was copied directly from the other. **A**, **H**, and **S** each possess independent textual authority for the reconstruction of the fifteenth-century text of the *Marvels*.

The excerpt in **L** rounds out this picture by pointing toward the existence of lost manuscripts of the *Marvels*. Neither **A** nor **S** could have been copied directly from **L**, given its status as a short excerpt. **L** is too early to have been excerpted from **A**. Nor could **L** have been excerpted from **S**, since **L** agrees with **H** as against **A** and **S**, for example, *tent* at line 2, where **A** and **S** have the trivializing, nonalliterating substitution *heede*. Thus textual evidence, like codicological evidence, shows that **L** is closely related to the stemmatic subfamily containing **A** and **S** but not the common ancestor of it. This conclusion, in turn, indicates the extent and diversity of the textual tradition of the *Marvels*. Comparison of **A**, **L**, and **S** adumbrates lost intermediary codices containing a trio of English verse prophecies, including the *Marvels of Merlin*, in two or more permutations.

 A is best understood as a partially reworked and therefore semi-reliable sixteenth-century copy of a Middle English poem. At least two **A** (and **L**) readings as against **H** and **S** likely represent the archetype of all surviving copies of the *Marvels*. These are 4 *felles* ("hills"),[18] where **H** and **S** have the nonrhyming common noun *feldes* "fields," and 37 *shall Kent*, preserving poetic syntactical inversion of auxiliary verb and subject, where **H** and **S** have *Kent shal* with prose word order. Among other texts of the *Marvels*, most read "fields" at line 4, with **H** and **S**, but "shall Kent" at line 37, with **A**. Many **A** and **H** (and **L**) readings as against **S** are also likely to represent the archetype of all surviving copies of the *Marvels*. Of those **A** and **H** readings noted above, especially strong candidates for archetypal readings are 3 *How*, necessary after 2 *tellethe*, and 24 *Thorowghe* and *redd*, where the line has become garbled in **S** due to a scribe's making "(the) red (rose)" the start of a new sentence. Inferentially, then, **S** represents a more boldly reworked copy of the fifteenth-century original than does **A**.

 Looking toward the future, a critical edition of the *Marvels*, taking into account all nine long texts and all four excerpts, is desirable. Such an edition would further contextualize **A** in the textual history of the *Marvels*. It would also enable a more detailed account of the poem's first historical context and its subsequent evolution in step with new developments in political history, contact with new readerships, and recombination with new prophetic texts.

 In view of the preceding discussion of the textual tradition of the *Marvels*, *NIMEV* 1253.5 should be merged with *NIMEV* 2613.5, adding **A** and the remainder of the long texts and excerpts identified by Jansen as witnesses to the poem. As Jansen remarked in her 1985 study, the obscure topical allusions and confusing textual history of the *Marvels* have kept the poem on the periphery of critical ken. Indeed, by collecting textual evidence of a Middle English verse prophecy from sundry sources and thereby disclosing a largely unremarked literary archive, Jansen made an exception of the *Marvels* in the wider field of English political prophecy. Many of the texts that appear alongside the *Marvels* in manuscript have never been printed, carry no modern titles, and bear an undocumented or only partially documented relationship to similar earlier, contemporary, and later manuscript texts.

 Though it does not figure prominently in current scholarship, political prophecy was a major locus of literary activity well into the seventeenth century in Latin and the British vernaculars. Prophecies influenced the decisions of kings, shaped public perception of national politics, and landed people in prison (or worse). In 1991, Jansen made two key contributions to the study of this literary genre: with Kathleen Jordan, a critical edition of the first of the two sixteenth-century manuscript compilations now bound together as Oxford, Bodleian Library, MS Rawlinson C.813; and the aforementioned monograph surveying the cultural, historical, and literary contexts of English political prophecy in the early sixteenth century.[19] The case of the text of the *Marvels* in **A** demonstrates that there are still discoveries to be made in incompletely catalogued and understudied post-1500 manuscript anthologies.

Boston College

NOTES

1. Sharon L. Jansen, "'The Marvels of Merlin' and the Authority of Tradition," *Studies in Medieval and Renaissance History* 8 (1985): 35–73. Cp. Sharon Jansen Jaech (as Sharon L. Jansen) and Kathleen H. Jordan, eds., *The Welles Anthology: MS. Rawlinson C. 813: A Critical Edition* (Binghamton: State University of New York, 1991), 281–288. I give the opening line from the earliest witness, London, British Library, MS Harley 2382: Jansen Jaech, "'Marvels,'" 60.
2. Sharon L. Jansen, *Political Protest and Prophecy under Henry VIII* (Woodbridge, UK: Boydell & Brewer, 1991), 165–166.
3. V. J. Scattergood, *Politics and Poetry in the Fifteenth Century* (New York: Barnes & Noble, 1972), 386–389 (*Marvels of Merlin*, ll. 1–8, at 389).
4. Jansen Jaech, "'Marvels,'" 37–40 (discussion) and 60–62 (text).
5. Ibid., 38–39 and n. 8, with references. For the dating of London, British Library, MS Harley 2382, see ibid., 38.
6. Ibid., 41–42 (state papers: discussion), 44–45 and n. 37 (anecdote about the servant), and 65 (state papers: text); and Jansen, *Political Protest*, 52–53 and 94 (anecdote about the servant).
7. Rossell Hope Robbins and John L. Cutler, *Supplement to the Index of Middle English Verse* (Lexington: University of Kentucky Press, 1965), *IMEV* 1253.5 and 2613.5.
8. Rossell Hope Robbins, "Poems Dealing with Contemporary Conditions," in *A Manual of the Writings in Middle English, 1050–1500*, ed. Albert E. Hartung, 10 vols. (New Haven: Connecticut Academy of Arts and Sciences, 1967–1998), 5:1385–1536 and 5:1631–1725 (bibliography), at 1716.
9. William A. Ringler, Jr., *Bibliography and Index of English Verse in Manuscript 1501–1558* (London: Mansell, 1992), and Julia Boffey and A. S. G.

Edwards, *A New Index of Middle English Verse* (London: British Library, 2005).
10. *Catalogue of Additions to the Manuscripts in the British Museum in the Years MDCCCLIV—MDCCLXXV*, 2 vols. (London, 1875–1877), 2:94–95.
11. For the scope of *NIMEV*, see Boffey and Edwards, *NIMEV*, xii–xiii. On the *Ireland Prophecy*, see Eric Weiskott, "The *Ireland Prophecy*: Text and Metrical Context," *Studies in Philology* (forthcoming).
12. Ringler, *Bibliography*, TM 43, 810, 1203, 1429 (=*NIMEV* 2834.3), 1509 (five lines from the prosified verse text that divides ll. 20 and 21 of the text of the *Marvels of Merlin* printed in this essay), 1857 (=*NIMEV* 3943), and 1907 (=*NIMEV* 4029). Two other previously unremarked English verse texts in MS Additional 24663 are "Then a dead man shall aryse and agrement make" (fol. 3r) (=*NIMEV* 3513.5) and "Marlyn saythe that a dead man shall aryse that was buryed in sight" (fol. 4r–v) (=Ringler, *Bibliography*, TM 5). Both poems are in cross-rhymed quatrains. Note that MS Additional 24663 may actually fall outside Ringler's date range: following the *Marvels* in this manuscript is "A straunge report of the cittie of Prage in Bohemia (yf it be trewe)" (fol. 6r) that refers to the year 1571 in the past tense.
13. A. S. G. Edwards, "Editing and Manuscript Form: Middle English Verse as Prose," *English Studies in Canada* 27 (2001): 15–28.
14. Jansen Jaech, "'Marvels,'" 47–48 (discussion) and 70–71 (text). On this manuscript, see also Jansen Jaech, "British Library MS Sloane 2578 and Popular Unrest in England, 1554–1556," *Manuscripta* 29 (1985): 30–41.
15. **L** also contains a long text of the *Marvels*: Jansen Jaech, "'Marvels,'" 40–41 (discussion) and 62–64 (text).
16. **A**, fol. 4r–v, and **S**, fol. 98r–v (within Jansen's no. 65: Jansen Jaech, "British Library MS Sloane 2578," 36).
17. Jansen Jaech, "British Library MS Sloane 2578," 31–32, dates **S** to 1554–1556 on the basis of evident allusions to political events of the reign of Mary I.
18. *Middle English Dictionary* Online, "fel (n.(2))."
19. Jansen and Jordan, *Welles Anthology*, and Jansen, *Political Protest*. On late-medieval and early-modern British political prophecy, see esp. Rupert Taylor, *The Political Prophecy in England* (New York: Columbia University Press, 1911); Jansen, *Political Protest*; Karen R. Moranski, "The *Prophetie Merlini*, Animal Symbolism, and the Development of Political Prophecy in Late Medieval England and Scotland," *Arthuriana* 8 (1998): 56–68; Tim Thornton, *Prophecy, Politics, and the People in Early Modern England* (Woodbridge, UK: Boydell & Brewer, 2006); and Morgan Kay, "Prophecy in Welsh Manuscripts," *Proceedings of the Harvard Celtic Colloquium* 26/27 (2006/2007): 73–108.

A Brief Note on Geoffrey Spirleng, Co-Scribe of MS Hunter 197 (U.1.1), and His Compilation of the Old Free Book of Norwich, NRO, NCR Case 17c

RUTH FROST

As Deborah Thorpe notes in the 2011 issue of *Journal of the Early Book Society*,[1] Geoffrey Spirleng (ca. 1426– ca.1494) was a "well trained and flexible" scribe.[2] He worked his way up within Sir John Fastolf's administrative circle, and later, during his tenure as the common clerk of Norwich, he made a copy of *The Canterbury Tales* along with his son Thomas.[3] Geoffrey Spirleng became Norwich's common clerk in May 1471. Reelected each year, he remained in office until 1491 and received a yearly salary of £4 6s 8d.[4] Among his many duties, Spirleng recorded the minutes of the assemblies of the mayor, aldermen, and common council; compiled the chamberlains' records; and maintained the register of freedoms to the city of Norwich, commonly called the Old Free Book.[5] As a professional civil servant, Spirleng swore an oath that he would make "trewe warantis entreis and recordes."[6] Yet for sixteen years Geoffrey Spirleng did not maintain the Old Free Book of Norwich at the same level of detail that previous common clerks had employed since the 1450s.

Starting in the early 1450s, the common clerks of Norwich organized the Old Free Book by occupation.[7] Mercers were grouped with mercers, for example, and drapers with drapers. The register noted each new freeman's name and occupation, gave his date of entry, and identified the mayor and common clerk.[8] Sometimes it included the chamberlains' names as well. In addition the Old Free Book distinguished between men who entered by patrimony (as sons of citizens) and men who entered as former apprentices of a citizen. Men who purchased their freedoms had no additional descriptions besides their name. If, therefore, information about apprenticeship or patrimony was not included, a reader of the freedom register could assume that an entrant had purchased his freedom.[9]

Before he became the common clerk in 1471, Spirleng had served as a common councillor of Norwich, in which capacity he had seen many men come before the assembly to swear their oaths as new freemen.[10] Indeed, we know about the changes in record-keeping within the Old Free Book because the Assembly Proceedings, civic documents also maintained by Geoffrey Spirleng, record the entries of those men who went before the mayor, sheriffs, and common council and swore the freeman's oath.[11] The names and fines of these men also appear in surviving chamberlains' account books and rolls.[12] (Men who were citizens by patrimony, however, appear only in the Old Free Book and not in the Assembly Proceedings or chamberlains' records, as they neither swore an oath of citizenship nor paid an entrance fine.)

In his early years as common clerk, Geoffrey Spirleng omitted information from the Old Free Book about the apprenticeship links of some men; a comparison with the Assembly Proceedings reveals that in 1471 and 1472 the Old Free Book noted the former masters for most of the men who entered by apprenticeship but not for all. However, in 1473, the Old Free Book only noted that two men had entered by apprenticeship, whereas the Assembly Proceedings showed that ten men had done so, and in 1474, the freedom register identified only one man as entering the freedom by apprenticeship, compared with nineteen in the Assembly Proceedings.[13] In 1475, the Old Free Book excluded all references to apprentices, and this exclusion continued, with only two exceptions, until 1488, when apprenticeship was fully reintroduced to the register of freedoms. While scholars can find the apprenticeship information in the Assembly Proceedings and surviving chamberlains' accounts, the exclusion of its references within the Old Free Book is nevertheless puzzling, especially given the experience and reputation of Spirleng, the close attention to detail that scholars have noted in his other work,[14] and the trust and responsibility placed upon him to maintain accurate civic documents.

Geoffrey Spirleng updated the minutes of the assembly meetings and other documents in the same manner as his predecessors, but he chose to break with precedent for the Old Free Book.[15] The question is: why? Omitting the description "nuper apprenticius Johannis Mundford" for the glazier William Stalon's entry, for example, saved some scribal time and ink, but it is unclear what additional advantages its exclusion might have offered, especially as other measures to save ink were not taken.[16] (Dropping the name of the mayor from every single entry would have saved much more effort and ink, yet this information continued to be recorded.) Given Spirleng's meticulous habits, it is likely that he suspended all apprenticeship references only after careful consideration. The patchy disappearance of the apprenticeship information in the early 1470s suggests that the initial omissions may have been inadvertent for 1471 and 1472. However, the omission of most apprenticeship references in 1473 and 1474 suggests that within two years of taking office Spirleng had adopted a deliberate change of policy regarding apprenticeship information within the Old Free Book.

The omission of apprenticeship references for over a decade seems to confirm this change of record-keeping policy. Spirleng continued to include references to paternity within the Old Free Book as this information was not readily available elsewhere. However, well aware that at least two other civic documents contained references to the apprenticeship ties of new citizens, Spirleng seems to have decided that it was superfluous to include the same information in the Old Free Book's entries.[17] His first omissions of apprenticeships in 1471 and 1472 may have been unintentional, but in 1473, fully settled into the job of common clerk and familiar with all the civic records, Spirleng seems to have deliberately implemented changes to the Old Free Book. Taken in this light, his inclusion of the few apprenticeship references in the Old Free Book for 1473 and 1474 was perhaps inadvertent, whereas his exclusion of apprenticeship information for the other entrants was the conscious result of a policy change.

To the question of why Geoffrey Spirleng omitted references to apprenticeships for so many years (or sanctioned their exclusion), one might further inquire why he reintroduced the apprenticeship information into Norwich's Old Free Book in 1488. As with its exclusion in the first place, the reintroduction of apprenticeship information seems likely to have been the result of a deliberate change of policy. An inquiry into an individual's citizenship may have revealed the register's gaps, and the resulting discussion may have prompted a policy reversal. Someone new to the common clerk's office or someone auditing its processes may have advocated the return of information related to apprenticeship. Spirleng himself may have found it time-consuming to consult another civic document if a question arose regarding a man's entry by apprenticeship.

It is also possible, although admittedly speculative, that a personal disagreement between the common clerk and the mayor led to the change in record-keeping. In 1487, the Assembly Proceedings describe an anomaly in Spirleng's election. On May 1, 1487, John Wellys was elected to his second term as mayor. According to the Proceedings, Wellys and Spirleng had had a long-standing dispute. As a result, the aldermen decreed that the common clerk's election on May 3, 1487, was to be suspended until the two men could have a private or public conversation ("quousque fiat interlo*quium* publi*cum* vel secre*tum* int*er* eos").[18] Despite this, the aldermen gave Geoffrey Spirleng permission to continue in office through the next year. In 1488, the aldermen elected a different mayor, and the aldermen reelected Spirleng without debate.[19] There is no evidence that animosity between Wellys and Spirleng had anything to do with the reintroduction of apprenticeship descriptors back to the Old Free Book, and it is wishful to speculate that an untrusting Mayor Wellys went through Spirleng's work with a careful eye, found the omissions, and demanded that the descriptions of apprenticeship and masters be returned. Nevertheless, the timing of the disagreement, and the parallel of its occurrence with the reappearance of apprenticeship entries within the Old Free Book, is tantalizing.[20]

Richard Beadle notes that "an extended reading of the documentary sources associated with him leaves the consistent impression that Spirleng was throughout his life a very busy and highly competent professional man, in whom shrewd but demanding employers were keen to invest large responsibilities and trust."[21] Geoffrey Spirleng, former employee of Sir John Fastolf and copyist of *The Canterbury Tales*, enjoyed a long and active career in Norwich. His decision to omit some information from that city's Old Free Book attests to the confidence he brought to his role as common clerk. Within a few years of taking office in 1471, he modified his maintenance of the register of freedoms by omitting references to apprentices, comfortable in exercising his judgment gained from years of clerical and administrative experience. Yet Geoffrey Spirleng reinstated apprenticeship information into the Old Free Book of Norwich in the late 1480s, suggesting that this "well trained and flexible" scribe continued to be flexible even towards the end of his long career.

University of British Columbia Okanagan

Acknowledgments

My thanks to Michael Treschow and to Karen Hodges for helpful conversations about aspects of this paper.

NOTES

1. Deborah Thorpe, "Documents and Books: A Case Study of Luket Nantron and Geoffrey Spirleng as Fifteenth-Century Administrators and Textwriters," *Journal of the Early Book Society* (2011): 195–215.

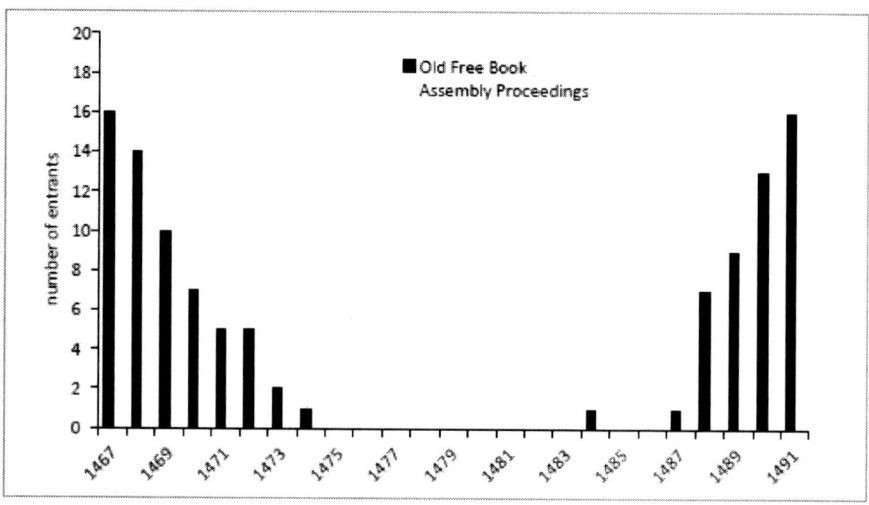

Figure 1: *Entries by apprenticeship in documents maintained by Geoffrey Spirleng or under his supervision - Old Free Book of Norwich compared with the city's Assembly Proceedings, 1467-1491*.[22] These are the yearly numbers of men identified in the Assembly Proceedings as entering by apprenticeship, as compared to the entries for apprenticeships in the Old Free Book. For the years in which discrepancies occurred the men continued to be entered into the Old Free Book, but no descriptions about apprenticeship appeared after their names. As the entries for the calendar years of 1467 and 1468 show, several apprenticeship descriptions were omitted prior to Spirleng's assumption of the role of common clerk in 1471. These seem to have been scribal errors. In contrast, however, around 1473 Spirleng appears to have made a concerted effort to omit apprenticeship information. The three references to apprenticeships in 1473 and 1474 may have been inadvertently included as he began to implement this change in policy.

  Deborah Thorpe is not alone in commenting on Geoffrey Spirleng's work and prowess; see Richard Beadle, "Geoffrey Spirleng (c. 1426- c. 1494): A Scribe of the *Canterbury Tales* in His Time," in *Of the Making of Books: Medieval Manuscripts, Their Scribes and Their Readers: Essays Presented to M. B. Parkes*, ed. Pamela Robinson and Rivkah Zim (Aldershot, UK: Scolar Press, 1997), 116–146; Daniel Wakelin, "When Scribes Won't Write: Gaps in Middle English Books," *Studies in the Age of Chaucer* 36 (2014): 249, 250, 257, 268, and 269; and Daniel Wakelin, *Scribal Correction and Literary Craft: English Manuscripts 1375–1510* (Cambridge, UK: Cambridge University Press, 2014), 64, 109, 230, 231, and 266.
2.   Thorpe, "Documents and Books," 208.
3.   Ibid., 195.
4.   Beadle, "Geoffrey Spirleng," 120 and 130.

5. Norfolk Record Office (hereafter NRO), Norwich Civic Records (hereafter NCR) Case 16d/1, Folio Books of Proceedings of the Municipal Assembly, Book 1 (1434–1491); NCR Case 16d/2, Book 2 (1491–1553) (hereafter referred to as Assembly Proceedings); NCR Case 17c, Freemen's Roll 1, 1317–1549 (hereafter referred to as Old Free Book); NRO, NCR Case 18a, Chamberlains' Account Book ; and NRO, NCR Case 7a-g, Chamberlains' Account Rolls.
6. William Hudson and John Cottingham Tingey, eds., *Records of the City of Norwich*, 2 vols. (Norwich, UK: Jarrold & Sons, 1906), i. cvii (clerk's duties), and i. 122 (Oath of the Common Clerk). This was similar to oaths in other towns. In York, for example, the common clerk was charged that "all things that shall be enterd of recorde, ye shall truly enroull and registre." See Barrie Dobson, "John Shirwood of York: A Common Clerk's Will of 1473," in *Much Heaving and Shoving: Late-Medieval Gentry and Their Concerns: Essays for Colin Richmond*, ed. Margaret Aston and Rosemary Horrox (Chipping, UK: Aston and Horrox, 2005), 114. For a discussion of the role of the common clerk in late-medieval London, see Caroline M. Barron, *London in the Later Middle Ages: Government and People 1200–1500* (Oxford: Oxford University Press, 2004), 185–188. Barron remarks that in London the common clerk was part of the city's "permanent civil service or town hall bureaucracy"; ibid., 173. David Palliser, *Medieval York 600–1540* (Oxford: Oxford University Press, 2014), 270, remarks that in York the "recorder and Common (town) Clerk were part of what Miller calls a new professional class, and both were often drawn from a group of interrelated gentry families."
7. See NRO, NCR Case 17c, fol. 53v, for the order made during Thomas Aleyn's mayoralty (1450–1451).
8. No woman entered the freedom during the years of this study. Very few women entered the freedom in general; see Penelope Dunn, "After the Black Death: Society and Economy in Late Fourteenth-Century Norwich" (PhD diss., University of East Anglia, 2003), 68.
9. Men who purchased their freedom usually paid 20s for the privilege. Those who entered by apprenticeship typically paid a fee of 13s 4d. Three men who entered the freedom between 1467 and 1491 had their entrance fees waived because of their positions: John Paston, "armig*er* et mercer," and Robert Thorpe, "gentilman *alias* mercer," both entered on the same day in 1483 (NRO, NCR Case 17c, fol. 57r; NCR Case 16d/1, fol. 120v), and the scrivener Andrew Pawe entered in 1491, shortly after his election as common clerk (NRO, NCR Case 17c, fol. 69v; NCR Case 16d/2, fol. 1r). John Paston was Sir John Paston III, 1444–1504. For more information on the entries of Thorpe and Paston and on parliamentary elections related to each man, see Francis Blomefield,

"The City of Norwich, Chapter 21: Of the City in the Time of Edward V," in *An Essay towards a Topographical History of the County of Norfolk: Volume 3, the History of the City and County of Norwich*, Part I (London: W. Miller, 1806), 171–172, available at http://www.british-history.ac.uk/topographical-hist-norfolk/vol3/pp171-172. In addition, the fees of about thirty-five men were waived because these individuals had been nominated for the freedom by the mayor and sheriffs. The city lost as much as 120s in yearly revenue by the forgiving of these men's entry fees. The mayors and sheriffs usually expanded their own personal support by choosing men who would have purchased their freedom.

10. Spirleng served as a Norwich common councillor from 1464 to 1472 and again in 1483. See Timothy Hawes, ed., *An Index to Norwich City Officers 1453–1835* (Norwich, UK: Norfolk and Norwich Genealogical Society, 1989), 144, under "Spyrlyng."
11. NRO, NCR Case 16d/1 and Case 16d/2; Hudson and Tingey, *Records of the City of Norwich*, i. cix, 129. By the terms of the Composition of 1415, the city of Norwich had twenty-four aldermen and sixty common councillors. See Ruth Frost, "The Urban Elite," in *Medieval Norwich*, ed. Carole Rawcliffe and Richard Wilson (London: Hambledon and London, 2004), 237.
12. The surviving chamberlains' accounts confirm the information found in the Assembly Proceedings, as the accounts record the amounts and names of those men who paid a fine to the city. The chamberlains' records and Assembly Proceedings differ significantly in only a few cases.
13. See Fig. 1.
14. For example, Wakelin, "When Scribes Won't Write," 250, notes Spirleng's apparent "dislike of incompleteness" when the scribe identified places where text was missing in an exemplar that he used for *The Canterbury Tales*.
15. His assistant clerk or clerks appear to have done the same. All the entries for the years in question note that Spirleng was the clerk, even entries where the hand differs from Spirleng's. For more examples of Spirleng's hand, see Thorpe, "Documents and Books," 212, fig. 1; and Beadle, "Geoffrey Spirleng," pls. 12, 13, 14, 15, 17.
16. For Stalon's entries, compare NRO, NCR Case 17c, fol. 68r to NRO, NCR Case 16d/1, fol. 122r.
17. This argument rather begs the question of why apprenticeship references continued to be included in both the assembly records and the chamberlain accounts rather than being included in only one source. The chamberlains' records probably recorded apprenticeship

information to show that men warranted paying the reduced entry fee of 13s 4d. The assembly minutes might have recorded the information because the men named their former masters when standing before the assembly.

18. NRO, NCR Case 16d/1, fol. 129r.
19. Ibid., fol. 131v.
20. Spirleng may have had disagreements with others as a young man. Thorpe, "Documents and Books," 203, notes that "it appears that the young Geoffrey Spirleng required guidance in the interpersonal skills that a man needed to function within a gentry circle. [Sir John] Fastolf wrote: '[…] I pray you to do sende for William Cole … and that Geffrey Spyrlyng forbere hym and gefe non occasion to displese hym.'" Thorpe, "Documents and Books," 203, goes on to note that Cole may have been "especially temperamental, or that Spirleng had yet to develop his skills of discretion."
21. Beadle, "Geoffrey Spirleng," 127. Although Spirleng continued to work for Fastolf until Sir John's death in 1459, Spirleng became a freeman of Norwich in 1457, enrolling as a scrivener; NRO, NCR Case 17c, fol. 69r; NCR Case 16d/1, fol. 32(2)v. He served as a Norwich common councillor from 1464 to 1472 and again in 1483. See Hawes, *Index to Norwich City Officers*, 144, under "Spyrlyng." Before he was elected common clerk in 1471, Spirleng began to work as the clerk of the Gild of St. George, a post he held from 1469 to March 1492. In addition, he was often called upon to help audit city and guild financial records. See Beadle, "Geoffrey Spirleng," 125.
22. In addition to the differing records for the years 1471 to 1487, apprenticeship figures between the Old Free Book and Assembly Proceedings do not correspond for 1467, 1468 or 1491. Figure 1 is drawn from N.R.O., NCR Case 17c, N.R.O., NCR Case 16d/1, and N.R.O., NCR Case 16d/2. The years correspond to January 1st to December 31st, but the dates have not been converted from the Old Style to the New.

Prenes en gre All Over Again

KATHLEEN L. SCOTT

One is continually surprised by medieval manuscripts, but in this instance it is a legal roll that succeeds in startling us. The phrase *prenes en gre*, usually found in literary and other non-legal texts, appears with a slightly different spelling in a plea roll of the King's Bench, having no apparent relevance to the pleas in whose company it appears. The court of the King's Bench (*curia regis*), a court of common law, was among the four most important courts in the English legal system in the Middle Ages, until it, with the other three courts (Common Pleas, Chancery, and Exchequer), was abolished and combined into one court in 1873. Initially, the court of the King's Bench was conducted in the presence of the king with his advisers and courtiers acting as judges wherever the king traveled within or outside the realm. This inconvenient situation endured from the late twelfth or early thirteenth century until 1421, when the court finally found a fixed seat in Westminster Hall.[1] The surviving plea rolls from the King's Bench court, now in The National Archives (TNA) at Kew, England, are enormous, in both size and number, and their decoration and illustration have received attention through the work of Erna Auerbach and other scholars.[2] The inscriptions of the King's Bench roll have, however, not as yet been examined extensively,[3] and this article will investigate only one: the phrase *prenes en gre*, which appears in the plea roll KB27/826 as *pernez en gre* and in two other manuscripts discussed below as *prandez en gre*.

In the late-medieval chronological sequence of the King's Bench rolls, most are prefaced by a heading in a large display script; this introductory paragraph states the site of the court, the term and year of the court sitting, the regnal year of the king, and his name.[4] In the roll under discussion here

(TNA KB27/826), the heading reads: "Placita coram domino Rege apud Westmonasterium de Termino Sancti Michelmis anno regni Regis Edwardi quarti post conquestum septmio" (Fig. 1).[5] The headings are followed by the name of the chief justice at the time that the roll was inscribed, here "J. Markham," that is, Sir John Markham, who was a justice of the King's Bench between 1444 and 1461 and who presided as chief justice between 1461 and 1468.[6] The phrase, *"per nez en gre,"* materializes on this first membrane in the King's Bench roll for Michelmas 1467, that is, year seven of Edward IV's reign.[7] It was written on the four visible turns of a scroll (hence the separations indicated above) wrapped illusionistically around a pleonastic stroke of the letter "J" (Fig. 2).

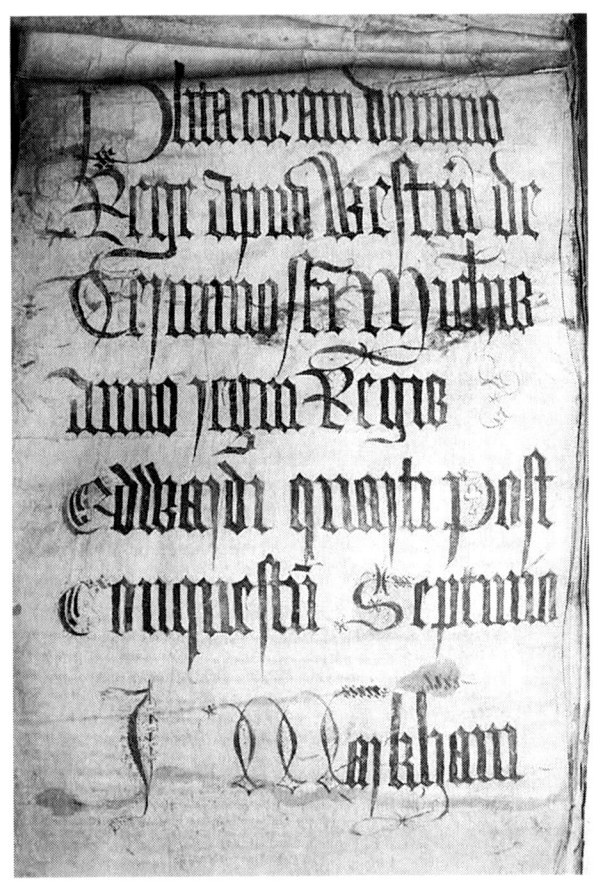

Figure 1. Kew, The National Archives UK, KB27/826, Michelmas term 1467, heading of roll followed by name of Chief Justice J[ohn] Markham.

Figure 2. Kew, The National Archives UK, KB27/826, Michelmas term 1467, detail of "J" with inscription *per nez en gre* on turns of scroll.

The phrase *prenes en gre*—found as a motto, tag, saying, and quotation and often occurring with a gift of some kind—has been translated in various ways: "Receive it willingly,"[8] "Receive or take [this . . .] with pleasure,"[9] "We hope we've pleased you,"[10] "Take kindly,"[11] "Tayk in thank,"[12] and for a book, "Take [and read me] willingly."[13] Because, as we shall see, *prenes en gre* was employed in so many different contexts, that is, in poetry, on a frontispiece, in scribal decoration, as the ending phrase of a text, on ivories and rings, as a heraldic motto, and here on a legal roll, I use the term "phrase" as a general catch-all for "motto," "tag," "quotation," and "saying."

The phrase seems to have had fairly widespread circulation in England in the fifteenth century and may have been introduced there—in addition to the close mercantile and other intercourse between France and England—by means of carvings on secular items as well as by French poetry, the latter transported by scribes such as Ricardus Franciscus (active 1447–1467).[14] Franciscus has been cautiously identified as French by several scholars,[15] particularly in view of his copying of the Statutes of the Order of the Garter in Nancy, Départementales de Meurthe et Moselle, MS H 80.[16] Nevertheless, his work is mainly known in English manuscripts, especially those of a literary nature;[17] and, as Martha Driver points out, Franciscus was largely "employed in copying books for English owners,"[18] with the majority of his works, according to Catherine Nall, being associated with Sir John Fastolf (1380–1459) or with readers associated with his household.[19] As a rule Franciscus wrote his own favorite phrases (he had more than one) in small scrolls wrapped around ascenders and sometimes descenders of letters,[20] often in the same manuscript together with numerous blank scrolls. In a few instances his *prenes* phrase concludes with *je vous en prie*,[21] which combined phrase I traced in a discussion of 1996 to a stanza of Chanson 31 by Charles d'Orléans:[22]

> Presentement ma chançon vous envoye,
> Or la prenés en gré, je vous en prie.[23]

> I now send you my chanson.
> Receive it willingly, I beg you.[24]

It is possible that this stanza was the source of the full phrase, but it is also certain that the first part of the phrase was widely used in France with the presentation of a gift and was almost certainly known independently of this and other poems to scribes, ivory workers, and likely the population of a well-endowed estate. The phrase is also found in two poems of Christine de Pisan. The first provides a precise designation as to its purpose: *Prenez en gre le don de vostre amant* ("Take willingly the gift of your lover").[25] It occurs in no. 81 of Christine's *Cent balades* as the refrain of all three stanzas; one is transcribed here:

> Si vous envoy ce petit dyamant,
> Prenez en gré le don de vostre amant.[26]

> In sending you this little diamond,
> Take willingly the gift of your lover.
> (trans. K. L. Scott)

This refrain, of course, suits and explains its appearance on such gifts as ivory combs and boxes carved with a courting scene as well as the "gift" of a poem.[27] I recently located a second use of the phrase by Christine in *Cent balades d'amant et de dame*, no. 68, as the refrain of three stanzas and a concluding couplet, spoken by the lover (L'amant):

> Ce dyamant avec de petit pris,
> Prenez en gré, doulce dame de pris.[28]
>
> This diamond of little price,
> Take willingly, gentle lady of great price.
> (trans. K. L. Scott)

Yet the *prenes* words could be plucked up and, as shown below, applied to other circumstances than to amorous declarations in a courtly love lyric or to the actual bestowing of a gift.

Whatever Franciscus's source for the phrase, his use of the *prenes en gre* phrase occurs mainly, as I say, in his copies of literary texts,[29] several of which appear in the following manuscripts: New York, Morgan Library and Museum M 126, John Gower, *Confessio Amantis* (ca. 1470), where the phrase is on folio 41v, "*prenes en gre mon* [*coeur/cuer* as the drawing of a heart]," written among other phrases and many blank scrolls on the ascenders;[30] Oxford, University College MS 85, a text of Alain Chartier, *Le quadrilogue invective* (copied between 1450 and 1470), where the phrase appears on pages 28, 64, 178, and 179;[31] and Oxford, Bodleian Library, MS Ashmole 764, *The First Foundation of the Office of Arms* (ca. 1475), with the phrase on folio 97r as in Charles d'Orléans's chanson, *prenes en gre je vous en prie* but in scrambled form.[32] Not all of Franciscus's literary texts were, however, so endorsed with the phrase; British Library MS Harley 4775, a copy of Jacobus de Voragine, *Legenda aurea (Gilte Legende)*, in English translation (ca. 1470), has, for example, ascenders with strapwork,[33] a religious phrase (*Aue ma ria*, fol. 227), blank, if well-drawn, scrolls,[34] and finally, two images of fish (fols. 94r, 164v), but not the *prenes* phrase. Books of Hours copied by Franciscus also seem to have lacked attraction for inscribed phrases; British Library MS Harley 2915, for instance, has none but shows tall ascenders with finishing strokes, strapwork, and a number of images on descenders, that is, dragons (fols. 91v, 94v), barbed roses (fols. 105v, 106r, 113v), curled sprigs with tiny flowers (fols. 159v, 185v), as well as a descender looped to form a heart (fol. 60v).[35]

Returning to the *pernez* phrase in the King's Bench plea roll, I note again that John Markham's period as chief justice extended from Trinity term 1461 (TNA KB27/801) to Michelmas term 1468 (TNA KB27/830), a span of approximately seven years, in which time the phrase occurs only once (TNA

KB27/826).³⁶ The scribe of the *pernez* heading (undoubtedly a clerk of the court) wrote a heading (without the phrase) in only one other plea roll with Markham's name (TNA KB27/815). Two notable characteristics of this scribal hand are, apart from the first line of the heading, use of a long-tailed "r" and internal rather than final use of long-tailed "s" (final "s" is two-compartment; Fig. 1).³⁷ The three downward strokes of the introductory capital "M" of "Markham" are formed by a series of loops infilled with decorative penwork ending in open rectangular spaces; two ending strokes at the top of the letter are finished with strapwork. Whoever the court scribe of this membrane may have been,³⁸ his script was clearly not that of Ricardus Franciscus; although Franciscus is known to have written semi- or pseudo-legal and charter-like documents³⁹ and although he can certainly be classed as a professional scribe, he is unlikely to have been a clerk employed in the court of the King's Bench. Furthermore, the rendering of Markham's name does not bear the extravagant ascenders or paraphs that Franciscus would surely have applied to it in such a circumstance.⁴⁰ The *pernez* phrase in the King's Bench roll is also unlikely to indicate a different Continental scribe working in London, given the use of the English long-tailed letters "r" and "s" and other conventional aspects of the display script and heading.

In order to give some sense of the wider context and general spread of the *prenes en gre* phrase, it may now be valuable to mention further instances apart from those of Ricardus Franciscus, the two French poets, and the inscription in the King's Bench plea roll. Four further English manuscripts known to me have the phrase, of which Oxford, Bodleian Library MS Laud Misc. 296, Miscellany, XV⁴, contains three works ending with the *prenes* phrase as *prandez en gre*:⁴¹ *Expositio in istad Ps cxviii*, folios 81r to 84v (Fig. 3); John Nyder, *Manuale Confessorum*, folios 85r to 128v (Fig. 4); and Johannes M., *De vini virtutibus*, folio 162r–v (Fig. 5).⁴² This newly identified manuscript is of particular interest because the phrase accompanies two religious texts, a subject not known to occur elsewhere with the phrase, and because the phrase makes an unavoidable argument for each text being presented as a "gift" to the reader. It is the clearest example we have in an English manuscript of the original "gifting" intent of phrase, whereas elsewhere its presence on a tiny scroll deep within a text is ambiguous, if not wholly unrelated to the context.⁴³ In Exeter, Cathedral Library MS 3529, Boccaccio, *Genealogae deorum* (XV³⁻⁴), probably copied from an edition printed in Cologne (ca. 1473), *Prandez en gre moun cur'* appears on a scroll, also below the last words of the text (fol. 166v; Fig. 6), if more finely presented in a shaded scroll than in the Laud Misc. instances.⁴⁴ In Oxford, Bodleian Library MS Ashmole 45, Part I, *The Erle of Tolous* (1520–1530), folio 2r, a full-page presentation frontispiece depicts a well-dressed young man near a speech scroll that bears the phrase as PRENES: ENGRE [sic], proffering a book to a young woman of

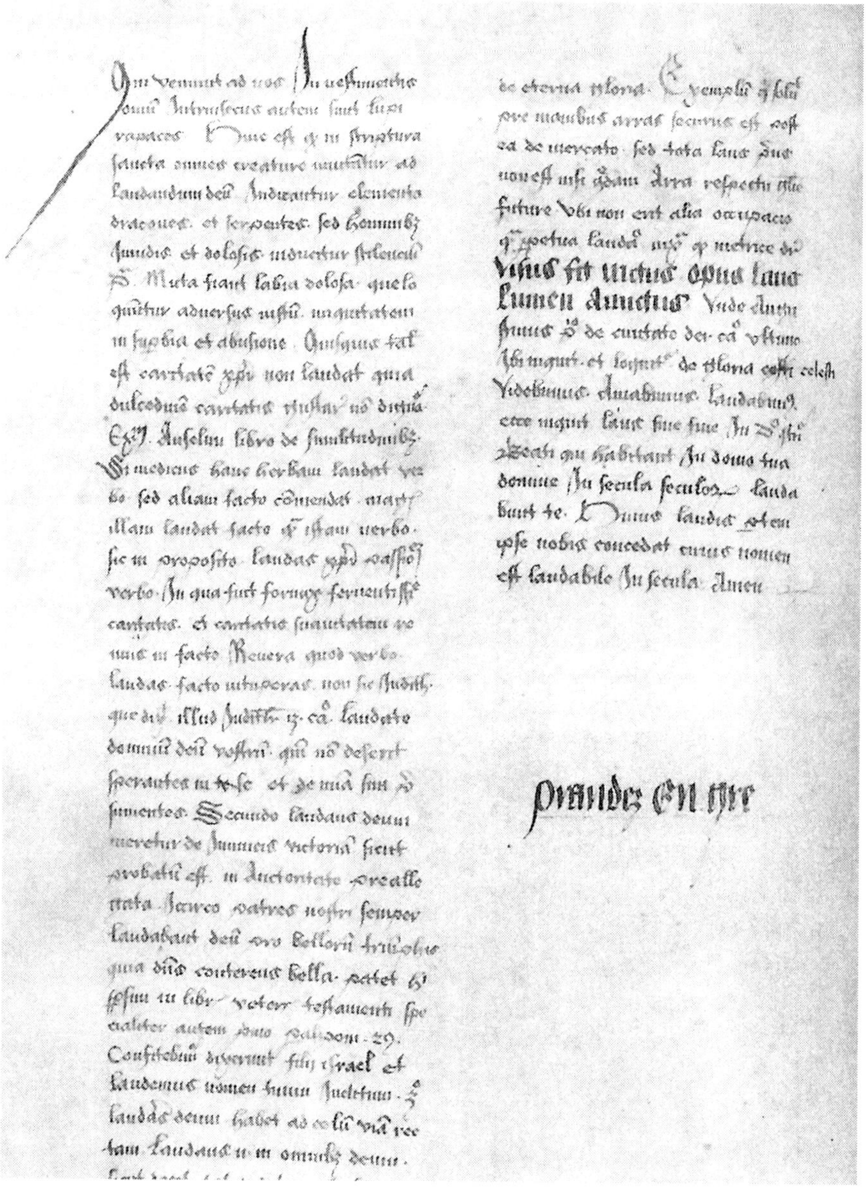

Figure 3. Oxford, Bodleian Library, MS Laud Misc. 296, *Expositio in istad PS* cxviiiI, fol. 84v, concluding page with phrase *prandez en gre*.

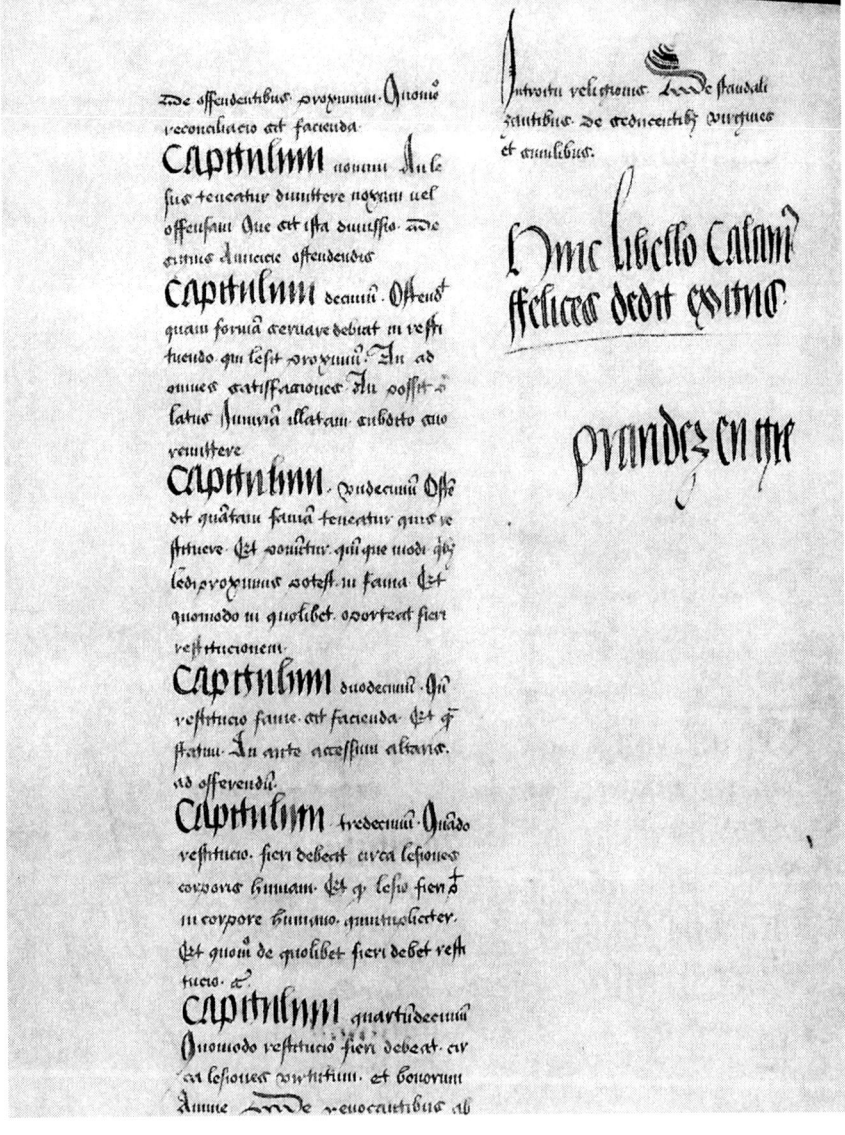

Figure 4. Oxford, Bodleian Library, MS Laud Misc. 296, John Nyder, *Manuale confessorum*, fol. 128v, concluding page with phrase *prandez en gre*.

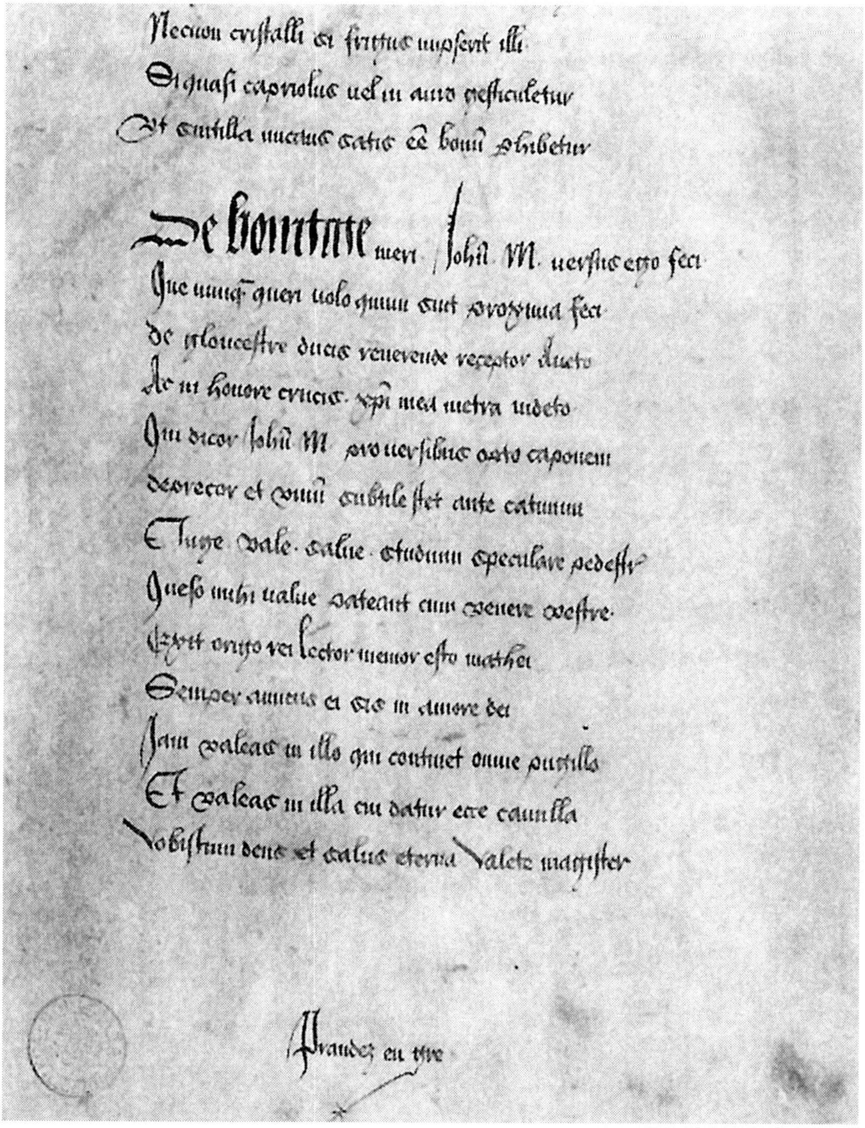

Figure 5. Oxford, Bodleian Library, MS Laud Misc. 296, Johannes M., *De vini virtutibus*, fol. 162v, concluding page with phrase *Prandez en gre*.

equal status; it is a gifting scene in which the phrase is self-explanatory with regard to the book[45] and in which the story itself has become "a gift object."[46] Last, John Skelton includes the phrase in his self-congratulatory "Garlande or Chapelet of Laurell" (1523) within the poem at the end of his "*Admonet Skeltonis omnes arbores dare locum viridi lauro juxt genus suum. Prennees en gre The Laurelle.*"[47] Here the phrase is once more found bestowing the text on the reader.

From Nancy Regalado, I learned that the expression can often be seen at the end of performance pieces such as a monologue, farce, or the last couplet of fool's plays (*sotties*), in which case she translates it as "I hope my performance pleases you";[48] and Nigel Ramsey informs me that *prenes en gre* adorns a two-sided ivory mirror case, carved on scrolls above two scenes of lovers.[49] One side shows a finely dressed young man in a chaperon, offering a flower to an equally finely attired young woman, with *Prenes* above; the other side finishes the phrase with *en gre*, above a similar scene of a young man offering a garland to his lady.[50] The mirror case is attributed to Northern Italy (possibly made in Milan, where French was spoken at the time) and dated

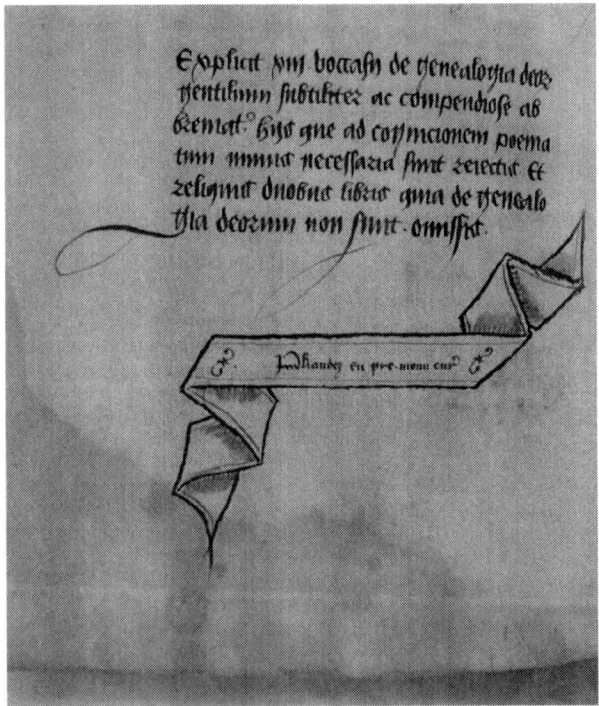

Figure 6. Exeter, Cathedral Library, MS 3529, Boccaccio, *Genealogae deorum*, fol. 166v, explicit and phrase *Prandez en gre moun cur* in shaded scroll.

around 1410.[51] Sarah Peverley alerted me to three other artifacts: a late-fourteenth-fifteenth century goblet inscribed with the phrase,[52] a wooden fifteenth-century comb with on one side *prenes en gre* and on the other *ce petit doun*,[53] and a posy ring with the phrase engraved inside.[54] These objects are almost certainly only a glimpse of secular items surviving with the phrase, and a search for more instances of the phrase on such luxury objects could well be undertaken. It can also be noted that the phrase was used as a heraldic motto around 1575 by Cuthbert, 7th Lord Ogle, of Bothal, Northumberland (London, College of Arms MS [cross], Glover's Visitation of the North 1569 and 1575, fol. 68v).[55] The Ogle motto is translated variously as "Accept in gratitude" and "Take in good will."

Why, finally, is the phrase *pernez en gre* written on the name of a chief justice in a King's Bench plea roll? Was it a motto or saying known to have been used by him? Or did it occur merely on the initiative of an anonymous court scribe? Was it meant to enhance the name? Or was it simply an enscrolled doodle slipped in by the scribe? Or perhaps among the clerks of the King's Bench there were some who found a certain cachet in attaching a motto to themselves or in displaying one on their work. At very least we have found another "nexus between the legal and literary worlds"[56]—and, one might add, the decorative worlds—though we are otherwise left at an impasse, unable to suggest an answer to these questions. It is only possible to pronounce with certainty that the King's Bench scribe knew of the phrase in England in 1467 and was impressed enough to blend it into his work so that the user of the roll would accept it with pleasure.[57]

Independent Scholar

Acknowledgments

I am grateful to Professor Marlene Hennessy for kindly reading a draft version of this essay and for her helpful remarks. Like Professor Rachelle Scott, Marlene has procured books for my research that I would otherwise been unable to obtain. Mary-Jo Arn has graciously shared her vast knowledge of Charles d'Orléan's poetry. Other contributors to the search for *prenes en gre* are acknowledged in the text. My husband, David K. Scott, has been invaluable in searching computer-land for me, Ellie Jones, Exeter Cathedral Archivist, has been kindness itself in arranging for a photo of MS 3529, and Susanne Jenks most helpful concerning TNA images. I am furthermore indebted to Dr. Jaclyn Rajsic for her extensive discussion of sources of "s" and "z."

NOTES

1. For a contemporary scene of the court of the King's Bench, ca. 1460, see London, Inner Temple Library, Inner Temple Misc. MS 188 (a detached leaf), in Richard Marks and Paul Williamson, eds., *Gothic: Art for England 1400–1547* (London: V&A Publications, 2003), 32.
2. Erna Auerbach, *Tudor Artists: A Study of Painters in the Royal Service and of Portraiture on Illuminated Documents from the Accession of Henry VIII to the Death of Elizabeth I* (London: Athlone, 1954); William Connor, "The Esholt Priory Charter of 1485 and Its Decoration," *Yorkshire Archaeological Journal* 80 (2008): 121–152; A. F. Sutton, "An Unfinished Celebration of the Yorkist Accession by a Clerk of Merchant Staplers of Calais," in *Rule, Redemption and Representations in Late Medieval England and France*, ed. L. Clark, The Fifteenth Century 8 (Woodbridge, UK: Boydell, 2008), 135–163, esp. 150. For illustration and decoration of the Common Pleas plea rolls, see Elizabeth A. Danbury and Kathleen L. Scott, "The Plea Rolls of the Court of Common Pleas: An Unused Source for the Art and History of Later Medieval England, 1422–1509," *The Antiquaries Journal* 95 (2015): 157–210.
3. Elizabeth Danbury has discussed certain inscriptions in the Court of the Common Pleas plea rolls in Danbury and Scott, "Pleas Rolls of the Court of Common Pleas," 174–177, 197–204.
4. The National Archives has allowed all of the rolls to be freely accessed at the Anglo-American Law Library of O'Quinn Law Library, University of Houston, http://aalt.law.uh.edu. For fuller details concerning this digital archive, see Danbury and Scott, "Plea Rolls of the Court of Common Pleas," 160 and n. 21.
5. Suspensions are rendered in italics. The date, name of the king, and name of the justice would, of course, vary through the years as well as through the four terms of Hilary, Easter, Trinity, and Michelmas. The heading may be translated as "Pleas before the King's Bench (or Court) at Westminster in the term of St. Michelmas year of the reign Edward fourth after the conquest seven."
6. J. H. Baker, *The Men of Court 1440 to 1550: A Prosopography of the Inns of Court and Chancery and the Courts of Law*, 2 vols. (London: Selden Society, 2012), 2:1060. Markham was knighted in 1461 and died on March 20, 1479. A copy of the statutes of Edward III to Richard II (Glasgow, University of Glasgow, Hunterian Library, MS 505, former V.8.8) was given by Markham to Humphrey Bourchier. The latter's inscription on the fourth, unnumbered folio from the rear boards records the gift; and Markham's name (?autograph) is on the last folio of the Statutes.

7. The concensus is that scribes used "s" and "z" interchangeably (Daniel Wakelin, correspondence, September 8, 2016; Martha Driver, correspondence, September 9, 2016; Jaclyn Rajsic, correspondence, September 10, 2016).
8. Barton Palmer, trans., Chanson 31, in *Poetry of Charles d'Orléans and His Circle: A Critical Edition of BnF MS. Fr. 25458, Charles d'Orléans's Personal Manuscript*, ed. John Fox and Mary-Jo Arn, Arizona Studies in the Middle Ages and the Renaissance 34 (Tempe, AZ, and Turnhout, Belgium: Arizona Center for Medieval and Renaissance Studies, 2010), 363.
9. Carol M. Meale, "'Prenes: engre': an early sixteenth-century presentation copy of *The Erle of Tolous*," in *Romance Reading on the Book: Essays on Medieval Narrative Presented to Maldwyn Mills*, ed. Jennifer Fellows, Rosalind Field, Gillian Rogers, and Judith Weiss (Cardiff: University of Wales Press, 1996), 230; Martha W. Driver, "'Me fault faire': French Makers of Manuscripts for English Patrons," in *Language and Culture in Medieval Britain: The French of England, c. 1000–c. 1500*, ed. Jocelyn Wogan-Browne, et al. (Woodbridge, UK, and Rochester, NY: York Medieval Press/Boydell, 2009), 420–443, at 430; Nicholas Perkins, "Introduction: The Materiality of Medieval Romance and *The Erle of Tolous*," in *Medieval Romance and Material Culture*, ed. Nicholas Perkins (Cambridge, UK: D. S. Brewer, 2015), 3 and pl. 1 (color).
10. This is the typical way in which fifteenth-century French *sotties* (fool's plays) ended; Nancy F. Regalado in correspondence with Mary-Jo Arn, February 2014.
11. Richard H. Randall, Jr., *Masterpieces of Ivory from the Walters Art Gallery* (New York and Baltimore, MD: Hudson Hills Press and Walters Art Gallery, 1985), 234, no. 348.
12. H. Oskar Sommer, *The Kalender of Shepherds: The Edition of Paris 1503 in Photographic Facsimile A Faithful Reprint of R. Pynson's Edition of London 1506* (London: Kegan Paul, Trench, Tribner & Co., 1892), 2:leaf gii. The Pynson edition is the source of the translation from the French "Song of Death," which begins: "Se mon regard ne vous vient a plaisir par sa hideur wui est espouantable prenez en gre congnoissans le desire." (If my esteem does not succeed in pleasing you because of its repulsiveness which is appalling, receive it kindly, conscious of my desire. . . . ; trans. K. L. Scott)
13. Perkins, "Introduction," 3. Perkins also notes two alternative interpretations: a self-deprecatory and a bawdy use of the phrase. For French definitions and usages of the word "gre," see Centre National de Ressources Textuelles et Lexicales, http://cnrtl.fr/definition/

gr%C3%A9; or Collins Online Dictionary, French to English, www.collinsdictionary.com/dictionary/french-english/gre, *s.v. gre*.

14. Lists of works by Ricardus Franciscus are in Lisa Jefferson, "Two Fifteenth-Century Manuscripts of the Statues of the Order of the Garter," *English Manuscript Studies 1100–1700*, ed. Peter Beal and Jeremy Griffiths, 5 (1995): 22; Catherine Nall, "Ricardus Franciscus Writes for William Worcester," *Journal of the Early Book Society* 11 (2008): 209-210; and Driver, "Me fault faire," 442–443.

15. See Richard Hamer, "Spellings of the Fifteenth-Century Scribe Ricardus Franciscus," in *Five Hundred Years of Words and Sounds: A Festschrift for Eric Dobson*, ed. E. G. Stanley and Douglas Gray (Cambridge, UK: D. S. Brewer, 1983), 69 ("He seems to have been French"); Carol M. Meale, "Patrons, Buyers and Owners: Book Production and Social Status," in *Book Production and Publishing in Britain: 1375–1475*, ed. Jeremy Griffiths and Derek Pearsall (Cambridge, UK: University Press, 1989), 202; Driver, "Me fault faire," 422; and Holly James-Maddocks and Deborah Thorpe, "A Petition Written by Ricardus Franciscus," *Journal of the Early Book Society* 15 (2012): 249. The latest expert analysis of Ricardus Franciscus's scribal characteristics did not reach a conclusion concerning his nationality; Martha W. Driver, "More Light on Ricardus Franciscus: Looking again at Morgan M. 126," *South Atlantic Review* 79 (2015): 20–35, at 30.

16. His signatures in this manuscript are reproduced in Jefferson, "Two Fifteenth-Century Manuscripts," pls. 1 and 2.

17. For a list of his literary manuscripts, see Linne R. Mooney, "Vernacular Literary Manuscripts and Their Scribes," in *The Production of Books in England 1350–1500*, ed. Alexandra Gillespie and Daniel Wakelin (Cambridge, UK: University Press, 2011), 204 n. 48.

18. Driver, "Me fault faire," 427; Driver, "More Light," 20.

19. Nall, "Ricardus Franciscus," 210. It may also be of interest that another justice of the King's Bench, Sir William Yelverton, was "one of Fastolf's most prominent executors" ca. 1470; he received considerable remuneration for the task, including two books (Richard Beadle, "Sir John Fastolf's French Books," in *Medieval Texts in Context*, ed. Graham D. Caie and Denis Renevey (London and New York: Routledge, 2008), 100–101).

20. A number of Franciscus's inscribed ascenders and descenders have been reproduced by Martha Driver: "Me fault faire," 430, fig. 32.5; and "Printing the *Confessio Amantis*: Caxton's Edition in Context," in *Re-Visioning Gower*, ed. R. F. Yeager (Asheville, NC: Pegasus Press, University of North Carolina, 1998), figs 10–13. Concerning Franciscus's "use of banderoles," see also Driver, "More Light," 21–22.

21. For a reproduction of the phrase, see J. J. G. Alexander, *The Decorated Letter* (New York: Braziller, 1978), 27, fig. 30, from Oxford, Bodleian Library, MS Ashmole 764, fol. 97r, "Explicit," with the long descender of "p" supporting a scroll with the saying written from bottom to top.
22. Kathleen L. Scott, *A Survey of Manuscripts Illuminated in the British Isles, vol. 6: Later Gothic Manuscripts 1390–1490*, 2 vols., gen. ed. J. J. G. Alexander (London: Harvey Miller, 1996), 2:319, no. 118.
23. Transcribed from John Fox and Mary-Jo Arn, eds., *Poetry of Charles d'Orléans and His Circle: A Critical Edition of BnF MS. Fr. 25458, Charles d'Orléans's Personal Manuscript*, Arizona Studies in the Middle Ages and the Renaissance 34 (Tempe, AZ, and Turnhout, Belgium: Arizona Center for Medieval and Renaissance Studies, 2010), 362, Chanson 31; see also Enid McLeod, *Charles of Orleans: Prince and Poet* (London: Chatto & Windus, 1969), 214. The wide circulation of the phrase is not discussed in either study.
24. See Palmer, Chanson 31, 363.
25. Randall, *Masterpieces*, 234, no. 348, noted without a reference.
26. From Maurice Roy, *Oeuvres poétiques de Christine de Pisan*, 3 vols. (Paris: Didot et Cie, 1886, 1891, 1896), 1:81. The *balades* were composed during the period 1399–1405; Christine de Pisan, *Ballades, Rondeaux, and Virelais: An Anthology*, ed. Kenneth Varty (Leicester, UK: Leicester University Press, 1965), ix–x.
27. Pisan was not the first to use the phrase in offering a poem as gift. After his invocation to Venus, Lucretius begins his poem *De rerum natura* with the verses: "For what's to come, open your ears, apply keen intellect / Far from cares, to true philosophy, lest you reject / Out of hand the gifts that I've assembled for your sake."; Lucretius, *The Nature of Things*, trans. A. E. Stallings (London: Penguin Books, 2007), 4: ll. 50–52.
28. Transcribed from Roy, *Oeuvres poétiques*, 3:277–278. Apart from *gré*, diacritics do not appear in the modern edition of the poem in Christine de Pizan, *Cent balades d'amant et de dame, Manuscrit Londres, British Library, Harley 4431*, ed. Jean-François Kosta-Théfraine (Rome: Éditions Paleo, 2010), 151–152 (fol. 390r of Harley 4431).
29. See n. 14 above for the most recent list of books and documents copied or written by Ricardus Franciscus. Two further documents possibly copied by Franciscus are mentioned in Driver, "Me fault faire," 443.
30. See the excellent Driver, "More Light," 20–35, for the latest discussion of this manuscript. Driver also discusses Morgan 126 and provides a full list of all sayings on ascenders written by Franciscus in Driver, "Printing the *Confessio*," 282 n. 27, 283.
31. Jean-Philippe Genet, ed., *Four English Political Tracts of the Later Middle Ages*, Camden 4th Series 18 (London: Royal Historical Society, 1977),

175; Scott, *Later Gothic Manuscripts*, no. 118 and earlier literature; Driver, "Me fault faire," 443.
32. Otto Pächt and J. J. G. Alexander, *Illuminated Manuscripts in the Bodleian Library Oxford* 1 (Oxford: Clarendon Press, 1973), no. 726; Driver, "Me fault faire," 443.
33. See e.g., fols. 91v, 95r, 107r, 177v, 178v, 192v, 193r, 204r, 212v, 223r.
34. See, e.g., fols. 91v, 95r, 100r, 104r, 107r, 119v, 126r, 139v, 164v, 173r, 193r, 196r.
35. Franciscus had as well the non-English habit for a scribe of announcing his name and initial letters as a half-page display as well as on ascenders and descenders; see, e.g., San Marino, CA, Huntington Library, HM 932, Statutes of the Archdeaconry of London, dated 1447, fol. 13v (Jefferson, "Two Fifteenth-Century Manuscripts, pl. 3; Scott, *Later Gothic Manuscripts*, 1: fig. 27, half-page, full name); New York, Pierpont-Morgan Library, M 126, John Gower, *Confessio Amantis*, fol. 65v, "quod Rychard" (Driver, "Me fault faire," 430, fig. 32.5), and fols. 39v and 65v ("qd R"); and Oxford, Bodleian Library, MS Laud Misc. 570, Christine de Pisan, *Othea*, etc., dated 1450, fol. 23v ("qd R.F.").
36. In the following plea roll (Hilary 1468, TNA KB27/827), a hand similar to that of the *pernez* inscription writes the heading, employing both long-tailed "r"s and "s"s; his script is, however, not of the same quality and cannot be assigned to the scribe of KB27/826.
37. For "s," see Fig. 1, l. 2, "Westm'" and l. 5, "Post." For "r," see l. 3, "termino" and l. 5, "Edwardi quarti." A few other headings in the rolls of this period show use of a long-tailed "s" only (TNA KB27/818, KB27/824, KB27/828, and KB27/830).
38. For biographies of the lawyers and clerks of courts of common law see Baker, *Men of Court* (n. 6 above).
39. A Grant of Arms for the Worshipful Company of Tallow Chandlers, issued by John Smert, Garter King of Arms, 24 September 1456 (Driver, "Me fault faire," 442); two manuscripts of Statutes of the Order of the Garter: Nancy, Archives Départementales de Meurthe et Moselle, MS H 80, dated 1467; and San Marino, CA, Huntington Library, MS HM 932, Statutes of the Archdeaconry of London, dated 1447 (Jefferson, "Two Fifteenth-Century Manuscripts," 18–35).
40. Note the elaboration on the ascenders in New York, Morgan Library and Museum, M 126 (Driver, "Printing the *Confessio*," figs. 11, 12); Philadelphia, Rosenbach Museum and Library 439/16, fol. 180r (Scott, *Later Gothic Manuscripts*, 1:fig. 438); Nancy, Archives Départmentales de Meurthe et Moselle, MS H.80, membrane 1 (James-Maddocks and Thorpe, "Petition," fig. 4); and the paraphs of Nancy, Archives Départementales de Meurthe et Moselle H 80, membranes 1, 2 (Jefferson,

"Two Fifteenth-Century Manuscripts," pls. 1, 2) as compared with that on "J. Markham" in TNA KB27/826, fig. 1. For a description of Franciscus's script, see Driver, "More Light," 21.
41. Only those texts with the *prandez en gre* phrase are noted by title.
42. The phrase is on fols. 84v, 128v, 162v. The three texts appear to me to be by the same scribe, if, perhaps, at somewhat different times.
43. As in New York, Morgan Library, M 126.
44. N. R. Ker, *Medieval Manuscripts in British Libraries*, vol. 2: *Abbottsford–Keele* (Oxford: Clarendon Press, 1977), 2:836–837. The manuscript title states that the copy was "de adquiscione D' patricii Grey de librario sancti Augustini extra Cant'"; Ker believed that the words in the scroll were by the main hand of the text, suggesting that the phrase may have been the motto of Patrick Grey, librarian of the Benedictine abbey of St. Augustine's, Canterbury, who was responsible for acquiring the manuscript (ibid., 2:836). This instance of the *prenes* phrase is also noted in Driver, "Printing the *Confessio*," 283 n. 28; and Michael P. Siddons, *A Dictionary of Mottoes in England and Wales*, New Series 20 (London: Harleian Society, 2014), 184.
45. The scene is discussed and reproduced in Meale, "Prenes: engre," 222, pl. 7; and Perkins, "Introduction," pl. 1; also noted in Driver, " Printing the *Confessio*," 283 n. 28.
46. Perkins, "Introduction," 2.
47. John Scattergood, ed., *John Skelton: The Complete English Poems* (New Haven, CT, and London: Yale University Press, 1983), 357. The *Garlande* was completed and published on October 3, 1523 (ibid., 18). I owe my knowledge of the occurrence of the phrase in Skelton's poem to Martha Driver, correspondence, December 21, 2015.
48. Nancy Regalado, correspondence, September 21, 2015.
49. Nigel Ramsey, correspondence, February 24, 2014.
50. Reproduced in Marvin C. Ross, "A Gothic Ivory Mirror-Case," *Journal of the Walters Art Gallery* 2 (1939): 109–111, figs 1, 2; Ross dates the case to the "early fifteenth-century" on the basis of the costume depicted. See also M. H. Longhurst, *English Ivories* (London: G. P. Putnam's Sons, 1926), 54. The back of the case is in the Walters Art Museum, Baltimore, Maryland, Inventory no. 7:1107; the front is in the Louvre, Paris, No. QA 115, on loan to the Cluny Museum. I am indebted to Sarah Peverley for the information concerning the Louvre case.
51. Randall, *Masterpieces*, 234, no. 348. The piece had earlier been described as French, Flemish or Burgundian; Ross, "Gothic Ivory," 109–111.
52. Sotheby's, "A Parcel-Gilt Silver 'Welcome' Beaker and Cover, Unidentified Marks, Probably 14/15th Century French," http://

www.sothebys.com/it/auctions/ecatalogue/2013/important-mobilier-sculptures-objets-art-pf1311/lot.84.html.

53. Paul Lacroix, *Science and Literature in the Middle Ages and at the Period of the Renaissance* (Paris: Bibliophile Jacob, 1878), 340, fig. 287, available as an ebook from the University of Adelaide at https://ebooks.adelaide.edu.au/l/literature/science-and-literature-in-the-middle-ages/chapter11.html. Longhurst refers to a further ivory comb in the "small museum" at Thetford, Norfolk, with *PRENES* on one side and *EN GRE* on the other, with roses, a tree at the ends of the panels, and cable borders, "all common Flemish and northern French work of the second half of the 15th century" (*English Ivories*, 54).

54. "PRENES EN GRE" is in black enamel on the interior of the ring. See the Portable Antiquities Scheme database at https://finds.org.uk/database/search/results/broadperiod/POST+MEDIEVAL/createdBy/56/workflow/3/county/East+Riding+of+Yorkshire. British Museum, Record ID: PAS-3785E3. See also the British Museum database at http://www.britishmuseum.org/research/collection_online/collection_object_details.aspx?objectId=1337102&partId=1. The museum number is 2002.0501.1; the phrase is translated as "Accept this willingly." See also Perkins, "Introduction," 2 n. 5.

55. Siddons, *Dictionary of Mottoes*, 184; also noted by Longhurst as the motto of some branches of the Ogle family; Longhurst (*English Ivories*, 54). A search on Google for "prenes en gre" brings up more information concerning the family and its motto.

56. James-Maddocks and Thorpe, "Petition," 256.

57. Driver observes that decorative and inscribed scrolls and initials were "more regularly employed in manuscripts copied in the 1470s or later" (Driver, "Printing the *Confessio*," 280); the King's Bench roll provides a slightly earlier dated instance in England. And as the legal term was that of Michelmas, the scribe may have had gift-giving on his mind.

Descriptive Reviews

VIRGINIA BLANTON, VERONICA O'MARA, AND PATRICIA STOOP, EDS.
Nuns' Literacies in Medieval Europe: The Kansas City Dialogue.
Medieval Women: Texts and Contexts, Volume 27.
Turnhout, Belgium: Brepols, 2015. xlv + 413 pp.
8 color plates and 26 B&W figures

It is rare to be able to describe a collection of essays, much less a volume of conference proceedings, as an exciting series of ground-breaking stories of survival and scholarship. But I can confidently do so for *Nun's Literacies in Medieval Europe: The Kansas City Dialogue*, the second in a series of three publications on nuns' literacies (the first by the same editors, *Nun's Literacies in Medieval Europe: The Hull Dialogue* [Turnhout: Brepols, 2013]). One of the strengths of this edited collection is its very broad geographical, linguistic, and chronological scope. Reading about such disparate situations helps to break us out of our sometimes narrow thinking about what women's literary culture could look like, and can introduce fresh questions into stale critical inquiries. In addition, the volume makes accessible a vast amount of important scholarly work in Italian, German, Dutch, Icelandic, Swedish, and Spanish, with many essays serving as gateways into material that would otherwise be difficult to navigate for English-language readers.

The first section demonstrates the great effort that nuns made to educate themselves and develop their institutions into bastions of intellectual learning and production. Virginia Blanton and Helene Scheck open with a beguiling vision of Leoba (d. 782), where a purple thread she pulls out of her body is interpreted by a wise old nun as the Word of God as well as the wisdom Leoba will spread through her own words. Leoba's *vita*, of an Anglo-Saxon nun on a mission to Saxony, shows how Carolingian educational and monastic reform encouraged the authority and agency of learned female communities – very learned, as this essay proves through an impressive collection of evidence. Moving forward several centuries, Ulrike Wiethaus explores the history and very specific details of literary practices that shaped life at the women's community of Helfta. Nuns not only taught each other how to read, but composed formally sophisticated new texts, and mastered theories of exegesis and hermeneutics. In her chapter on the sister scribes in the Brussels convent of Jericho, Patricia Stoop explains how women's communities are responsible for two-thirds of about 500 manuscripts surviving from religious institutions in the Low Countries, an astonishing statistic. The Augustinian convent "must have been one of the main centres of vernacular book production in the Low Countries" (47), and 29 manuscripts written by its nuns survive. Next, Andrea Knox outlines the fascinating history of Irish Dominican nuns in late medieval Spain: they formed a "durable educational infrastructure focusing upon schools for girls and academic curricula with an emphasis on literacy" (67). Irish, Spanish, and Latin swirled throughout these textual communities, where many nuns managed to resist the Inquisition's enforcement of the Index of banned books by refusing male functionaries access to the female-only areas including the libraries and scriptoria. These brave women not only preserved books, "they moved literary culture forward" (84). Together, the essays in this section suggest the care nuns took to educate each other, how highly intelligent and skilled women often came to lead these intellectual powerhouses, and how nuns had real influence on the history of learning.

The next section focuses on the paleographical evidence for nuns' written culture. Despite a lack of surviving records or modern scholarly interest, Antonella Ambrosio pushes forward in her important mission to trace the literacy of Neopolitan convents, by analyzing a late fifteenth-century accounts ledger written (if somewhat ineptly) by a nun. Italian laywomen were not taught to write, so nuns were the only women with even limited writing skills in this period – in stark contrast to the Swedish convent of Vadstena, the subject of the next essay by Nils Dverstorp. At the Birgittine motherhouse the nuns participated in all steps of book production and at a high level of skill. Dverstorp examines how one manuscript, seemingly with multiple hands, in fact seems to show the evolution of a single anonymous nun's writing abilities. If only it were so easy even to identify manuscripts written by unnamed or named nuns in England, Veronica O'Mara rightly laments in this section's last essay, on nuns and writing in late-medieval England. O'Mara follows up her essay on the same topic in the previous *Hull Dialogue* volume by examining three likely manuscripts in which nuns have written. In her words, "it is only by such painstaking forensic investigation that we can build up a fuller picture of scribal literacy" (147) for not only women but also men.

Karen Blough's essay on the "Implications for Female Monastic Literacy in the Reliefs from St. Liudger's at Werden" is a real masterpiece about a masterpiece. Sixteen robed, seated female figures, each with a book prominently in their laps, appear to converse with each other in this lively mid-eleventh-century set of reliefs, probably meant for the male monastery's crypt altars, Blough argues. She convincingly suggests they evoke both the virgin martyrs, and more importantly, "the learned canonesses of Essen, who for the monks of Werden were the highly visible, contemporary embodiments of a tradition of intellectual exchange among religious women" (164). The next two essays in this section contrast the relative paucity of identifiable convent book production in the Lucchese region of Italy (Loretta Vandi) with the embarrassment of riches enjoyed by scholars of women's literary culture in German-speaking regions. Anne Winston-Allen surveys the absolutely astonishing scribal production by these late-medieval nuns, who copied whole libraries, illuminated dozens if not hundreds of books, and introduced much creative innovation in style and practice. (Scholars of regions with fewer survivals are advised to try not to compare and despair.)

The penultimate section focuses more closely on analyzing texts themselves, from Ireland to Iceland to Germany to the Low Countries. Maive Callan points out the misogynistic history of critics' dismissing the claims of texts to be by women and argues persuasively that first millennium Irish poems such as Líadain's Lament do in fact contain women's voices "speaking to us through the centuries" (227). Svanhildur Óskarsdóttir suggests that an idiosyncratic miscellany from late medieval Iceland was likely compiled for a nunnery, specifically the one at Reynistaður. Another amazing survival provides the focus of the next essay, by Eva Schlotheuber: three letter books containing copies of 1,794 letters to and from the Benedictine nuns in Lüne. Their advanced Latinity and devotion earned them quite a lot of authority at the time, and Schlotheuber's contribution will surely inspire further scholarly research. In the Low Countries, meanwhile, an active group of nuns at the Arnhem Sint-Agnes convent both wrote their own manuscripts and also fostered an unusually intense mystical culture, as demonstrated by three remarkable sixteenth-century mystical texts in Middle Dutch closely associated with their convent, as Kees Schepers explains.

Andrew Rabin opens the final section by examining nuns and the law in Anglo-Saxon England, arguing that "participation in the production and reception of juridical texts afforded religious women access to a form of agency that was otherwise unattainable" (305). Moving forward to later medieval England, Emilie Amt offers some nuanced analysis of the slim evidence for literary culture at Godstow Abbey. She brings our attention to an interesting archival source: the receipts for collection of pension payments after the Dissolution, signed – or not – by the ex-nuns and ex-monks. Darcy

Donahue concludes the volume with her essay on Ana de San Bartolomé's version of the Discalced Carmelite reform. This nun miraculously learned how to write with the help and encouragement of Teresa of Ávila herself, and the texts that result provide a crucial insight into late medieval Spanish and French religious life.

Overall the volume is impeccably prepared and proofread. The color plates and plentiful black and white plates contribute greatly to the essays' arguments. It is a shame the book is so expensive (€100), but hopefully enough libraries will invest in either the hard copy or digital version so that its contents can find as wide a readership as possible and influence the future of many fields of study. This volume overwhelmingly proves that despite the various barriers of their medieval worlds, and despite their often dismissive neglect by modern critics, many medieval nuns achieved deep learning and fostered lively literary cultures. If we persist in saying this is "surprising," it is only because we continue to underestimate women's potential for intellectual production, and indeed underestimate the profound intellectual contributions of the entire Middle Ages.

Laura Saetveit Miles, University of Bergen, Norway

MARGARET CONNOLLY AND RALUCA RADULESCU, EDS.
Insular Books: Vernacular Manuscript Miscellanies in Late Medieval Britain.
Proceedings of the British Academy 201.
Oxford: Oxford University Press, 2015. xviii + 330 pp.

This collection of essays grew out of a conference hosted by the British Academy in 2012, and as the title of the volume suggests, the conference and these subsequent papers all address, in one form or another, miscellanies from late medieval Britain. This is, admittedly, a broad topic which no single volume could hope to encompass or to provide definitive analyses of, and wisely the editors make no such claims. Instead, they define their goals thus: "Two novel and ambitious avenues for investigation therefore form the core of the present collection of essays: defining the miscellany, and assessing ways in which modern scholarship can best engage with and exploit the complex questions that the miscellany raises, on the one hand; and the associated issue—though of no lesser importance—the cultural significance of this type of manuscript, that is the ways in which examination of the miscellany may reveal processes and interactions that are otherwise obscured in editions or critical studies of individual texts" (2–3). The fifteen essays that follow take up this challenge in a variety of ways. Since almost every essay in this collection is likely germane to the research interests of this journal's readership, I will begin by providing a cursory summary of each.

In Chapter 2, "Texts in Conversation: Charlemagne Epics and Romances in Insular Plural-text Codices" (the first chapter following the Introduction), Marianne Ailes and Phillipa Hardman offer a comparison of French- and English-language manuscripts of Charlemagne romances, demonstrating that the former tend to be thematically coherent compilations, while the latter are more miscellaneous. In Chapter 3, "Multilingualism, the Harley Scribe, and Johannes Jacobi," Keith Busby provides a valuable contextualization of the work of the Harley Scribe, looking at multilingual miscellanies from France and Italy. Susanna Fein follows Busby's focus on the Harley Scribe with "Literary Scribes: The Harley Scribe and Robert Thornton as Case Studies," in which she suggests that these two scribes should be placed somewhere between the creative agency of literary authors and the passivity of slavish copyists. (Such a quick summary cannot do justice to the fascinating and convincing examples that Fein has marshalled in this essay.) Next, Ad Putter offers "The Organisation of Multilingual Miscellanies: The Contrasting Fortunes of Middle English Lyrics and Romances," in which he troubles the standard scholarly narrative that sees miscellanies becoming increasingly monolingual as England progresses through the thirteenth, fourteenth, and fifteenth centuries. As Putter shows, such a narrative works for manuscripts of romance but not for lyrics.

In Chapter 6, "John Northwood's Miscellany Revisited," Wendy Scase presents a new analysis of London, British Library MS Additional 37787, showing that, contrary to previous analyses, this manuscript was a miscellany produced in several distinct units and that only a small portion of it should be attributed to John Northwood, monk of Bordesley Abbey. Raluca Radulescu then gives us "Vying for Attention: The Contents of Dublin, Trinity College, MS 432," in which she argues that this manuscript is "less haphazard in the accretion of items than previously believed," and that it is, rather, "tantalisingly homogeneous" (127). Then, in Chapter 8, "The Chivalric Miscellany: Classifying John Paston's 'Grete Boke'," Andrew Taylor uses London, British Library MS Lansdowne 285 as a case study to explore how types of medieval books simultaneously opened up and delimited different identities—in this case, John Paston's identity as chivalric parvenu and ne'er-do-well. In Chapter 9, "Amateur Book Production and the Miscellany in Late Medieval East Anglia: Tanner 407 and Beinecke 365," Carol Meale sets out to demonstrate that, in the bold words of her opening sentence, "There is no way in which the imposition of a modern taxonomy onto medieval codices can be anything other than problematical" (157). To make this case, Meale proposes that some books are best thought of as "personal compilations" (159), that is, codices which mediate the idiosyncratic interests of the compiler, and in essence, offer scholars the chance to engage in some thick sociological description of individual readers, using the two manuscripts of her title to investigate how different manuscripts manifest their compilers' identities differently.

Chapter 10 (Ceridwen Lloyd-Morgan's "Writing without Borders: Multilingual Content in Welsh Miscellanies from Wales, the Marches, and beyond") takes us to medieval Wales. In this survey of medieval Welsh prose manuscripts, Lloyd-Morgan shows that such codices tend to be multilingual, challenging the too-easy assumption that Welsh was for the Welsh and

English for the English. Dafydd Johnston follows this with "Welsh Bardic Miscellanies," which, with its focus on verse miscellanies, provides a nice companion to Lloyd-Morgan's analysis of prose manuscripts. Ultimately, Johnston suggests that this corpus has been ill-served by the typical text-based approach to editing, which selects a few texts from various manuscripts to present to readers. Instead, he suggests, we need a new editorial approach to such manuscripts, one that can properly express the cultural significance and shifting complexities of the "itinerant poets, scribes, and patrons which produced these miscellanies" (207).

We next turn north with Emily Wingfield's "*Lancelot of the Laik* and the Literary Manuscript Miscellany in 15th- and 16th-century Scotland." In this survey, Wingfield shows that Scottish manuscripts of this period used Middle English materials liberally, rarely employed French or Latin, and tended towards the secular rather than the religious. She ends her chapter with an analysis of Cambridge, University Library MS Kk.1.5, shedding new light on its scribes and process of compilation. This is followed by Chapter 13, "Entertainment Networks, Reading Communities, and the Early Tudor Anthology: Oxford, Bodleian Library, MS Rawlinson C. 813," in which Deborah Youngs argues that this manuscript, more commonly known as the Welles Anthology, should be located within the complex social matrix of the English gentry, who exhibited multiple, often overlapping, cultural and political affiliations with both courtly and provincial literary culture. Chapter 14, William Marx's "Aberystwyth, National Library of Wales, MS Peniarth 12: The Development of a Bilingual Miscellany—Welsh and English," returns us to the Welsh literary scene. In this chapter, Marx analyzes Peniarth 12, a compilation whose core comprises Welsh and Middle English translations of Honorius Augustodunensis' *Elucidarium*, demonstrating the likelihood that Hugh Evans, Dean of St Asaph Cathedral under Elizabeth I, was likely responsible for bringing the manuscript together.

The penultimate chapter is Julia Boffey and A. S. G. Edwards's "Towards a Taxonomy of Middle English Manuscript Assemblages," which problematizes previous attempts to categorize Middle English manuscripts. As they demonstrate, many manuscripts grew accretively over time, frustrating scholarly attempts to identify a single, overarching thematic coherence to such volumes. Boffey and Edwards thus issue a word of caution to scholars who would posit "a controlling design" in a manuscript's compilation (279). The final chapter is Margaret Connolly's "The Whole Book and the Whole Picture: Editions and Facsimiles of Medieval Miscellanies and Their Influence," in which she surveys the history of facsimile production, showing how editors' choices about which manuscripts to reproduce in facsimile form have the potential to offer us a false impression of what the overall field of Middle English manuscripts really was like. This collection then closes with Ardis

Butterfield's Afterword, a short, pithy reflection on the differences between Continental French miscellanies, which tend to be much more thematically coherent and self-conscious productions, and insular books, which Butterfield sees "as operating under different, looser assumptions" (303).

As I hope is obvious from my chapter summaries, for *JEBS*'s readership at least, this is one of those rare edited collections that would merit reading from beginning to end, for the essays are uniformly interesting, thought-provoking, and well-researched. Each has something to offer the book historian, from the neophyte to the seasoned, grizzled codicologist. As someone who has edited or co-edited three collections, I can attest to how Sisyphean it can be trying to achieve coherence across a collection (it's no coincidence that editors of such volumes routinely whisper to fellow editors, when out of earshot of others, that the process is not unlike herding cats), and this is a problem that, on occasion, crops up in this collection. There is a wide diversity of types of essays in this collection. Some, for example (e.g., Lloyd-Morgan, Johnston, Wingfield, and Boffey and Edwards) serve as master classes, surveying their topic and introducing readers to a number of manuscripts. Others (e.g., Scase, Radulescu, Youngs, and Marx) present focused analyses of individual codices. Yet others (e.g., Fein, Putter, Taylor, and Meale) press a methodological argument about how scholars ought to categorize medieval books. And while such diversity can obviously be a strength, demonstrating how rich the field of manuscript studies is and how complex working with such books can be, it did leave this reviewer occasionally puzzled about what the volume's aims were. If it was simply to bring together scholarship on the miscellany, content with the fact that book history is a "big tent" (to co-opt American political parlance—or a "broad church," if you prefer the British equivalent), then this volume certainly satisfies that criterion.

A few other, more niggling inconsistencies did present themselves across this volume. Two consecutive chapters, for example, make conflicting claims about when the term "commonplace book" was first applied to Middle English manuscripts (150, 173). There is also an unresolved contradiction between Lloyd-Morgan's insistence that "There can be little doubt that access to material deriving from several languages within the written culture was the norm, and to contrast manuscripts written entirely in Welsh with those written in two or more languages is to make a false distinction" (191), with Marx's contention that "A significant feature of these miscellanies of Welsh provenance was that where they contained Middle English, English was very much a minority language" (247). But more significant is the issue of terminology, for some of the authors treat the categories with which we are all familiar (e.g., *miscellany, household book, commonplace book, anthology*) as a live question whose definition must be wrestled with, and as one that can shed light on a manuscript's production and meaning-making (e.g.,

Connolly's Introduction [pp. 5–8], Busby, Taylor, Meale), while others treat the categories as having stable, settled definitions (e.g., Ailes and Hardman, Wingfield, Marx). As a result, when one reads this book through from beginning to end, one does not leave with a clear sense of whether the terminology even matters. I do not necessarily intend this as a criticism of the volume, for such divergence of opinion may simply signal that this is a complicated issue which belies simple definitions. But most readers will come to this volume already familiar with some of the famous attempts to define (or to trouble the very act of defining) miscellanies by Ralph Hanna, Derek Pearsall, Julia Boffey and John Thompson. This volume, rather than leaving the reader with a definitive impression of what the miscellany is, leaves the reader with the impression that miscellanies are complex, baggy monsters that we do not yet know how to categorize. There is much more work to be done in this area, and this fine collection of essays will no doubt spur more such work. To the readers of this journal, I cannot commend it highly enough.

Michael Johnston, Purdue University

AIDAN CONTI, ORIETTA DA ROLD, AND PHILIP SHAW, EDS.
Writing Europe, 500-1450: Texts and Contexts.
Essays and Studies 2015. The English Association.
Cambridge: D.S. Brewer, 2015. xvi + 198 pp. 26 B&W figs.

Writing Europe contains an interesting and diverse range of papers, mainly written by younger scholars including three doctoral students. The volume explores textual culture in a European context, and contributions discuss books, literacy and language in England, Wales, Scandinavia, Italy, Frisia, and Bulgaria. This range of topics offers a series of case studies of texts produced in specific historical contexts, and the reader is largely left to infer connections between the different national milieux.

In their introductory essay, "Medieval Manuscript Studies: A European Perspective," Orietta Da Rold and Marilena Maniaci disarmingly disclaim any intention of offering a comprehensive overview of the contemporary state of the subject but "rather a series of thoughts on some aspects and issues" (1). This series of thoughts takes in developments in codicology, paleography, and the newer approaches of digital paleography and neuropaleography. Their footnotes provide recent bibliographies, although many works cited are unfortunately not in English.

Digital paleography gets its own chapter, "The DigiPal Project for European Scripts and Decorations," and describes a project based in King's College, London, with short contributions from those involved. Stewart Brookes explains the purpose and function of this computer-based method of paleography, while Peter Stokes, Matilda Watson, and Débora Marques de Matos discuss its application in their respective research fields of Old English, Scandinavian, and Sephardic manuscripts. One of the difficulties of this approach is in imposing a standard template that enables the computer to recognize repeated patterns in an individual's handwriting, without constraining one's description of letter-forms too rigidly to a pre-determined model. A scribe's handwriting over a period of time can be subject to various subconscious influences, such as how tired he may be, how he is feeling, and so on. Nor can the element of subjectivity in the researcher's judgement of what is characteristic of a hand or style be eliminated.

Nadia Togni, in "Italian Giant Bibles: The Circulation and Use of the Book at the Time of the Ecclesiastical Reform in the Eleventh and Twelfth Centuries," argues that such Bibles (whose characteristic features she lists, 60) were produced in and sent from Rome to religious institutions which accepted the program of ecclesiastical reform promoted by Pope Gregory VII (1073 to 1085). Her focus is specifically on Italian Bibles, but similar Bibles are found elsewhere in Europe. Are they also a consequence of the Gregorian Reform? She is right to observe that manuscripts are the products of historical circumstances, and it would be interesting if she drew out the implications of her findings for Bibles produced beyond Italy. Rolf H. Bremmer, Jr., on the other hand, in "Isolation or Network? *Arengas* and Colophon Verse in Frisian Manuscripts around 1300," draws out the international aspect that the use of *arenga* and colophon in Frisian charters reveals. That the scribes were able to patch together phrases from a common European store for both the *arenga* (the preamble to a charter setting it within a religious framework) and the colophon shows pragmatic literacy was further advanced in Frisia about 1300 than hitherto realized.

Annina Seiler, in "Writing the Germanic Languages: The Early History of the Digraphs <th>, <ch> and <uu>," discusses the problem of creating an orthographical system from the Latin alphabet for sounds which existed only in the Germanic languages. She argues that the use of the digraphs <th>, <ch>, and <uu> in early Old English spelling was probably modelled on the Merovingian example where the scribes of charters had adopted them to maintain a letter-sound correlation in spelling the names of Frankish witnesses. In "The New Heathens: Anti-Jewish Hostility in Early English Literature," George Younge traces the growth of anti-Semitic hostility in post-Conquest England, a development that can be attributed to biblical commentaries which emphasized Jewish culpability for the crucifixion of Christ together with the increasingly visible presence of wealthy Jews in towns and cities.

Looking beyond England, Aidan Conti, in "Latin composition in Medieval Norway," surveys the corpus of Latin composed in that country. Most Latin is to be found in letters and documents written before 1590, mainly in the large body of correspondence to and from the papacy to the Norwegian church. The amount of Latin composed in Norway (as opposed to copied) is relatively small, since Norway did not sustain the literary activity it had initially seen in the twelfth century. However, while the vernacular was used for runic inscriptions on rune-stones, monuments and church buildings, brief inscriptions in Latin exist on runic sticks, lead plates and bands, and pieces of bone. This suggests Latin had a wider circulation than previously thought.

In "Translating Europe in Medieval Wales," Helen Fulton discusses the influence after the Edwardian conquest of Wales in 1282 of European works, both in Latin and French, on Welsh literature. French courtly romances of Arthur and Charlemagne were adapted in translation to fit a Welsh setting, consequently "Welsh Arthur is less like a French king and more like a Welsh chieftain" (167). A crucial role in making French texts available in Welsh seems to have been played by Hopcyn ap Tomas ab Einion from Glamorgan (fl. c. 1337 to 1408), who commissioned not only Aberystwyth, National Library of Wales, Peniarth MS 11, but also Oxford, Jesus College, MS 111, the "Red Book of Hergest," a volume that contains almost the entire canon of medieval Welsh literature.

The final essay by Svetlana Tsonkova, "Charms among the Chants: Verbal Magic in Medieval Bulgarian Manuscripts," discusses her research on oral charms. These are mainly preserved in prayer books intended for the parish priest as an integral part of the text rather than as additions or marginalia. They had an apotropaic function designed to cope with practical day-to-day concerns, such as the charms she quotes against dog bites and urinary retention, and reflect the priest's role in any crisis to heal his parishioners.

Many of the contributors are non-native English speakers. While full of admiration for those who write in a language not their own, and recognizing the difficulty an editor can have in intervening in an author's text without misrepresenting what the author wants to say, I feel that the editors could usefully have offered some minor corrections. Thus a miscellany is said to contain "pieces of historical chronicles" (178) when I assume the writer means "extracts"; elsewhere there is confusion between "conservation" and "preservation" in the statement that manuscripts are listed "with their places of conservation" (64), when location is meant. And the editors really should have corrected the wording of what is said to be one of the characteristics of late eleventh- and twelfth-century Bibles, "The use of a standardised Carolingian minuscule font" (60). Unusually and admirably, measurements are given for the initials depicted on pages 62 and 63. Regrettably, too many scholars do not recognize the necessity of indicating scale when providing illustrations in support of their arguments.

Pamela Robinson, Institute of English Studies, University of London

JANET COWEN, ED.
On Famous Women:
The Middle English Translation of Boccaccio's 'De Mulieribus Claris.'
Edited from London, British Library, MS Additional 10304.
Middle English Texts, 52. Heidelberg: Winter, 2015. li + 131 pp.

As Janet Cowen herself notes, this is a "timely" (xi) edition of *On Famous Women*, the only known copy of an anonymous Middle English verse translation of Boccaccio's Latin prose text *De Mulieribus Claris*, previously only available in extracts dating from 1892 and a full but inaccessible text from 1924. In the introduction Cowen writes with authority and with an expertise born of a close engagement with this text over many years, as she deals with the features expected in any scholarly edition: text (xi), manuscript (xi–xix), source (xx–xxiii), translation (xxiii–xxvii), linguistic profile (xxvii–xxxviii), versification (xxxviii–xlix), and editorial policy (xlix–li). Her task has not been straightforward, partly because of the inherent complexities of her source text and partly because the manuscript, London, British Library, MS Additional 10304 (which was acquired by the British Museum in 1836 after the sale of the magnificent library of the book collector, Richard Heber), has not previously received the scrutiny it deserves. As Cowen explains so cogently, *De Mulieribus Claris*, which is dated to between 1361 and 1362, had several phases of authorial editing, with either seven or nine redactions, depending on which expert is believed. In its final form, it consists of one hundred and six chapters (together with dedicatory and concluding material), mainly concerning famous women of Graeco-Roman antiquity, with only the last six chapters devoted to post-classical times. This emphasis on pagan goddesses and heroines is justified in Boccaccio's proem (xx) and broadly replicated in the Middle English (ll. 169–210), mostly on the grounds that Christian women are already adequately dealt with in hagiographical tradition.

Cowen's discussion of the Middle English translator's selection of material, possibly dependent on an anonymous French prose intermediary, is especially interesting. The translator starts in order with Boccaccio's first ten lives and then proceeds to slot the rest of his eleven lives into a pattern that may have developed as the work proceeded. The plan remained open-ended as the translator hoped to add more in the future: "If it fortune to be acceptable / And please the herers, forth I will procede / To the residue of ladyes notable" (ll. 1786–88). The lives vary in length and detail, with Tamaris (the Athenian painter) only meriting two stanzas, albeit with the important point that she was "a peyntrys" (l.1638), the first use of the term in the *Middle English Dictionary*. In her introduction and thorough commentary, Cowen constantly guides the reader in how the Middle English translator has abbreviated, expanded, or transposed the lives in his source. In associating the dialect with East Anglia, more specifically Norfolk, the editor produces a careful linguistic analysis but also widens the focus by considering how the language here relates to that of another important writer from the East Anglian area, John Lydgate. This comparison gives the linguistic analysis more substance, something that characterizes the introduction as a whole. Cowen has clearly thought very carefully about her arguments. For instance, rather than citing the usual superficial notion about exemplary female lives as a model for women readers, she notes that "in the standard rhetorical tradition examples of strong women functioned not as models for women, but as exhortations to men" (xxv).

It can be overwhelming for a reader to struggle through a thicket of footnotes or risk losing sight of the main argument by being referred to other authorities to validate virtually every point. In many ways we have gone from one extreme to the other, in that earlier scholars were very spartan and haphazard with their citation of references, while some modern scholars are prone to allow their arguments to become so overrun by secondary material that the reader cannot see the wood for the trees. The current editor shows commendable restraint in this respect. Yet there are times in the introduction (though not in the commentary or glossary, which are both fully developed) when she could perhaps have been a little more expansive in her treatment of explanatory material and references. While this economy does not detract from her main points, here and there the reader would have benefited from being told a little more. For example, on the first page of the introduction (xi), it is noted that "*FW* is one of only two known translations of *DMC* into English before modern times," supported by a note that simply says "For the other see Wright 1943." Rather than sending readers to the relevant EETS volume to check this, it would have been useful to have been told that this edition of forty-six lives is none other than that by Henry Parker (1480/1–1556), Lord Morley, an intimate of the English royal court from boyhood.

Another example of such economy comes later, in the discussion of the hands. Cowen points out that the Latin verse and rubric at the beginning of the text are in a humanistic hand (see her figure 1) and then says in footnote six that the use of such hands "is rare in English vernacular manuscripts of this time" (xvi), followed by a reference to Daniel Wakelin's *Humanism, Reading, and English Literature 1430 to 1530*, page 60, note 126. There may be no more to be added, but the interested reader might wish to know how "rare" is "rare" in Cowen's opinion. She herself (xi) makes the point that the use of humanistic letter forms in the vernacular script (see her figure 2) might point to a date nearer to 1460 than to 1440 (the dates originally provided for the manuscript by Ian Doyle). In fact, given that she also notes that the binding is associated with one dated to 1481 (xii), a little more consideration might have been devoted to the possibility of a later overall dating.

Nevertheless, in the general scheme of things, such economies are trivial points. Editors (sometimes guided by general editors) will always have a different regard for what they think is relevant or necessary, in the same way that readers will appreciate the given material to varying extents. While personally (as an editor of prose texts), I was not so engaged with over ten pages on versification, I would nevertheless stoutly defend Cowen's right as an editor who knows this text better than anyone to use the opportunity to point out to readers what she has learned and to pass it on to us. This is not simply a case of readers needing to be educated about things that only mildly interest them or about which they may be uncaring. Rather it is only by telling us about the problematics of the versification of this text that Cowen can set it in context beside other writers of the period (for instance, in the sometime vexed debate over the metrical value of final "e" in Chaucerian and related texts). More importantly, by doing so she can also substantiate some of her editorial decisions. And it is for this very reason (as well as for dialectal considerations) that she obtained permission from the series editors to italicize her expansions, something that is exceptionally rare in published Middle English texts these days, even though it used to be *de rigeur* when most of us began our editing careers.

To edit a text that has not been edited before or has been edited mostly in an early or inaccessible edition is a major responsibility. In this edition Cowen has risen admirably to the challenge. Anyone working on the depiction of female lives, vernacular translation, or the presentation of pagan antiquity in the Middle Ages will be certain to find much of interest in this fine edition.

Veronica O'Mara, University of Hull

SUSANNA FEIN, ED.
The Auchinleck Manuscript: New Perspectives.
York: York Medieval Press, 2016.
xi + 253 pp., 6 B&W figs.

In *The Auchinleck Manuscript: New Perspectives*, Susanna Fein presents thirteen essays (most of which originate from the 2008 meeting of the London Old and Middle English Seminar), packaged with a bibliography, an index of manuscripts cited, and a general index. The essays are summarized in a short introduction in which Fein also outlines those issues that have formed the main points of scholarly inquiry into this famous fourteenth-century manuscript, succinctly framed as a series of questions: "Who were its makers? Its users? How was it made? And what end did it serve?" (4). Fein notes that access to the manuscript has been facilitated by the print facsimile edited by Derek Pearsall and Iain Cunningham, and by the development of the digital facsimile by David Burnley and Alison Wiggins hosted by the National Library of Scotland. The contributors to the volume variously rely on these surrogates in citing readings and other evidence from the manuscript, with the exception of Ralph Hanna whose observations are based on first-hand examination of what he terms a "live book" (209). His essay is the final one in the collection, and he uses it to make some controversial suggestions: first in denying the separate existence of Scribe 6 (who is only Scribe 1 on another day), and then in suggesting that the manuscript's production may have been less consistently planned than is usually assumed. Conversely, A. S. G. Edwards finds that Auchinleck's overall shape and sequence of texts "suggests some deliberate controlling principle that probably existed from the outset" (34). However, he too argues for a different slant on what is typically envisaged. His essay concentrates on the manuscript's early sections in which the contents are largely of a religious nature and derived more from

Latin than from Anglo-Norman, which leads him to suggest that the balance of contents in the completed, undamaged codex might have been less romance dominated than is now the case.

These are valuable new perspectives on matters of textual production. Two other especially detailed and illuminating discussions of aspects of the making of Auchinleck that have previously escaped exhaustive scrutiny are offered by Timothy Shonk and Míceál F. Vaughan. Shonk's essay contains a closely observed analysis of paraph forms, helpfully tabulated in an appendix. His findings are mixed, and he can suggest no definitive conclusions about the distribution of paraphs in Auchinleck, but he successfully articulates how a wider search for the activities of paraphers might extend existing knowledge of communities of bookmakers in the early fourteenth century. Vaughan ventures into the relatively untrodden field of scribal correction, observing the presence of a variety of conventions and practices in Auchinleck, which leads him to question the assumption that Scribe 1 was responsible for all such emendations. Vaughan acknowledges the difficulty in identifying who did what and when, even allowing that some corrections may have been made by early readers of the volume – a rare mention of matters related to reception, an area that receives scant attention in this collection.

The scope of this volume largely reflects current preoccupations in the study of medieval English literature, with much attention directed to codicological issues, though not to the exclusion of literary analysis. Derek Pearsall's essay assessing "The Auchinleck Manuscript Forty Years On" addresses a more fundamental matter than book production: the unresolved issue of the authorship of Auchinleck's many texts. Textual and literary matters, as well as different notions of compilation, also concern Helen Phillips who draws analogies between Auchinleck and its close contemporary, British Library MS Harley 2253, and the later literary compilation of Chaucer's *Canterbury Tales*. Several contributors concentrate on individual romances. In "The Auchinleck *Adam and Eve:* An Exemplary Family Story," Cathy Hume extends the idea that the manuscript as a whole was designed for family reading. Patrick Butler's essay contends that a message about multilingualism may be found in some of the texts of this famously monolingual compilation, particularly in the Prologue to *Of Arthour and of Merlin*. Yet Emily Rundle, starting with the same text in her analysis of "Scribe 3's Literary Project: Pedagogies of Reading in Auchinleck's Booklet 3," finds an emphasis on Englishness. That Englishness is implicitly accepted by Venetia Bridges who ponders the "Absent Presence: Auchinleck and *Kyng Alisaunder*," noting that the ancient Greek historical focus of this romance makes it unlike the manuscript's other contents; it is this lack of fit with perceptions of a governing principle of Englishness that she believes is the cause of the relative critical neglect of this romance. Marisa Libbon focuses on another king and another incomplete text in her essay "The Invention of King Richard," raising a question about just how much of this incomplete text might now be missing, and querying the imperfectness of its ending. This topic is more properly the preserve of Siobhan Bly Calkin's careful account of "Endings in the Auchinleck Manuscript," which explores ideas about endings, perfect or otherwise, and strategies for closure, noting how the variety of traditional and non-traditional forms of finishing texts in Auchinleck may problematize modern attempts to fill in its codicological gaps.

It is surprising – and pleasing – to find that there is still much to learn about this most celebrated early fourteenth-century codex. As Hanna comments: "the book has scarcely been exhausted of its secrets, and is certainly worthy of much more detailed examination" (221). In this regard it is also rather disappointing that readers, owners, annotators, and users receive almost no consideration here. An exception is Ann Higgins's essay, "*Sir Tristrem*, a Few Fragments, and the Northern Identity of the Auchinleck Manuscript." Higgins's thesis is that Auchinleck was compiled in London for a regional client who took it north when it was finished. Sketching this scenario requires, as she admits "a certain amount of speculation and risk" (109), but it is bravely done, and no one else ventures any thoughts in this regard. However her attempt to connect this supposed northern commission with the "hard physical evidence" (124) of the manuscript's later history in Scotland is impeded by some misinterpretations and factual inaccuracies, notably in relation to the foundation of the University of St Andrews. There are one or two errors elsewhere in the volume: the print facsimile edited by Derek Pearsall and Iain Cunningham was published in 1977 (not 1979, as given on page 1 and in the Bibliography), and on page 189 the title of Murray J. Evans's book is given correctly as *Rereading Middle English Romance* in the text but as *Rereading Middle English Manuscripts* in the supporting footnote and the Bibliography.

The free availability of the digital facsimile of the manuscript from the website of the National Library of Scotland removes the need for much illustration here, but the six images that are included are well reproduced, and particularly in Shonk's essay, are very helpful to the reader's understanding of the argument. Though generally useful, the essays mostly stand alone, even where there are manifest points of interrelation: there is not much cross-referencing between individual chapters, and given the volume's conference origins, one might certainly have expected more. Collectively the essays in this volume enhance our knowledge of the manuscript officially known as National Library of Scotland, Advocates' MS 19.2.1 and offer fresh perspectives which are illuminating in themselves, and which more importantly may also serve to reveal new paths for future enquiry.

Margaret Connolly, University of St Andrews

SCALA ARTS AND HERITAGE PUBLISHERS

JULIE GARDHAM
Ingenious Impressions: Fifteenth-century printed books from the University of Glasgow Library.
London: Scala, 2016. 80 pp. 70 color plates.

The foreword to this charming little book (7½ x 6½ in.) explains its rationale: it "explores the development and subsequent afterlives of [incunabula], drawing on the extensive research of a five-year project to catalogue the University of Glasgow's outstanding collection" (4). The collection houses the largest number of incunabula in Scotland, over one thousand books, and the present small volume was produced as part of a drive (which included an exhibition in the Hunterian Art Gallery in 2015) to encourage further knowledge and use of the collection in the light of the Glasgow Incunabula Project (available at www.gla.ac.uk/services/incunabula/). After a brief context-setting introduction by Jack Baldwin (of the Project), thirty-five incunabula are described and illustrated, each on a two-page spread with either full-page or several smaller illustrations, all in color. The first is a Netherlandish or German blockbook Apocalypse of the 1460s and the last are two German incunables of 1489 with inscriptions of ownership by Conrad Wubberdingk of Rintelln in Lower Saxony (interestingly, one is on witchcraft and the other on the priesthood). The emphasis is on Continental printers, although William Caxton and Wynkyn de Worde are included with illustrations from *The Myrrour of the World* (1489, bought by the vicar of Much Wenlock, Shropshire in 1510), the *Statuta Angliae: XI Henry VII* (1496, with a hand-colored woodcut of the king's arms on the verso of the title page), and *The Miracles of our Lady* (printed about 1496, bought by William Hunter for 15s. 6d. at the book sale of the collector John Ratcliffe in 1776).

M. E. J. HUGHES
The Pepys Library and the Historic Collections of Magdalene College Cambridge.
London: Scala, 2015. 88 pp. 101 color plates.

This much larger book (10½ x 7¾ in.) is equally lavishly illustrated but performs more functions: not just to introduce readers to the collections of the Pepys Library and the Old Library of Magdalene College but to serve "unashamedly" as "a celebration of that history we inhabit as an intellectual community" (5). As such, the illustrations of manuscripts and books are interspersed with photographs of people and archives important to the college. For example, the brief introduction to Cambridge books and Magdalene's two historic libraries includes not only two plates of birds (from a medieval artist's model book and the *Prenostica pitagorice considerationis*, respectively) and a leaf from an illustrated manuscript of the Englished *Metamorphoses* bought by Samuel Pepys, but also Pepys's book stamp and a photograph of the Pepys Library itself. There follow sections on the "Pepys Library" (including "The Library of Samuel Pepys," "The Pepys Building," "Pepys the Collector," "The Diary," and "Furnishing a Library"), on "The Old Library" (including "The Old Library: Heart of the College," "Building a Collection," "Treasures of the Old Library," "Special Collections," and "Objects in the Collections"), on "The Archives," and on "The Work of the Historic Libraries" (including "Exhibitions," "Conservation," "Scholars and Readers"). Although "The Archives" contains only one section ("The Magdalene College Archives"), the diversity of approach is demonstrated by the fact that there are illustrations of an indenture of 1643; twentieth- and twenty-first-century calligraphy on book covers, book plates, book labels, and stone; the college's order book, with a note of the sending down of Charles Steward Parnell for brawling; the 1555/1565 statutes; the register for 1602 to 1603; photographs of Nelson Mandela at Magdalene in 2001, and other photographs from the archives, including the college porter in the Cambridge Pancake Race on Shrove Tuesday, 1959.

Throughout this lavishly illustrated book, the captions are full, interesting and informative, and one is left with a sense not just of the two historic libraries but of the life of the college itself (the avowed intention of the book). The whole ends with a "List of (Fellow) Librarians," a "Selected Bibliography" and "Acknowledgements."

SCALA ARTS AND HERITAGE PUBLISHERS

JAMES KELLY, ED.
Treasures of Ushaw College: Durham's Hidden Gem.
London: Scala, 2015. 160 pp. 97 color plates.

Slightly smaller than the Magdalene book (10 x 8¼ in.), but with the same intention, to publicize and celebrate its heritage and holdings, *Treasures of Ushaw College* mingles past and present photographs of Ushaw with excellent plates of items from its collection. Until recently the future of Ushaw was by no means certain, as indicated by the final sentence of Eamon Duffy's historical introduction: "By 2011 ... the seminarians were moved to Wideman's financially better-endowed Midland seminary at Oscott, and Ushaw closed its doors" (31). As well as this "Introduction: Historical," which traces the history of Ushaw as a Roman Catholic seminary founded in 1808, there is an "Introduction: Architectural," in which Sophie Andreae takes the story a little further: "Since [2011], and through the good offices of Durham University, there has been a burgeoning interest in Ushaw and its remarkable buildings and associated collections which previously were so little known beyond a small number of experts" (46). Neither the foreword, by the Archbishop of Westminster, Cardinal Vincent Nichols, nor the preface and acknowledgements by the editor James Kelly, refers to the recent problems.

However, it seems that the tide has turned, and Ushaw's amazing nineteenth-century buildings and stunning artefacts are well celebrated in this volume. Not that they had been uncelebrated earlier: shortly before the closure of Ushaw, *Ushaw College 1808-2008: A Celebration*, compiled and edited by W. J. Campbell on behalf of Saint Cuthbert's Society (Keighley: PBK, 2008), had celebrated the two hundred years of the college, opening with a carefully-worded foreword by the then Archbishop of Westminster, Cardinal Cormac Murphy-O'Connor: "It is to the credit of the St Cuthbert's Society – the umbrella organisation of alumni, ordained and lay, friends and supporters of the College – that they caused this Bicentenary Memorial Book to be created and published. While confessing our complete trust in the Lord's providential love, we can pray that the future of Ushaw may be as rich and fruitful as its past. *Ad multos annos!*" (vi). In the present volume, James Kelly too refers to "the biggest debt of thanks" as due to the St Cuthbert's Society.

It seems that the Archbishop's confidence was not misplaced, although it is astonishing to think that this great collection, both standing architecture and individual artefacts, might have been consigned to moth-balling or even sale. The architecture and artefacts were, of course, designed and donated to celebrate God. After the Catholic Emancipation Act of 1829 and under Monsignor Charles Newsham's presidency, new buildings, including a new chapel, were built to the designs of A. W. Pugin, and on his death, his son E. W. Pugin, and of the similarly Roman Catholic architects, Joseph and Charles Hansom. Many of the artefacts illustrated in this book relate to the use of the stunning Pugin chapel – furnishings, vestments, plate, and even relics.

However, *Treasures of Ushaw College* begins with a manuscript. The first item, "Local Survivors from before the Reformation," is introduced by Ian Doyle, former Keeper of Rare Books at Durham, and illustrated (across the double spread which is characteristic of each item in this book) by an item from one of the several books from Durham Cathedral Priory held at Ushaw, a fragment of binding material from the Christmas liturgy (Northumbria, eighth century). Each item in the book is introduced by a suitable expert, in the case of the manuscripts and early printed books, an expert from the Department of History at Durham: a Book of Hours from about 1408 to 1409 is introduced by Richard Gameson, the late-fifteenth-century Esh Missal by Margaret Harvey, Hartmann Schedel's *World Chronicle* (1493) by Katherine Krick, and Andreas Knopken's *In epistolam ad Romanos* (1525) by David Gehring. (Other printed books are beyond our period.) While the books of Ushaw (despite their actual numbers) occupy only twenty of the forty-six items displayed, this testifies to the riches and breadth of the Ushaw collection. For once the term "treasures" is not inappropriate as the title of this splendid and uplifting volume.

Susan Powell, University of Salford

DAVID GREER
Manuscript Inscriptions in Early England Printed Music.
Aldershot: Ashgate, 2015. 226 pp. 36 figs.

What happened to a music edition once it left the printing house? Until recently, itineraries of printed music have attracted remarkably little comment – a matter too bibliographically esoteric for musicologists and too niche for book historians. Drawing upon a lifetime of bibliographical off-cuts, David Greer's study is a welcome pioneer in an as yet disappointingly underpopulated field.

It is principally a hand-list of printed music books, arranged alphabetically by library of deposit (following the efficient sigla developed by the *Répertoire international des sources musicales*: so, GB-Llp denotes the Lambeth Palace Library in London and USA-Wc, the Library of Congress). Brief notices are provided for each copy and its current state, along with the transcriptions or descriptions of the annotations themselves. This constitutes Part II (63-189).

Part I comprises five short chapters in which Greer surveys the corpus and discusses his selection criteria (Chapter One, consisting of a five-page list of publications from about 1520 to 1640, nearly 200 in all), and then categorizes the annotations to be found in early printed music editions: ex libris inscriptions and other signs of ownership; added text and music; numbers (usually page or folio numbers, but sometimes prices); and other additions not covered by these categories – scribbles, colorings-in, criticisms germane and otherwise, theoretical explanations and diagrams.

Garnered over the course of many decades as part of scholarly projects long since published and garlanded, Greer's observations might in former times have made their way to an archive or learned library in the guise of antiquarian notes. As Greer is at pains to point out, this was not a defined bibliographical project in its own right, and this accounts for the strengths and weaknesses of this study.

In order to keep the study to manageable proportions, and reflecting the author's long-term interests, selection criteria were necessarily stringent. "Printed music" means, usually, polyphonic music by native composers printed in England or for the English market, with some kind of handmade annotations that are not "modern" (in practice this means a focus on the sixteenth and seventeenth centuries). This excludes printed music for Sarum use and any vernacular psalters that do not quite make the grade as "musically significant" (3). This is understandable, but it means that some important but neglected witnesses go unheard and potentially informative parcels of evidence are excluded.

But this is a splendid exercise in the gathering, sifting, categorizing and description of data, even the most inane. Put to work, these scraps of evidence help to pin down the owners of music books, to reassemble tract volumes that were more recently dismembered, and to affiliate component partbooks from dispersed sets. So easily overlooked as graphic noise, a set of coarse children's drawings serves here to affiliate long-dispersed music books now found in UCLA, Harvard, the Huntington and the Royal Academy of Music in London.

If there is a second edition, one might hope for an index of the nearly 200 editions listed in Chapter One. As things stand, the reader cannot easily follow up the intriguing bibliographical trails suggested in Greer's catalogue. Anyone researching the post-production history of the landmark six-partbook *Cantiones* by Thomas Tallis and William Byrd (STC 23666, 1575), for instance, would be better off starting with the hand-list in John Milsom's edition of the *Cantiones* (London: Stainer & Bell, 2014). Greer reminds us that one set of *Cantiones* ended up (mostly) in the Brussels Bibliothèque Royale, courtesy of F. J. Fétis, and that this copy is signed "Ric: Langley"; but it is Milsom who provides the essential information needed to link the Brussels partbooks with the orphaned Superius partbook now in the Bodleian Library, also signed by one Richard Langley.

Delving into the detail of Greer's hand-list whets the appetite without sating it. The dates of annotations are seldom specified, necessitating arduous air miles on the part of a reader wishing to test hypotheses or investigate a potential line of inquiry (thumbnail illustrations are sparse: could this have been a web project?). Might the Joannes Yelding, owner of the BL copy of Thomas Ford's *Musicke of Sundrie Kinds* (STC11166, 1607), have been the John Yelding presented by Viscount Montagu to the rectory of St Clement, Hastings in 1576? Or might he have been the yeoman of Battle involved in litigation in 1716? Dating the signature would help us to rule at least one of them out of contention. And might the John Palgrave, one-time owner of the LoC copy of the 1575 *Cantiones*, be associable with the Augustin and Margaret Pagrave [sic] whose names appear in a British Library copy of the same publication (K.3.f.9)? Although Greer does not note the coincidence, the suspicion that the bearers of this uncommon name were of the same gentry family is quickened with the discovery that the Palgraves were Norfolk neighbors of the Pastons, the notable family of recusant music-lovers.

In raising so many questions of this kind, *Manuscript Inscriptions* serves its intended purpose handsomely. Its success will best be measured by how quickly and how comprehensively it is superseded.

Magnus Williamson, Newcastle University

PATRICK J. HORNER
The Index of Middle English Prose: Handlist XXI: Manuscripts in the Hatton and e Musaeo Collections, Bodleian Library, Oxford.
Cambridge: D. S. Brewer, 2014. xx + 109 pp.

Patrick Horner's first *Index of Middle English Prose* volume (*IMEP* 3) was published in 1986; it dealt with the Digby manuscripts in the Bodleian Library and was followed the next year by the Douce manuscripts (*IMEP* 4). The Ashmole collection was indexed in 1992, "smaller Bodleian collections" in 1998, and the Laudian collection in 2000 (*IMEP* 9, 12, 16). In the current volume Brother Patrick returns to the Bodleian Library to index the Hatton and e Musaeo collections.[1]

The Hatton manuscripts came to the Bodleian in 1671 when they were sold at the death of Christopher Hatton, first Baron Hatton and eventual heir of the Elizabethan courtier of the same name. The manuscripts were not in fact Hatton's own. We are told that "prior to the civil war...Hatton had engaged with a number of scholars, including William Dugdale, in collecting and transcribing medieval records" (xiii). In doing so he had borrowed at least 116 manuscripts (the present Hatton collection), many from monastic and cathedral libraries (especially Worcester Cathedral) which he did not return. All but four Anglo-Saxon codices (Junius MSS 22, 23, 24, 99, later donated to the Bodleian) were sold to the Bodleian's principal agent for £156. Other Anglo-Saxon manuscripts were also among the sale manuscripts, including Hatton MSS 20 (the Alfred translation of Gregory the Great's *Cura Pastoralis*), 30 and 42 (which belonged to St Dunstan), 48 (the earliest manuscript of St Benedict's Rule), 76 (the Old English *Herbarium*), and MSS 112-16 (homilies of Aelfric and Wulfstan). Only MSS 20, 76, and 113-16 are indexed here, and only because they have Middle English (and, in the case of MS 20, Latin) glosses which require their inclusion in Macaronic Index D.

Of course, the Hatton collection also contains fully Middle English manuscripts, including Richard Rolle's commentaries on the Psalter and the Ten Commandments, Nicholas Love's *Mirror of the Blessed Life of Jesus Christ*, and the *Brut* chronicle (MSS 12, 31, 50), as well as lesser material. The e Musaeo collection (so called because from the mid-seventeenth century acquisitions were stored "in the museum," i.e., in a cupboard in the office of the librarian, Thomas Barlow) contains more Middle English material: an imperfect copy of John of Trevisa's Bartholomeus Anglicus (MS 16), another copy of Love's *Mirror* and of the *Brut* chronicle (MSS 35 and 39),[2] the Wycliffite New Testament (MS 110),[3] Suso's *Horologium sapiencie* in Middle English (MS 111); two manuscripts of Mandeville's *Travels* (MSS 116 and 124), an interesting Carthusian compilation in verse and prose (MS 160), and more Rolle (MS 232). Apart from the usual medical recipes, there are two manuscripts of Chaucer's *Treatise on the Astrolabe* (MSS 54, 116) and other important medical treatises (in MSS 52, 116, and 146).

Of those manuscripts the present reviewer knows very well, MSS Hatton 96 and e Musaeo 180, the descriptions seem accurate. It is a pity that the *sanctorale* sermons (listed as items [4]-[63]) in Hatton MS 96 are not individually indexed, since they have not yet been identified, and the many *Festial* sermons (and versions of the same *Festial* sermon) in the same manuscript, even though identified, should each be listed with incipit and explicit. (The listing of each sermon in a collection was, at one time at least, IMEP policy, although not now cited in the General Introduction). Given the editing of e Musaeo 180 by Stephen Morrison, individual listing of the sermons is perhaps not necessary, although the value of incipits and explicits for every item in IMEP is that future discoveries of the same collection, or sermons from the same collection, may be recognized. That this seems no longer fundamental to IMEP weakens it as a tool for establishing the corpus of Middle English sermon material.

One might say a little more about the Macaronic Index and *IMEP*. The General Introduction to all *IMEP* volumes lists "a few general features of the Handlist," among which is "2. Macaronic materials appear in an Appendix and are recorded only by opening lines" (v). As noted above, the "macaronic" manuscripts of D (Writings in Latin, Old and Middle English) are in fact all written in Old English and are macaronic only in that they have glosses in Middle English (one in Latin also).[4] Two other sections of the Macaronic Index (A: Writings in Latin and Middle English, B: Writings in French and Middle English) often feature similar Middle English glosses, in Latin manuscripts ([A1] to [A4]) and in Anglo-Norman manuscripts ([B1] and [B2]). Section C (Writings in Latin, French, and Middle English) contains only one item which may be truly macaronic, as I understand the term (that is, written in a mixture of languages), since it is described as "a glossary of plant names in Latin, French, and Middle English" ([C1]), but there is no incipit from which to attempt to determine this. Of the remaining manuscripts in the Macaronic Index ([A5] to [A11]), only [A5] strikes me as genuinely macaronic, the others containing Latin or English headings to English or Latin material, and the like. At the very least, it seems desirable that there should be more advice given to the users of IMEP (and perhaps to the individual editors) as to exactly what "macaronic" means. One might, for example, expect to find the English *Quinta Tabula* of the *Speculum christiani* ([A6]) or the English testimony of Sir John Oldcastle ([A11]) in the main body of the index and not hidden in an ambiguous macaronic index.[5]

Susan Powell, University of Salford

NOTES

1. The American spellings in his Introduction have, oddly, been allowed to stand.
2. Not "e Mus 23,35" (xiv).
3. Not "e Mus 111" (xiv).
4. As noted by Horner ([D2]), MS 76 should perhaps be recognized as Middle English but is not so recognized in this Index (seemingly because it is not in the *Index of Printed Middle English Prose*, but see General Introduction, p. vi (8.)).
5. They are listed in the main body of the text, but only with cross-references to the Macaronic Index.

MICHAEL JOHNSTON AND MICHAEL VAN DUSSEN, EDS.
The Medieval Manuscript Book: Cultural Approaches.
Cambridge: Cambridge University Press, 2015.
Pp. xii, 302.

In my graduate seminar on medieval communication, we devote much of the semester to the scholarship on manuscripts, including works by many of the great paleographers and codicologists of the past fifty years. When we eventually turn to print, the contrast with the scholarship on manuscripts is striking. The field of manuscript studies has produced nothing that compares to the powerful synthetic arguments for print culture that one finds in the work of scholars such as Elizabeth Eisenstein, whose thesis we may not fully accept but which nonetheless has given a vital stimulus to studies on print. I cannot think of one book that historicizes manuscript culture in this way. Many essay collections have broad-sounding titles that introduce a series of narrowly focused studies. Michael Johnston and Michael Van Dussen nicely summarize the current situation: "Almost all of the foundational theoretical work...has been done by scholars of print" (11). Technically focused studies, whether on specific features of manuscript production or on individual authors and texts–what they label the "service industry" model of scholarship–are of course essential to moving the field ahead. But we kid ourselves if we think this work, unmediated, amounts to cultural history.

The present volume does not completely overturn the status quo, but it comes closer than most do, and just as important, it draws attention to the challenges we face. Its focus is the later period, 1100 to 1500, which saw "a revolution in the technology of the book" (2). In their introduction, Johnston and Van Dussen propose three theses that may move us closer to a more synthetic understanding of late medieval manuscript culture. First, they argue for the manuscript not only as a product but as a process. To put it in philosophical terms, one might say that the manuscript was always becoming, never being. It was "in constant flux" (5). It could change at any time and was susceptible to reshaping through addition or subtraction. As a result, the late medieval manuscript inherently tended toward miscellaneity. Second, because manuscripts constantly evolved, we must go beyond the "moment of original production" to consider the entire life cycle of a manuscript (6). Production is of course important, but exclusive focus on that "original intent" ignores the important moments that come later and that shape how a manuscript is assembled, used, stored, refurbished, and resold. Many books that were originally produced for a specific reader or readers soon entered the secondhand book market – a topic about which we know next to nothing. Third, the inherent instability of the medieval manuscript encouraged "decentralized" authority, as the manuscript moved beyond control of the author and came within reach of an enlarged reading public. In part this also had to do with material and cultural changes–paper, increasing literacy, growth of the vernaculars–that democratized book production.

The editors envision this collection as an overview of the major themes of the "social life of manuscripts" (12). There are no case studies. Instead, the twelve essays that follow draw on evidence from specific manuscripts to make broader arguments about manuscript culture. Some of the essays feel like helpful introductions to specific themes or features of the manuscript book. Erik Kwakkel argues that the makers and readers of medieval manuscripts made choices that can be decoded to reveal a manuscript's original purpose and use. In a similar vein, Pascale Bourgain provides an overview of the circulation of texts in manuscript culture, and Lucie Doležalová explores Czech manuscripts to reflect on multilingualism and how to interpret a given choice of language.

Other essays advance more conceptual arguments, and here we begin to see fault lines in our understanding of manuscript culture. Seth Lerer proposes the category of the "premodern book" to describe a handwritten or printed object that "was understood to be an individual object in its own time" (19). He then offers this category as the basis for a new periodization to move us beyond a teleological drive "*from* script *to* print" (emphasis in the original, 19). This proposal fits well with Jeffrey Todd Knight's argument (in his essay on "the complex entanglement of print and manuscript") that we should think of the transition from manuscript to print not as two separate stages, but as (in the words of Robert Fraser) "a multivalent process that spirals off in several directions, and in which many different combinations of orality, literacy, and print culture are both possible and recorded as matters of fact" (79). Yet where Lerer and Knight emphasize the ambiguity of the late medieval book situated between manuscript and print, Stephen G. Nichols sees the manuscript book as inherently opposed to print. For Nichols, the parchment page functions as a "manuscript matrix" "inviting continual representational and interpretive activity," "a place of radical contingencies" (39). All of this, of course, assumes a sharp break with print.

Other essays explore how modern institutions structure our encounter with medieval sources (Siân Echard), digital technology and medieval manuscripts (Martin K. Foys), miscellaneity (Arthur Bahr), vernacular authorship and control of manuscript production (Andrew Taylor), and the manuscript history of French and Italian literature (Keith Busby and Christopher Kleinhenz). An Afterword by Kathryn Kerby-Fulton suggests that paleographers have already made enormous but overlooked "conceptual contributions" that may help in the realization of Johnston's and Van Dussen's project.

This is an excellent collection for beginning to think in a more synthetic way about late medieval manuscript culture. Scholars of medieval manuscripts do not have the benefit of a central thesis such as Eisenstein provided for print that can serve to orient their discussion. Perhaps they never will. But this volume is a step in the right direction.

Daniel Hobbins, University of Notre Dame

CAROLYNE LARRINGTON AND DIANE PURKISS, EDS.
Magical Tales: Myth, Legend and Enchantment in Children's Books.
Oxford: Bodleian Library, 2013. 192 pp. 70 color illustrations.

Reviewing a work about children's books seems an odd choice for the Early Book Society, but this short collection of academic essays is about the influence of texts from our "early book period" on children's literature, and the authors make a strong case for its academic relevance, in that exercises in medievalism continue to keep traditions (such as that of Arthurian literature) alive, re-invent the ideas in such literature in interesting ways and bring it to a new audience every new generation. The subject is certainly a popular one nowadays, with the Harry Potter series and works by Philip Pullman, and many others, for both children and adults. This book was originally published to accompany an exhibition at the Bodleian Library in 2013 called "Magical Books: from the Middle Ages to Middle-earth," but because no mention is made of the exhibition in the book (!), it must stand alone. It is, in any case, not a catalogue but an independent collection of essays with a slightly different focus than the exhibition.

The editors do not draw a clear distinction between "adult" or "children's" fiction, and they are right not to attempt it. The border cannot be defined. Many writers wrote for both audiences, and their style or subject matter is not necessarily that different when they appear to address a different age of reader (contrast *The Hobbit* and *The Lord of the Rings*). The publisher's packaging only betrays how the publisher saw the target readership at the time of publication.

I have some criticisms of the book, but first the praise. Each essay is a revelatory and enjoyable read, by experts who know their subject. The book is beautifully printed (in China) with handsome illustrations, many of early books, and is fully referenced and indexed. The editors first contribute an introduction (1–12), which begins with the provocative statement "Books are magical" (1) because of their secrets and surprises and their deployment of magic in their texts. I would accept this but by emphasizing "magic" and "enchantment," the book fails to acknowledge that mystery is important in adult fiction, too, especially in detective and fantasy fiction.

Diane Purkiss, English tutor at Keble College, Oxford, next examines the influence of medieval and early modern magic manuscripts on children's literature (13–46). She cites examples such as the Bodleian MS Ashmole 1406 and the miniature spellbook (Bodleian MS e.Mus 243), both early-seventeenth-century in their final form, but containing medieval texts, and both used by Alan Garner in his mystical novels. Carolyne Larrington, tutor in medieval English at St John's College, Oxford, follows with a study of modern re-workings of the Norse legends, a literary fashion that arose simultaneously with scholarly interest in the Vikings (47–80). She emphasizes collections of Viking legends (Keary, 1857; Wägner, 1880; Picard, 1953; Crossley-Holland, 1980) rather than retellings of individual stories such as *Grettir the Strong*, which are often found in children's literature. H.A. Guerber's anthology is not mentioned. There is some consideration of the influence of Wagner's Ring Cycle and William Morris here (but not of Morris's influence on book design, important for late Victorian and Edwardian children's historical novels with their handsome pictorial covers). An important and relevant writer of Norse resettings, Henry Treece, is not even mentioned, and Wagner was not the only composer to be influential in spreading the word on mythology: Jean Sibelius promoted the Kalevala, for example, and Rutland Boughton, the Celtic.

The Norsemen are followed by David Clark, a senior lecturer of medieval literature at Leicester University, on "magical" aspects of the Middle Ages in children's fantasy literature (81-112). This essay begins with George MacDonald, and covers E. Nesbit, Rudyard Kipling, C. S. Lewis, J. R. R. Tolkien, Alan Garner, Susan Cooper and a few others to take the survey to the present day. Anna Caughey, a lecturer in Old and Middle English at Keble College, Oxford, is next on Arthurian literature for children (113-51), which of course emphasizes Thomas Malory and illustrates the post-medieval decline in his popularity, revived after the new editions of 1816 to 1817 and now the subject of a truly enormous number of re-workings. King Arthur's association with the Boy Scout movement was something I had not noticed before. It was a bit surprising to find Rosemary Sutcliff mentioned only in passing as a writer who had also done some traditional re-settings of Arthurian stories; and another important character who is a modern reworking of the Arthurian theme of the wandering knight, who solves problems in the places he visits, and then leaves, is not mentioned at all: Dr Who.

Finally, Hannah Field, a Ph.D. student at Somerville College, writes on eighteenth- and nineteenth-century children's moveable books (the cognitive link here being that these are "magical," which indeed they are). This last essay was very enjoyable and might appear less relevant to this journal's interests, if it were not for the revelation at the start that moveable books are an invention of the early book period: the author points out that Ramón Lull used such devices in his *Ars Magna* of 1305, as did Peter Apian and Vesalius in 1540 and 1543, in books on the cosmos and the human body. The book concludes with the endnotes for the essays, brief profiles of the authors and an index, and each chapter is also treated to a useful list of further reading.

My main criticism is that the book is partisan. It emphasizes the Bodleian Library's collections rather than the subject as a whole, and it emphasizes writers with Oxford connections. Although many great libraries have published celebratory books about their treasures, this one is pretending to be a general book on the subject. If the book had been consciously presented as a companion to the exhibition, this bias would be entirely acceptable, but standing on its own, it looks like a wilful denial of the world beyond Oxford.

There is a fashion in some academic publishing to give a book an all-encompassing title, and then a subtitle which tells the true content (e.g., Oxford has recently published Erin Michelle Goeres' *The Poetics of Commemoration*, which is subtitled *Skaldic Verse and Social Memory, c. 890–1070*). Such misrepresentation irritates and deceives, and the readers are only interested in the real content, expressed in the sub-title, not the misleading abstract one. In this case the Bodleian has given the book both a general title and subtitle, and the reader yearns for a book on that broader subject, rather than the exhibition companion which the book really is.

Tolkien, Lewis and Garner are repeatedly discussed, because they have Oxford connections and the Bodleian holds some of their manuscripts, and the Opie Collection of Children's Literature, for the same reason. These writers are certainly important and influential, and the Opie Collection may be magnificent, but they are not the whole picture and I felt they were mentioned too often in a book claiming to be a general survey. The British Library is only mentioned once, in passing, as an example of another library holding "arcana," yet the British Library is the leading collection for everything, not least medieval manuscripts, and it is a library that has always catalogued all copyright receipts, in all subject areas and made them available to all readers, whereas the other copyright libraries, especially those of Oxford and Cambridge (which is never mentioned, by the way), are selective in what they retain. I am a publisher: not everything I have donated to the Bodleian Library has been catalogued. It is only the acquisition of the Opie Collection which has made the Bodleian a leading collector of children's books. At the time of their first publication, such titles were frequently rejected.

I enjoyed the acknowledgement that Duke Humfrey's Library in the Bodleian was used for the Hogwarts library in the films of the Harry Potter series, but even this detail could have been accompanied by a mention of the beguiling library in *The Name of the Rose*, and that bizarre college library in *Buffy the Vampire Slayer*, though the Library of Death in Terry Pratchett's *Hogfather* is mentioned in passing here (absurdly, this is the only mention of Pratchett in this book!).

There is an important children's writer who had no Oxford connection, but who is central to the subject of the book because he wrote historical fiction with supernatural elements, and he is of legendary popularity because he was an extremely good writer: Robert Westall. He is not mentioned once. The book discusses attempts to sanitize Arthurian literature to make it more accessible to children, but Westall wrote best-sellers which included such dark themes as medieval child sacrifice (in *The Stones of Muncaster Cathedral*), suggesting perhaps that it is not the children who do not want to read about "dark" subjects, but the adults; and that some writers can accomplish a great novel on such material without any obvious display of sanitizing. Susanna Clarke's best-selling *Jonathan Strange and Mr Norrell* (2004) is another obvious book that is simply ignored.

Some whole subject areas are also ignored. Robin Hood is mentioned only twice, and then only to say that the Arthurian writers Andrew Lang and Howard Pyle also wrote on Robin Hood. This is a glaring omission, very important for both "myths and legends" and for children's books. Robin Hood deserves a whole chapter. The Arthurian chapter ends with some wise comments on the recent BBC *Merlin* series, but Robin Hood has also been treated to a politically correct BBC reworking, and there was a missed opportunity for comparison here. Too late for this book, the recent 2015 series from ITV on *Beowulf: Return to the Shield Lands* continued the daft politically correct recasting of traditional literature, with some of the names being the only left-over connection with the original text.

Other traditional tales such as Cinderella, the Pied Piper, and Dick Whittington, which are medieval in origin, are also hardly mentioned at all, and nursery rhymes are only really considered in the context of moveable books. The brothers Grimm only appear twice, as an aside, and only one Hans Christian Andersen story is mentioned, and that because it was a moveable book. Ghost stories, with their great antiquarian traditions, and many famous children's settings, are not mentioned. Vampires and werewolves are as popular today as they were in the early twentieth century, but their modern audiences are mostly "young adults." They are also excluded, but they are medieval myths.

An interesting problem in the history of medievalist children's literature is the conflict between historical and fantasy settings, a challenge which I have encountered in my own collecting of historical fiction. I feel that fantasy elements in the real world, such as any supernatural agency, can be interesting because they express the beliefs of the characters, and rewritings of medieval literature, however magical (such as *Beowulf*), are still important. But what about medieval-like details transferred to what appear to be parallel universes or other planets? The world of Tolkien's *Lord of the Rings* series might as well be another planet even if the author argued it was a prehistoric Earth. C. S. Lewis's *Narnia* series is set in a parallel universe accessible from this world. The new television program *Beowulf* is certainly set in some parallel dimension. I prefer to reject such material if the real Middle Ages on planet Earth is my declared focus.

Nevertheless, the relationship between the real and the unreal allows for interesting observations of both worlds, but "true" historical fiction is hardly mentioned at all in this book, and children's settings were a high proportion of the number of books in that genre until the late 1960s, when the number of new titles for adults started to expand enormously, but for children it declined. That relationship between truth and imagination challenges us to think, but it seems to me that complete immersion in fantasy worlds, without the restraining tension of reality, means leaving something of our humanity behind. This book is an academic one, and it could have explored this tension, which is at the heart of much of our culture, and perhaps that is where the border lies between childhood and adulthood.

The Bodleian Library deserves praise for taking children's literature seriously, even if this book is misleadingly partisan. Children's literature is, after all, written by adults, published by adults and bought by adults. It influences the development of any literary tradition, and it has a subtle influence on medieval studies. It is far too important to be left in the hands of children.

Shaun Tyas, Paul Watkins Publishing

ANGELA M. LUCAS
The Index of Middle English Prose: Handlist XXII: Manuscripts in Christ's, Emmanuel, Jesus, Selwyn and Sidney Sussex Colleges, Peterhouse and Trinity Hall, Cambridge.
Cambridge: D. S. Brewer, 2016. xxiv + 173 pp.

The college libraries of the University of Cambridge might be expected to be rich in medieval holdings. However, there are at least three caveats. One is that university libraries were Latin libraries, whereas IMEP indexes only English prose. The other is that the colleges covered in this Handlist were largely of sixteenth-century foundation and would mostly have been furnished with printed books rather than manuscripts, certainly in the case of Christ's College, refounded by Lady Margaret Beaufort in 1505, who herself furnished the chapel with printed books and the library with at least thirty-nine printed volumes in theology, law and medicine.[1] A third caveat is that books were lost as a result of three successive sixteenth-century purges: in 1535, under Henry VIII; in 1549, under Edward VI; and in 1557, under Mary Tudor.[2] Many of the manuscripts are, in fact, donations of the seventeenth century and later.

This Handlist does not, therefore, contain as many manuscripts, nor as many interesting items, as one might imagine. Jesus College was founded between 1496 and 1516, Emmanuel in 1584, Sidney Sussex in 1596, and Selwyn, not until 1878. Selwyn's single indexed manuscript ("a selection of readings from the New Testament in English" [xvii]) seems to have been a bequest of 1894. Even Peterhouse (founded 1284 and the earliest of the Cambridge colleges) and Trinity Hall (1350) have only seventeen and three manuscripts respectively with some (minimal) English prose.

To illustrate just how minimal the English prose may be, Christ's College MS 11 has only "I nel not go with þe," and Jesus College MS Q.B.1 has only "Remembyr remembyr that I owe you for iij d. obol for lace goldingham." There are a number of English prayers, and medical recipes are predictably common in the ephemeral prose category.

However, this is not to dismiss the value of this volume. The English prayers include an English version of the Fifteen Oes (Sidney Sussex College MS 37), and the scattered medical recipes are offset by an imperfect *Chirurgie* of Guy de Chauliac in Jesus College MS Q.G.23 (absent from the Library at the time of M. R. James's cataloguing and so not catalogued until now),[3] and the English translation of the *Sirurgie* of Henri de Mondeville in Peterhouse MS 118. It is interesting that there are several manuscripts of Wycliffe, which was not, of course, printed until the era of scholarly editions. The Wycliffite Bible and two Wycliffite New Testaments are in Emmanuel College (MSS 21, 34 and 108), and New Testaments are also recorded in Christ's (MS 10), Jesus (MSS Q.B.13 and Q.D.6, donated in 1685 and 1602 respectively) and Sidney Sussex (MS 99). Fragments of Wycliffite Sunday Gospel sermons are in Peterhouse 69, and both Gospel and Epistle sermons in Christ's College MS 7. "The Twelve Conclusions of the Lollards" is incorporated into the anti-Lollard tract of Roger Dymok in Trinity Hall MS 17.

More orthodox texts are found in Emmanuel College MS 248 and Sidney Sussex College MS 55 (the "Great Sentence of Cursing"), the latter also containing *The Lay Folk's Catechism*. The sermons of Sidney Sussex College MS 74 have long been known from the work of Alan Fletcher and Helen Spencer, although the extensive material in the latter's *English Preaching in the Late Middle Ages* (Oxford, Clarendon, 1993) is not mentioned here. Quite properly, the sermons are individually recorded, as is IMEP policy (but see IMEP XXI also reviewed here).

Jesus College MS Q.D.4 has the *Abbey of the Holy Ghost and Charter of the Abbey of the Holy Ghost*, and Rolle is found in Sidney Sussex College MS 89. Peterhouse has *Barlam and Josaphat* (MS 257), while the plum of the Peterhouse manuscripts must be the unique copy (MS 75.1) of what was long thought to be Chaucer's *Equatorie of Planetis*. (Kari Anne Rand's most recent work, which firmly ascribes it to John Westwyk, is not mentioned.)[4]

The volume follows the usual IMEP conventions in terms of contents. Quite why some of the items in the Macaronic Index are not in the main index is a puzzle, at least to someone working at second hand with only the incipits and explicits to guide her. For example, Emmanuel College MS 69 has an English tract on phlebotomy and John of Arderne's *Fistula in ano* (also in English), but they are listed in the Macaronic Index under

Works in Latin, French, and English ([C1], [C2]). (The extensive and accessible reserach on this manuscript is not mentioned.)[5]

Susan Powell, University of Salford

NOTES

1. Susan Powell, "Lady Margaret Beaufort and her Books," *The Library*, 6th series, 20 (1998), 197-240 (236-38 and n. 257). (The 1623 donations book is the only source of evidence for the thirty-nine library volumes.)
2. For a comprehensive account of Cambridge libraries and their holdings, see *The University and College Libraries of Cambridge*, ed. Peter D. Clarke, Corpus of British Medieval Library Catalogues 10 (London: The British Library in association with the British Academy, 2002), Introduction (by Roger Lovatt), *passim* (reviewed in *JEBS* 12, 2009).
3. Although indexed (p. 170, but not p. 169) as Chauliac, Peterhouse MS 118 [6] and [7] only draw on the work.
4. K.A. Rand, "The Authorship of the *Equatorie of the Planetis* revisited," *Studia Neophilologica*, 87 (2015): 15-35.
5. Linda Ehrsam Voigts and Patricia Deery Kurtz, *Scientific and Medical Writings in Old and Middle English: An Electronic Reference* (Ann Arbor: University of Michigan Press, 2000), available on the Medieval Academy of America website. It is used by Horner in IMEP XXI, also reviewed here.

PETER E. PORMANN, ED., WITH JANE EAGEN.
*A Descriptive Catalogue of the Hebrew Manuscripts of
Corpus Christi College, Oxford.*
Cambridge: D. S. Brewer for Corpus Christi College, Oxford, 2015.
Pp. x + 122. 33 color plates and two figures.

Peter Pormann begins a lengthy and apologetic introduction by pointing out his lack of competence for cataloguing this important group of manuscripts. A Corpus graduate, with specialities in Greco-Arabic science (not Hebrew biblical copying or Latin script), he relates that he was set to the task by his former Corpus tutor (in the run-up to the 500th anniversary of the Corpus Christi's founding in 1517, a topic bruited in the introduction). Pormann's unsuitability for this task is a shame, because these books are treasures. Seven of the thirteen volumes described here – three are post-medieval – are what is known as *superscriptiones*. That is, they present the Hebrew text, most usually biblical, with a painstakingly literal interlinear Latin translation (one that usually attends closely to and carefully marks the morphology of Hebrew, e.g., initial *waw* presented apart from the root as "et"). In addition, they routinely include a parallel rendition of the Vulgate. The volumes thus provide alternate access to the *hebraica veritas* that underlies Christian scripture (and might also be used to provide instruction in Hebrew more broadly). Unfortunately, other than images, glitzily colored but not at actual size (no ratios provided), Pormann really has nothing to add to the stellar account which treats most of these books (and all the *superscriptiones*) by Judith Olszowy-Schlanger in *Les Manuscrits hébreux dans l'Angleterre médiévale: Étude historique et paléographique* (Paris and Louvain: Peeters, 2003).

Problems begin with Pormann's conception of the project. The volume shows persistent confusions between what a catalogue does and what an edition does. Manuscript detail is buried under a rash of other things, potentially useful enough – but in a separate publication. Pormann's handling of MS 469 (109) shows that he is aware that catalogues are supposed to include collations of their books and that these are vital to discussing their original production. But this is the only occasion on which he does provide such information. He does not consistently follow the long-established practice of citing vertical dimensions of leaf and writing area before horizontal ones; he gets it right most of the time, but these are persistent occasions when he does not (see 56, 72, 93). The description of MS 7 offers no comment on the ruling system, but Figure 15 (50) shows a manuscript ruled in blind/dry-point. This would be highly unusual to rare in a contemporary Anglo-Latin book. But it may be a sign that this is a Jewish scribe accustomed to copying torah (the liturgical scroll of the law); a torah is always ruled, but in blind, for the only ink that can go on the scroll is text, the very *dabar adonai/verbum Dei*.

At page 54 note 92, Pormann needs more than a footnote to address the painted openings of books in Hebrew biblical manuscripts. Traditionally in this culture, representational ornament is a form of idolatry; in this case, the decoration to be supplied testifies to connections between Jewish and Christian bookmen, since it is a version of the champ initial, frequent in circumambient book-culture from the thirteenth century. In the Hebrew context, the initial word appears in gold leaf on a blue and magenta ground. Such interchanges represent a very basic point about Hebrew book-history, persistently emphasized by the dean of the field, Malachi Beit-Arie. Most disconcertingly, bibliographical detail that should have been subjected to special attention is presented with a lack of care. Jane Eagen at page 103 pronounces a late seventeenth-century binding "roughly contemporary with the text," but the book was produced in France, s. xii ex. On page 57, in his discussion of MS 9a, I think – I find the locution too obscure to be entirely certain–Pormann's description has reversed the two parts of the book: isn't it the first portion that is presented *hebraice* (and to Western eyes reads back to front), the second presented *latine*?

There is a larger narrative here as well that Pormann does not address, the question of medieval English poly-lingualism. One of Pormann's manuscripts (MS 10, p. 72) includes an English glossing note (which he appears not to understand). Another note which he seems not to know how to deal with (although this book contains a Continentally-produced Rashi commentary, and there is a reasonably extensive literature discussing Rashi's presentation of Romance words in Hebrew clothing) presents in Hebrew characters the French names for the stones on the high priest's ephod (MS 165, p. 101). For the record: the last stone in the first line is "topaz," and the second line has "charbuncle," "saphire," and "beryl" (although I would demur in trying to guess what the Romance forms signalled by the Hebrew spellings are). Indeed, English is distinctly rare in such volumes, but in insularly produced books, as Olszowy-Schlanger's more recent researches have publicized, Anglo-Norman is present in great profusion.

The book appears not to have been proofread, and typos abound (references by page, paragraph, line or lines): 4.3.2-3, "Robert Bacon" (read "Roger Bacon"), 20.1.3, "year" (for "years"), 42.6.2, "Folios 37v is" (read "Folio 37v is"), and so on. Cursory comparisons of plates and their descriptions suggest to me that Pormann's reportage of manuscript detail misrepresents the books a good deal too frequently. Here are a few examples: 16.22.10-11, "reptiliauerunt" (not "reptilianunt" and perfectly clear in the plate in spite of demurrers in the text); 60, the single superscriptio (super)ficie (not a non-existent "super facie"); 64, *superscriptio* at line 1 should read "posicio" (not "positor") and "emptus" (not "emptor"), and line 3 "requies" (not "requiescens"); 80, the first line of the Latin at the page foot "latinum" (not "latinitatem"). At page 75, describing marginalia (line 5), Pormann apparently fails to recognize the normal late medieval representation of the Arabic number "17." And while Pormann is sometimes unduly finicky, but again inconsistently so, in presenting abbreviated Latin forms (marking unwritten letters in a manner more appropriate in a transcription than in a catalogue), he seems persistently unaware of one abbreviated form he reproduces again and again without comment: "ar" (see page 49, *superscriptio* at line 5, here representing, as most usually, both Hebrew es- and ha-). This represents the full word "articulus"; the scrupulous authors of *superscriptiones* use the form – Latin, after all, has no articles – to indicate an element that is to be ignored in Latin.

An outstanding collection deserves much better than this.

Ralph Hanna, Keble College, Oxford

JACLYN RAJSIC, ERIK KOOPER, AND DOMINIQUE HOCHE, EDS.
The Prose Brut *and Other Late Medieval Chronicles. Books Have Their Histories: Essays in Honour of Lister M. Matheson.* Woodbridge: York Medieval Press/Boydell Press, 2016. xxv + 246 pp.

The diverse essays in this volume, which offer a fitting tribute to Lister Matheson (1948-2012) from former students and academic colleagues, deal with Latin and vernacular writings on English history and how those texts entered into conversation with each other as translations, sources, or other kinds of influences, and have come down to us in the present day. They represent the work of scholars—many of them Early Book Society members—with whom Lister Matheson exchanged ideas and shared conference platforms over a career spent dealing with the issues and topics under consideration. Following an introduction by the editors that argues for the coherence of the collection as a whole, there is a brief memoir celebrating the life and achievement of the honoree. The remaining thirteen essays are presented in three parts: I, Uses of History; II, The Prose *Brut*; III, Receptions [sic] and Afterlives of Late Medieval Chronicles. There are a number of overlapping themes and ideas that straddle these sections, but broadly speaking, the first part deals with the socio-political and didactic function of English history writing, the second with outlying texts belonging to the English Prose *Brut* tradition, and the third with late medieval books containing chronicles (and Prose *Bruts*) and their later owners and readers.

The introduction stresses that the volume is a memorial to Lister's influence as both a scholar and teacher, and it is followed by an appropriately affectionate personal memoir by Julia Marvin which picks up on this theme. It turns out in this essay that it is not only books that have their histories but also the modern human beings that write about them: Lister is remembered by Marvin as a scholar whose geniality was legendary at the Medieval Chronicle Society conferences and Kalamazoo conference sessions listed in the extensive curriculum vitae positioned, a little unusually, in the prefatory matter of the volume (xvii–xxv). Perhaps it is worth adding here that he also made an earlier but still-remembered contribution as a doctoral student working on *Brut* texts under Michael Samuels' supervision in the Department of English Language at Glasgow; his Early Book Society contributions were always lively and engaging, and latterly, as an International Fellow, he became a mainstay of the "Imagining History" research project at Queen's Belfast. Books do have their histories, and as the list of Matheson's publications shows, it is the Prose *Brut*, in all its multitudinous and formidable textual permutations and forms that largely shaped Matheson's intellectual interests and development as a professional and very humane scholar.

Part I opens with Krista A. Murchison's discussion of ideas of piety, community and local history in *Le Livere de Reis de Engleterre*, an early fourteenth-century Anglo-Norman prose work. Murchison usefully argues against the artificial divide modern scholarship is sometimes keen to set up between secular and religious histories in the later Middle Ages, reminding us instead of the continuum from universal to national histories that can be observed chiefly because of continuing clerical engagement in the writing and production of chronicle and history writing in both Latin and the vernacular. The following essays, by Christine M. Rose on the fifteenth-century Middle English translation of Nicholas Trevet's fourteenth-century universal chronicle, *Les Cronicles*, and by Alexander L. Kaufman on John Warkworth's *Chronicle*, implicitly support this point, largely through their examination of the place of miracles, portents and wonders across a variety of vernacular chronicle writing traditions. Dan Embree's essay then offers an analysis of different fifteenth-century chronicle writing styles (characterized as the lawyer's and the herald's) in two apparently eye-witness accounts of a similar period of insurgency in Edward IV's reign: *The Chronicle of the Rebellion in Lincolnshire* and *The Historie of the Arrivall of Edward IV in England*.

The essays in Part II (on the Middle English Prose *Brut*) revisit some of the unresolved issues and problems that Lister Matheson's research has raised. Erik Kooper's study of the Latin *Brut* chronicle text in Longleat House MS 55, and Jaclyn Rajsic's study of an English *Brut* chronicle on a roll, identify and rescue new items for the larger *Brut* corpus by arguing for a broad generic categorization of such items, at the same time as they question whether the Prose *Brut* is served well by being categorized as a single text with many later versions rather than as a writing tradition. William Marx's study of Peculiar Versions of the ME Prose *Brut* follows similar lines of enquiry from the point of view of an editor engaged in the problem of understanding what motivated the emergence of two of these assorted versions. Neil Weijer's study of the early printed editions of *The Chronicles of England* picks up on Marx's point in relation to how far later printers felt free to remake the English Prose *Brut* in a drive to reconcile the early history of England with universal history and other external histories, particularly Roman ones which had huge appeal for sixteenth-century English readers.

Modern editors are often prone to make a distinction between the production, dissemination, and afterlife of medieval texts, but the collapse of such a distinction remains a potent theme in Part III. Heather Pagan's study of Nicholas Trevet's *Les Cronicles* is exemplary in this respect, demonstrating the longevity of an interest in the Anglo-Norman prose text among fifteenth- and sixteenth-century English gentry readers, as well as the later and better-known antiquarian fascination with Trevet. Similarly, Elizabeth J. Bryan's work deciphering the interest in the Middle English Prose *Brut* of Matthew Parker and his circle argues for continuing scholarly interest in the work, a point also made in the next essay, Edward Donald Kennedy's fascinating study of Thomas Hearne and English chronicles. Caroline D. Eckhardt's account of *Castleford's Chronicle* treats the text as a witness to the development of the *Brut* tradition in a northern English context, tracing its surviving manuscript from its Yorkshire origins as an imperfect collaboration between two main scribes and a rubricator through to its eighteenth-century arrival in continental Europe among the household goods of a Londoner working in Germany, who may well have shared some similar bureaucratic interests and civic responsibilities as much earlier metropolitan readers of the text. In the final essay in the volume, A. S. G. Edwards considers the movement of *Brut* manuscripts from a completely different perspective, by analyzing the commercial value and the implications (for scholars working on manuscript provenance) of placing *Bruts* for sale. A valuable appendix describes the manuscripts of the ME Prose *Brut* that were sold or otherwise disposed of during the twentieth century.

John Thompson, Queen's University, Belfast

KARI ANNE RAND
The Index of Middle English Prose:
Index to Volumes I to XX.
Cambridge: D. S. Brewer, 2014. ix + 603 pp.

This volume begins boldly with the statement that "*The Index of Middle English Prose* is our most important reference tool for non-verse texts in manuscripts written in English between 1200 and 1500" (vi). Having achieved what she has done here, Kari Anne Rand would be entitled to begin with such a proud claim. Yet she is not speaking about the current enterprise but about the twenty volumes that comprise *The Index of Middle English Prose*. To list the summary contents from the Huntington Library in California in volume I to Corpus Christi Cambridge in volume XX takes from pages 1 to 133. This is nearly a book in itself, but there are almost another five hundred pages to follow, made up of an index of incipits (134–362), index of rubrics and titles (363–465), and a general index (466–600).

The summary list is extremely useful, as it allows an instant overview of the contents of a fair proportion of Middle English prose manuscripts. Rand even prepared three of the summary lists herself, together with the addition of two more by other colleagues (Patrick Horner and Oliver Pickering). Like the summary list, the index of incipits is linked to the volume numbers. This is very helpful, as not everyone is going to recall automatically that, for instance, the Ashmole Collection in the Bodleian Library is in volume IX or the Peniarth Collection in the National Library of Wales is in volume XIV. Unfortunately, this same link is not maintained in the later indexes. Perhaps this was for practical reasons, as there may not have been enough horizontal space in the index to rubrics and titles to accommodate all that was needed in the line, while the provision of the volume number would have been impracticable in the more crowded entries in the general index.

In the same way as a workman (or woman) is only as good as his tools, so Rand has been dependent on the prior compilation skills of those responsible for the twenty volumes here. As any careful user of these books will suspect (even if it may be churlish to say it), some volumes are better than others. While each compiler brought his or her own skills to the exercise, in the same way as good editors are born and not made, so it is with cataloguers and indexers. These days everyone is supposed to be able to rustle up an index, but proper indexing requires serious expertise and concentrated application. Yet Rand could only work with what she was given, and as she comments, the preparation of the volume "presented a considerable challenge" owing to the indexers' "divergent approaches to indexing," where the "situation is perhaps best described as confusing" (vi). She then proceeds to describe the vagaries of the indexes that exist and what she did to remedy the situation. It would not have been feasible to have rethought the indexing terms from scratch; neither would it have been advisable, as it would only have led to some of the individual indexes of the twenty volumes becoming almost unserviceable. In the production of the indexes above, she does her best to present the material in a streamlined way. Inevitably, because of the genesis of the indexes, there are some oddities. For instance, in the section on "Sermons" (574–75), some texts are listed separately under titles, such as "Sermon, unknown occasion," whereas most of the others are understandably indexed together under the "Sermons" category. There are also other (patchy) refinements, such as "Septuagesima, sermons for." Yet such small duplications and inconsistencies are problems with which we can cope: those interested in sermons will just realize that they should check all available references at this point. At times the sheer number of manuscripts in a single entry can threaten to become unmanageable. That for "Prayers" (555), for example, has about sixty texts, while the entry for "Recipes," usefully subdivided, extends to five and a half pages (560–66). And yet it is far easier to have all these texts in one place rather than to have to search across twenty volumes.

As with any enterprise of this nature, closer inspection can reveal minor flaws. But the discovery of such imperfections is mostly dependent on the random knowledge or wavering scrutiny of the reader or reviewer. In other words, anyone can list errors that he or she has found either by accident or — worse still — has actively sought out. One very simple example will suffice. In a passing glance at the general index (573), I noticed that the name of "Alicia Scheynton" was linked to Fitzwilliam Museum, MS McClean 89, when in fact it should be to MS McClean 123 because Alicia Scheynton was a fifteenth-century owner of the latter manuscript that belonged to the Fontevraud convent of Nuneaton in Warwickshire. The fact that I have noticed this error does not give me (or anyone else) license to assume anything about the overall quality of Rand's indexing here. Clearly some little slip occurred at this point either in the computer search or the checking as MS McClean 123 follows on directly from MS McClean 89 in volume XVIII (67).The assembly of these vast indexes has clearly been a gargantuan task, and one can only begin to imagine the unquantifiable degree of checking and cross-checking that would have been involved. Most of us would have quailed at the prospect, and so it is a tribute to Rand's absolute tenacity and selflessness that she saw this project through to completion.

Inevitably, however, there is an elephant in the room. Throughout it has been noted that indexes to twenty volumes have been produced (and Rand herself was responsible for three of these). But when this present work was nearing publication, another volume of *The Index of Middle English Prose* was finished, and since the publication of her index, yet another has appeared. This means that no sooner had Rand's index been printed than it was partly out of date.

This and the other "shortcomings" of this exercise are largely owing to the fact that, when the Index of Middle English Prose project was set up some forty years ago by A. S. G. Edwards, N. F. Blake, and others, it was an enterprise before its time in many ways. As a project that sought co-operation across national and international boundaries, that drew on skills bibliographical, historical, palaeographical, and textual, and that was ambitious and far-reaching, it was the sort of project that in later years would have been a candidate for research council funding. Some degree of funding (difficult as it would have been to achieve) would have enabled or even forced greater centralization in terms of the original indexing, as well as speedier production of the individual volumes, some travel costs for contributors who in most cases had to self-fund this service to the academic community, and — most especially — the opportunity to take advantage of some element of online methodology when this became available.

Yet the funding situation today (albeit with its frustratingly changing priorities and the instability of online platforms) did not obtain four decades ago, and it is useless to bemoan this. Essentially, what Rand's volume does now is to encourage us to take stock of the current situation, to think afresh, and to try to work out the best way forward for cataloguing and indexing future work. As she herself says, "Scholars would be best served by digitised access to the indexes, but until funding can be found for digitisation and the maintenance of such a database, the present printed finding-tool...will be of considerable help to researchers (including compilers of future volumes), and will provide a starting point when a digitisation project eventually gets under way" (vi). Despite any caveats, the volume produced by Rand will be of inestimable benefit in this process and we are all truly in her debt.

Veronica O'Mara, University of Hull

JONATHAN WILCOX, ED.
Scraped, Stroked, and Bound: Materially Engaged Readings of Medieval Manuscripts. Utrecht Studies in Medieval Literacy, 23. Turnhout: Brepols, 2013.
xvi + 237 pp. 14 color plates + 26 B&W figs.

Scraped, Stroked, and Bound publishes the proceedings of a seminar held at the Obermann Center for Advanced Studies at the University of Iowa attended by medievalists interested in the medieval book and contemporary makers of handmade books. The belief that those who study medieval manuscripts in their own right rather than simply as bearers of text can gain insight into craft production from engaging with those who make books by hand today is not an original one. Nevertheless, one might hope that craft-conscious awareness will lead to a greater understanding of the world of practice that produced such manuscripts. Unfortunately, not all the papers are particularly helpful in this respect to the reader.

Among the craft-based essays, Gary Frost's "Material Quality of Medieval Bookbindings" is not easy to follow. Citing navigability as an advantage of the codex format he writes, "This is the attribute of haptic communication in which the manipulation of the mechanical format conveys additional meaning without distracting comprehension of content. Primate dexterity and a deeply embedded capacity for hands to prompt the mind are fully optimised by the codex mechanism" (133). If he means a book is easy to handle, open and turn its pages to find one's place, why not say so? Jesse Mayer gives recipe-like instructions for "Parchment Production: A Brief Account," while Cheryl Jacobsen in "A Modern Scribe Views Scribes of the Past" provides useful hand-drawn diagrams to illustrate *ductus* and pen angle. Her recommendation that the way to understand the formation of a medieval letter-form is to copy it from the manuscript is sound, though I would dispute her claim that this process has been frowned upon by paleographers (86).

It was certainly not the case, for instance, with Neil Ker or Malcolm Parkes. Timothy Barrett's "Parchment, Paper, and Artisanal Research Techniques" is intriguing. His research into why medieval paper is sturdier and stronger than later papers suggests that medieval papermakers used more gelatine to size their paper than later manufacturers.

The other essays are mostly concerned with manuscripts earlier than those usually discussed in *JEBS*. Three focus on Anglo-Saxon volumes. Thus Matthew T. Hussey, in "Anglo-Saxon Scribal *Habitus* and Frankish Aesthetics in an Early Uncial Manuscript," discusses a scribe whose *habitus* or ingrained training was in Insular Half-Uncial but in a copy of Isidore's *Synonyma* (Würzburg, Universitätsbibliothek, HS M.p.th.f.79), probably produced at Worcester about 800, attempted to write Frankish Uncial. Patrick W. Conner, in "On the Nature of Matched Scribal Hands," that is, collaborating scribes who were taught to match the hands they wrote as closely as possible, seeks a sociological theory to explain this "shared competence." Might it not simply be that scribes were well-trained in a house-style (a term he does not use) because it was considered that a manuscript looked better if all the hands in it wrote in the same disciplined way? In "Dismembering and Reconstructing MS Durham, Cathedral Library, A.IV.19," Karen Louise Jolly writes on the palaeography and codicology of the well-known tenth-century Durham Collectar, glossed by Aldred the provost.

Another liturgical manuscript is discussed by Constance H. Berman, in "The Cistercian Manuscript, Trent 1711, Version One and Its Exemplar," significant as a witness to the creation of the Cistercian order. Berman's analysis of this twelfth-century manuscript's structure reveals that an original core, Trent One, containing a monastic customary without the "typical" Cistercian elements, was updated by adding quires at the beginning and end of the volume, Trent Two. Her findings suggest the creation of the Order occurred through "increments and experiments" rather than dating as long-assumed to the 1130s (169). Also focussed on a twelfth-century book is Jennifer Borland's "Unruly Reading: The Consuming Role of Touch in the Experience of a Medieval Manuscript": Munich, Bayerische Staatsbibliothek, Clm. 1133, from Benediktbeuern, Bavaria, is a composite volume containing saints' lives of which only one, the *Passion of St Margaret*, is illustrated with pen and ink drawings. Possibly it had originally circulated as an independent *libellus*. All the drawings of the evil characters who persecuted Margaret have been deliberately defaced with a sharp instrument, suggesting a powerful emotional response by a reader. Interestingly, other manuscripts from Bavaria of Margaret's life show similar treatment, which raises the question why? And what is our own response to such treatment?

A seventeen-page recital of institutions in the USA offering programs in book arts and traditional bookbinding precedes a brief mention of two other early manuscripts and their binding techniques by Elsi Vassdal Ellis in "The East-West. Then-Now Binding Nexus." The author does not supply the shelfmarks for these manuscripts in her essay: the Cuthbert Gospel, formerly the Stonyhurst Gospel, was bought by the British Library in 2012 and is now shelved as Additional MS 89000, while the shelfmark of the Kassel Bede of the *Historia Ecclesiastica* is Kassel, Gesamthochschulbibliothek 4° HS Theol.2.

The final essay by Martha Rust, "'*Lymned to his awne vse*': The Illuminated Realm of John Lacy, Artisan and Anchorite, in MS Oxford, St John's College Library, 94," interprets as an epitaph an inscription (fol. 1) requesting prayers for Lacy's soul and the wish that the prayer book he had written and illustrated for himself should pass on his death to someone else, reflecting also on Lacy's metaphorical entombment as an anchorite. Unfortunately, there is no mention of the many other examples of such inscriptions. And could the word "vse" have had any significance for Lacy since he was an anchorite at the Dominican convent of Newcastle-upon-Tyne, for the friars had the use but not possession of their books?

Four epigraphs precede the whole collection of papers: three relating to scribes (the colophons of Aldred and Lacy and the titulus to the well-known portrait of Eadwine in the Canterbury Psalter, Trinity College Cambridge MS R. 17. 1) and a riddle from the Exeter Book (Exeter Cathedral MS 3501) to which the solution is a book.

Pamela Robinson, Institute of English Studies, University of London

About the Authors

Margaret Connolly teaches palaeography and medieval literature at the University of St Andrews and is a general editor of the Middle English Texts series. Her most recent publication is a collection of essays, *Insular Books: Vernacular Manuscript Miscellanies in Late Medieval Britain* (2015), which she edited jointly with Raluca Radulescu. She has also published a volume for the *Index of Middle English Prose* series, editions of Middle English religious prose texts, and the monograph *John Shirley: Book Production and the Noble Household in Fifteenth-Century England* (1998).

Rory G. Critten is a Lecturer in Old and Middle English literature at the University of Bern, Switzerland. His publications treat late Middle English and Middle French writing; he has also published on the history of modern languages education in England. His current monograph project examines the rhetorical currency of the pose of the self-publishing author in the fifteenth century (provisional title: *Books Under Pressure: Self-Publication in Fifteenth-Century England*).

Alex da Costa is a University Lecturer in the English Department at Cambridge University and a Fellow of Newnham College. Her first book, *Reforming Printing: Syon Abbey's Defence of Orthodoxy* (Oxford University Press, 2012), examined Syon Abbey's early Reformation printing. She has also published on printed pilgrimage guides, the negotiation of censorship, and changing paratexts. She is currently working on a book exploring how printing practices changed the experience and way in which people read between 1476 and 1557.

Martha W. Driver is Distinguished Professor of English and Women's and Gender Studies at Pace University in New York City. A co-founder of the Early Book Society for the study of manuscripts and printing history, she writes about illustration from manuscript to print, manuscript and book production, and the early history of printing. In addition to publishing some 55 articles in these areas, she has edited twenty-one journals over nineteen years, including *Film & History: Medieval Period in Film* and the *Journal of the Early Book Society*. Her books about pictures (from manuscript miniatures to woodcuts to film) include *The Image in Print: Book Illustration in Late Medieval England* (British Library Publications and University of Toronto), *An Index of Images in English MSS*, fascicle four, with Michael Orr (Brepols), and *The Medieval Hero on Screen* and *Shakespeare and the Middle Ages*, with Sid Ray (McFarland). She contributed to and edited *Preaching the Word in*

Manuscript and Print in Late Medieval England: Essays in Honour of Susan Powell with Veronica O'Mara (Brepols, 2013). She also oversees the Texts & Transitions book series published by Brepols.

Susanna Fein is Professor of English at Kent State University and editor of *The Chaucer Review*. Her research involves Middle English poetry with emphases on manuscript studies, lyrics, alliterative verse, and Chaucer. Her books include editions of MS Douce 302 (the Audelay manuscript) and MS Harley 2253 (Medieval Institute Publications, 2009, 2014 to 2015). She has also edited essay collections on the manuscripts copied by Robert Thornton (with Michael Johnston) and on the Auchinleck manuscript (York Medieval Press, 2014, 2016). Her latest book is *Chaucer: Visual Approaches* (Penn State University Press, 2016), co-edited with David Raybin.

Ruth Frost is an Associate Professor of History at the Okanagan campus of the University of British Columbia. She has previously published on the urban elite of late medieval Norwich.

Ralph Hanna is Professor of Palaeography emeritus and emeritus fellow of Keble College, Oxford. His most recent major publication is *Editing Medieval Texts* (Liverpool, 2015). Other publications include editions for the Early English Text Society, *Richard Rolle: Uncollected Verse and Prose, with Related Northern Texts* (o.s. 329, 2007) and *Speculum Vitae: A Reading, Editions I and II* (o.s. 331-2, 2008).

Marjorie Harrington is a Ph.D. candidate in English at the University of Notre Dame and the 2016 to 2017 Helen Ann Mins Robbins Fellow in Medieval Studies at the University of Rochester. Her primary research interests include Early Middle English lyrics, manuscript studies, and medieval translation practices.

Daniel Hobbins is Associate Professor of history at the University of Notre Dame. He is the author of *Authorship and Publicity before Print: Jean Gerson and the Transformation of Late Medieval Learning* (2009). His research interests include medieval authorship, Joan of Arc, and the contexts of printing.

Michael Johnston is an Associate Professor of English at Purdue University. He specializes in the production and circulation of literary manuscripts in fourteenth- and fifteenth-century England.

Laura Saetveit Miles is Associate Professor (førsteamanuensis) in English literature at the Department of Foreign Languages, University of Bergen,

Norway. Her research encompasses medieval religious culture, visionary writings, women's reading practices, and modern feminist theory. She has published on Syon Abbey and St. Bridget, as well as on Julian of Norwich. Her 2014 *Speculum* article on the early history of Mary's book at the Annunciation will be followed up by a book on the subject.

Veronica O'Mara is a Professor in the Department of English at the University of Hull. Her main research areas are Middle English religious literature, female literacy, preaching, and the relationship between manuscript and print. She has recently edited (with Martha W. Driver) *Preaching the Word in Manuscript and Print in Late Medieval England: Essays in Honour of Susan Powell*, Sermo, 11 (Turnhout: Brepols, 2013), and (with Virginia Blanton and Patricia Stoop) *Nuns' Literacies in Medieval Europe: The Hull Dialogue*, Medieval Women: Texts and Contexts, 26 (Turnhout: Brepols, 2013), and *Nuns' Literacies in Medieval Europe: The Kansas City Dialogue*, Medieval Women: Texts and Contexts, 27 (Turnhout: Brepols, 2015).

Niamh Pattwell is a Lecturer in Middle English literature at University College Dublin, where she is also Director of the M.A. in Medieval English Literature and Culture. She has published in the area of medieval manuscripts and early books with a particular interest in vernacular, pastoral literature. She produced an edition of the *Exornatorium Curatorum* with the Heidelberg, MET series in 2013. She is currently working on a volume of the *Index of Middle English Prose* for Trinity College Dublin with John Scattergood.

Susan (Sue) Powell is Professor Emeritus of Medieval Texts and Culture (University of Salford) and a Research Associate at the Centre for Medieval Studies, University of York. She is currently a Visiting Research Fellow at the Institute of English Studies, University of London. She is an editor of manuscripts and early printed books, and her research focusses on religious and devotional texts and institutions. Her latest book, co-edited with Vincent Gillespie, is *A Companion to the Early Printed Book in Britain 1476-1558* (Cambridge: Brewer, 2014), and she is currently preparing an edition of the household papers of Lady Margaret Beaufort for the British Academy (Records of Social and Economic History).

Pamela Robinson is Senior Research Fellow at the Institute of English Studies, University of London. She is currently compiling a *Catalogue of Medieval Manuscripts containing Latin commentaries on Aristotle in London Libraries*, as part of a British Academy project to compile inventories of such manuscripts in British libraries.

Valerie Schutte earned her Ph.D. in History from the University of Akron. She is author of *Mary I and the Art of Book Dedications: Royal Women, Power, and Persuasion* (2015) and co-editor of *The Birth of a Queen: Essays on the Quincentenary of Mary I* (2016), both in the Palgrave Macmillan Queenship and Power series. She has two more edited collections in early stages and has published articles on Shakespeare, royal Tudor women, and print. Forthcoming publications include several essays comparing book dedications to Mary and Elizabeth Tudor, an article on counsel given to Katherine Howard, nine entries in *A Bibliographical Encyclopedia of Early Modern Englishwomen, Exemplary Lives and Memorable Acts, 1500-1650* (Ashgate), and an analysis of historical novels featuring Katherine Howard.

Kathleen L. Scott is an independent scholar whose main areas of research are the illustrations and borders of fifteenth-century English manuscripts. Her current undertaking is as general editor of *An Index of Images in English Manuscripts from c. 1380 to c. 1509*, a series of fascicles by contributing scholars that records imagery of all kinds in manuscripts of the period.

John Thompson is Emeritus Professor of English Textual Cultures at Queen's University, Belfast. He has been a member of the Early Book Society since its inception and has been the Research Director of the AHRC-funded "Imagining History" project at Queen's University, Belfast, examining, through a process he described as cultural mapping, the texts and traditions of the so-called "English Prose *Brut* Tradition." His work on large corpus Middle English works and their afterlives is continuing.

Shaun Tyas is an independent publisher of academic history, with a personal interest in the Middle Ages, bibliography, medievalism, and architecture.

Daniel Wakelin is Jeremy Griffiths Professor of Medieval English Palaeography in the University of Oxford and a Fellow of St Hilda's College. His recent publications include *Scribal Corrections and Literary Craft: English Manuscripts 1375-1510* (Cambridge University Press, 2014) and "When Scribes Won't Write: Gaps in Middle English Books," *Studies in the Age of Chaucer*, 36 (2014), 249-78. He has also contributed essays to *Probable Truth: Editing Medieval Texts from Britain*, edited by Vincent Gillespie and Anne Hudson (Brepols, 2013) and to *A Companion to the Early Printed Book in Britain*.

Eric Weiskott is Assistant Professor of English at Boston College. His essays on early English poetics appear in *Anglo-Saxon England, Journal of English and Germanic Philology, Modern Philology, Review of English Studies*, and *Yearbook of Langland Studies*, among others. His first book, *English Alliterative*

Verse: Poetic Tradition and Literary History, is forthcoming from Cambridge University Press. With Irina Dumitrescu, he is editing a collection of essays tentatively titled *Early English Poetics and the History of Style*.

Rebecca West is a Ph.D. student in the Medieval Institute at the University of Notre Dame. Her research interests include Medieval English and Old Icelandic language and literature. Her current research focuses on the conversion of Northern Europe, especially the manner in which the process of translation develops and transforms texts and ideas.

Magnus Williamson is Professor of Early Music at Newcastle University, UK, and works on music in the fifteenth and sixteenth centuries, particularly in England. He is General Editor of the British Academy editorial series, Early English Church Music (www.eecm.ac.uk), and is Principal Investigator of the Arts & Humanities Research Council-funded Tudor Partbooks project (www.tudorpartbooks.ac.uk).

Oliver Wort lives and works in pleasing exile in Aachen, Germany. He once held a British Academy Postdoctoral Research Fellowship at the University of Cambridge, and before this, he was for a short time an Associate Professor in the Faculty of Languages and Cultures at the University of Kyushu, in Japan. His main research interest is Reformation literature.

The nineteenth volume of the *Journal of the Early Book Society*
was published in Fall 2016
by Pace University Press

Cover and Interior Layouts by Taylor Lear
The journal was typeset in Arno Pro
and printed by Lightning Source in La Vergne, Tennessee

Pace University Press

Director: Sherman Raskin
Associate Director: Manuela Soares
Graduate Assistants: Rachel Diebel and Taylor Lear
Student Aide: Kelsey O'Brien-Enders

CPSIA information can be obtained
at www.ICGtesting.com
Printed in the USA
BVOW01s0319181116
468275BV00010B/23/P